THE **BIG** BOOK OF **WATER-COLOR**

THE **BIG** BOOK OF **WATER-COLOR**

THE MUST-HAVE GUIDE TO PAINTING

MALLERY JANE

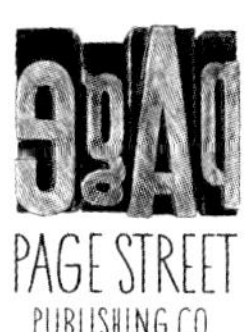

PAGE STREET
PUBLISHING CO.

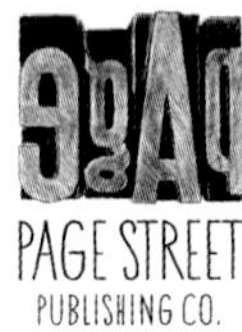

PAGE STREET
PUBLISHING CO.

Copyright © 2024 Mallery Jane

First published in 2024 by
Page Street Publishing Co.
27 Congress Street, Suite 1511
Salem, MA 01970
www.pagestreetpublishing.com

Distributed by Macmillan, sales in Canada by The Canadian Manda Group.

28 27 26 25 24   1 2 3 4 5

ISBN-13: 979-8-89003-084-9

Library of Congress Control Number: 2023949738

Edited by Sadie Hofmeester
Cover design by Mallery Jane and Laura Benton
Book design by Laura Benton for Page Street Publishing Co.
Art and photography by Mallery Jane

Printed and bound in China

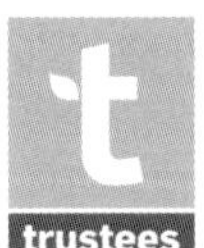

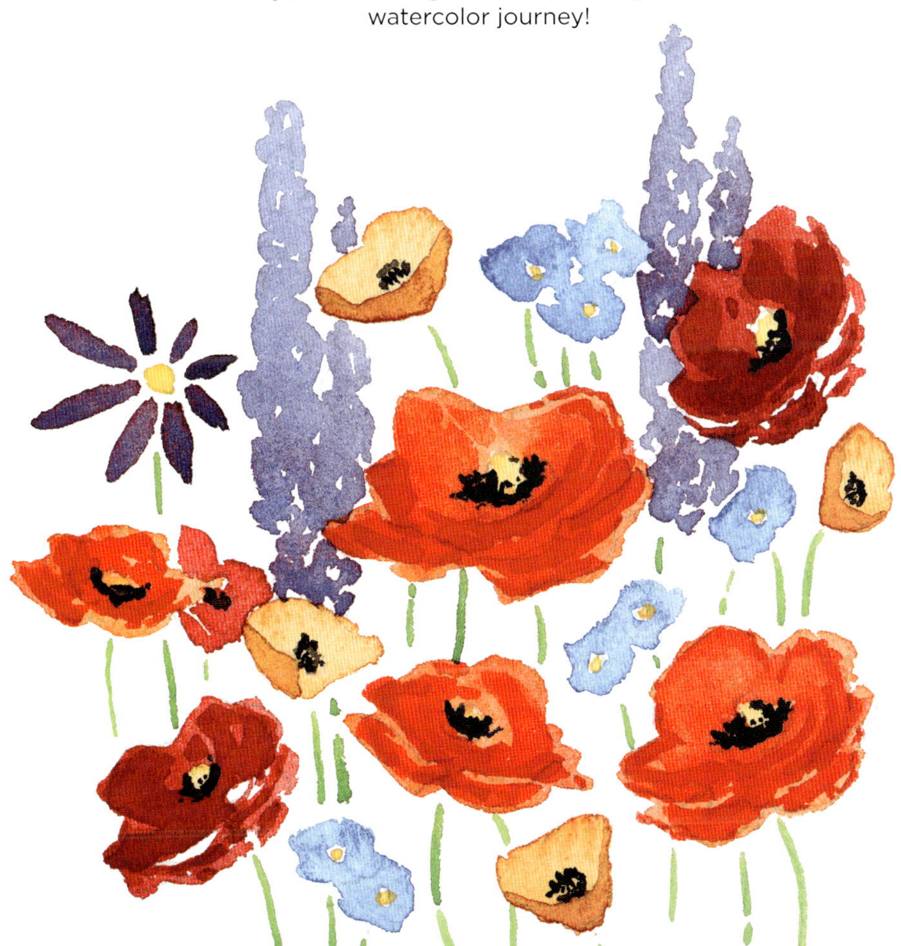

CONTENTS

INTRODUCTION

Hi there! I am so happy you are here and ready to sit down to paint and create! Whether you are brand-new to watercolor or have been painting for some time, I created this book to help you feel inspired and learn some techniques in this beautiful medium.

We feel accomplished when we work with our hands and can show a finished product. For me, this comes in all different forms throughout the day. I love to paint, cook and even clean because I can see the difference at the end. I've written this book to help carve out a small portion of your day to sit down and have that feeling of, "Wow, I just did that!"

I graduated from college and taught art in schools for seven years before becoming a full-time artist and creating online art courses. I realized how much I love to help others learn the little tips and tricks I use with watercolor. Throughout this book, I sprinkle knowledge gained over the past decade.

One of the beautiful parts of painting, especially in watercolor, are the endless options you have each step of the way. Depending on the different watercolor techniques, colors and materials, I could sit down and paint an orange differently each time. Having so many options can make watercolor fun but also intimidating. This book aims to help beginners learn the techniques while painting fun subjects. If you are an intermediate painter, this book will also help inspire you on the days you aren't sure what to paint and help you approach your subject in various ways, challenging you to think differently in watercolor.

Throughout the book, you will notice a paint palette at the beginning of each project. Inside each palette shows the difficulty level of that project as easy, intermediate or challenging. You will also notice QR codes sprinkled throughout the book. These lessons include a paint-along video with me!

My goal with this book is to transport you into each painting, whether it be the crisp feeling of fall, the sensation of eating sushi, the discovery of a seashell at the beach, the experience of a sunset across the desert, the pleasure of picking wildflowers or the awe of standing by the Golden Gate Bridge. As you go through the tutorials, let yourself be caught up in the painting and immersed in the moment, where you let go of your worries about tomorrow and the troubles from yesterday. Enjoy the process and have fun learning different ways to use watercolor!

mallery jane

WATERCOLOR FUNDAMENTALS

Throughout this book, we use lots of techniques and watercolor methods. Before you even get painting, you want to be familiar with the tools of the trade, which is why this chapter starts off with the materials used throughout the book. Next up, we dive into key techniques and terminology before finishing up the fundamentals review with a bit of basic color theory. All the words in **bold** that you'll encounter throughout the book are explained in this chapter so you can easily reference those watercolor fundamentals whenever you need a refresher. This chapter will become your best friend because we'll use these terms all the time!

But before we dive into all that, there are a couple of logistics to get out of the way first. As you work your way through this book, you'll notice that the first step of each project is always the same: trace or sketch. While you can sketch out your own **subject**, if you want to get right to the painting, please head to the Templates section (page 225) in the back of this book. These traceable sketch templates are printed on perforated pages, so you can tear them out for easier tracing. I recommend placing the template beneath your paper and pressing both to a window or using a light table for the easiest tracing experience. As you trace the templates, keep your pencil marks light. Then you're free to paint!

Another note to keep in mind: Unless otherwise stated, let your painting dry between each step. I know, I know—this isn't the most exciting part of watercolor painting. But, letting each step dry completely allows you to build layers and layers of paint. If you're feeling impatient, you can always make your painting dry faster by carefully using a hair dryer. Or you can do as I do and enjoy a cup of coffee as your painting dries.

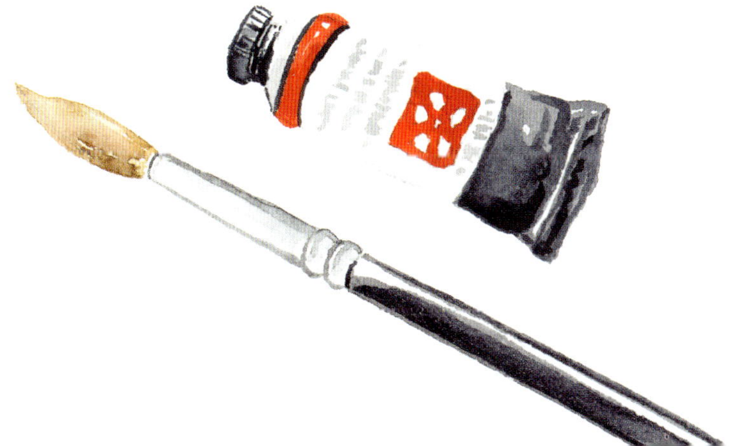

MATERIALS

Before you begin painting your way through the book, you'll want to gather your supplies. Alongside a cup of clean water and a paper towel or cloth, you'll need the following:

PENCIL: You want a pencil that is light because watercolor is a medium that is semi-transparent. I typically use a Staedtler® Mars® Lumograph® 2H.

ERASER: In some of these paintings, I will instruct you to lightly erase your pencil markings. Instead of using any eraser, I encourage you to use a kneaded eraser. The one I use is a Faber-Castell® kneaded eraser.

BRUSHES: I prefer to mainly paint with a size 8 round brush. It helps me stay loose by not getting too detailed with a smaller brush. There are a few occasions when I will pull out a size 4 or 2 for more minor details at the end of a painting. However, you will notice that for most of these paintings, I use a size 8.

There are two types of brushes: synthetic and natural hair. The most significant difference between them is that synthetic brushes hold less water but are excellent for detail and cheaper than natural brushes. On the other hand, since natural brushes hold more water than their synthetic counterparts, they are great for adding large swaths of color to a painting. If you are starting in watercolor, I suggest using synthetic, as it is a little easier to work with and more affordable. Below are the brushes I will use throughout this book.

- Princeton Aqua Elite™ Round Size 8
- Princeton Aqua Elite Round Size 4
- Artegría Round Quill Size 2 (Mop Brush)
- Escoda® Perla Series 1430 Pointed Round Size 14

PAINTS: I use a mixture of brands for my paint tubes, but the majority of my paints are Winsor & Newton™. I have a mixture of artist grade and professional grade paints. As a beginner, I highly recommend the artist grade paints; they are still great quality but much more affordable.

There are also watercolor palettes that come with pans of paint ready for you to use. These can be more affordable and a great beginner-friendly way to start. I used tubes for the book because I could pick the exact colors I wanted. I used to use a Winsor & Newton 16-pan palette, but unfortunately, they changed the colors inside the palette. I didn't like not knowing if the colors would be the same or not when it came time to replace my palette again. Results also vary slightly between the pans and tubes because the pans are more concentrated than the tubes. Knowing this can help you figure out how much water to add as you paint. If you have pans, add a little extra water, whereas if you have tubes, you don't have to add as much water.

Another note: Because the pans stay hardened, they are rougher on your brush when scrubbing the paint versus working with the tube paint. With tube paint, your brush doesn't have to scrub. Both pros and cons exist, so use whichever works within your budget and preference!

If you choose to use paint tubes, organize your palette in a way that works best for your creative workflow. For those of you who may be curious, below are the colors I use and in the order that I organize them on my palette. I know it may seem like madness, but it works for me. For instance, I don't want to place my Ultramarine Blue next to my Indigo, as the **hues** are so dark and I don't want to accidently grab the wrong color.

- **Yellow Ochre** (Winsor & Newton: Professional, Series 1, Permanence AA)
- **Lemon Yellow** (Daler-Rowney®: Aquafine)
- **Cadmium Orange** (Winsor & Newton: Professional, Series 4, Permanence A)
- **Quinacridone Gold** (Winsor & Newton: Professional, Series 3, Permanence A)
- **Winsor Red** (Winsor & Newton: Professional, Series 1, Permanence A)
- **Alizarin Crimson** (Winsor & Newton: Professional, Series 1, Permanence B)
- **Ultramarine Blue** (Da Vinci: Professional Quality)
- **Cobalt Blue** (Daniel Smith Extra Fine™: Premium Artist Grade, Series 3)
- **Cerulean Blue** (Winsor & Newton: Artist Grade, Series 3, Permanence AA)
- **Cobalt Teal Blue** (Daniel Smith Extra Fine: Premium Artist Grade, Series 2)
- **Indigo** (Daniel Smith Extra Fine: Premium Artist Grade, Series 1)
- **Green Gold** (Winsor & Newton: Professional, Series 2, Permanence A)
- **Winsor Green** (Winsor & Newton: Artist Grade, Series 1, Permanence A)
- **Neutral Tint** (Winsor & Newton: Professional, Series 1, Permanence A)
- **Permanent White Gouache** (Winsor & Newton: Designers Gouache, Series 1, Permanence A)

The last paint on my palette is White Gouache. Gouache is a water-based medium similar to watercolor. However, it can be opaque. When combining the gouache with watercolor, we can achieve a semi-opaque medium.

PAPER: Watercolor paper comes in a variety of sizes, brands and types. You can have cold press or hot press watercolor paper. Cold press has a "tooth" or **texture/** roughness to the paper, which makes it easier to use because it is more absorbent and holds onto the pigment and water. Hot press watercolor paper is smooth, which can be trickier to work with, so I recommend sticking to cold press. Watercolor paper comes in a variety of thickness, so I would stick to paper that is 110 to 140 pounds (160 to 210 gsm) because it can hold more water and won't soak through as easily as thinner paper. For the projects in this book, I used Arches® Cold Press Watercolor Paper, 140 pounds (210 gsm).

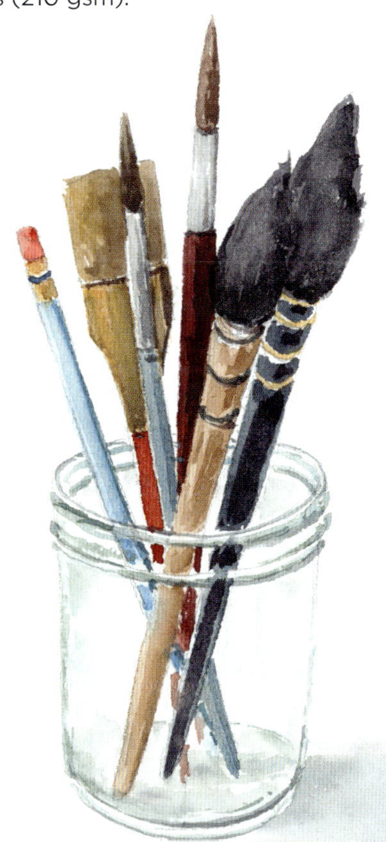

SLANTED DRAWING BOARD/ TABLETOP EASEL: I paint on a slanted surface, which can help the paint naturally flow downward, preventing it from staying flat on the paper and causing puddles. I use the Falling in Art Large 5-Position Wood Drafting Table Easel. However, the only project that requires a slanted easel is Northern Lights (page 72). A cheap option would be to cut a piece of cardboard, tape your painting to the cardboard and rest it on a stack of books so that it is at a slight downward angle. All the other projects can be painted on a flat surface. If you notice puddling, take a clean, dry brush and absorb the excess paint.

PAINTER'S TAPE: On many of these projects, you will want to use painter's tape. Not only can you tape your paper to your desk, but you can often create fun borders as well. I like to use Tssart's Acid-Free Masking Art Tape, 0.6 inches (1.5 cm) wide. It is okay to use masking tape instead of painter's tape; however, I would recommend testing the brand first to make sure it will keep out the water without **bleeding**. Another huge thing you will want to test is that it won't rip your watercolor paper when you pull off the tape.

DRAWING GUM/GUM PASTE/ MASKING FLUID: Despite all the different names, drawing gum, gum paste and masking fluid are all the same thing. These products allow you to mask an area of your paper. By masking areas, you keep the white of your page while painting; this is especially helpful for placing **highlights** or preventing **bleeding** into an area where you know you don't want any paint to be. The brand I use is Pébéo Easy Peel.

To apply drawing gum, I usually use an old paintbrush because the drawing gum paste destroys the bristles over time; make sure to rinse your brush immediately after to help save the bristles. You can also use other household items to apply the drawing gum. For example, a toothpick is perfect for small dots like snow, or a Q-tip® works excellently for larger circles.

RUBBER CEMENT ERASER: To remove the drawing gum, you will want to use a rubber cement eraser. I use the Crafter's Toolkit™ Glue and Residue Eraser.

PEN: While I don't use one for each piece, when I want an extra pop, I'll use a Sharpie® Felt-Tip Pen (Size 0.4 mm) to outline my painting or add in some deeper **shadows**.

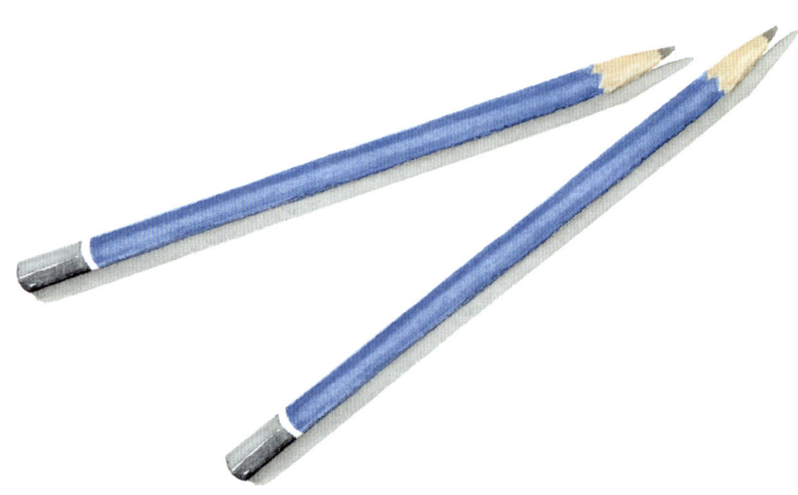

KEY TECHNIQUES AND TERMINOLOGY

The best way to learn is to do! Each painting in this book uses basic techniques that build upon each other, so you'll be mastering watercolor as you paint. But before we begin, let's all get on the same page and lay out some definitions.

LOAD/LOADING: When we **load** our brushes, we always want to get them wet in our water before adding our paint, so first swirl your brush around in your cup of water. Now, go with the color you want and grab some of the paint with the tip of your brush. Place this on your palette and swirl it around to feel the consistency. I highly recommend never going straight from grabbing the paint to your paper. It is easier to judge how much water and paint you have if you go to your palette first.

WASH: A **wash** is simply putting paint on your paper in an area. Throughout this book, we refer to a **wash** as paint mixed with water on our palette and then applied to the paper. There are three different types of color **washes** (**flat, gradient** and **varie-gated**) and two techniques used to apply these **washes: wet-in-wet** or **wet-on-dry**. Because the different application techniques help showcase the differences between the types, we'll start there.

Wet-In-Wet

WET-IN-WET: Also known as wet-on-wet, this is when we paint into a surface that is already wet with paint or clear water. Painting **wet-in-wet** can help create a stroke-free **wash**. Keep in mind that adding paint to wet paper will always give you a lighter **value** (to learn more about **values**, see page 22) versus adding the same exact paint to dry paper. When we are doing the **wet-in-wet** technique, we often begin by painting color into clean water; we call this a **clear water wash**.

CLEAR WATER WASH: When applying a **clear water wash**, **load** your brush with clean water and paint in the **wash** with no color pigment. This is typically used for starting a **wet-in-wet** application.

Wet-On-Dry

*Gradient Wash
Wet-In-Wet*

*Gradient Wash
Wet-On-Dry*

WET-ON-DRY: Whenever we apply a **wash** to dry paper, we are using *wet* paint on *dry* paper, hence the name **wet-on-dry**.

In this book, I often refer to a **wet-on-dry wash** as just a **wash**, or I don't reference it at all and just say "paint." I do this because a **wet-on-dry wash** happens so frequently. However, I will always mention the **wet-in-wet** technique by name because it is important for you to know when you need to paint into something wet without it drying before you have time to work in the area.

FLAT WASH: A **flat wash** is usually a large area painted in an even, uniformed manner with one color. However, this type of **wash** can also be used in smaller areas to apply a smooth **wash** of color (see, for instance, Step 2 in the Eucalyptus painting on page 26).

GRADIENT WASH: A **gradient wash** gradually moves from a dark **value** to a light **value**. This is perfect for painting skies. To apply a **gradient wash**, you could use either the **wet-in-wet** or **wet-on-dry** technique.

To apply a **gradient wash** using **wet-in-wet**, first wet the area of your paper with your paintbrush dipped in fresh water (**clear water wash**). Next, take your color and apply it to the top of the area; this will be our darkest **value**. As you come down the paper, use less paint by diluting it with more water, allowing the **value** to get lighter and lighter each time. Using a slanted surface will allow gravity to naturally pull the paint downward.

To apply a **gradient wash** using **wet-on-dry**, you follow the same steps except instead of wetting the paper first, you apply the paint directly to dry paper. Applying a **gradient wash** on dry paper is easier to avoid **blooms**, but you have to work quicker because you are working on dry paper. Experiment to see if you like working **wet-on-dry** or **wet-in-wet**, as there are pros and cons to both.

VARIEGATED WASH: A **variegated wash** will have two or more colors. This works great for a sunset. To use a **variegated wash**, you can use either the **wet-in-wet** or **wet-on-dry** technique.

To apply a **variegated wash** using **wet-in-wet**, wet the area of the paper first with your water (**clear water wash**). Next, grab your first color and paint the top area. Now you can grab your next color and paint along the edge of your first color so the two colors blend. You can continue doing this with as many colors as you'd like.

To apply a **variegated wash** using **wet-on-dry**, you follow the same steps except instead of wetting the paper first, you apply your paint directly to dry paper. Applying a **variegated wash** on dry paper is easier to avoid **blooms**, but you have to work quicker to ensure smooth transitions between colors. Experiment to see if you prefer working **wet-on-dry** or **wet-in-wet**, as there are pros and cons to both.

> **HELPFUL TIP:** Using a slanted surface or board that you can tilt will make applying a **gradient** and **variegated wash** so much easier.

Variegated Wash Wet-In-Wet

Variegated Wash Wet-On-Dry

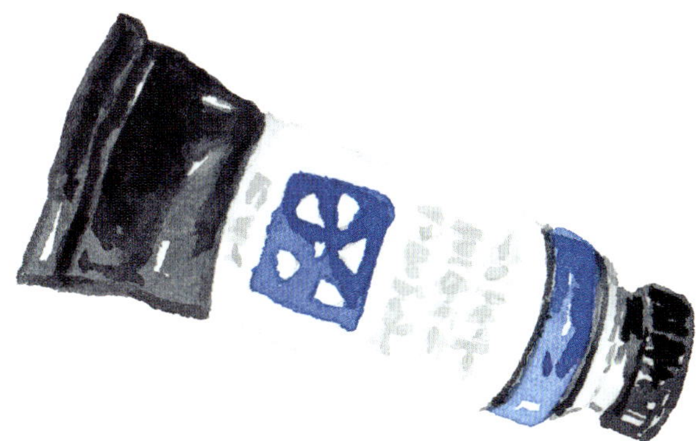

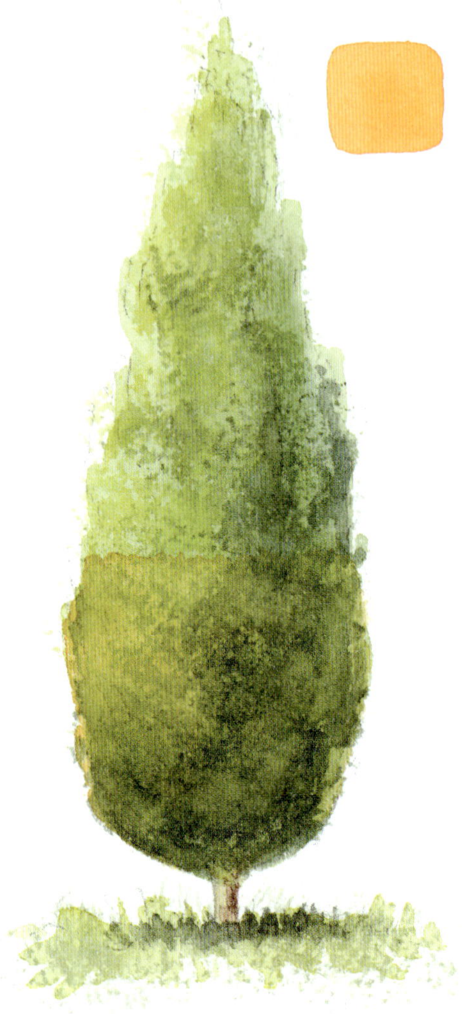

Glaze

GLAZE: If I had to choose one technique as my favorite, it would be glazing! A **glaze** is simply applying a layer on top of a completely dried previous layer of paint. You can layer multiple colors on top of each other, and each time you would be applying a **glaze**. Each time you add a **glaze**, you are modifying the color and **tone** of your painting. It is almost like mixing colors on your paper. In the example on the left, I painted a Quinacridone Gold **glaze** on the bottom half of the tree to warm the foliage color. You can see the difference between the lighter, cooler color on the top of the tree and the warmer **tone** on the bottom half of the tree; that's the power of a **glaze**!

TEXTURE: We often think of **texture** relating to touch, but we also can see **texture**. When painting, you can depict visual **texture** with smooth or rough strokes.

DRY BRUSH: To **dry brush**, you still wet your brush in the water, but after that, you want to get as much water off on your paper towel as possible. Then, you can grab your paint and apply it to the paper. Because there is very little water on the brush, you will notice little spaces of the white paper showing through. These gaps create wonderful **texture** and interest. Using a **dry brush** technique is especially excellent for achieving **texture** with fur or grass.

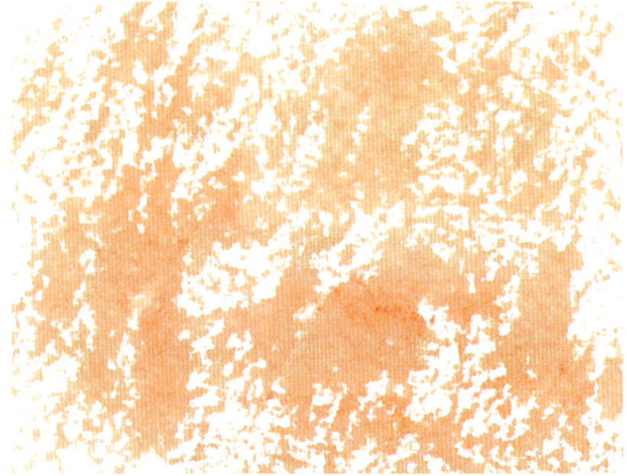

Dry Brush

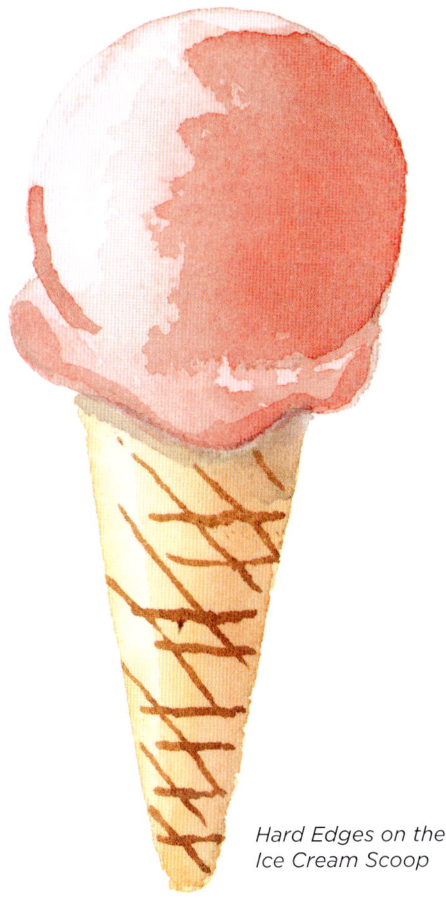

Hard Edges on the Ice Cream Scoop

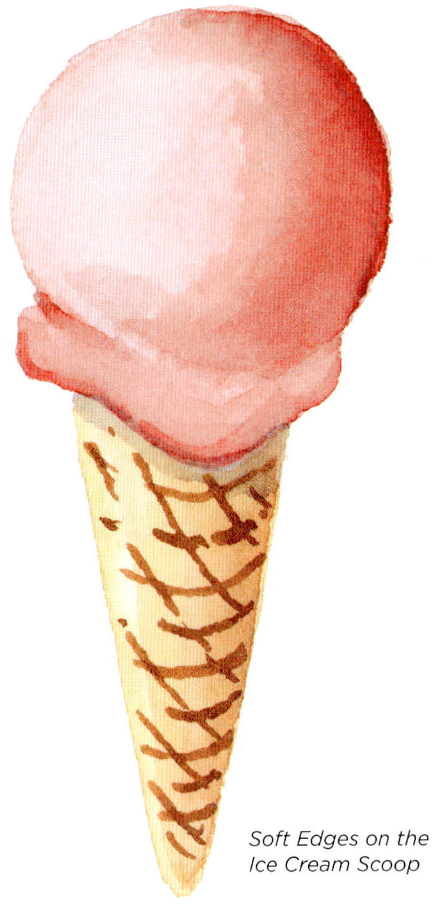

Soft Edges on the Ice Cream Scoop

HARD EDGE: **Hard edges** are created when you don't blend, or **soften**, the edges of your paint. Similar to **dry brushing**, **hard edges** can help add **texture** to a piece. To create a **hard edge**, you always want to paint on dry paper. If you have water or paint that's still wet on your paper, let it dry if you wish to apply a **hard edge**. All you have to do is paint a stroke and leave it to create a **hard edge**. It is much simpler than creating a **soft edge**.

SOFT EDGE: Unlike a **hard edge**, a **soft edge** is blended to create a smooth look. To create a blended or **soft edge**, first paint the area with a **wash**. Second, rinse your brush quickly and come back along the edge with a damp brush to disperse the edge. Keep in mind, once an edge starts to dry, you can no longer **soften** it, so planning in advance can help make sure you work quickly and know when and where to **soften** the edges. This method is best for smaller areas because it is more precise. Another way to **soften** an edge is to wet the area of your paper first with a **clear water wash**. When you place your paint on the paper, the water will help **soften** the edge. This option is best for larger areas, like skies, where unpredictable blending is expected.

Lift/Lifting

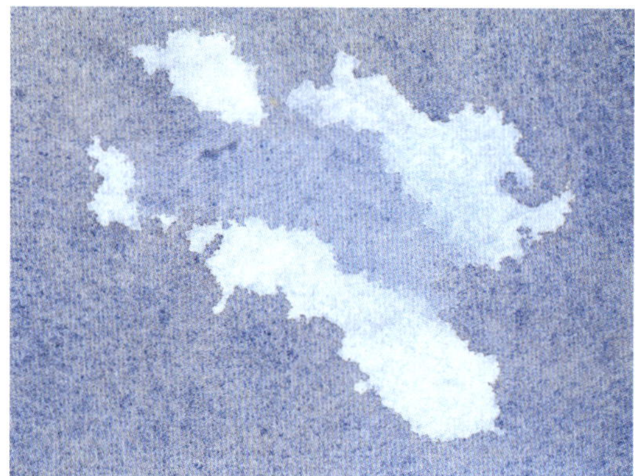

Blot/Blotting

LIFT/LIFTING: **Lifting** refers to removing color (paint) off your paper. To **lift**, take a clean, damp brush and grab the area of pigment you want to lighten or remove from the watercolor paper (the paint on the paper should still be wet so it can "**lift**" off). You can repeat this process to remove more pigment. Be careful not to scrub the paper with your brush; it should be a quick wipe of the brush, followed by rinsing your brush and wiping it on your paper towel before you repeat as needed. If you work the area too much, you could potentially start to rub the paper off.

There are multiple uses of **lifting** in watercolor. You may want to **lift** because of a mistake, and it can act as an eraser. However, keep in mind that some colors will come off more easily than others. **Lifting** can also help lighten an area to create a **highlight** or a lighter **value** within an area. You can also use **lifting** to help **soften** an edge.

BLOT/BLOTTING: **Blotting** is another form of removing paint from your paper using a paper towel or tissue. When arranging the paper towel or tissue, bunch it up tight because you can have more control versus holding it loose. This works great to create clouds or **texture** by removing some of the pigment from the paper. How much pressure you use will determine how much paint is removed from your paper. The more pressure you apply, the more paint will come off.

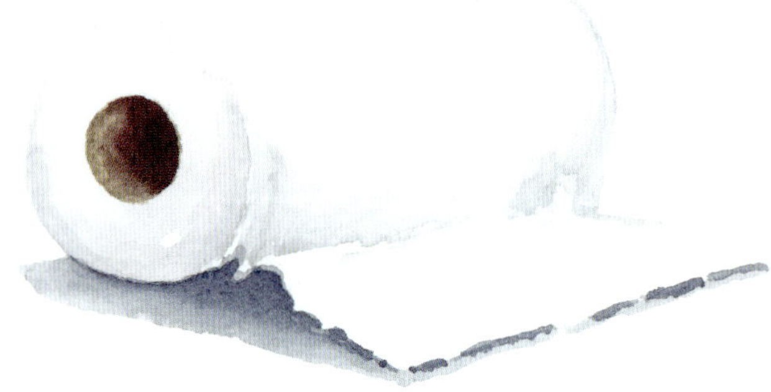

SPLATTER/SPLATTERING:

Splattering is good for creating an added pop or movement to your painting. For example, in the Happy Birthday Cake painting (page 108), it helps add to the flickering of the candles. In a winter painting, you can create a snowfall effect by **splattering** white gouache on your painting. To **splatter**, **load** your brush with a lot of water and paint so that it is almost dripping. With the pointer finger on your hand that isn't holding the brush, hit the paintbrush so the contact sends the paint flying toward the paper in a sporadic spray. The first few splatters will have bigger droplets because there is more paint/water on the brush. As you keep splattering, the drops will get smaller. If you only want smaller dots, splatter over a scrap piece of paper first until you are getting the desired size and then splatter over your painting.

BLEED/BLEEDING:

Bleeding is created when you touch your paintbrush against an area that is wet. This is a great technique to use when you want the colors to smoothly blend, or **bleed**, into each other. For example, in the Colorful Coral piece (page 120), the top color and bottom color come together in the middle and **bleed** nicely, creating a seamless transition of color. However, even when you don't want the colors to mix, **bleeding** can happen accidently, and it's very frustrating. To avoid **bleeds**, make sure the first **wash** of color is dry on your paper before painting another color next to it. Certain paints and pigments drag other colors into them (they "pull" them in), while others tend to be pulled. As always, experiment with your paints because some paints and pigments **bleed** and pull differently, so you don't want to be surprised on a painting.

BLOOM:

Watercolor **blooms**, also called backruns or cauliflowers, happen when you drip paint onto a semi-dry area on your paper. The drip creates a marking similar to a flower or cauliflower, hence the name.

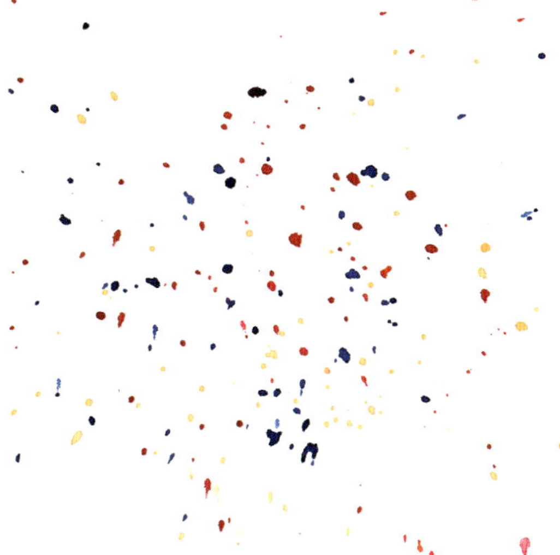

Splatter/Splattering

Bleed/Bleeding

Bloom

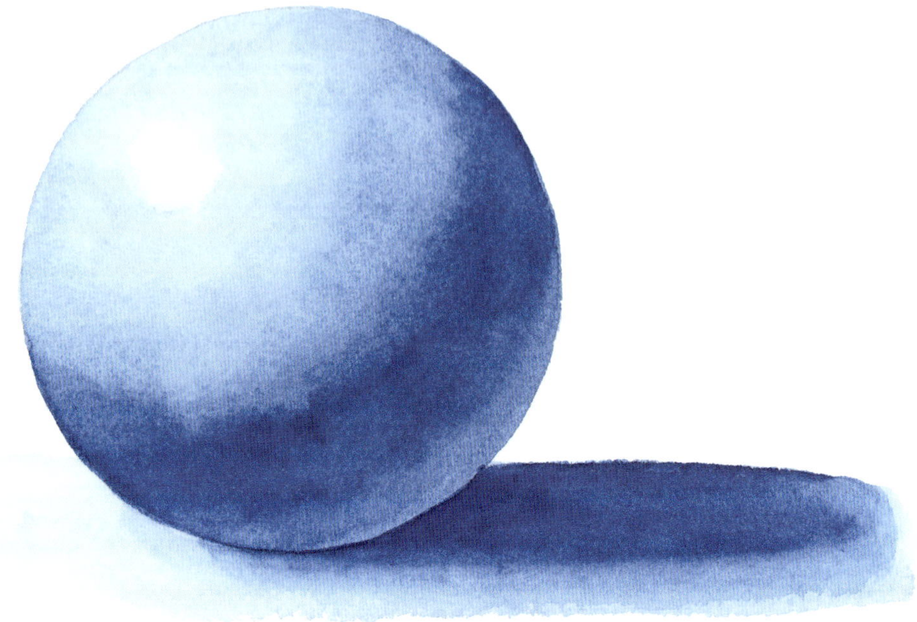

SUBJECT: The **subject** is the topic of focus, the main image in the painting.

LIGHT SOURCE: A **light source** generates light and shows the direction your light is coming from.

HIGHLIGHT: Highlights can give your painting more dimension. They are simple to implement by leaving little areas of the lightest **value** (usually this is the white of the paper). Preserving the white of the page for highlights is an artistic choice you will need to make at the beginning of the painting. However, if you forget to add the **highlight** at the beginning, you can always use white gouache at the end. It is fascinating that something so small as a **highlight** can elevate your paintings.

SHADOW: This is technically called Form **Shadow**, but I will be referring to it in my book as **shadow**. The form **shadow** is the area of the object that is in **shadow**.

CAST SHADOW: This is the **shadow** being "cast" from the object on the ground or surface. A **cast shadow** is made when an object blocks the light.

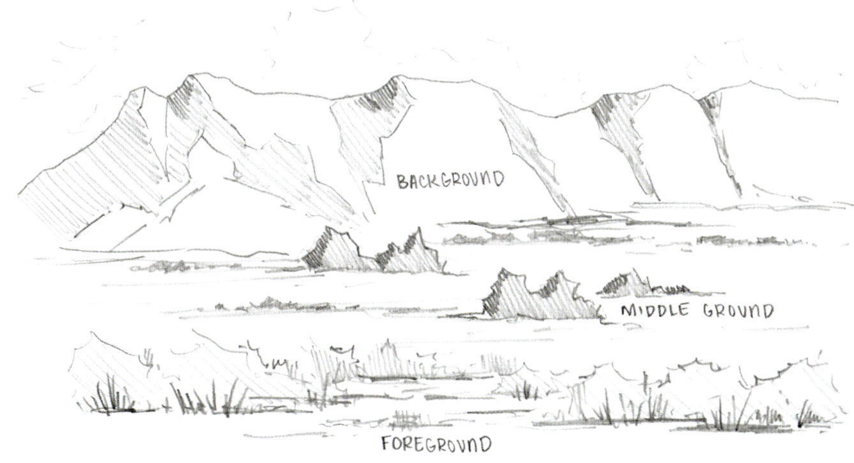

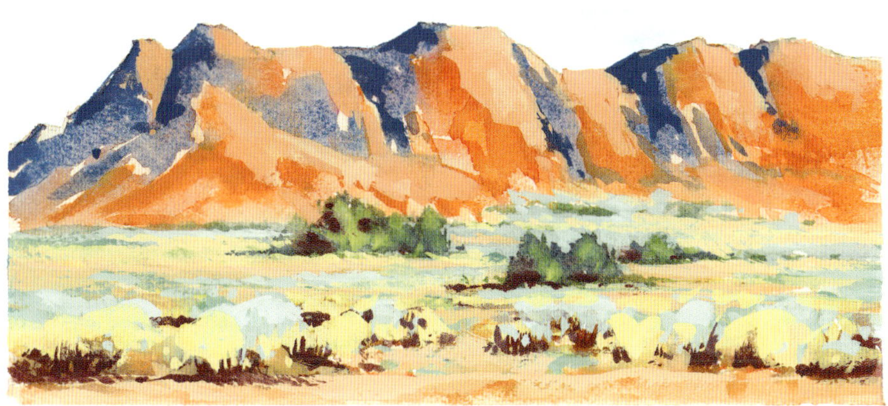

FOREGROUND: The area closest to the front of the painting is the **foreground**. Objects in the **foreground** should be larger and more **saturated** to help appear closer.

MIDDLE GROUND: The **middle ground** is the area between the **foreground** and the **background**.

BACKGROUND: The **background** is the farthest area away in the painting. Usually, objects in the **background** will appear smaller and duller to help enhance the look of being in the distance.

BASIC COLOR THEORY

Color theory is one of the building blocks of art that deals with the combining and mixing of colors based on the color wheel. Understanding these basics will greatly improve your paintings because you will learn which colors work well with one another. To be honest, color theory is one of my favorite things to use and to teach, and it's the topic I receive the most questions on. For example, I love using color theory to choose **complementary colors** to create my **shadows**.

VALUES: This concept refers to the lightness and darkness of a color. In watercolor, we can change the **value** by adding more or less water to our pigment. Adding more water will lighten the **value**. To darken the **value**, we can add less water.

WATER-TO-PAINT RATIO: The more water mixed with our paint, the lighter the color will be; the less water we use, the darker our color will be. I've included a quick reference to use for estimating the percentage of **water-to-paint ratios** to create different **values** below. If you want to practice **water-to-paint ratio**, visit the Snowy Mountain project on page 156.

Throughout this book, I will instruct you to add more water or less water to the swatch to change the **value** of the color. If not otherwise noted to lighten or darken your **value**, assume that the mixture is made up of 50 percent paint to 50 percent water.

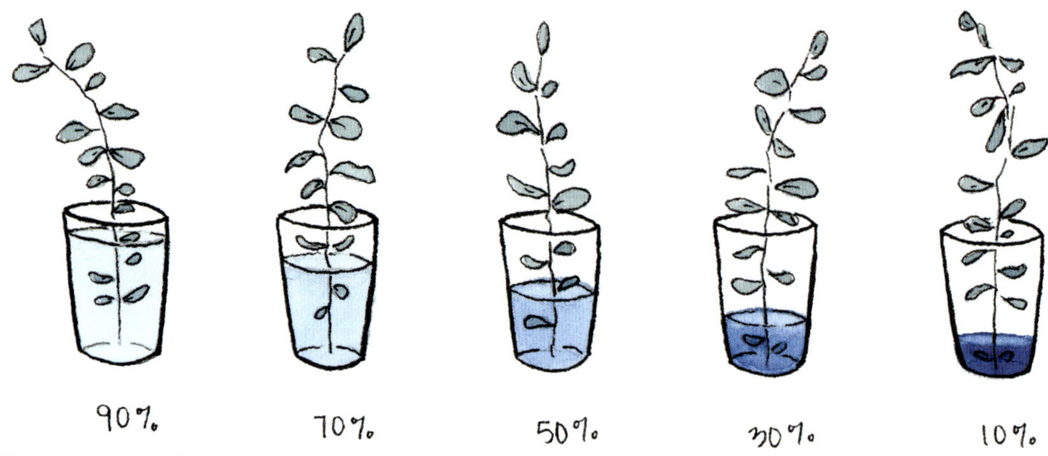

Water-to-Paint Ratio

Value Scale

VALUE SCALE: A **value scale** shows the light and darkness of a color in an organized system. Above is a **value scale** using Ultramarine Blue. The darkest **value** is at the right, and each swatch to the left gets lighter in **value** by adding more water.

A great exercise to understand **value** is to paint a monochromatic painting, which uses only one color with variations in the **value/saturation/temperature**. The Snowy Mountain painting on page 156 is a monochromatic creation.

TEMPERATURE: The **temperature** of a color refers to how warm or cool it is. Each color can have variations in **tone**.

SATURATION: Saturation refers to the purity of the color, or how intense the color is. Low **saturation** refers to muted colors, while high **saturation** refers to bright colors. **Saturation** is different from **value** because **value** deals with the darkness or lightness of the color, whereas **saturation** deals with how bright or dull the color is. You can have a bright color with a dark or light **value**.

COMPLEMENTARY COLORS: When looking at the color wheel, **complementary colors** are across from each other. For example, blue and orange are **complementary colors**. When using these side by side, they can create high contrast. When mixed, they cancel each other out to make a neutral color. I love using **complementary colors** to create my **shadows**. You'll create your own **shadows** using **complementary colors** in several paintings in this book, including the Mushrooms (page 106), Lemon Shark (page 138) and Pumpkin (page 174).

ANALOGOUS COLORS: When looking at the color wheel, **analogous colors** are any three colors right next to each other, for example, red, red-orange and orange. These colors work beautifully together because they share similar properties.

HUE: The term refers to the color. This is the color right out of your paint tube or palette.

TONE: This word refers to the characteristic of the color. **Tone** refers to how warm or cool, bright or dull, light or dark a color is.

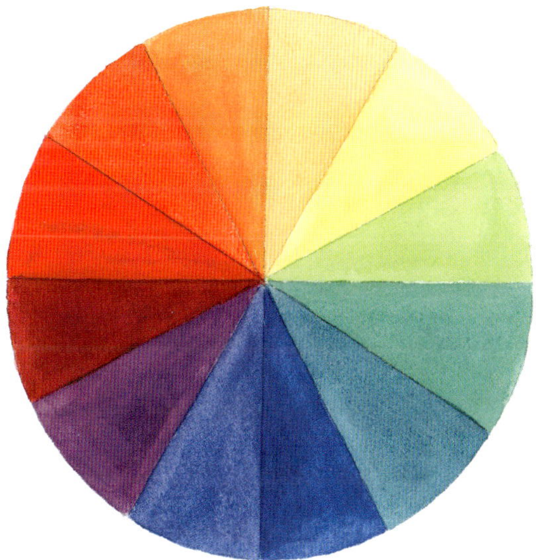

Color Wheel

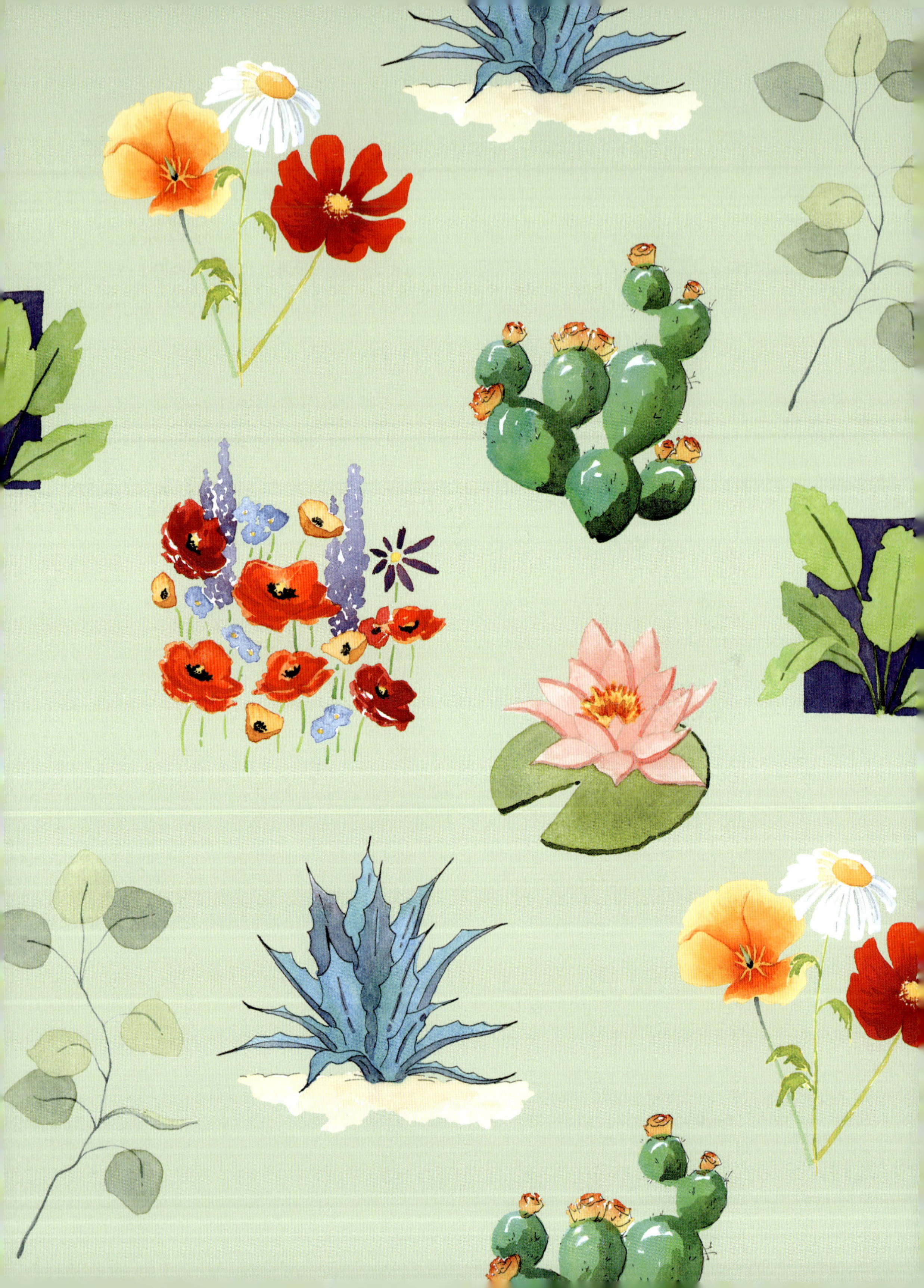

BOTANICALS

In this chapter, you will learn how to paint various flowers, plants and cacti while learning different techniques! One of my favorite things about painting botanicals is having a lot of freedom in my paint strokes since I am using organic shapes. This is quite different from painting a geometric object, like a building, where the strokes must be straight and more precise. If you are new to watercolor, I suggest diving into botanicals first because they are beginner-friendly!

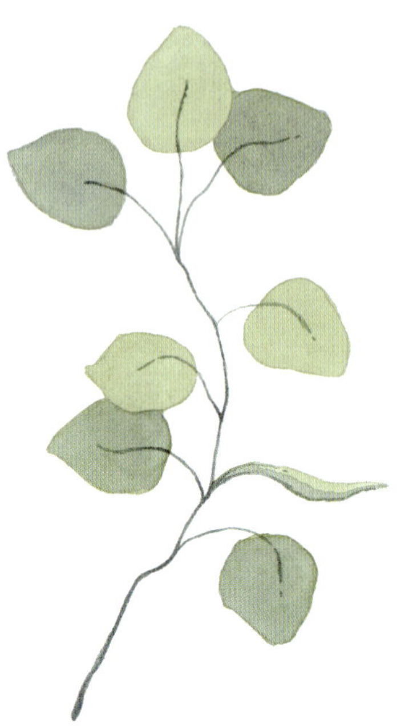

EUCALYPTUS

It is easy to overcomplicate a painting. There's a common assumption that the more details and the longer we spend on a painting, the better it will be. Sometimes, this can be true; however, I've also found that more simplified portrayal, like this Eucalyptus, can be more elegant. "Less is more," I say to myself when I start overdoing it and getting frustrated! This painting is a great practice for restraint and is wonderful when you want to keep it simple while still creating something beautiful.

MATERIALS

Pencil

Watercolor paper

Size 8 round brush

Size 2 round brush (optional)

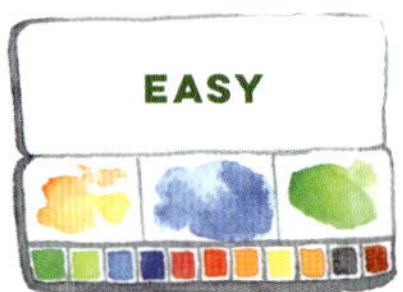

COLORS

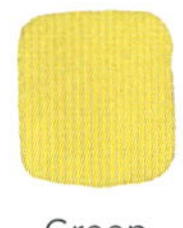
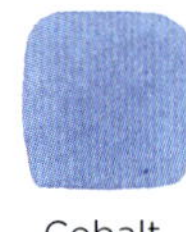
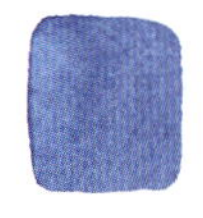
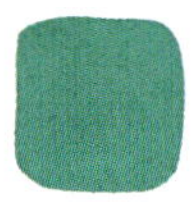
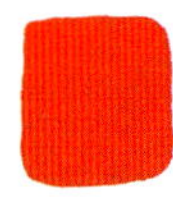

| Green Gold | Cobalt Blue | Ultramarine Blue | Winsor Green | Winsor Red |

STEP 1: Trace (page 225) or lightly sketch the eucalyptus stem and leaves in pencil on your watercolor paper.

STEP 2: On your palette, mix Green Gold (60%) and Cobalt Blue (40%) together. Use this cool green mixture and a size 8 round brush to paint in the leaves of the eucalyptus plant.

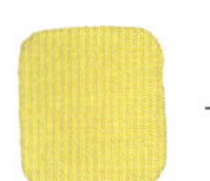
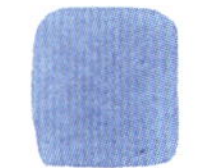
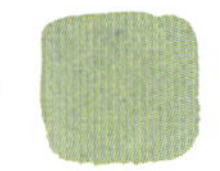

Green Gold (60%) + Cobalt Blue (40%) =

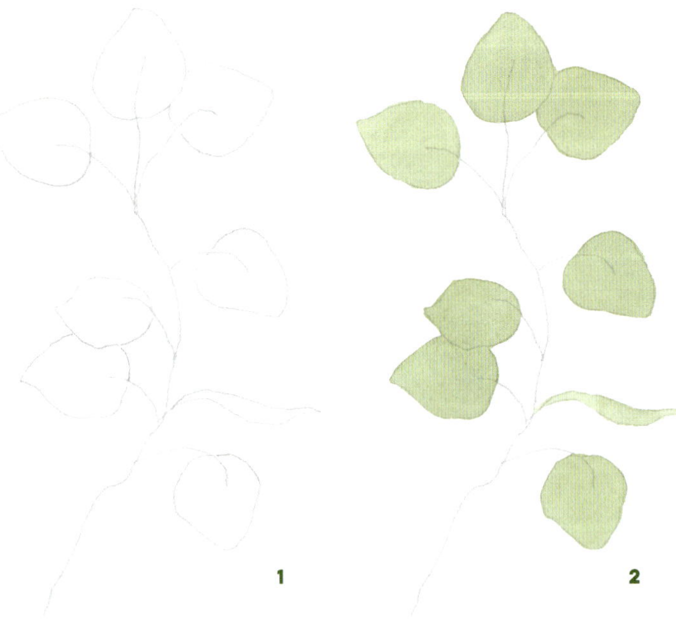

1

2

STEP 3: Paint an Ultramarine Blue **glaze** over four of the leaves. Don't apply a **glaze** to every leaf in order to keep some variation in color. To add depth to the horizontal leaf, paint the glaze only on the bottom half.

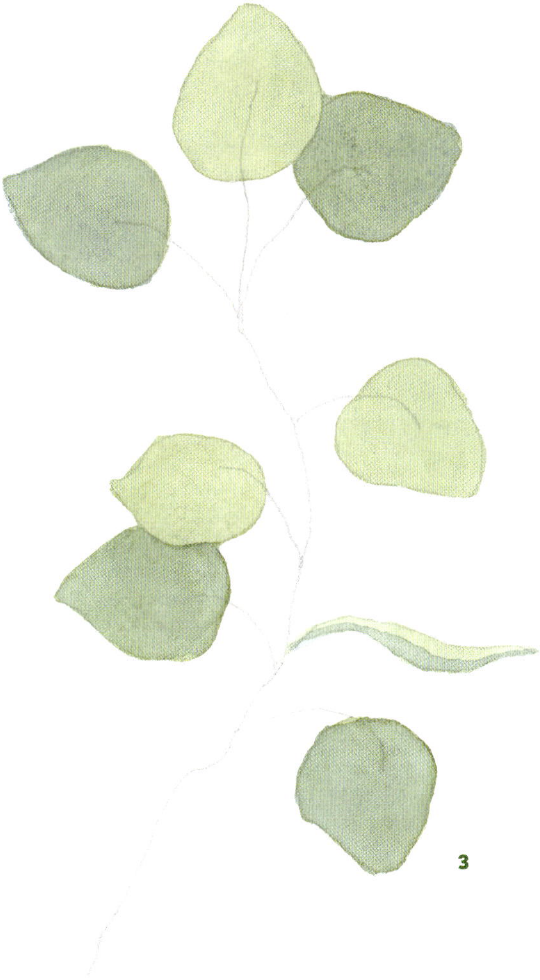

STEP 4: Combine Winsor Green (70%) with Winsor Red (30%) on your palette. Paint in the stem of the eucalyptus plant using this mixture. You may want to use a size 2 round brush since the lines are thin.

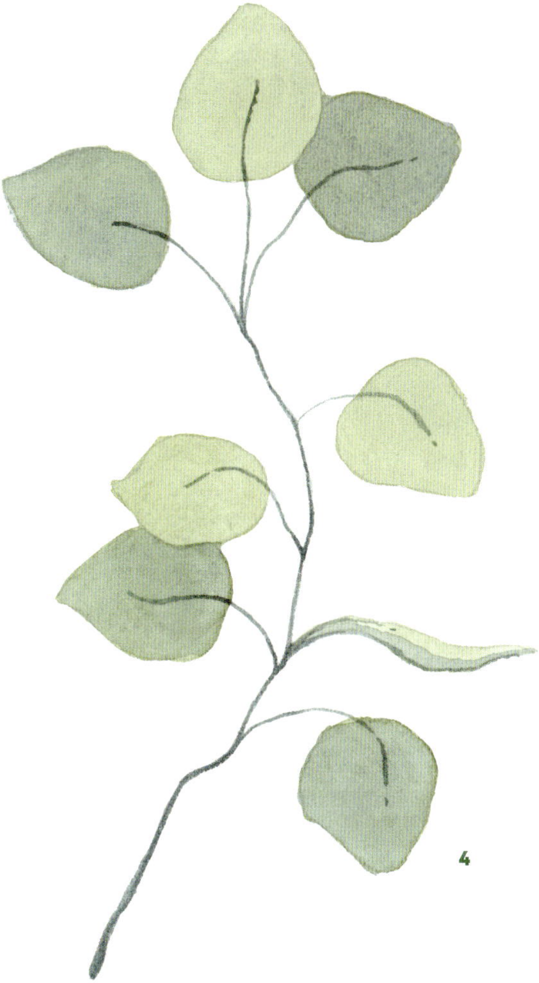

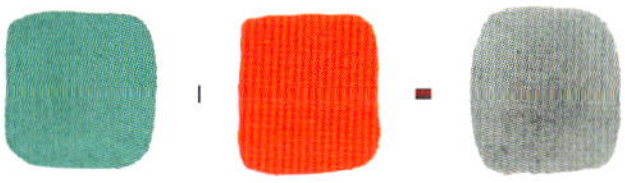

Winsor Green (70%)   Winsor Red (30%)

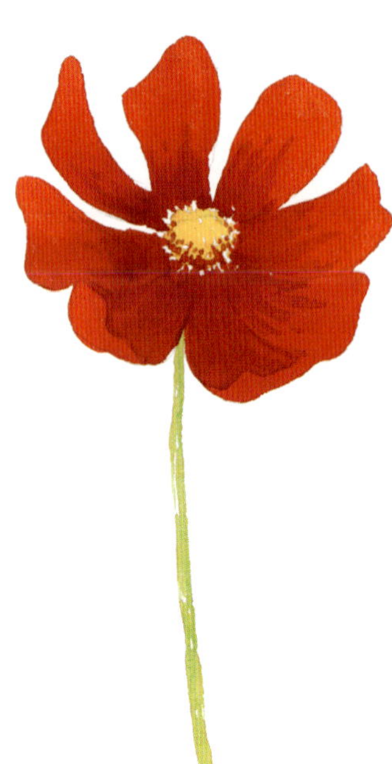

COSMO

One of my favorite flowers is the cosmo; I love the shape of the petals and how big the center pollen is. They also come in various colors, which are so lively to paint. When we apply the pollen for this Cosmo flower, it appears to be a circular shape. However, if you look closely, it isn't perfect because there are lots of irregular dots that create a textured look instead of a smooth, solid circle of paint.

MATERIALS

Pencil

Watercolor paper

Size 8 round brush

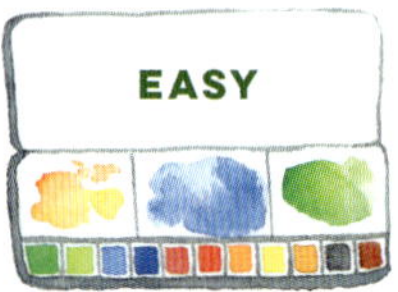

COLORS

 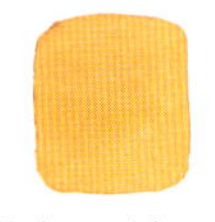 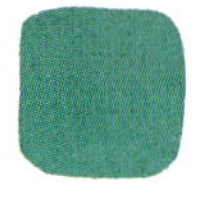 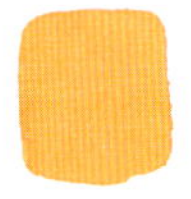 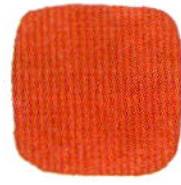

| Lemon Yellow | Quinacridone Gold | Winsor Green | Cadmium Orange | Alizarin Crimson |

STEP 1: Trace (page 225) or lightly sketch the cosmo flower and stem in pencil on your watercolor paper.

STEP 2: Lightly erase the pencil marks until they are just dark enough to see as a reference. Start painting the inside of the flower with a size 8 round brush. Apply Lemon Yellow first using small dots, then follow with dots of Quinacridone Gold to create a variety of yellows within the pollen area. Leave little white spots of your paper poking through.

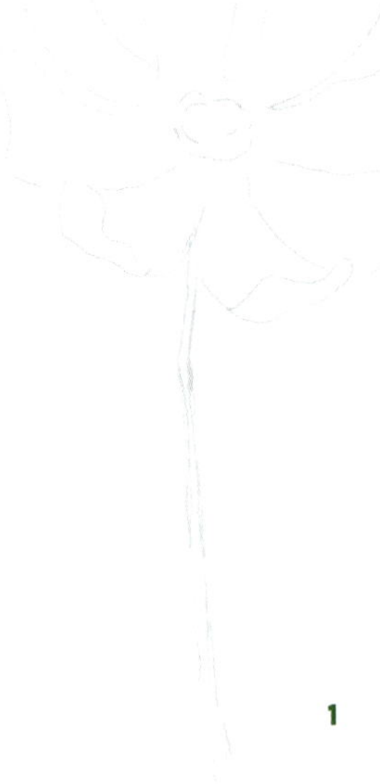

To paint the stem, mix Quinacridone Gold (60%) with Winsor Green (40%). I purposely don't paint in the stem completely, leaving tiny areas of the white paper showing through. This is a stylistic choice I make to break up the solid block of color. However, you can fill in the stem completely if you would like.

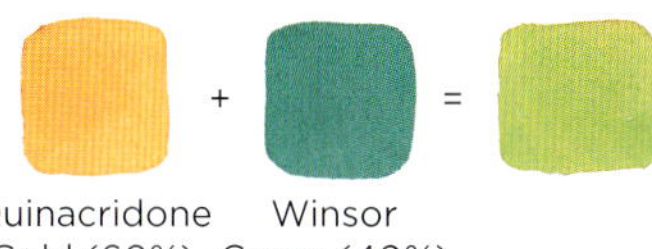

Quinacridone Gold (60%) + Winsor Green (40%)

STEP 3: Begin this step using the **wet-in-wet** technique. Because it is a lot of area to cover, you can focus on each petal at a time. Mix Cadmium Orange (50%) with Alizarin Crimson (50%) to paint on the petals. You won't want to paint all the way to the pollen; leave a little white of the paper showing. While the paint is wet, take Alizarin Crimson and drop it in near the pollen of the flower to create a darker **value** to provide depth to the center of the petals.

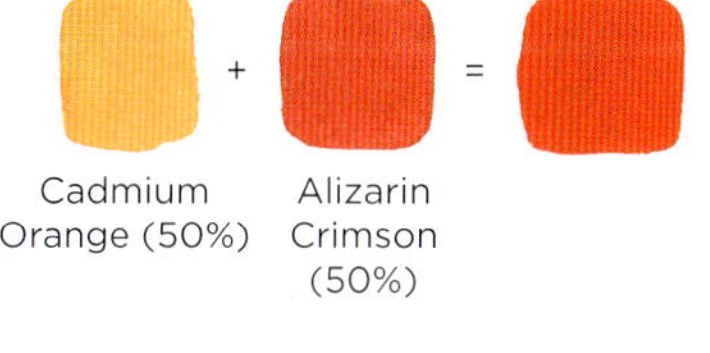

Cadmium Orange (50%) + Alizarin Crimson (50%)

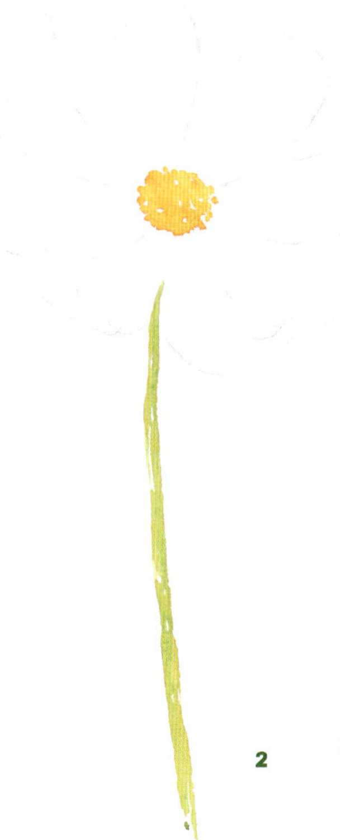

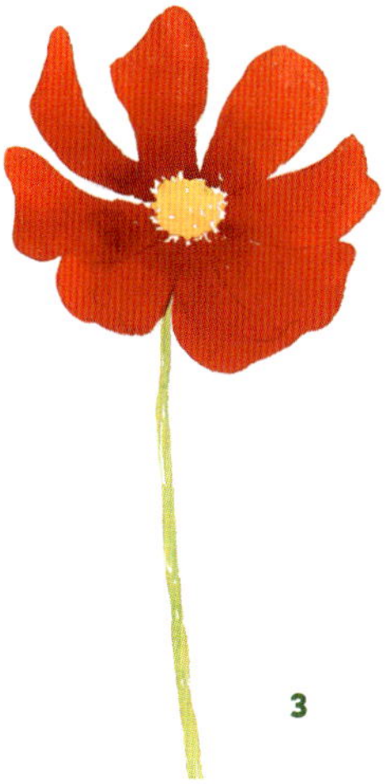

STEP 4: In the pollen, dot in another layer of Quinacridone Gold. Focus on the bottom border. Let that dry.

Add another layer of Alizarin Crimson on the petals to create dimension. Work your way from the center, near the pollen, bringing your paint toward the tips of the petals in thin strokes. Don't paint the tips of the petals. Allow some of your first layer to show through in areas. The bottom two petals will have more of the Alizarin Crimson to add depth and to show the petals curling.

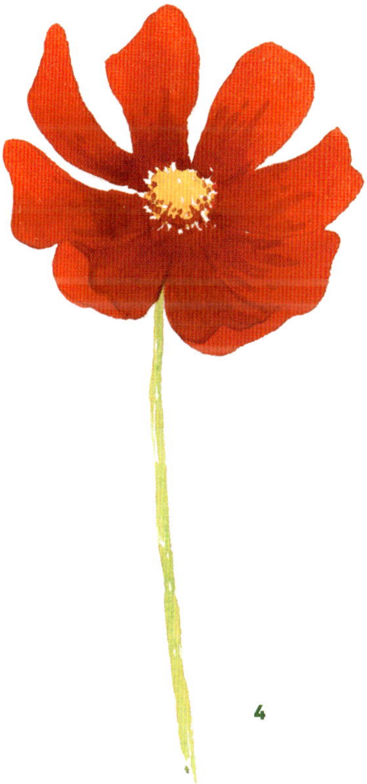

TULIP PRICKLY PEAR

When I was going to Arizona State University, I remember how gorgeous the desert was when all the cacti bloomed with flowers. One of my favorite desert plants was the tulip prickly pear because the yellow and orange flowers stood out so starkly against the green of the cactus. In this Tulip Prickly Pear, use ink to create the spiky **texture**. Ink is one technique used to accentuate and easily add **texture** to your painting.

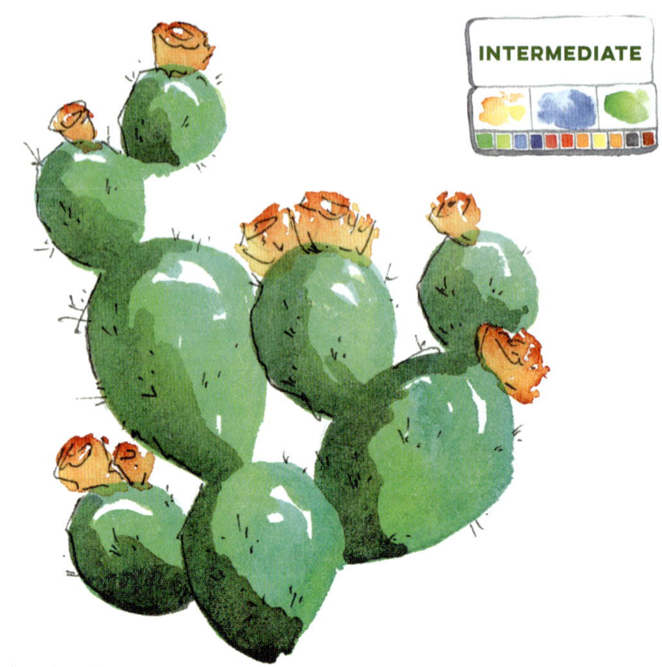

MATERIALS

Pencil

Watercolor paper

Size 8 round brush

Sharpie felt-tip pen (optional)

COLORS

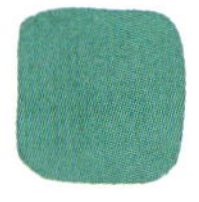

Winsor Green

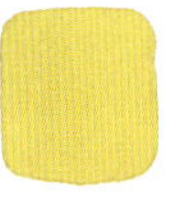

Green Gold

Quinacridone Gold

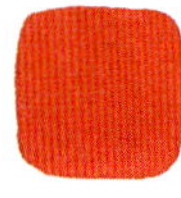

Alizarin Crimson

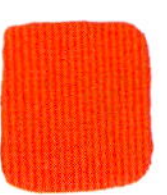

Winsor Red

STEP 1: With a pencil, lightly trace (page 227) or sketch the tulip prickly pear cactus on your water-color paper.

1

STEP 2: Lightly erase your pencil marks. For the main body of the cactus, apply a Winsor Green **wash** with a size 8 round brush. While it is wet, add in Green Gold throughout the pads, but focus on the left sides (**wet-in-wet**). Leave white spaces for **highlights**.

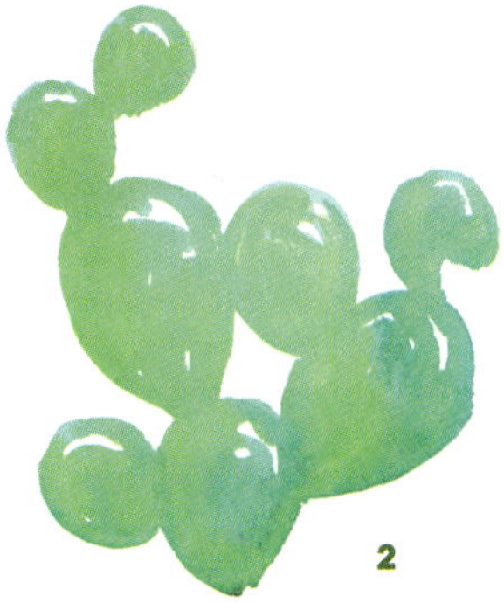

STEP 3: Use Quinacridone Gold to paint the flowers. Once they are filled in, quickly drop in Alizarin Crimson on the top (**wet-in-wet**) and let those colors blend beautifully together!

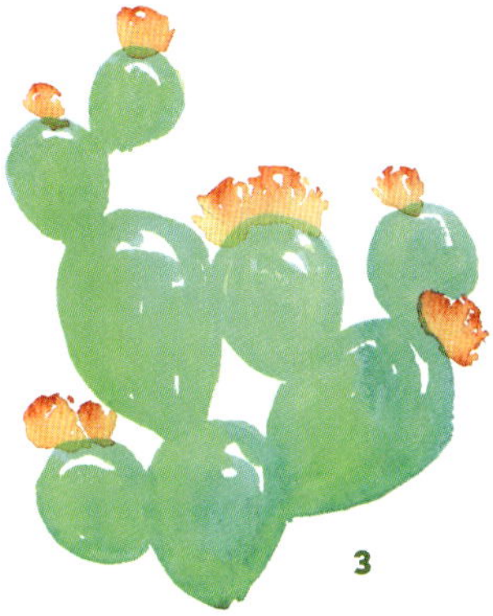

STEP 4: Add a **shadow** on the left side of the cactus pads. Use a mixture of Winsor Green (60%) and Winsor Red (40%). Apply a smaller amount toward the top and let the **shadows** get larger toward the middle and bottom. For each cactus pad, try to do this in one to two strokes to keep it loose. Leave a **hard edge**.

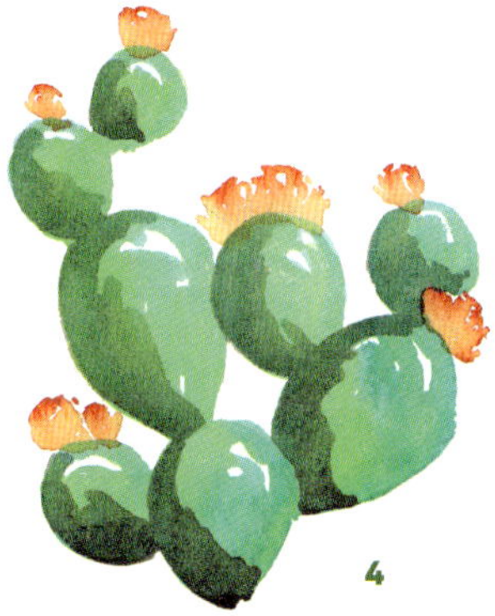

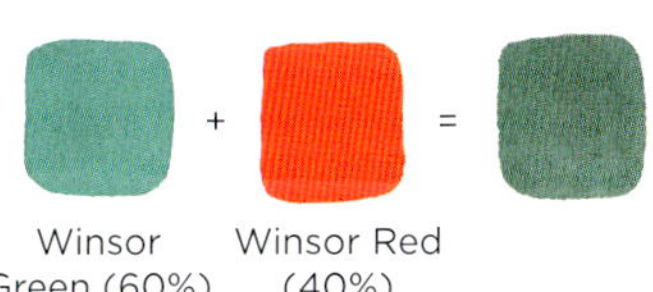

Winsor Green (60%) + Winsor Red (40%) =

STEP 5: Adding ink on top is a stylistic choice and is always optional. If you choose to use ink, outline the left side of the cactus pads. Make tiny marks for the needles, applying them to the middle of the pads and on the outside edges. For the flowers, use the ink to make swirls on the tops and outline the left edges.

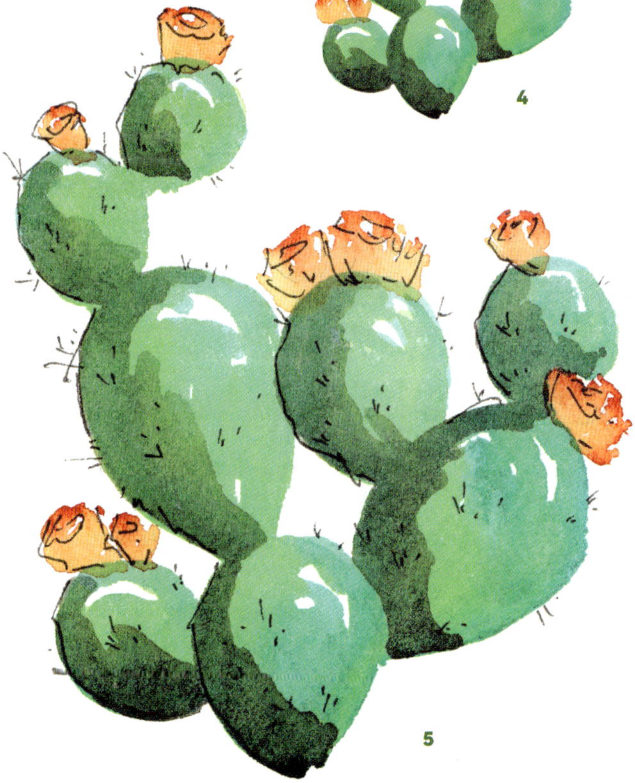

DAISY

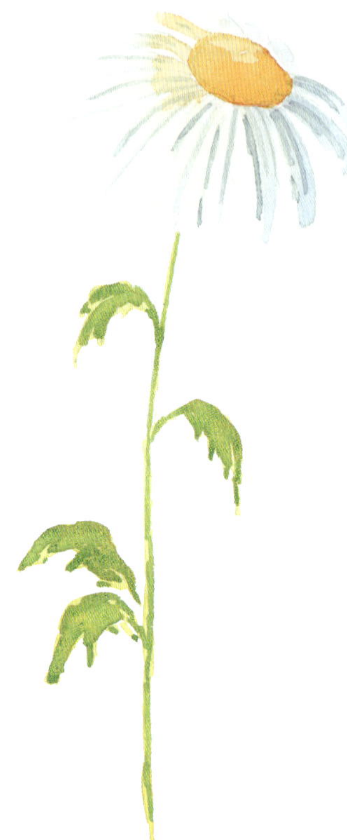

White **subjects** can be challenging. Even though the daisy appears white, the **light source** and **shadows** will reflect color onto the petals. For this Daisy, use light yellows where the sun is hitting and light blues for the **shadow** area. To create lighter **values**, use more water in the mixture than normal. Looking at other white objects closely can help identify the different colors hidden within white. Studying snow, for example, is a great way to see how **shadows** create a light blue cast on the white ground, while the sun lends a pale yellow **tone** to the snow.

MATERIALS

Pencil

Watercolor paper

Size 8 round brush

Size 2 round brush (optional)

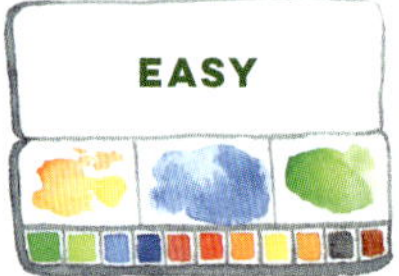

COLORS

  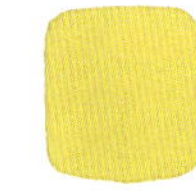 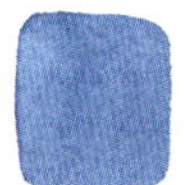

Quinacridone Gold   Cadmium Orange   Green Gold   Ultramarine Blue

 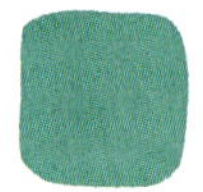 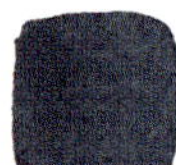

Neutral Tint   Winsor Green   Indigo

STEP 1: With a pencil, trace (page 227) or sketch the daisy on your watercolor paper.

STEP 2: Lightly erase your pencil marks. **Load** your size 8 round brush with Quinacridone Gold; use more water than paint to lighten the **value**. Paint the center of the flower, which is the pollen area. While it is wet, drop in Cadmium Orange to the bottom right-hand side of the pollen (**wet-in-wet**), which will darken the rim. Wait for this to dry (I did not, and my pollen color bled onto five of my petals on the left. This still worked out well, but if it had been on the right-hand side, it wouldn't have worked because that is the **shadow** side).

Now create a lighter **value** of Quinacridone Gold by adding even more water so that the color is barely visible. Apply this paint to the forward-facing petals. You don't need to completely paint the petals; let some of the white paper be visible. Add Green Gold to the stem and leaves.

STEP 3: Mix Ultramarine Blue (70%) with Neutral Tint (30%) to add the **shadow** on the flower petals. Use light **values**, so add plenty of water in your color mixture. Apply a larger amount to the right-hand petals. Paint thin strokes on the left-hand side petals where the sunlight is hitting. You can size down to a size 2 round brush for the thin strokes if you prefer.

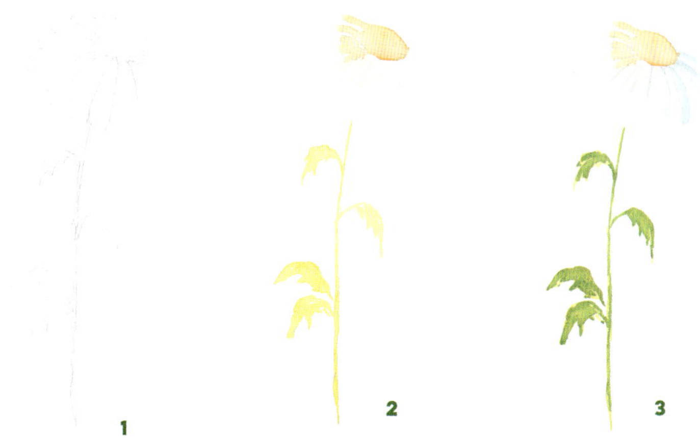

Combine Cadmium Orange (60%) with Winsor Green (40%) on your palette, mixing a darker **value** to create depth, and apply it to the stems and leaves area. Be careful to not completely cover up the first layer.

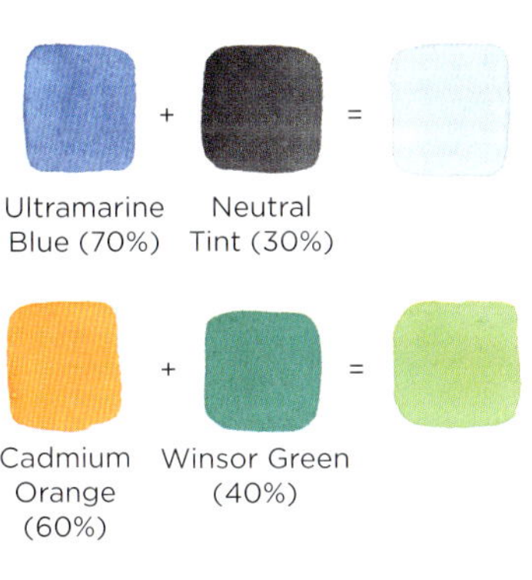

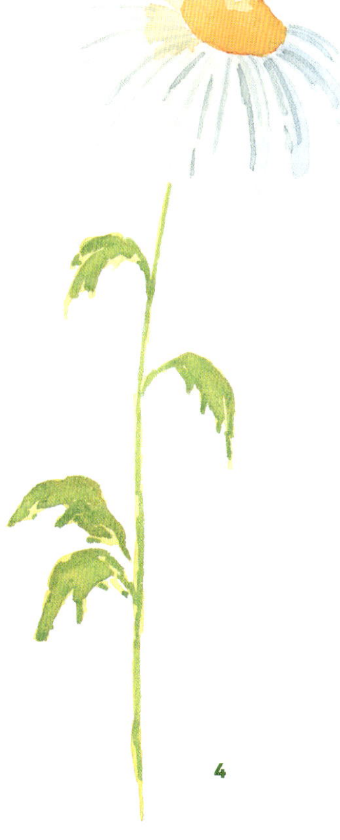

STEP 4: To darken the pollen, use Quinacridone Gold to **glaze** the majority of the area, except on the top left corner. Leave the first layer in that corner for the **highlight**. Mix Indigo with some water (a little bit less than you used when mixing your colors in Step 3) to add a line down the middle of each petal to create definition.

CHINESE MONEY PLANT

For this Chinese Money Plant painting, there are A LOT of leaves of the same shape over and over. To create depth and allow some of the leaves to look like they are behind others, overlap the leaves and paint the ones in the back with a darker **value**. By painting some of the leaves darker, we are creating a **shadow** and helping differentiate which leaves are in front and which are in the back.

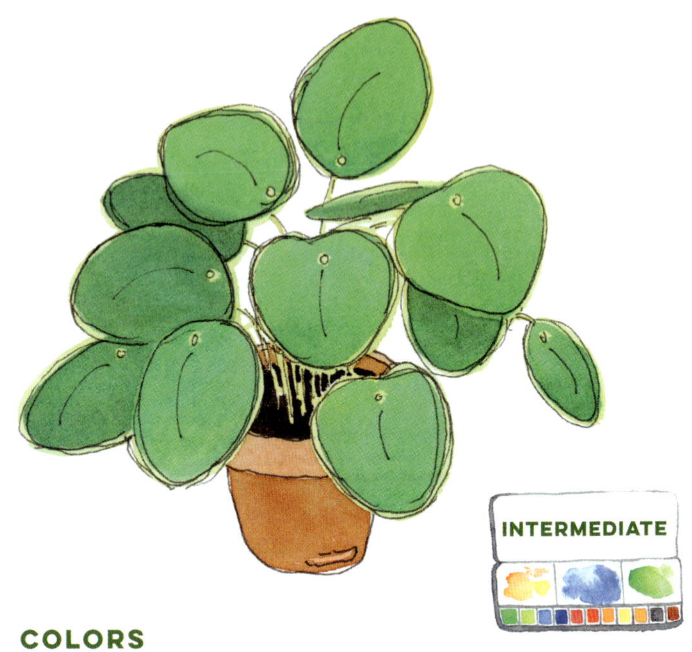

MATERIALS

Pencil

Watercolor paper

Drawing gum paste

Old brush

Size 8 round brush

Rubber cement eraser

Sharpie felt-tip pen (optional)

COLORS

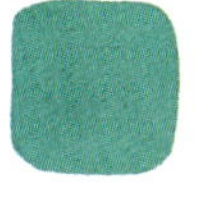
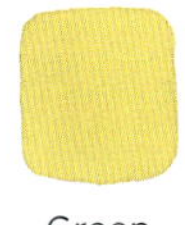

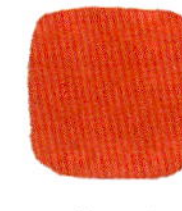
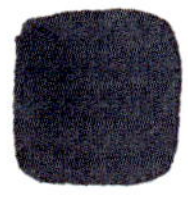
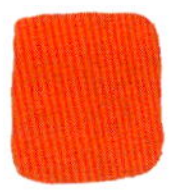

Winsor Green	Green Gold	Cadmium Orange	Alizarin Crimson	Indigo	Winsor Red

STEP 1: Trace (page 227) or lightly sketch the Chinese money plant in pencil on your watercolor paper.

1

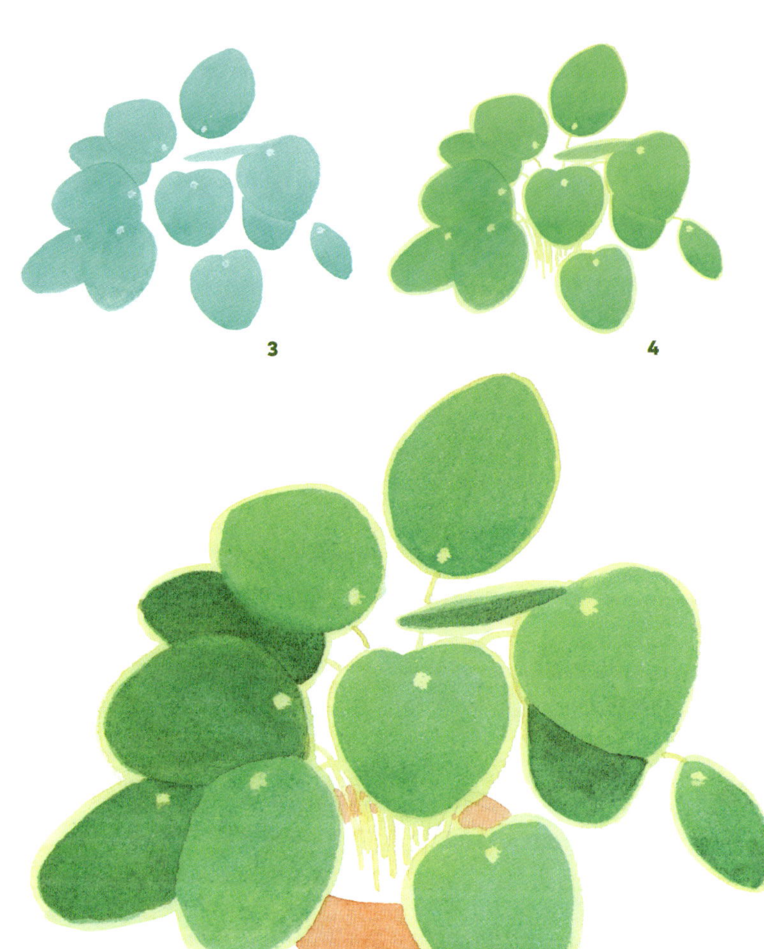

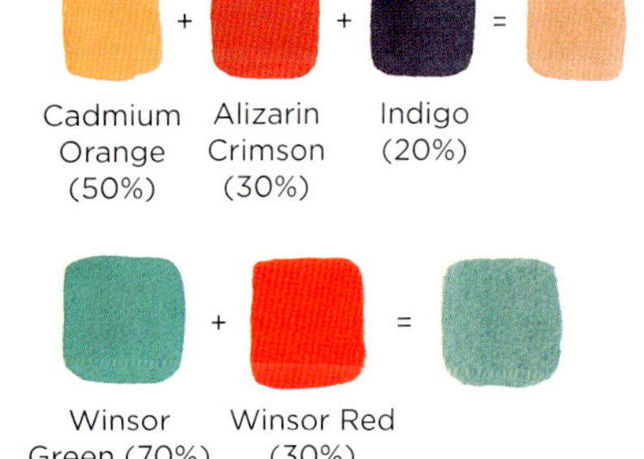

STEP 2: Lightly erase your pencil marks. Add drawing gum paste with an old brush onto the **highlight** area of the leaves as small dots.

STEP 3: With a size 8 round brush, paint in the leaves using Winsor Green, going over the drawing gum paste. Let the painting completely dry, then remove the drawing gum paste with a rubber cement eraser.

STEP 4: Apply a Green Gold **glaze** over the leaves and extend the **glaze** so that there is a Green Gold border around each leaf. Carry the Green Gold down into the stems.

STEP 5: To get the traditional terra-cotta pot color, mix on your palette Cadmium Orange (50%) with Alizarin Crimson (30%) and Indigo (20%). Use this mixture to paint in the pot.

To add variety and break up the leaves, add **shadows** to six of the leaves. Combine Winsor Green (70%) and Winsor Red (30%) on your palette. Paint this **glaze** on three leaves on the left and three leaves on the right.

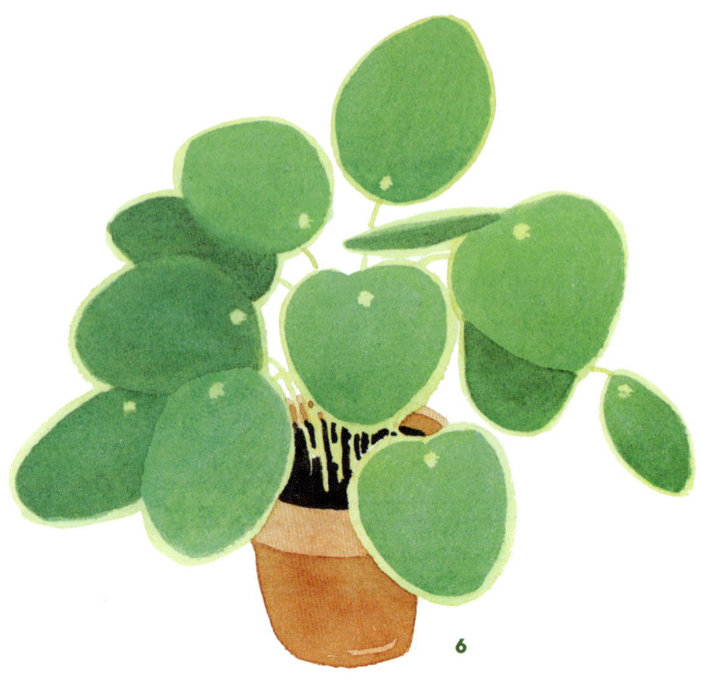

6

STEP 6: Darken the outside of the pot and the inside rim of the pot. Use the same color mixture on your palette from Step 5: Cadmium Orange (50%) with Alizarin Crimson (30%) and Indigo (20%). Adding a second layer of the same color will darken the pot. When you paint the outside layer of the pot, leave markings of your first layer coming through on the bottom right-hand corner to act as a **highlight**. Let the pot dry before moving forward.

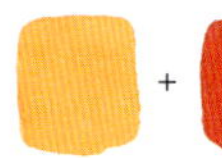 + 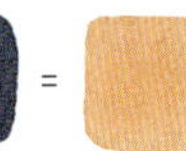 =

Cadmium Orange (50%)   Alizarin Crimson (30%)   Indigo (20%)

Take Winsor Red (80%) and mix it with Winsor Green (20%) on your palette. Use this color to paint in the dirt inside the pot. Avoid painting over the stems.

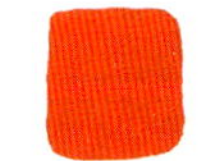 + 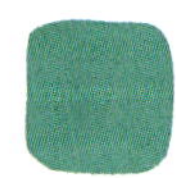 = 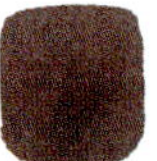

Winsor Red (80%)   Winsor Green (20%)

STEP 7: This step is optional if you want to add ink on top of the painting. I chose to use a Sharpie to add ink in a sketch-like style where I made multiple lines over and over to make it look looser and a little messy. I also added a line down the middle of each leaf.

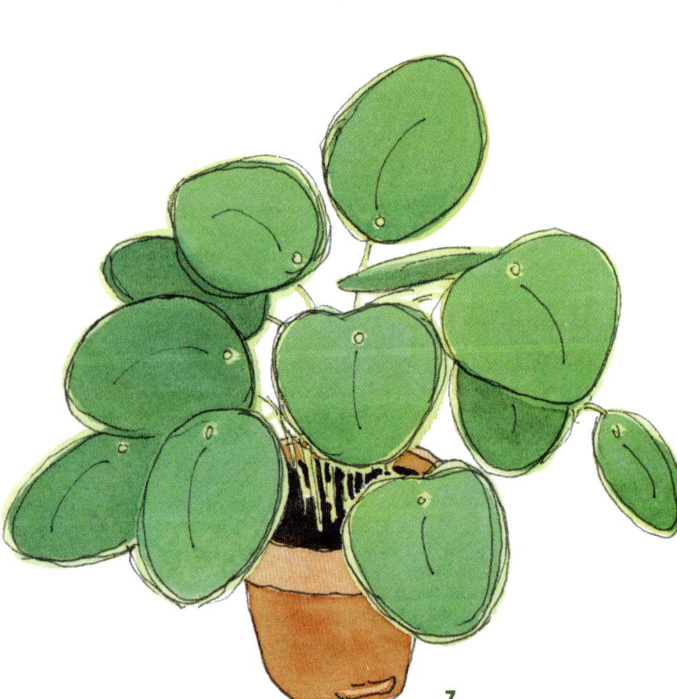

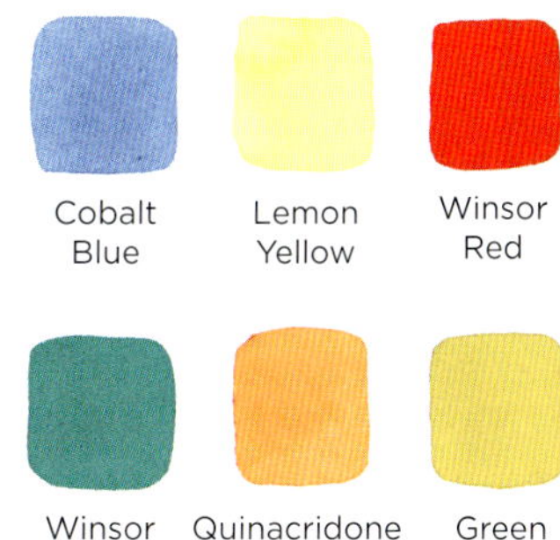

SUNFLOWERS

A great way to emphasize your **subject** is to play with the border around it. In this Sunflower painting, the sky keeps to a rectangular border, but the greenery around the sunflowers exceeds the border in an irregular pattern. The viewer's eye will naturally go to the sunflowers because they appear to be "popping" out of the frame. This painting is challenging for a few reasons. First, you must paint around the flowers; things get trickier whenever areas need to be avoided. The flowers also get outlined, which requires a steady hand to make the strokes thin and precise. Although this sounds more intimidating, having a smaller brush can be your best friend for these challenges!

MATERIALS

Pencil

Watercolor paper

Size 8 round brush

Size 2 round brush

STEP 1: Trace (page 229) or lightly sketch the sunflower composition with a pencil on your watercolor paper.

1

STEP 2: Lightly erase your pencil markings. Using the size 8 round brush, paint a Cobalt Blue **wash** onto the top half of your paper for the sky.

STEP 3: Paint Lemon Yellow over all the sunflowers.

STEP 4: Combine Winsor Red (70%) with Winsor Green (30%) on your palette, then paint in the centers of the sunflowers. Let that dry.

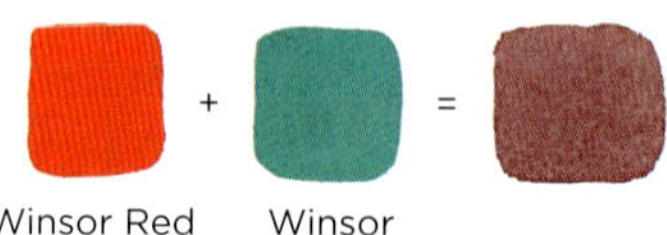

Switch to a size 2 round brush. **Load** that brush with Quinacridone Gold, then outline your flower petals and paint a line in the middle of each petal.

2

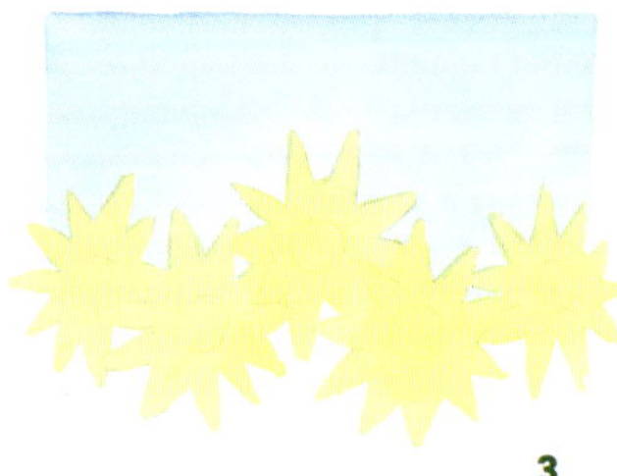

3

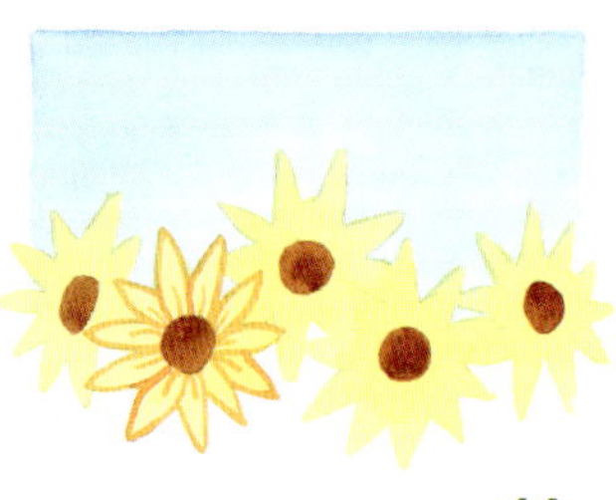

4A

4B

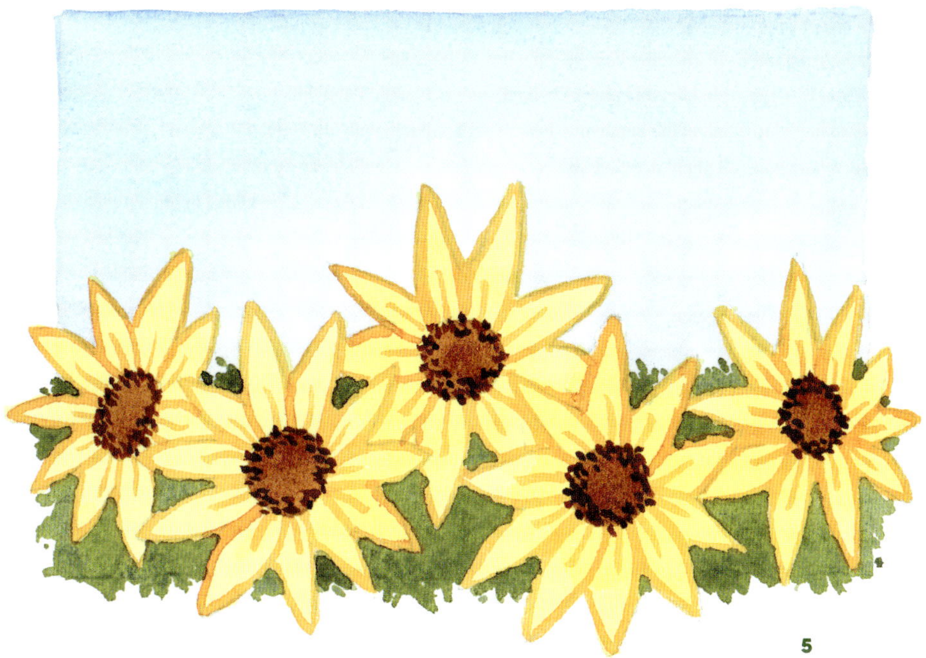

STEP 5: On your palette mix Green Gold (50%) with Cobalt Blue (50%). Switch back to a size 8 round brush and paint this green mixture around the sunflowers. On the edges, apply the green mixture in jagged strokes and little dots to imply the **texture** of grass.

Now, take some of the Winsor Red (70%) and Winsor Green (30%) mix from Step 4 but add less water to darken the **value**. Dot some brown on the center of the sunflowers to add depth.

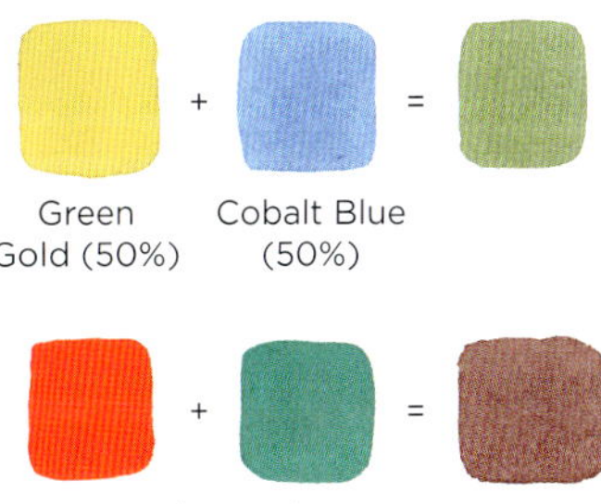

LILY PAD

A simple way to help create dimension in your artwork is to add a **shadow** in a darker **value** to your object. In this Lily Pad project, you will apply a darker pink to the edges of the flower and a darker green to the edge of the lily pad. As you paint, you'll see how all of a sudden, it goes from looking flat to popping out!

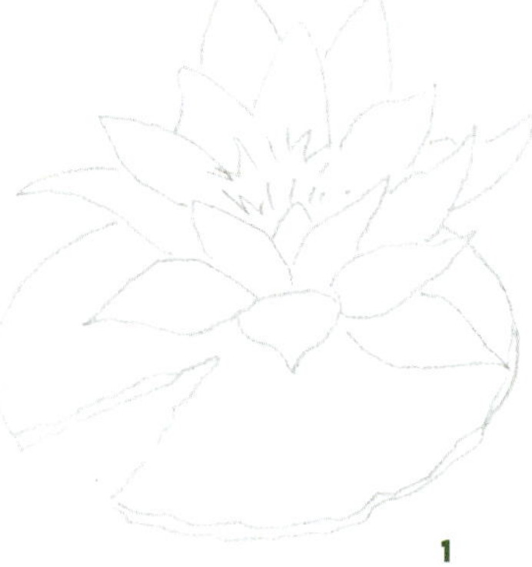

MATERIALS

Pencil
Watercolor paper
Size 8 round brush

COLORS

Lemon Yellow

Cadmium Orange

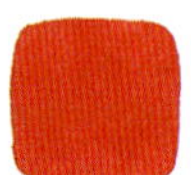

Alizarin Crimson

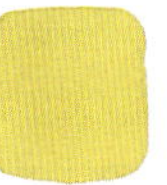

Green Gold

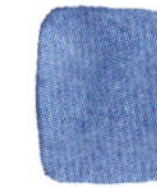

Ultramarine Blue

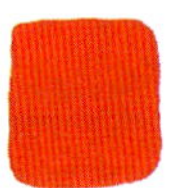

Winsor Red

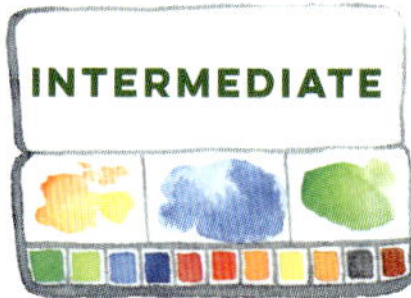

STEP 1: With a pencil, trace (page 225) or sketch the lily pad onto your watercolor paper.

STEP 2: With a size 8 round brush, paint a Lemon Yellow **wash** in the center of the lily flower. Using **wet-in-wet**, drop in Cadmium Orange while the Lemon Yellow is still wet. Let that dry.

Take a light **value** of Alizarin Crimson and paint in the lily petals on the flower.

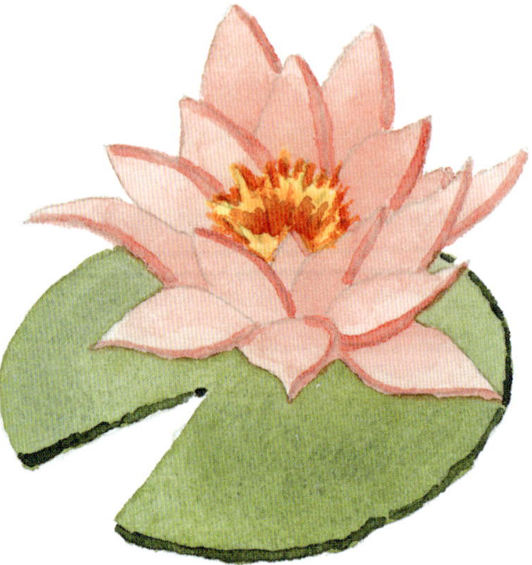

1

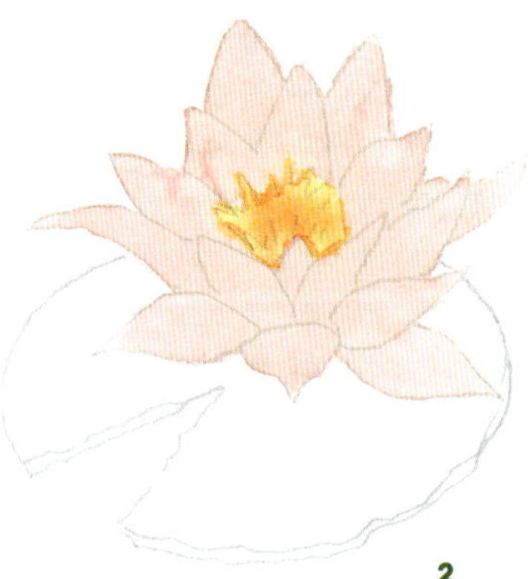

2

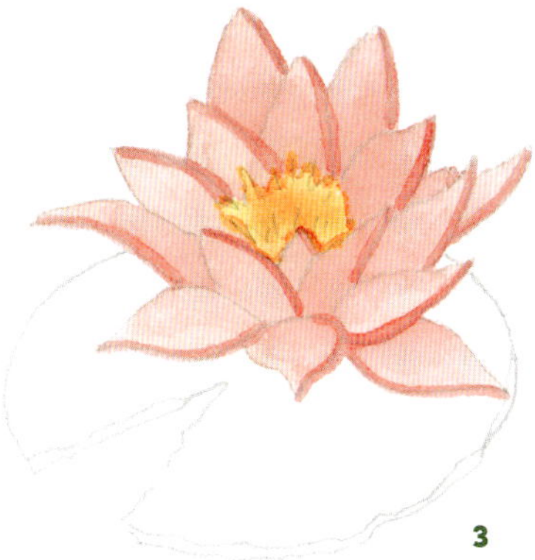

STEP 3: Add a second layer on the lily flower petals using the same light **value** of Alizarin Crimson from Step 2. Don't paint in the flower petals completely; leave areas of the first layer coming through, especially on the petals in the **foreground**. Leave less of the first layer showing on the petals in the **background** and the bottom petals to create a sense of depth. Let that dry.

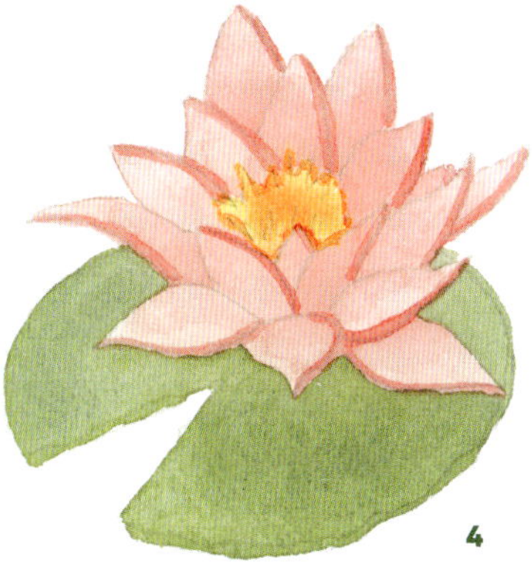

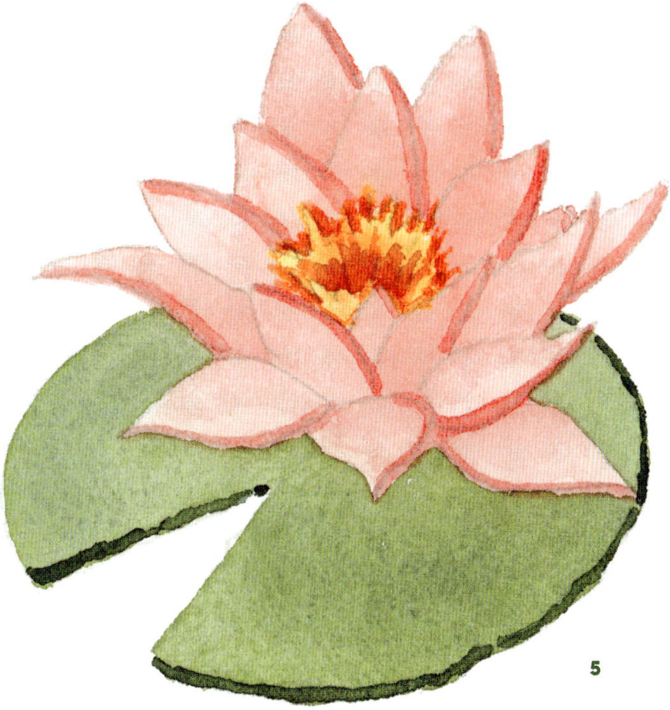

Take Alizarin Crimson and don't add as much water as you did in Step 2 in order to achieve a darker **value**. The color should still be pink. With this color, outline one of the lines on each flower petal.

STEP 4: Combine Green Gold (60%) with Ultramarine Blue (40%) on your palette. Use this mixture to paint the lily pad.

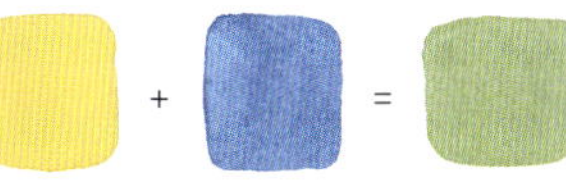

Green Gold (60%)   Ultramarine Blue (40%)

STEP 5: Mix on your palette Ultramarine Blue (60%) and Green Gold (40%). Take this color and paint in the edging on the lily pad.

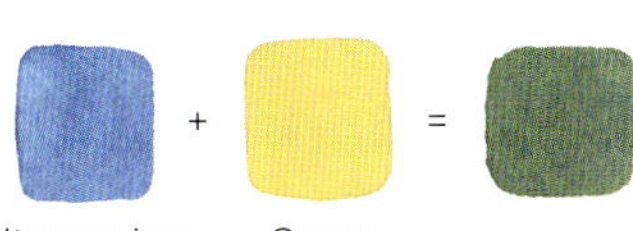

Ultramarine Blue (60%)   Green Gold (40%)

Mix Cadmium Orange (60%) with Winsor Red (40%) on your palette. Add this mixture in the tips on the yellow center of the lily flower. When you paint it in, use thin little lines as if they were little spikes.

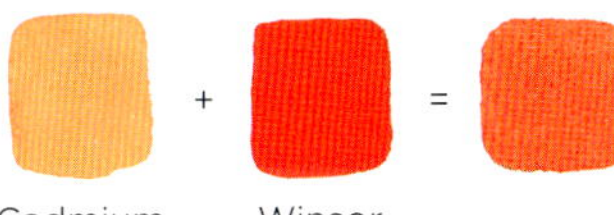

Cadmium Orange (60%)   Winsor Red (40%)

FIDDLE LEAF FIG

One of the best ways to experiment with stylistic direction is by playing with the **background**. With this composition, the **background** part of the painting is made by allowing the color to become a part of the **subject**; in this case, it is our pot. Here, I've chosen a peachy-pink color because those colors are the opposite of the greens we use on the leaves, making them **complementary colors** on the color wheel. **Complementary colors** (page 23) work well next to each other to create contrast). There are endless choices when applying a **background**, so think outside of the box and experiment!

MATERIALS

Pencil
Watercolor paper
Size 8 round brush

COLORS

Indigo

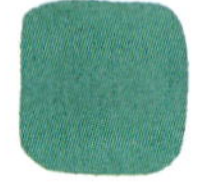

Winsor Green

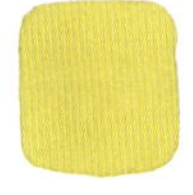

Green Gold

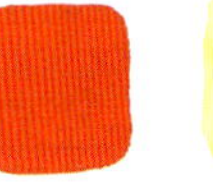

Winsor Red

Lemon Yellow

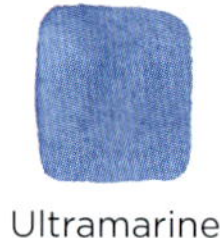

Ultramarine Blue

Cadmium Orange

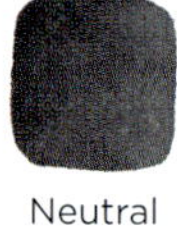

Neutral Tint

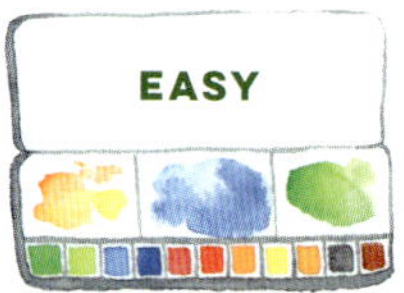

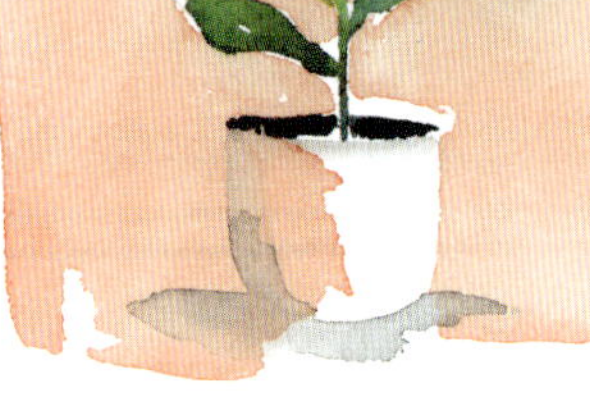

STEP 1: Lightly trace (page 231) or sketch the fiddle leaf fig on your watercolor paper with a pencil.

STEP 2: Lightly erase the pencil marks. Mix Indigo (60%) with Winsor Green (40%) on your palette. Use this mixture and a size 8 round brush to paint a **wash** over the leaves and stems. While still wet, add Green Gold into the mixture. Lay the Green Gold in the center of each leaf for a fun **bleeding** look.

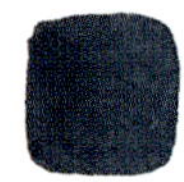 + 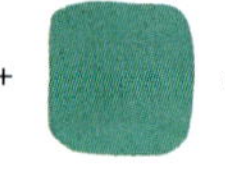 = 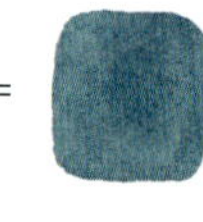

Indigo (60%)   Winsor Green (40%)

1

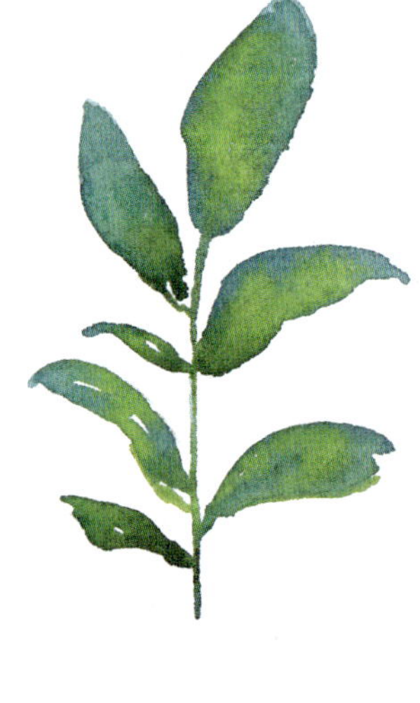

2

STEP 3: Take Winsor Red (70%) and combine it with Lemon Yellow (30%) on your palette. Clean your brush, then apply a **clear water wash** behind the plant (**background**) and the left side of the pot. Once the **clear water wash** is added, use the **wet-in-wet** technique to add the red-and-yellow mixture in the **clear water wash** areas. I chose to leave little areas of white around the leaves and the pot as a stylistic choice to make the paint more rough and sketchy feeling. You can paint all the way to the edging if you want.

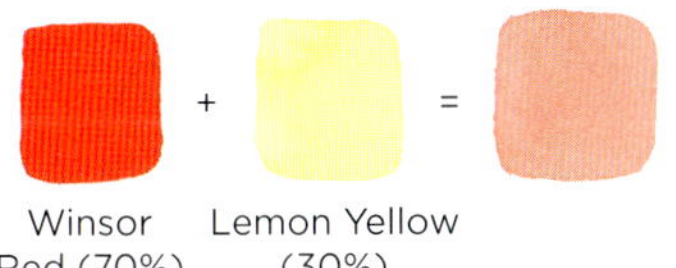

Winsor Red (70%)   +   Lemon Yellow (30%)   =

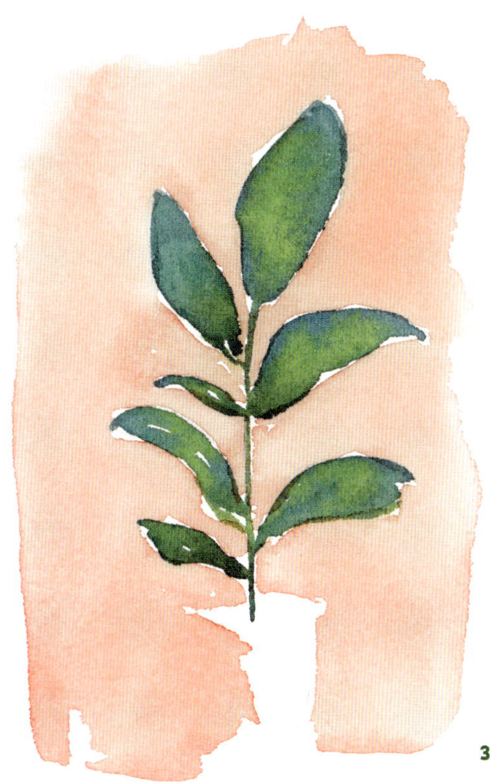

3

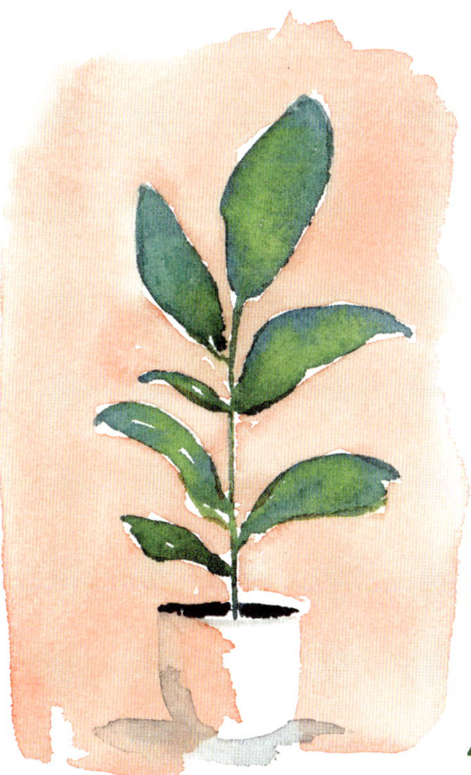

4

STEP 4: On your palette, mix Ultramarine Blue (70%) with Cadmium Orange (30%), then paint the dirt inside the potted plant. Once you paint in the dirt, **load** your brush with a light **value** of Neutral Tint. Use that light color to paint in the **shadow** on the bottom left side of the pot and on the ground. The **light source** is coming from behind the pot on the right-hand side, which is why the **cast shadow** is in the **foreground** and mainly to the left.

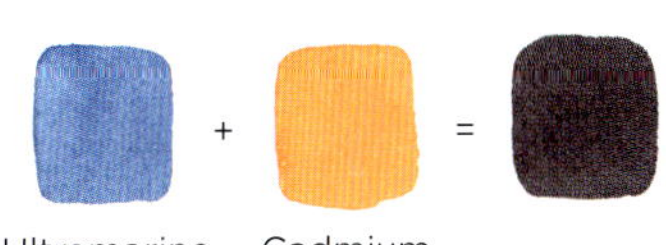

Ultramarine Blue (70%)   +   Cadmium Orange (30%)   =

DAFFODIL

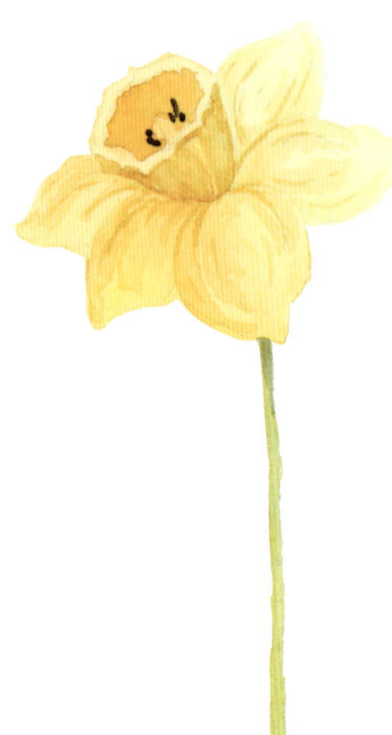

When you have an object that appears all one color, like a yellow daffodil, there is usually more to the story. To make your **subject** appear three-dimensional, you need to use multiple colors of yellow and **values** to help create dimension. Notice in this Daffodil painting, the inside of the center of the flower is darkened to help distinguish the inside from the outside **value**. If you have trouble defining an object, look at the **values** and decide if lightening or darkening an area can help. Another example of this is the Chinese Money Plant painting (page 34), which uses a darker **value** on some leaves to help distinguish which leaves are forward and which are behind.

MATERIALS

Pencil

Watercolor paper

Size 8 round brush

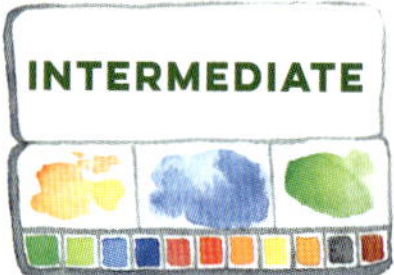

COLORS

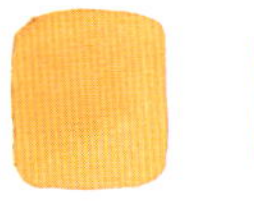

Lemon Yellow   Quinacridone Gold   Cadmium Orange

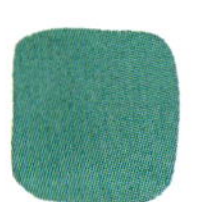
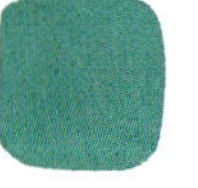
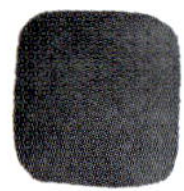

Winsor Green   Neutral Tint

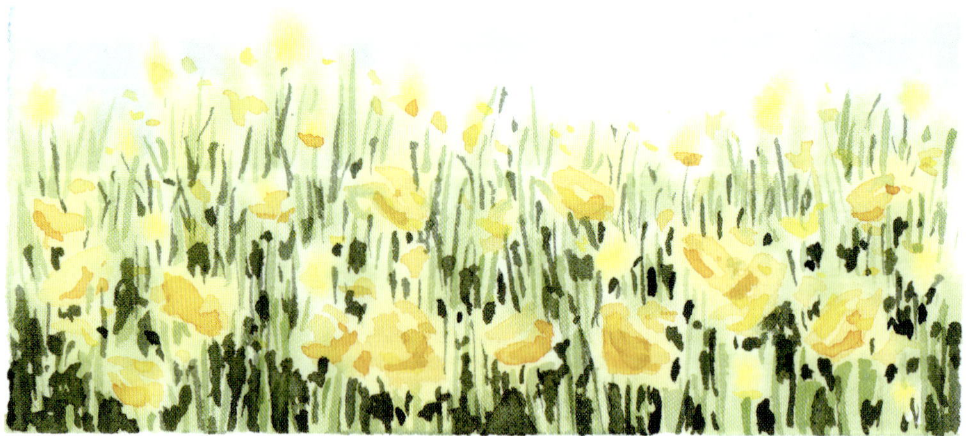

STEP 1: With a pencil, trace (page 229) or sketch the daffodil on your water-color paper.

STEP 2: Lightly erase the pencil marks with a size 8 round brush, paint Lemon Yellow over the whole flower. Don't let this dry; for the remainder of this step, work **wet-in-wet**. Drop in Quinacridone Gold to the left three petals and the center flower. Add Cadmium Orange to the very center of the flower. If the top two petals are too dark, you can **lift** some color off. **Lift** the paint that is on the rim of the center flower. This provides a bit of a **highlight** to show where the **light source** is coming from.

STEP 3: On your palette, mix Quinacridone Gold (60%) and Winsor Green (40%). Use that mixture to paint the stem. Add a Quinacridone Gold **glaze** to the middle of the center flower, but don't cover in the very center where the pollen will go. Add some detailing on the petals also using Quinacridone Gold by starting at the base and pulling the paint along the sides of the petals. Add a variety of strokes, making sure to let the first layer show through in some places.

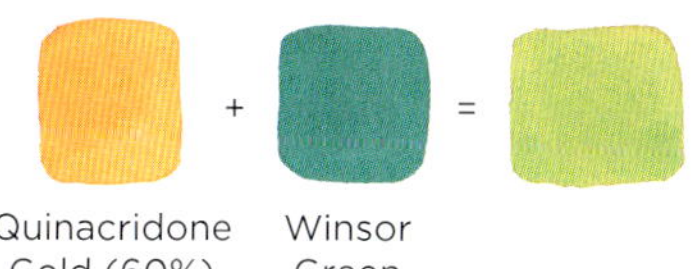

Quinacridone
Gold (60%)

Winsor
Green
(40%)

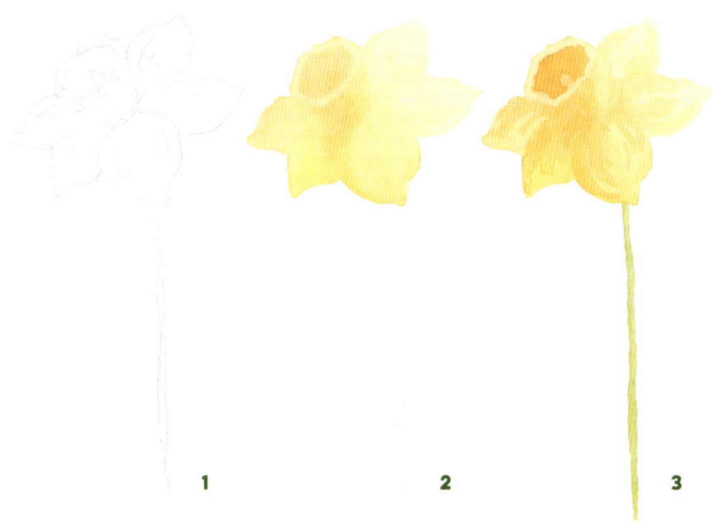

STEP 4: Use Neutral Tint for the pollen by adding two dots on the left side and three on the right. Add Quinacridone Gold underneath the rim of the center flower and a few thin lines on the petals. Take a watered-down Neutral Tint and add a **shadow** on the left side of the stem under the flower.

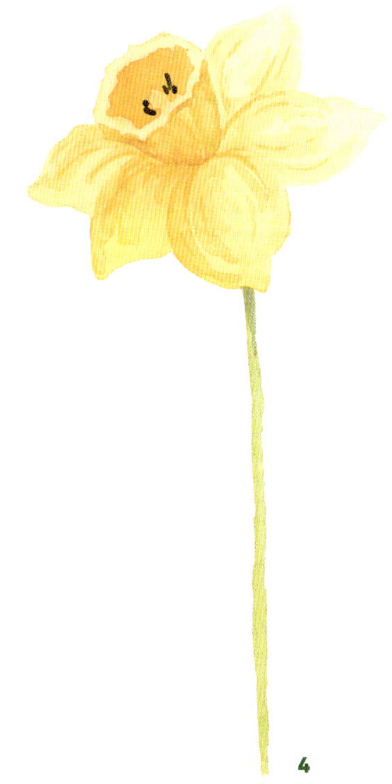

BLUE AGAVE

On the blue agave plant, there are little spiky points at the ends of each leaf. To create this effect on this Blue Agave painting, I used ink at the beginning to make these spiky points instead of trying to create them with a brush, which would be more challenging. The ink also helps accentuate the sharpness of the leaves. To help differentiate the leaves from the front to the back, a **glaze** is added, creating depth within the plant.

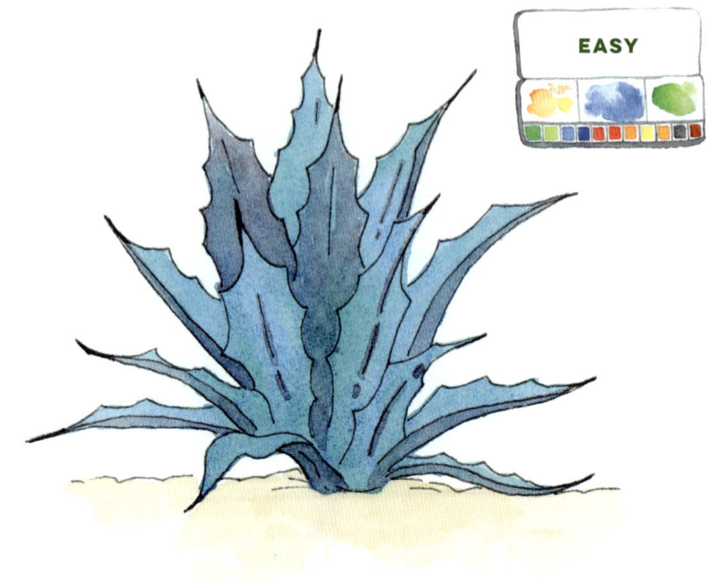

MATERIALS

Watercolor paper

Sharpie felt-tip pen

Pencil (optional)

Size 8 round brush

COLORS

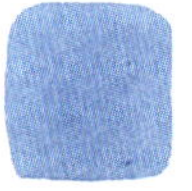
Cobalt Blue

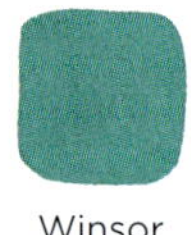
Winsor Green

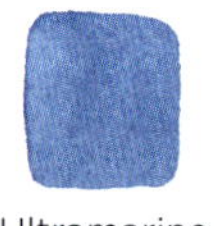
Ultramarine Blue

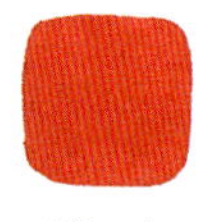
Alizarin Crimson

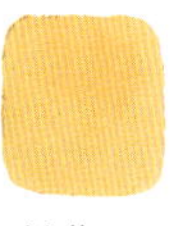
Yellow Ochre

STEP 1: On your watercolor paper, trace (page 229) or sketch the blue agave using your Sharpie. If you aren't comfortable going in with ink right away, draw it out using pencil first, then trace over your pencil markings with ink.

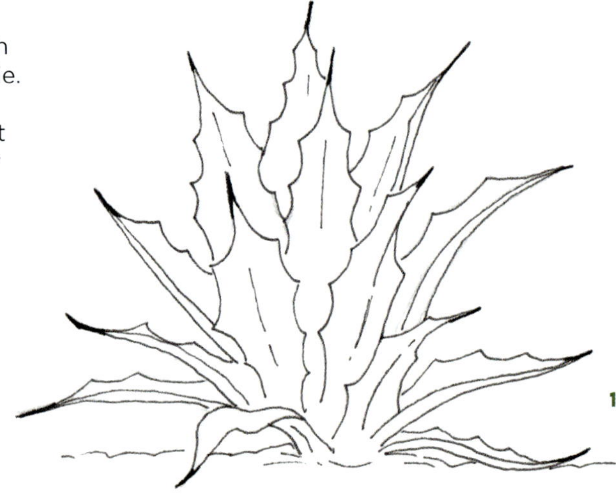

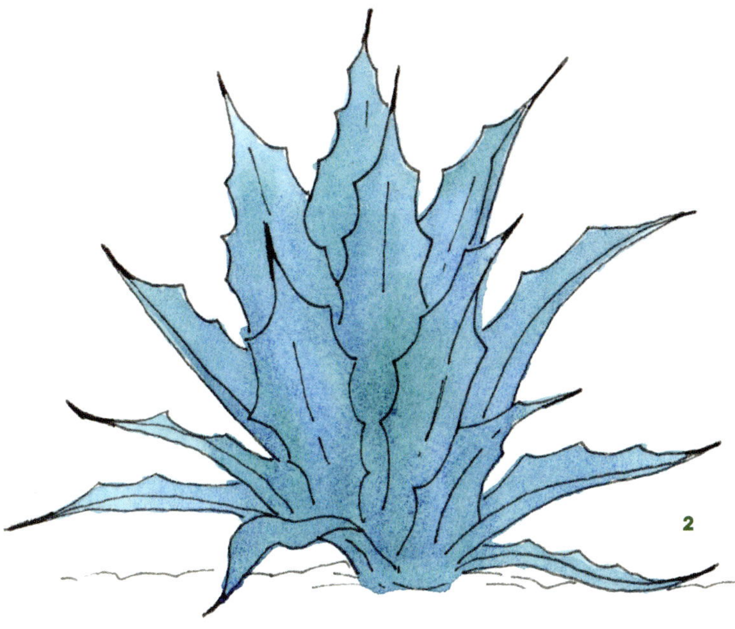

STEP 2: For this step, use the **wet-in-wet** technique and a size 8 round brush. Paint Cobalt Blue over the plant and, while that is still wet, drop Winsor Green in random areas to create variety in the coloring.

STEP 3: Combine Alizarin Crimson (70%) and Ultramarine Blue (30%) on your palette. Use this mixture to **glaze** the plant leaves and create a darker **value**. Fill in two leaves completely; this helps separate those two leaves from the rest to give dimension. On some leaves, you can add the color to the edges to show depth. Once that is dry, add Yellow Ochre with a **dry brush** on the ground as sand.

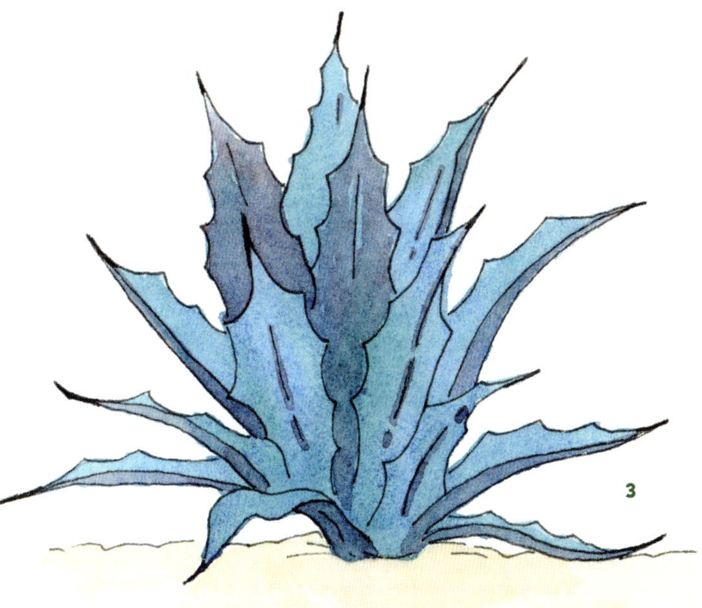

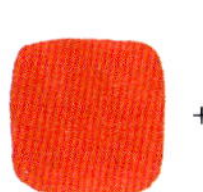 + 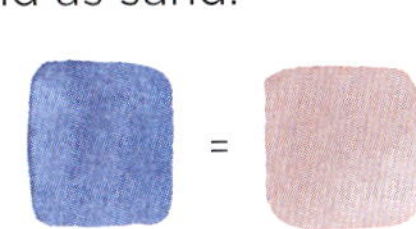 =

Alizarin Crimson (70%)

Ultramarine Blue (30%)

BANANA LEAVES

There are multiple ways to paint things. There is no perfect one-size-fits-all to watercolor. In this Banana Leaf painting, I applied a **glaze** to the leaves in **shadow**, but I also could have darkened those leaves on the first layer while everything was still wet. While the final looks are slightly different, both methods show dimension from the **shadows**. Try experimenting with your banana leaves by painting them multiple times in various ways to challenge yourself. The beauty of watercolor is the freedom; you have endless options for how to paint a **subject**!

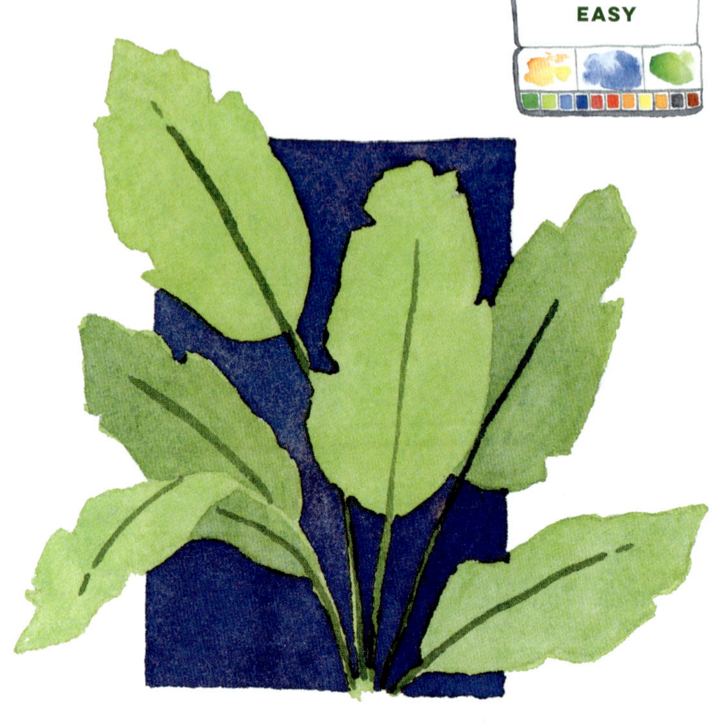

MATERIALS

Pencil

Watercolor paper

Size 8 round brush

COLORS

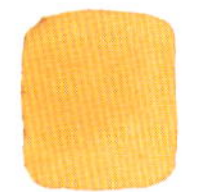
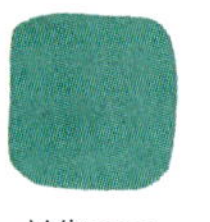
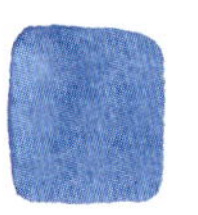
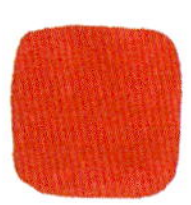

Quinacridone Gold

Winsor Green

Ultramarine Blue

Alizarin Crimson

STEP 1: Trace (page 231) or sketch the banana leaves with a pencil on your watercolor paper.

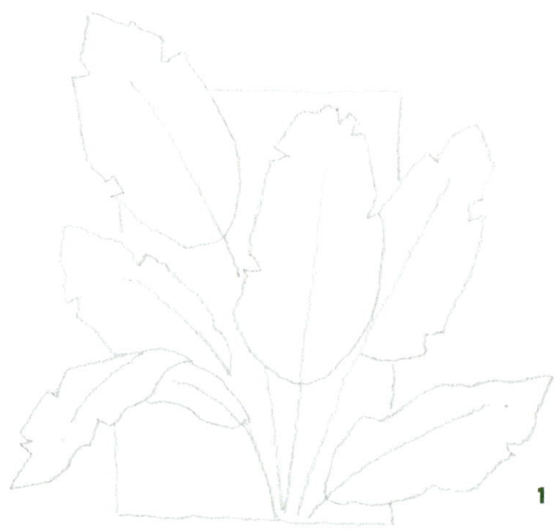

STEP 2: Lightly erase the pencil marks. Make a green mixture on your palette using Quinacridone Gold (70%) with Winsor Green (30%). Use a size 8 round brush to paint this mixture as a **wash** over all the leaves and stems.

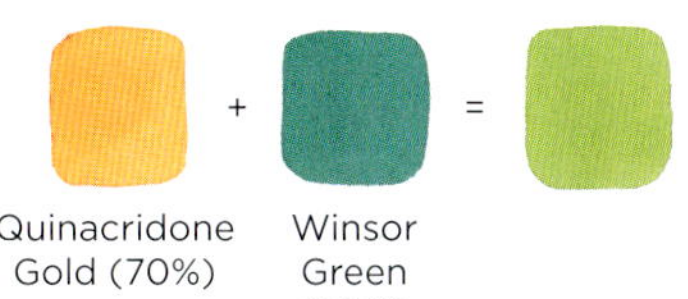

Quinacridone Gold (70%)   +   Winsor Green (30%)   =

STEP 3: Take a light **value** of Ultramarine Blue and paint a **shadow** on three of the banana leaves. The banana leaf on the bottom left is slightly **lighter** in **value** because **shadows** vary in real life. The fourth leaf you will add the **shadow** to is on the underside of the flopped leaf.

STEP 4: Mix Quinacridone Gold (60%) and Ultramarine Blue (40%) on your palette. Use this mixture to paint a line down each banana leaf and down each stem.

Quinacridone Gold (60%)   +   Ultramarine Blue (40%)   =

STEP 5: On your palette, mix Ultramarine Blue (80%) and Alizarine Crimson (20%) and paint in the **background** with this color. One way to help your object "pop out" is to paint a smaller **background**, allowing the object to exceed the borders.

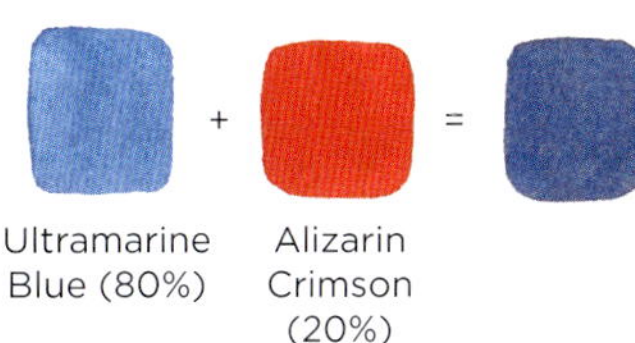

Ultramarine Blue (80%)   +   Alizarin Crimson (20%)   =

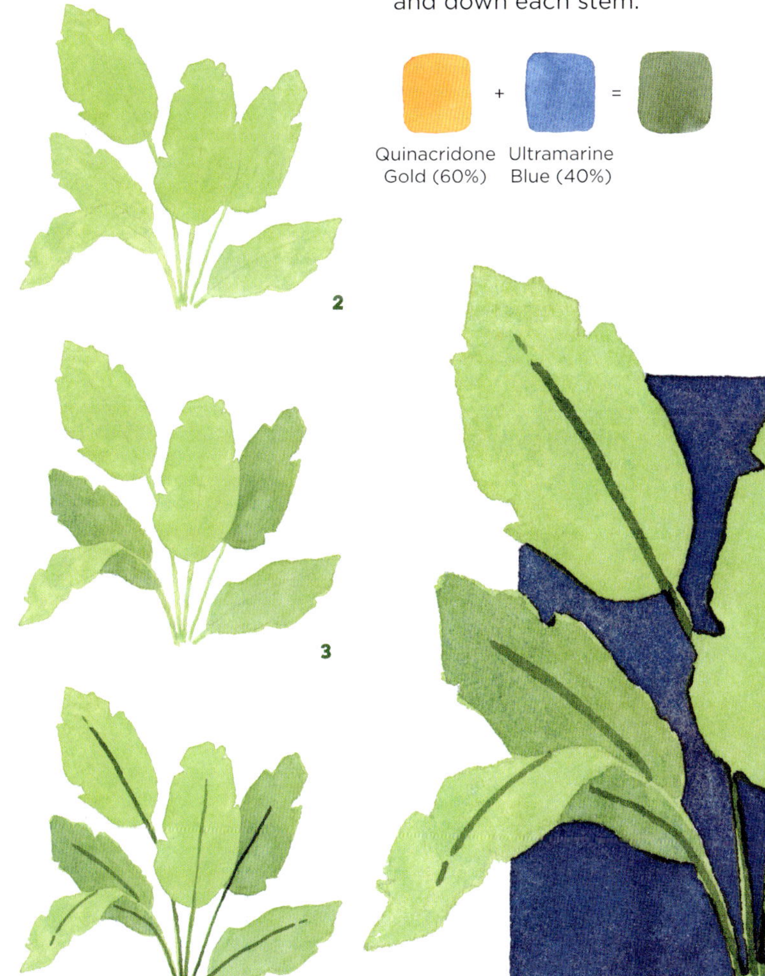

2

3

4

5

FLOWER BOUQUET

A good rule of thumb when painting multiples of an object is to paint in odd groupings instead of even groupings. It helps create visual tension because humans tend to seek out patterns and balance in paintings. By creating an odd grouping, you keep your viewer more engaged for longer. This Flower Bouquet painting only has three flowers; if we had placed four, it would have become static and too balanced, which doesn't engage the viewer.

MATERIALS

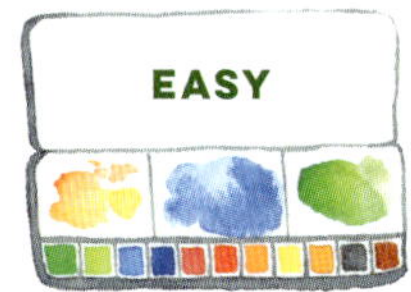

Pencil
Watercolor paper
Size 8 round brush

COLORS

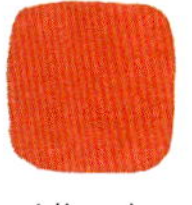
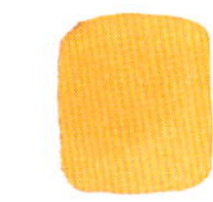
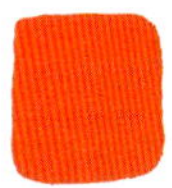

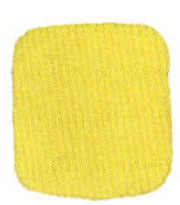
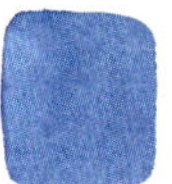

| Winsor Green | Alizarin Crimson | Quinacridone Gold | Winsor Red | Lemon Yellow | Green Gold | Ultramarine Blue |

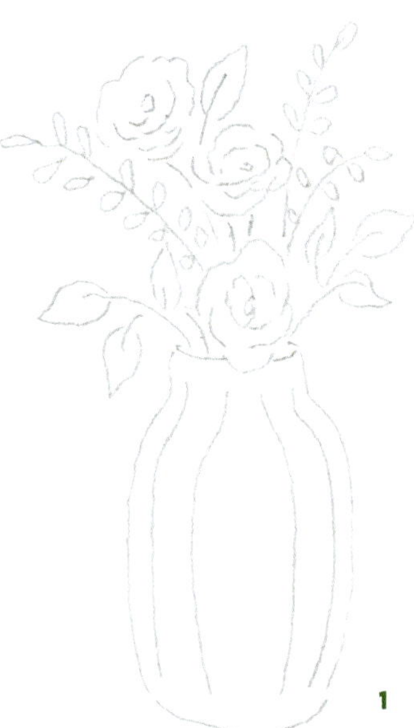

STEP 1: With a pencil, trace (page 229) or sketch the flower bouquet on your watercolor paper.

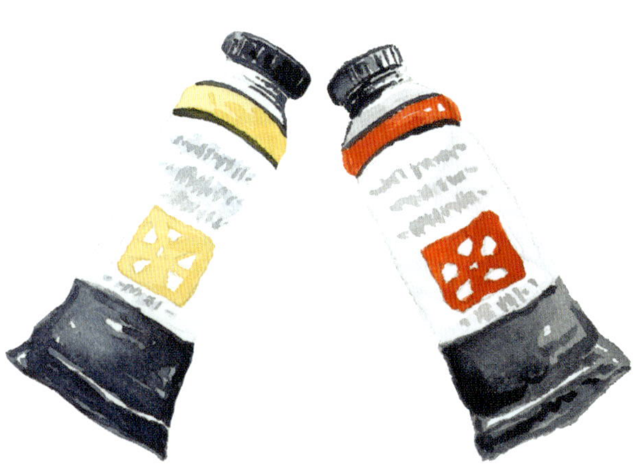

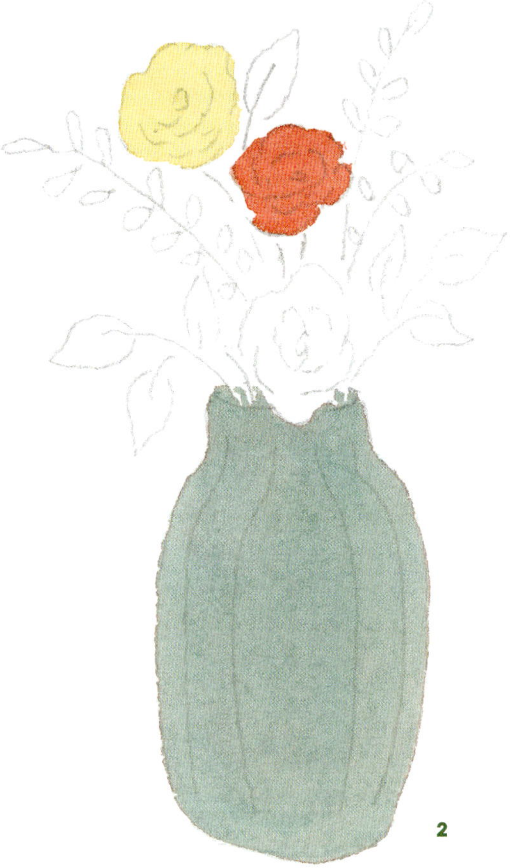

STEP 2: Mix Winsor Green (60%) and Alizarin Crimson (40%) on your palette. Use this mixture and a size 8 round brush to paint in the vase.

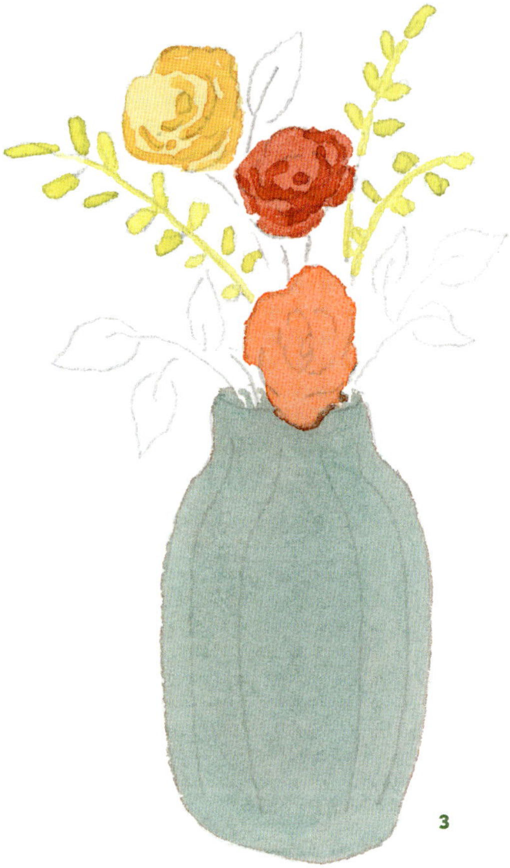

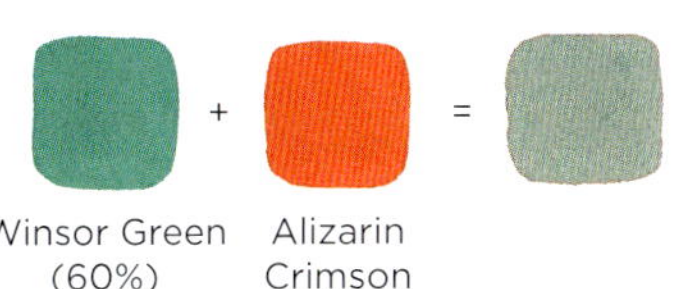

Winsor Green (60%) + Alizarin Crimson (40%) =

Take Quinacridone Gold and paint the very top flower. For the middle flower, paint it in using Alizarin Crimson.

STEP 3: On your palette, combine Winsor Red (70%) with Lemon Yellow (30%). Paint in the bottom flower with this color mixture. Try to avoid letting this color touch the dark green vase; if the vase is at all damp, the green will **bleed** into your flower.

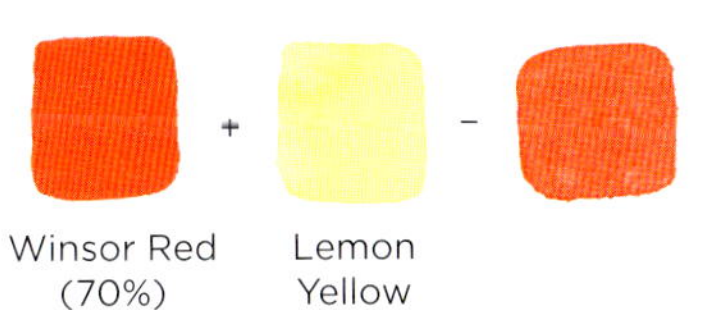

Winsor Red (70%) + Lemon Yellow (30%) =

Load your brush with Quinacridone Gold and apply the paint heavily on the right side of the top flower for detailing the **shadows**. Now add **shadows** to the middle flower using Alizarin Crimson. Focus the **shadow** on the right side as well.

Paint in the tiny leaves and branches with Green Gold.

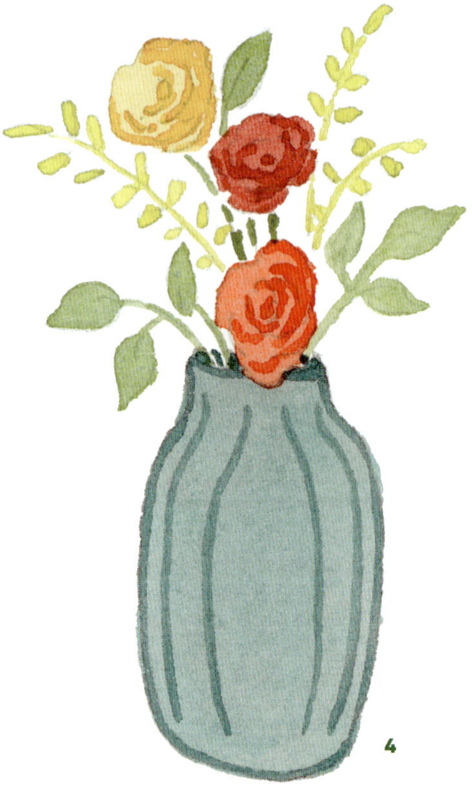

STEP 4: To add the details on the vase, start by using Winsor Green (60%) combined with Alizarin Crimson (40%) on your palette. Use the mixture to outline the vase, add four arched lines on the vase and darken the inside hole of the vase. Let this dry before moving forward.

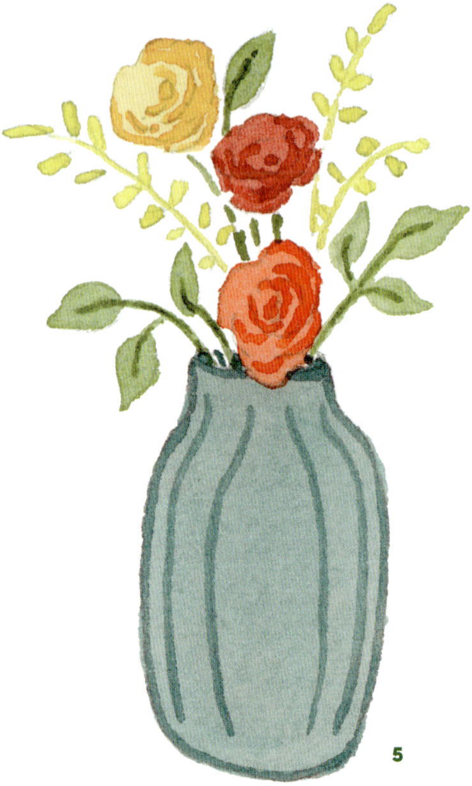

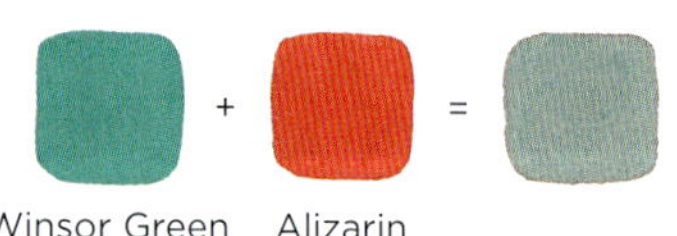

Winsor Green (60%) + Alizarin Crimson (40%) =

Use the same peach mixture from Step 3, Winsor Red (70%) with Lemon Yellow (30%), to add the **shadows** on the right side of the bottom flower.

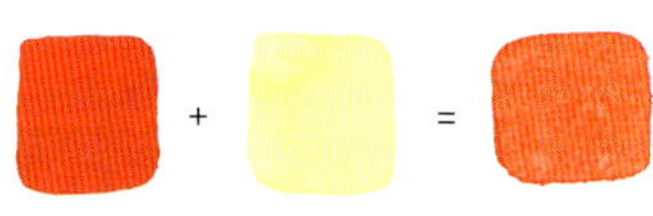

Winsor Red (70%) + Lemon Yellow (30%) =

On your palette, mix Green Gold (50%) with Ultramarine Blue (50%). Paint in the big leaves and stems with this mixture.

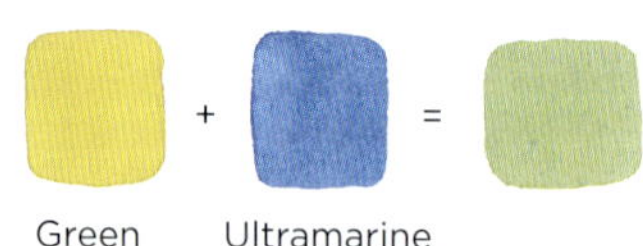

Green Gold (50%) + Ultramarine Blue (50%) =

STEP 5: Paint in the darker details on the big leaves and stems using the same color mixture of Green Gold and Ultramarine Blue made in Step 4.

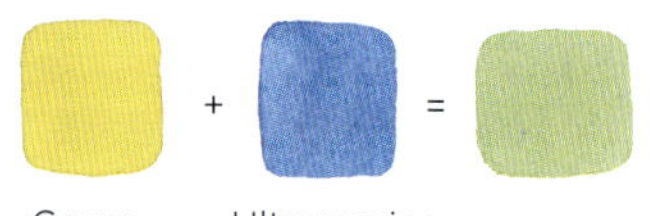

Green Gold (50%) + Ultramarine Blue (50%) =

WILDFLOWERS

As an artist, each time you paint a **subject** or scene, you must decide where to simplify and where to add more detail. In this Wildflowers painting, focus on the gold and red poppies by adding more layers with dimension while going less detailed on the blue and purple flowers by only applying one layer. Balancing less detailed and more complex areas prevents the scene from getting too messy.

MATERIALS

Pencil

Watercolor paper

Size 8 round brush

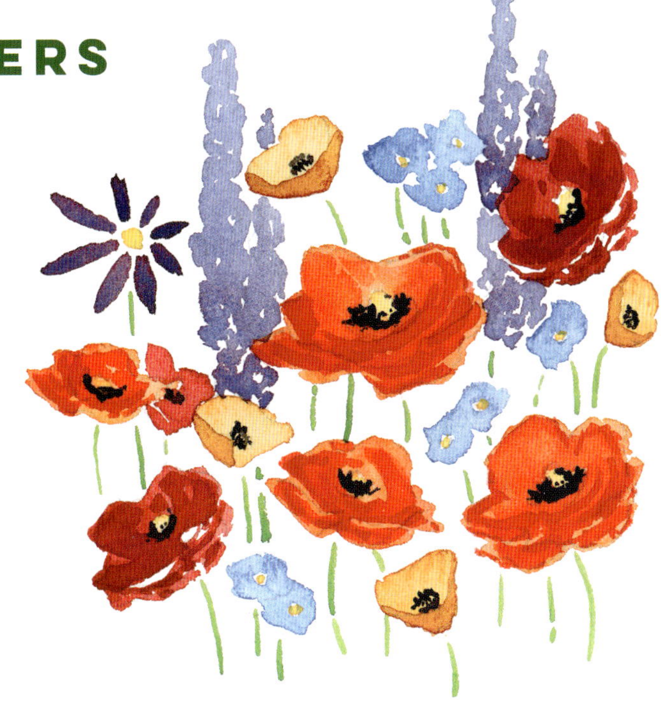

COLORS

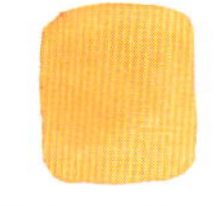
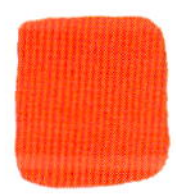
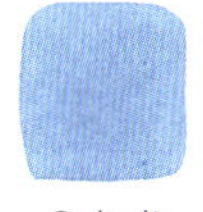
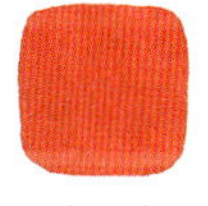
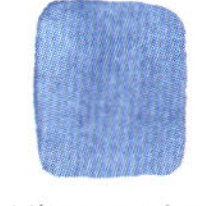

Quinacridone Gold   Winsor Red   Cobalt Blue   Alizarin Crimson   Ultramarine Blue   Lemon Yellow

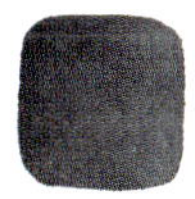
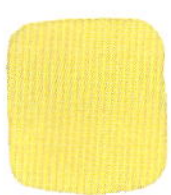
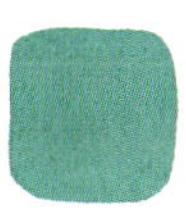

Neutral Tint   Green Gold   Winsor Green

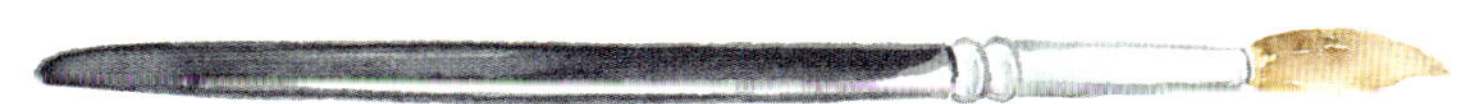

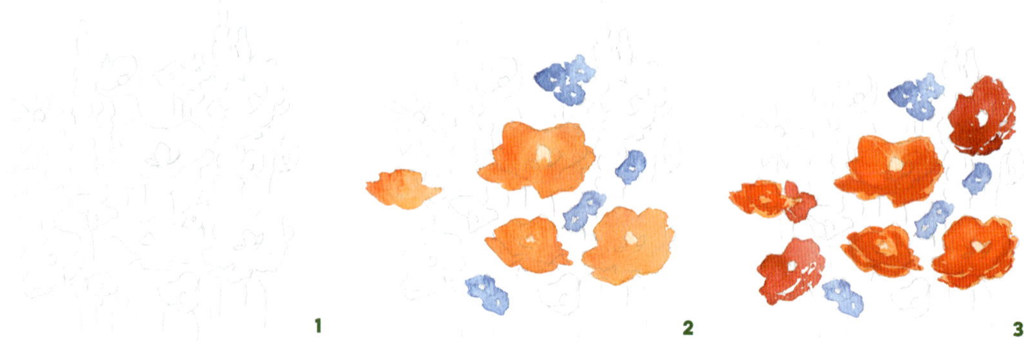

STEP 1: Use a pencil to trace (page 231) or sketch the wildflowers onto your watercolor paper.

STEP 2: Lightly erase the pencil marks. **Load** your size 8 round brush with Quinacridone Gold and lay that color on four of the red poppies in the front. Using the **wet-in-wet** technique, paint Winsor Red into the Quinacridone Gold. Try not to get the Winsor Red in the center of the poppies. If the red does **bleed** into any of the centers, **blot** it away with your towel or a Q-tip® cotton swab (dot the center of the poppies). To create a more vibrant effect, you can add even more Quinacridone Gold in the petals of the poppies.

Clean and **load** your brush with Cobalt Blue and add that to the little flowers. Make sure to leave the center of the flower white so you can go back in and add the pollen later.

STEP 3: Add Winsor Red on top of the four red poppies painted in Step 2. When you apply this Winsor Red, leave gaps so that the first layer will show through. This Winsor Red will be painted more heavily at the base of each of the red poppies.

Use Alizarin Crimson to paint in three additional poppies. Leave white at the bottom edging of the flower and in the center as well.

STEP 4: Paint in four poppies with Quinacridone Gold. Now add Lemon Yellow to the inside of all the flowers. Let that dry before moving forward.

Add additional Alizarin Crimson to the three Alizarin Crimson poppies we worked on in Step 3; this helps to add just a bit of dimension to the petals and helps the flowers feel three-dimensional. Experiment painting on **soft** and **hard edges** (see page 17 for more details on this technique).

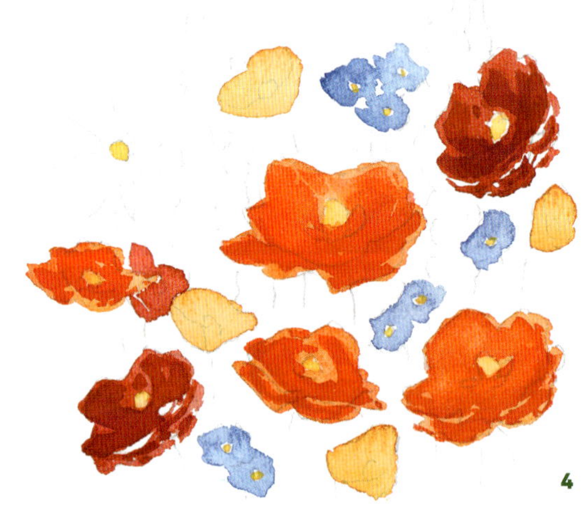

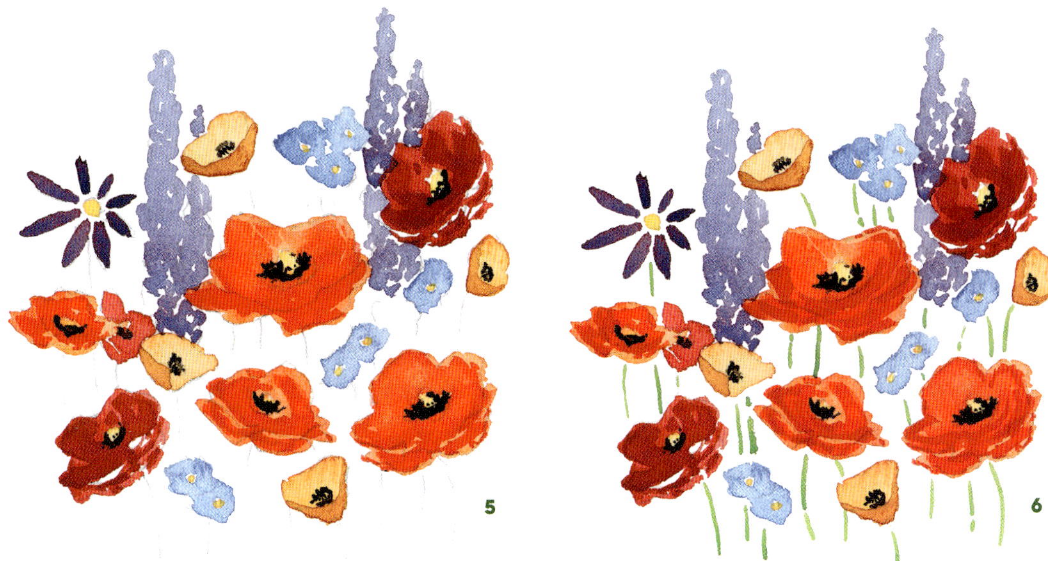

STEP 5: Mix Cobalt Blue (60%) with Alizarin Crimson (40%) and put that on the tall flowers in the back. Leave white spaces near the middle as you add the color onto the flowers.

 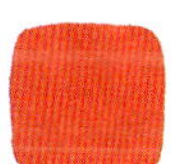 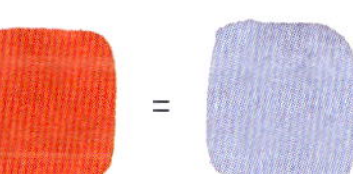

Cobalt Blue (60%)　　Alizarin Crimson (40%)

Take a mixture of Alizarin Crimson (60%) with Ultramarine Blue (40%) and add that to the flower with the Lemon Yellow center that you haven't painted yet (on the left side of the paper).

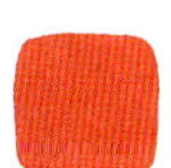 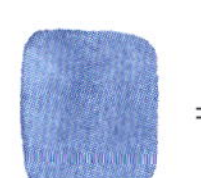

Alizarin Crimson (60%)　　Ultramarine Blue (40%)

Add Quinacridone Gold to the outside petals of the four Quinacridone Gold poppies. We are doing this to give the poppies dimension, which will give definition between the outside and inside of the flower.

In a dotting motion, add Neutral Tint to the area around the center of each poppy. Keep the paint to just around the yellow pollen area—don't let it extend too far up the petals.

STEP 6: On your palette, mix Green Gold (70%) with Winsor Green (30%). Paint all the flower stems with this green.

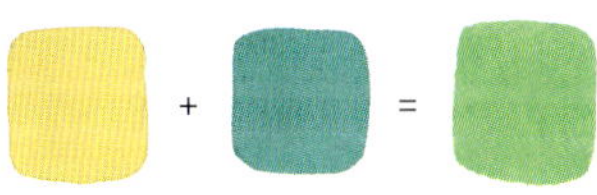

Green Gold (70%)　　Winsor Green (30%)

Add a second layer of Winsor Red to the four Winsor Red poppies. You are pretty much just outlining the outermost petals with the color. The purpose of this is to provide a bit more dimension and help the flowers stand out.

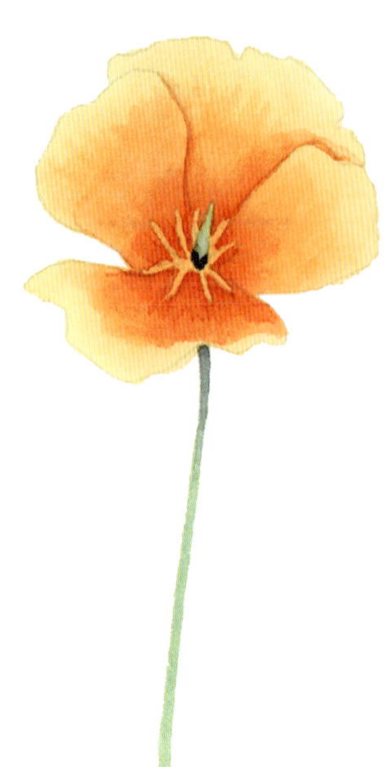

CALIFORNIA POPPY

This California Poppy is an excellent example of using a **variegated wash**. While the **variegated wash** for this painting is not used in the sky the way it usually is, the effect it will have on the petal shape is similar. The easiest way to choose colors that will work well together for this type of **wash** is by using **analogous colors**, which are colors right next to each other on the color wheel; these will blend together beautifully.

MATERIALS

Pencil
Watercolor paper
Size 8 round brush

COLORS

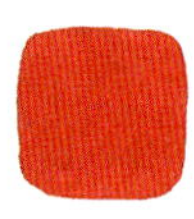
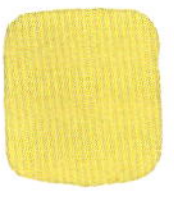

| Cadmium Orange | Lemon Yellow | Alizarin Crimson | Green Gold | Winsor Green |

STEP 1: Trace (page 227) or lightly sketch the California poppy in pencil on your watercolor paper.

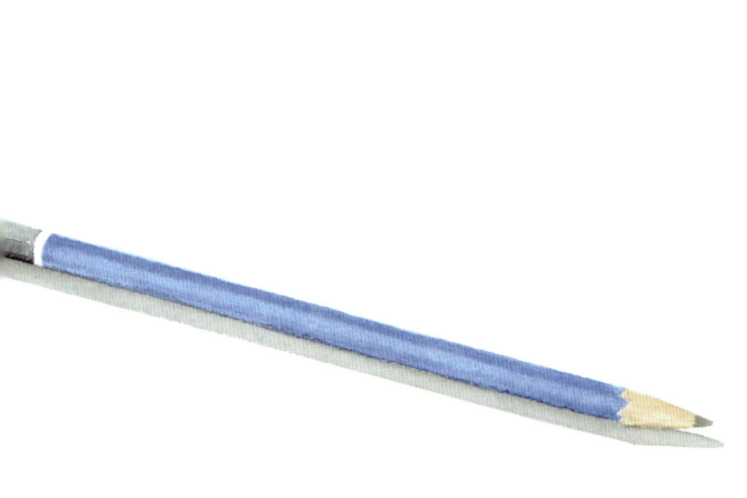

1

STEP 2: With a size 8 round brush, paint a **clear water wash** over the whole flower except for one area in the very center. You will be using the **wet-in-wet** technique as you paint your **variegated wash**. **Load** your brush with Cadmium Orange and start painting from the center of the flower, avoiding the center spike. Don't paint the Cadmium Orange all the way to the edges of the petals; stop before you get midway. Once you've painted the Cadmium Orange around the center, clean your brush and **load** it with Lemon Yellow. Start painting in the Lemon Yellow where the Cadmium Orange ended and allow those colors to **bleed**. Clean and **load** your brush with Lemon Yellow again, then finish painting to the edges of the flower petals with the Lemon Yellow.

STEP 3: On your palette, mix Cadmium Orange (60%) and Alizarin Crimson (40%). Start in the center again, but this time avoid the center spike and the radiating spikes as well. Paint this mixture outward toward the petals but don't pull it all the way to the edge. Take it about 75 percent toward the petals.

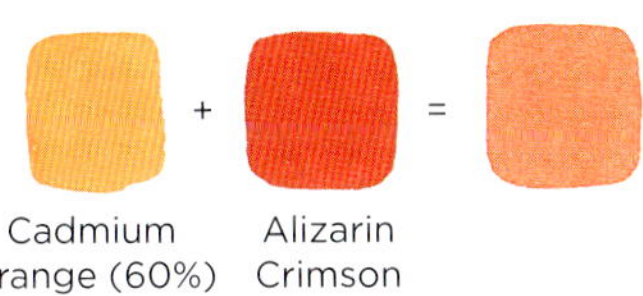

Cadmium Orange (60%)   +   Alizarin Crimson (40%)   =

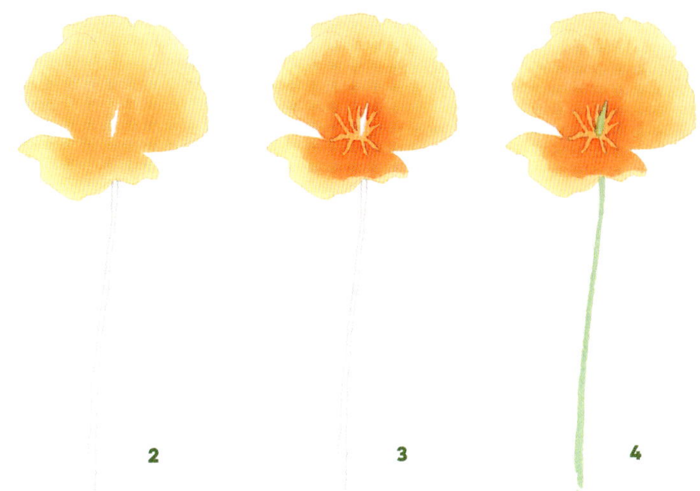

2   3   4

STEP 4: Mix Green Gold (60%) and Winsor Green (40%) on your palette. Use this mixture to paint in the center spike and the stem of your poppy.

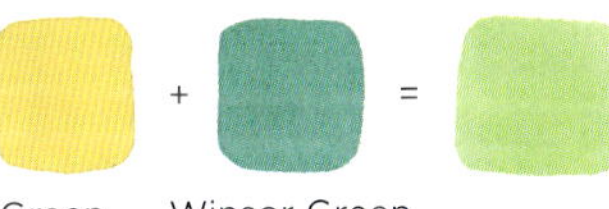

Green Gold (60%)   +   Winsor Green (40%)   =

STEP 5: Use the same mixture from Step 3, Cadmium Orange (60%) and Alizarin Crimson (40%), to paint a darker **value** around the center. Make sure to avoid the spikes again. With the same mixture, paint the left and right petals along the inside edge of the center.

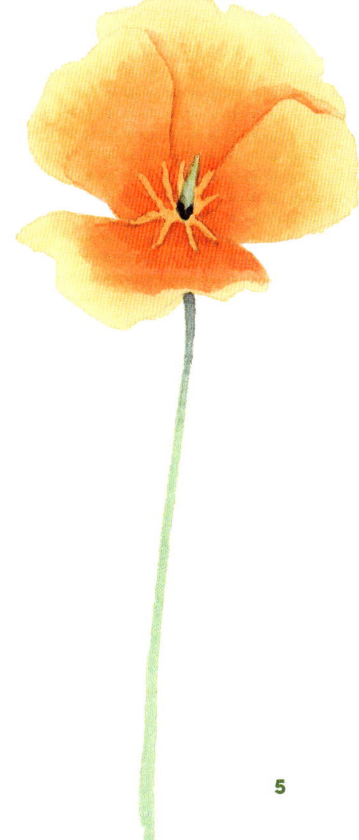

5

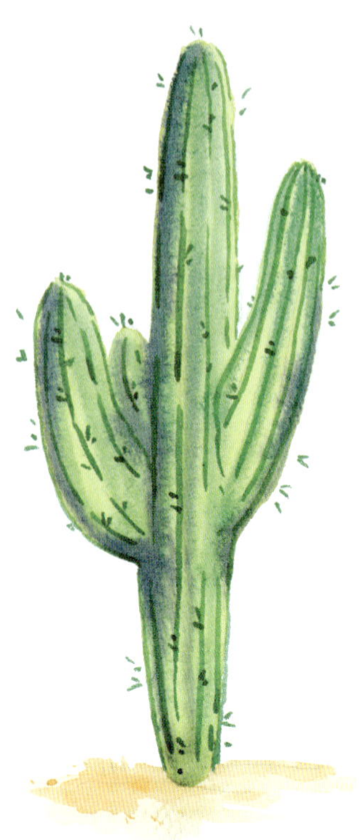

SAGUARO

When you need to add a lot of the same details, be careful not to add too many. This will save you time and eliminate frustration. In this Saguaro project, a few of the needles will go a long way. The viewer can immediately identify that the cactus is spiky, even without meticulously painting thousands of needles.

MATERIALS

Pencil
Watercolor paper
Size 8 round brush
Size 2 round brush (optional)

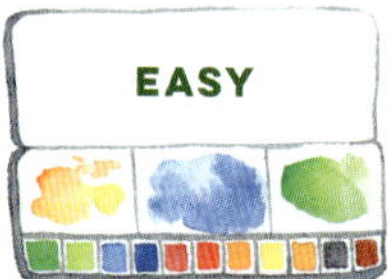

COLORS

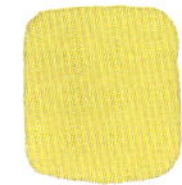
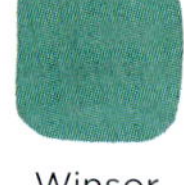
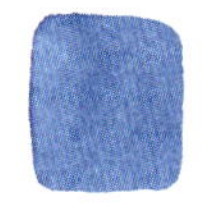
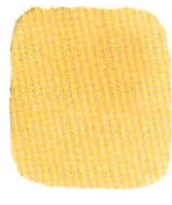

| Green Gold | Winsor Green | Ultramarine Blue | Yellow Ochre | Cadmium Orange |

STEP 1: With a pencil, lightly trace (page 233) or sketch the saguaro on your watercolor paper.

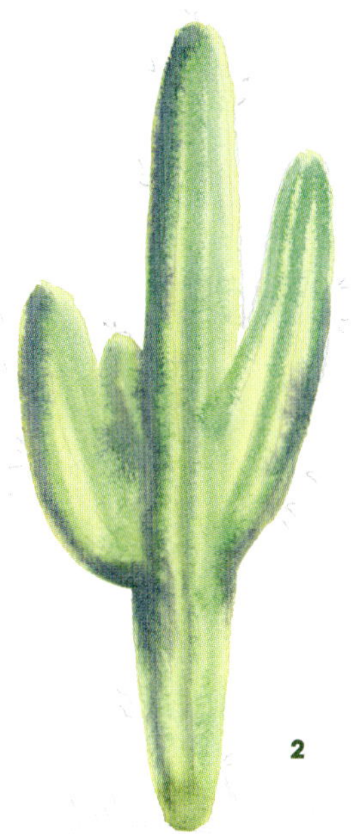

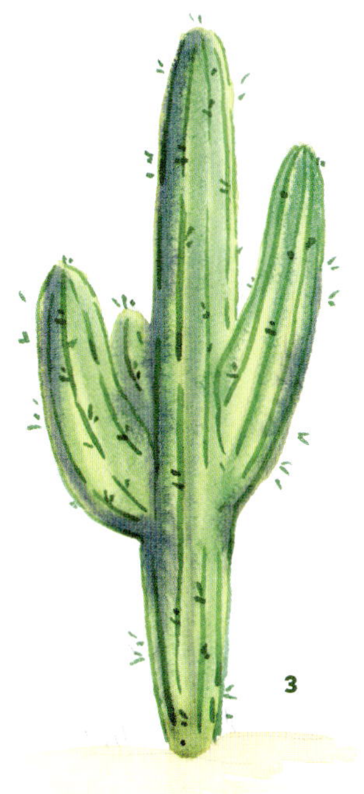

STEP 2: If your pencil lines are too dark, lightly erase until there is just enough left to use as a reference. Then with a size 8 round brush, use Green Gold to paint a **wash** over the entire cactus. Don't let this dry; for the remainder of this step, you will be using the **wet-in-wet** technique. Add in Winsor Green with a vertical stripe motion. Lay in Ultramarine Blue as a **shadow** on the outside edging of each arm and the left side of the main pillar.

STEP 3: Apply Yellow Ochre to the ground. Next, mix Cadmium Orange (60%) with Winsor Green (40%) on your palette. (You can size down to a size 2 round brush if you don't feel comfortable using the size 8 round brush). Use that mixture to do some thin vertical stripes down the cactus, leaving some spaces so it isn't always a continuous line. The gaps provide variety. Also, use this color to add little lines as the needles along the vertical stripes on the inside and the outside edging of the cactus. For the outside edging needles, I don't always connect them to the cactus, so it appears like they are hovering. The reason I did this is because it creates more movement and feels like the sharp spikes are jumping out. Feel free to play around with your preference for needle placement.

STEP 4: Darken the ground using another layer of Yellow Ochre to create a **cast shadow** on the left side. To achieve that gritty sand **texture**, add a variety of different strokes with little dots as well.

Cadmium Orange (60%) + Winsor Green (40%) =

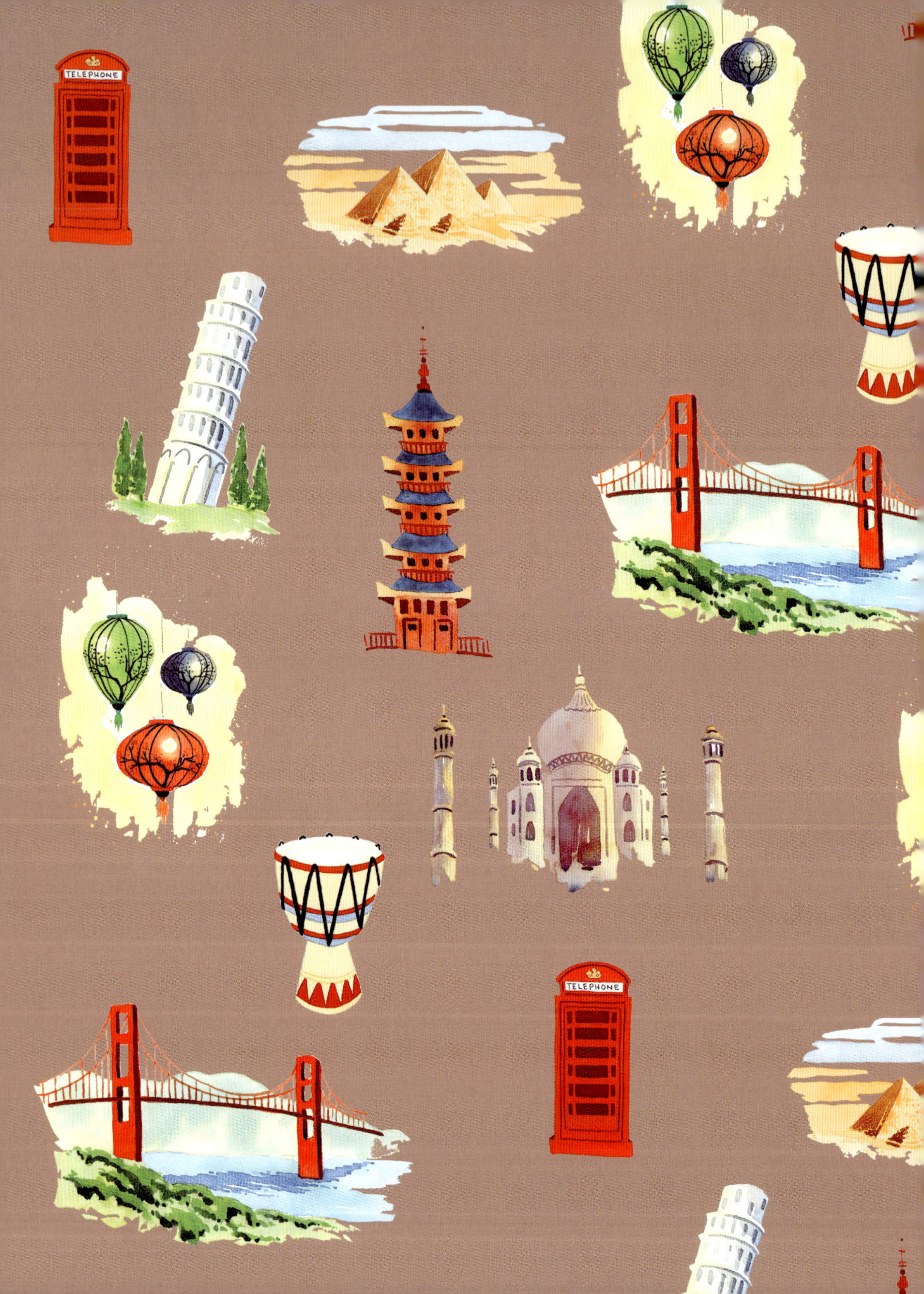
TELEPHONE
TELEPHONE

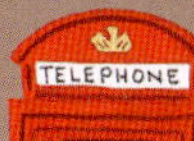

AROUND THE WORLD

This chapter is about being transported to many beautiful places around the world! One of the best parts of painting is becoming immersed in what you are creating and feeling connected to your **subject**, even if you have never seen it in real life. Around the World is a fun section that focuses on that feeling; you get to feel like you are at the San Francisco Golden Gate Bridge (page 87) or in Paris during autumn (page 79). I've found that when I paint places I've never been and finally see them in real life, they mean so much more because I've already spent time appreciating the beautiful colors, **textures** and details.

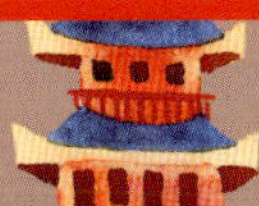

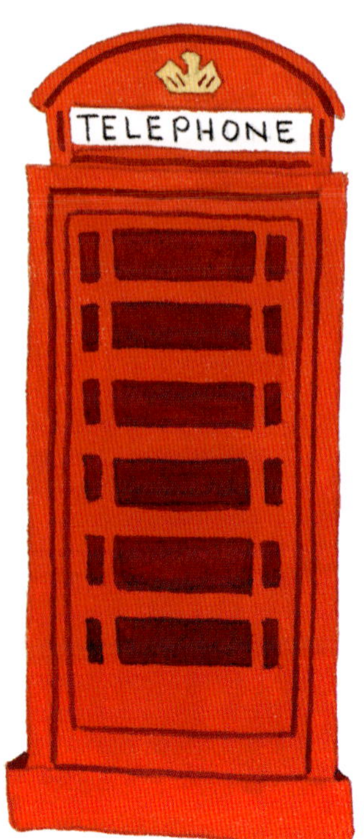

LONDON PHONE BOOTH

It is extremely important to use a big brush when you have a large area to cover. This will help avoid unevenness within the **wash**. If you use too small of a brush, you will see the brushstrokes and it won't look uniform. Be brave here! Working with a larger brush can feel scary when you're starting out, but I promise you'll be happier with the result, especially for covering the large area on your phone booth!

MATERIALS

Pencil

Watercolor paper

Size 2 round brush

Size 14 round brush

Sharpie felt-tip pen

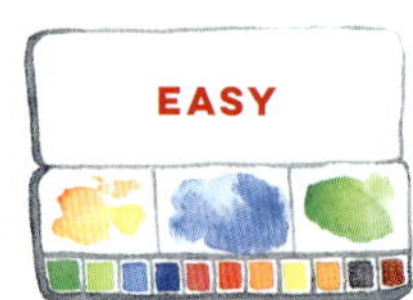

COLORS

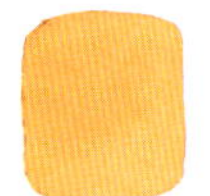 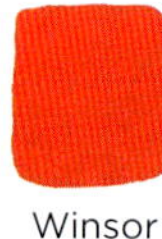  

Quinacridone Gold   Winsor Red   Lemon Yellow   Cobalt Blue

STEP 1: With a pencil, trace (page 233) or sketch lightly the London phone booth onto the watercolor paper.

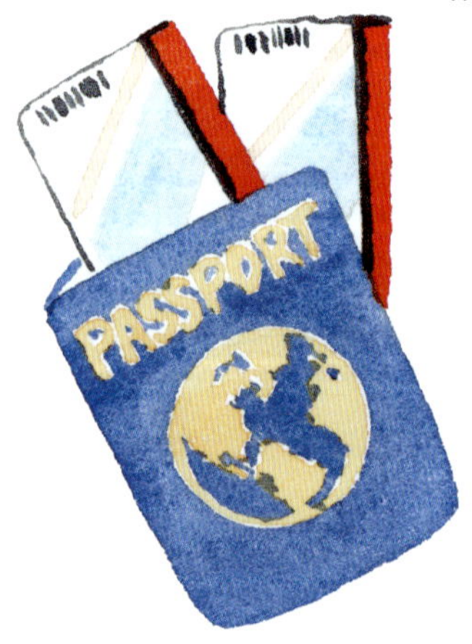

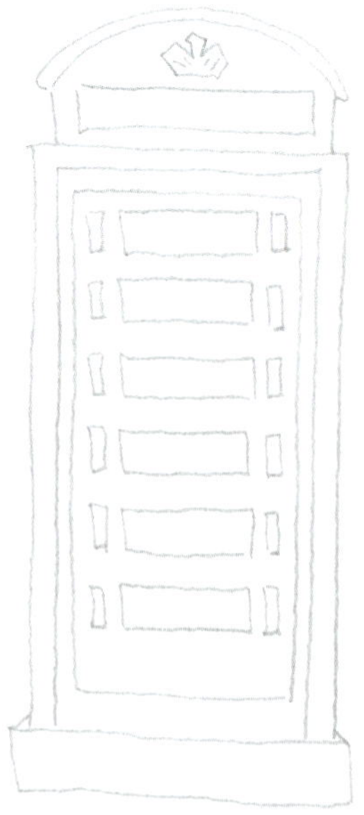

1

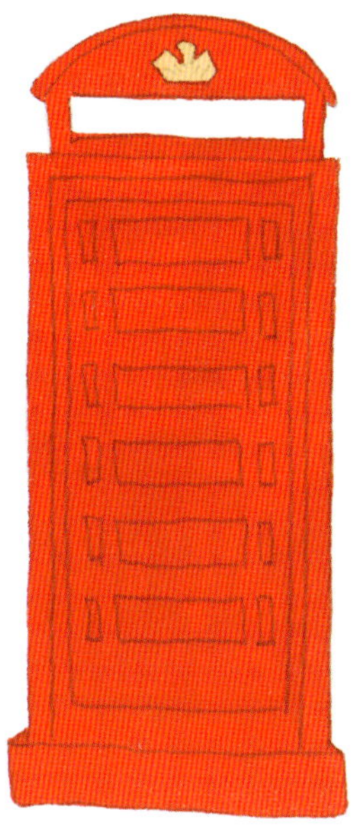

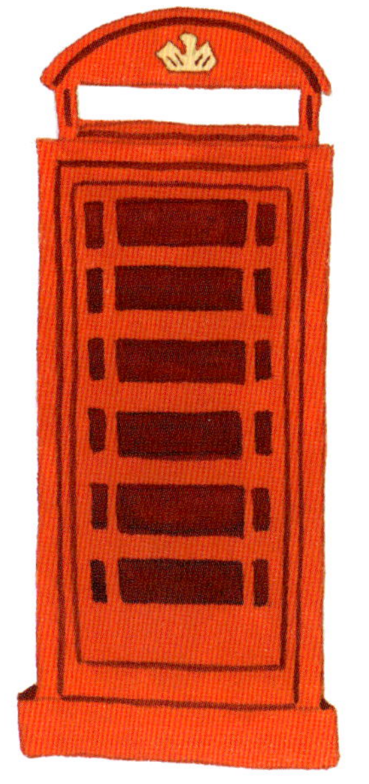

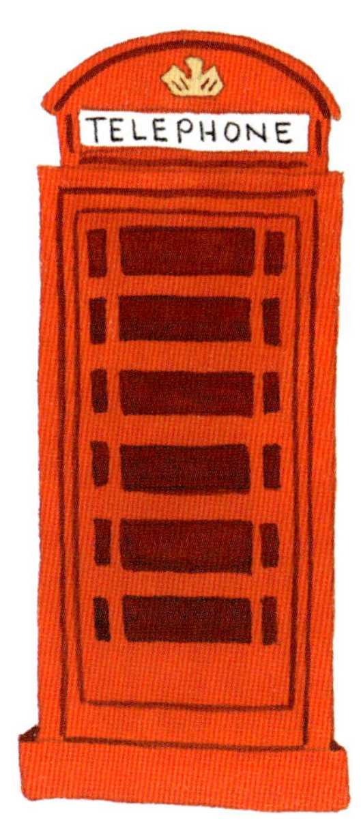

2   3   4

STEP 2: Use your size 2 round brush and Quinacridone Gold to paint in the crown at the top of the phone booth. Let that dry.

Make sure you mix a large amount of this next mixture on your palette because you will cover a large area and don't want to run out of this color. Mix Winsor Red (70%) with Lemon Yellow (30%) on your palette. Use a size 14 round brush to paint the entire phone booth except for the gold crown you just painted and the white banner underneath it.

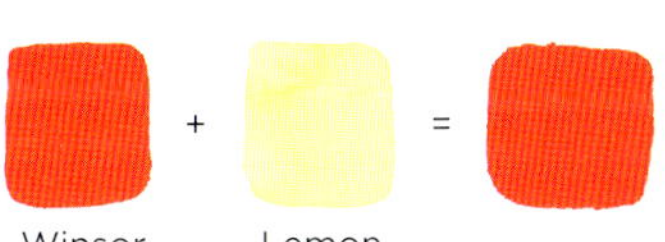

STEP 3: On your palette, mix Cobalt Blue (60%) and Winsor Red (40%). Switch to a size 2 round brush and paint in all the dark details using this mixture.

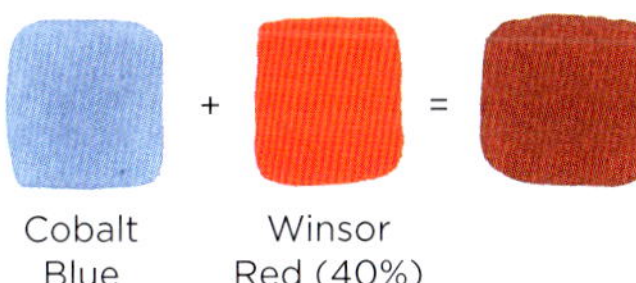

STEP 4: Writing "TELEPHONE" in your white rectangle banner can be tricky. To avoid errors, start by penciling the letters where you want them. Even I, as a professional artist, write out the letters in pencil before inking them to avoid mistakes. Then, once you're happy with placement (and have double-checked the spelling), go over the pencil with your Sharpie.

THE PYRAMIDS OF EGYPT

Contrast can be a powerful tool in a painting because it can make the **subject** pop. There are many ways to achieve contrast, but one of the easiest ways is to use light and dark **values**. In this pyramid painting, notice the difference between Step 4 and Step 5. The **shadows** really bring this composition to life.

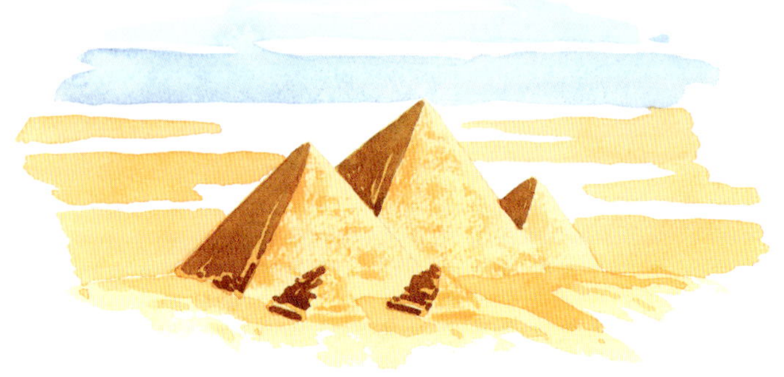

MATERIALS

Pencil
Watercolor paper
Size 8 round brush

COLORS

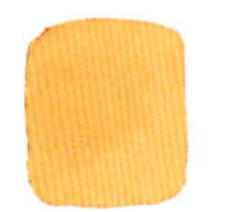
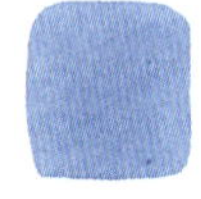

Quinacridone Gold

Cobalt Blue

Cadmium Orange

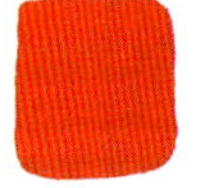
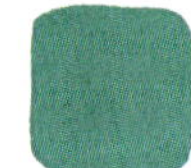

Winsor Red

Winsor Green

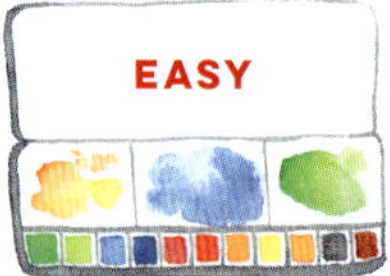

STEP 1: Using a pencil, trace (page 233) or sketch the pyramids on your watercolor paper.

STEP 2: Lightly erase your pencil marks. Use your size 8 round brush to paint the pyramids and **foreground** with Quinacrid-one Gold. Leave the bottom edging jagged for a cool effect that looks like sand. Take Cobalt Blue and lay it into the top of the sky in three horizontal lines, leaving white spacing between. Don't paint the sky all the way down to the pyramids.

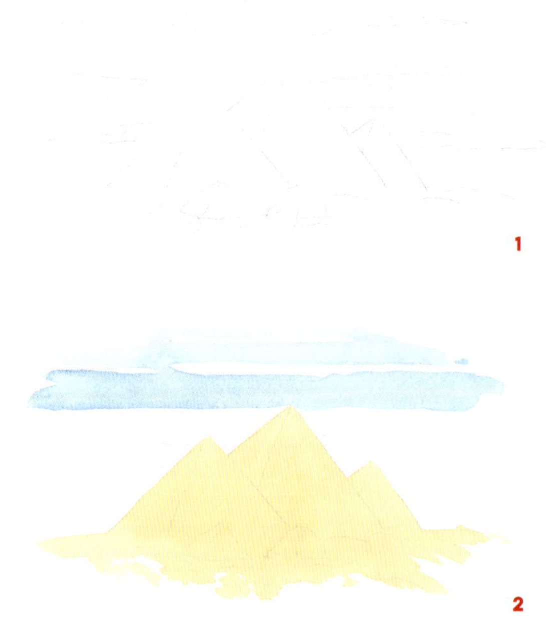

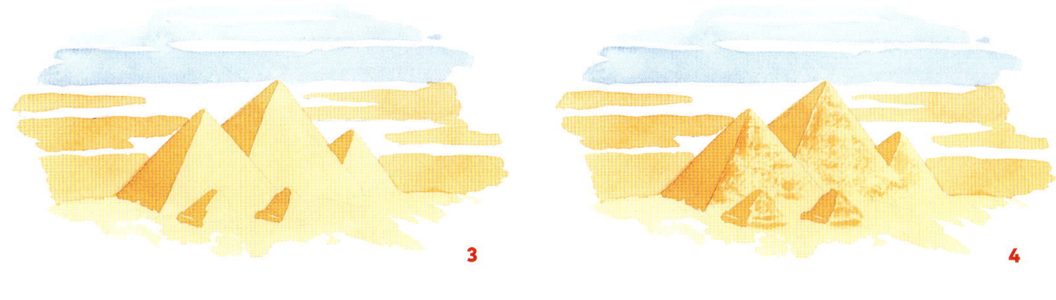

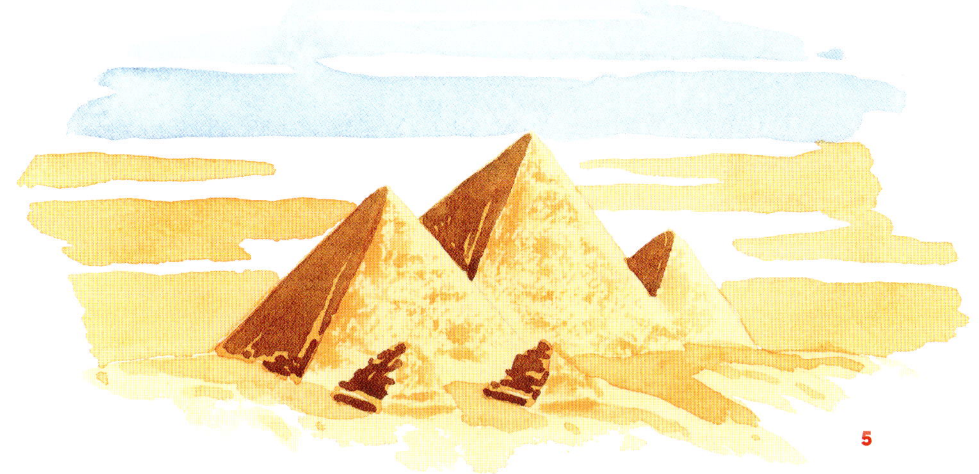

STEP 3: Use less water with the Quinacridone Gold than used in Step 1 to create a darker **value** and paint the **shadow** side on the pyramids. Let those dry before moving forward. Then, **load** your brush with Cadmium Orange and paint the sky under the Cobalt Blue layers and around the pyramids, leaving white gaps to represent clouds. This is painting the negative space, which is also done on the Eiffel Tower painting (page 79).

STEP 4: With Quinacridone Gold, use a **dry brush texture** (page 16) to create the look of bricks.

STEP 5: Mix Winsor Red (80%) and Winsor Green (20%) on your palette and add a second **shadow** to the sides of the pyramids to really make them pop. As you paint the sides, leave gaps for your previous layer to show through. Then, add a glaze of Quinacridone Gold on the top of the sand to create extra dimension.

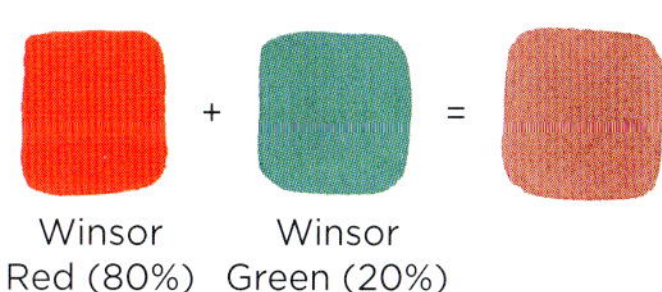

LEANING TOWER OF PISA

Architecture can be intimidating to paint because of the perfect details like windows, archways, doors and so forth. To simplify and make buildings easier to paint, don't get caught up in painting perfectly straight lines. Keep your window shapes as blobs because they will still convey to the viewer that they are windows when seeing the whole painting. This iconic leaning tower is a great way to practice simplifying a very detailed and complex **subject**.

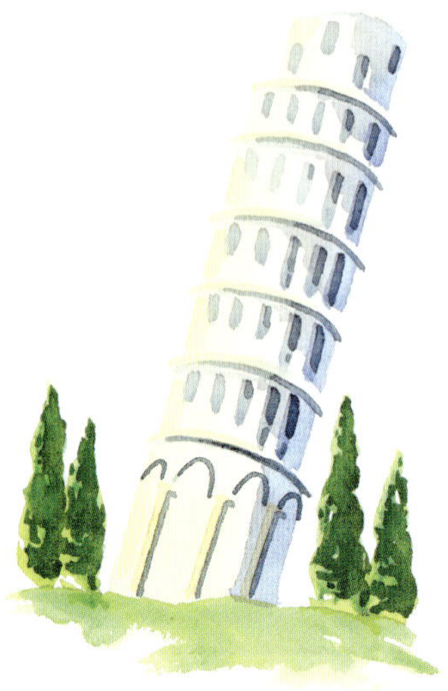

MATERIALS

Pencil
Watercolor paper
Size 8 round brush

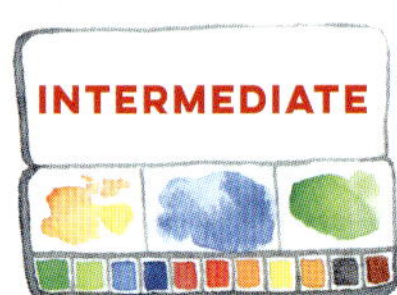

COLORS

 Quinacridone Gold
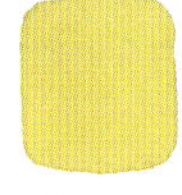 Green Gold
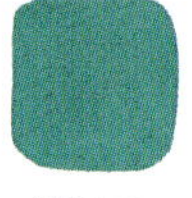 Winsor Green
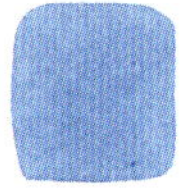 Cobalt Blue
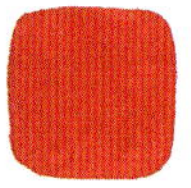 Alizarin Crimson
 Cadmium Orange
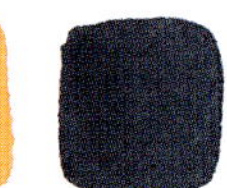 Indigo

1

2

STEP 1: Take your pencil and trace (page 237) or sketch the Leaning Tower of Pisa on your watercolor paper.

STEP 2: Lightly erase your pencil marks. With a size 8 round brush, paint a light **value** of Quinacridone Gold on the tower, leaving the right edge white. Let that dry.

Use Green Gold to paint the trees. While the Green Gold is wet, **load** your brush with Winsor Green and dab it into the trees (**wet-in-wet**).

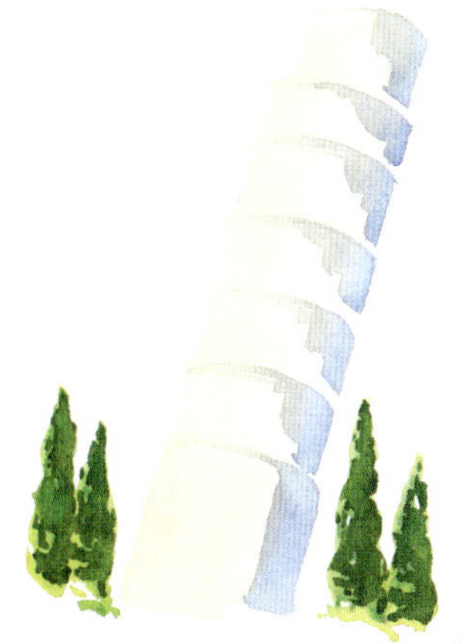

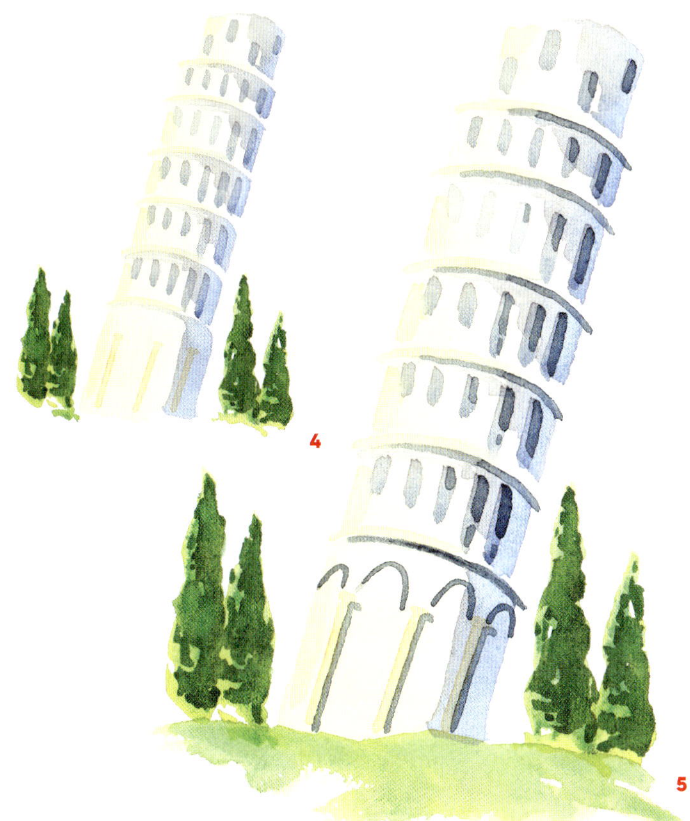

STEP 3: Create a mixture of Cobalt Blue (80%) and Alizarin Crimson (20%) on your palette. Apply this as a **shadow** on the tower's right edge. While it is wet, pull a little of the color under each balcony. Add a **shadow** to the trees using a mixture of Cadmium Orange (60%) and Winsor Green (40%). Make sure you leave some gaps for the first layer of the trees to show through.

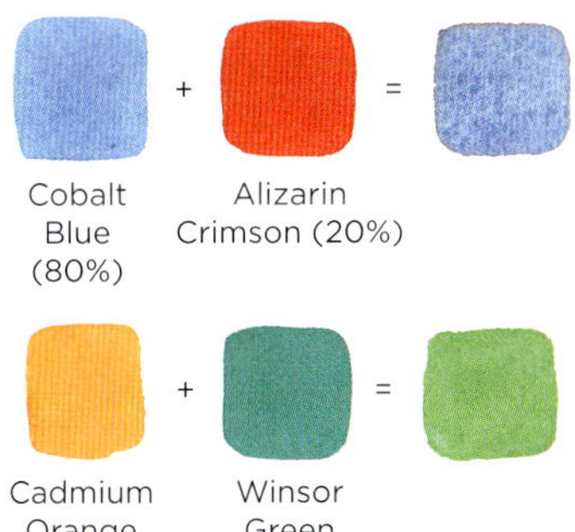

Cobalt Blue (80%)	+	Alizarin Crimson (20%)	=	

Cadmium Orange (60%)	+	Winsor Green (40%)	=	

STEP 4: Take the same tower shadow mixture in Step 3, Cobalt Blue (80%) and Alizarin Crimson (20%), but add more water to create a **lighter value**. Use this to add windows. The windows will be longer on the right side of the building and smaller on the left. Try to dab these in using one stroke. You don't want perfect lines; you want to stay loose and painterly.

To add a little more of a **highlight**, take Quinacridone Gold and add it to the left side of the tower. Pull that paint across the lips of the balconies. Also use the Quinacridone Gold to add to the beams at the base of the tower.

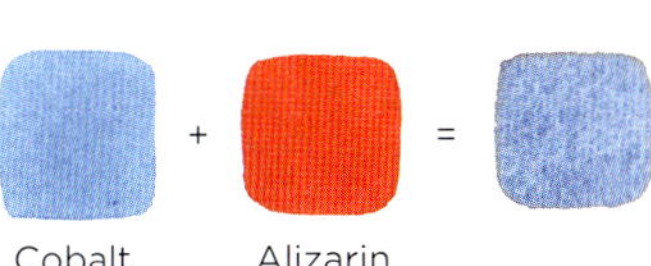

Cobalt Blue (80%)	+	Alizarin Crimson (20%)	=	

STEP 5: **Load** your brush with Indigo and paint that as a **shadow** underneath the balconies. Steer to the right side of the tower. Also add the Indigo to the windows that are more in **shadow** as well. Use the Indigo on the bottom beams to also add a **shadow**.

Combine on your palette again a mix of Cadmium Orange (60%) and Winsor Green (40%), then paint that as your **foreground**.

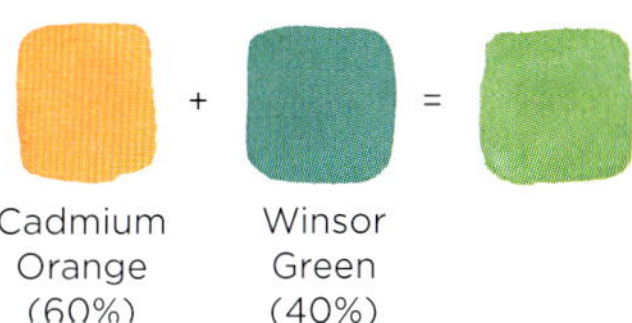

Cadmium Orange (60%)	+	Winsor Green (40%)	=	

VESPA®

When starting a **subject** with many different parts, first paint the largest area. Always start with the largest brush and work down to the smallest. Working from the largest to smallest brush will help to avoid getting caught up in little details at the start. A good rule of thumb is to only use your smallest brush for the last 10 to 20 percent of your painting.

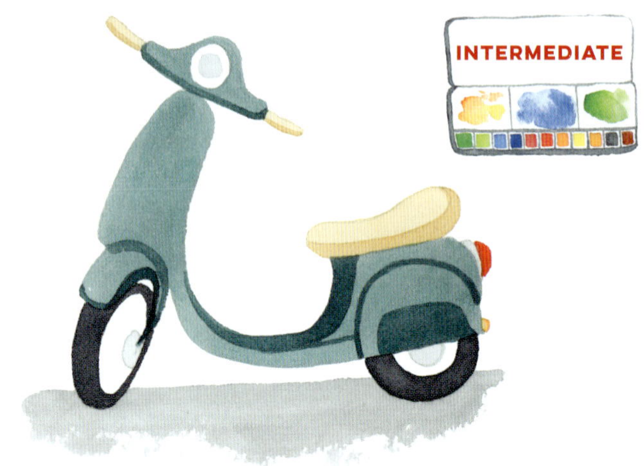

MATERIALS

Watercolor paper
Pencil
Size 8 round brush

COLORS

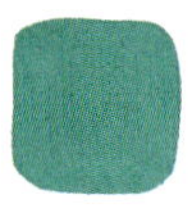
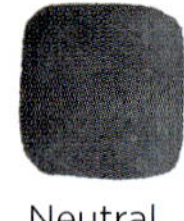

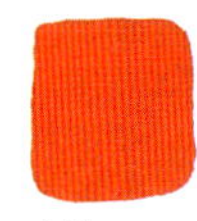

| Winsor Green | Neutral Tint | Yellow Ochre | Winsor Red | Cadmium Orange |

STEP 1: On your watercolor paper, trace (page 237) or sketch the Vespa® using a pencil.

STEP 2: Lightly erase the pencil marks. Mix Winsor Green (70%) with Neutral Tint (30%) on your palette. Use this mixture and your size 8 round brush to paint the body of the Vespa. Let that dry before moving forward.

Paint the seat and handlebars in Yellow Ochre.

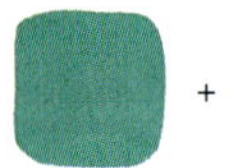 + 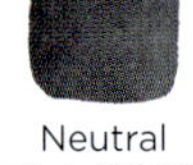 = 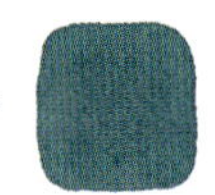

Winsor Green (70%)   Neutral Tint (30%)

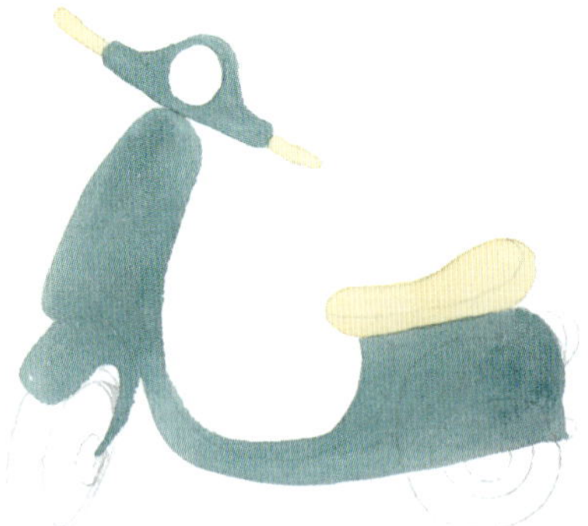

STEP 3: Lighten the **value** of Neutral Tint by using extra water. Add this light gray color to the center of the light between the handlebars, the casing holding the back light and the tire rims. Apply a Yellow Ochre **glaze** to darken the side of the seat. Use this same **glaze** on the bottom part of the handlebars as a **shadow**.

STEP 4: For the light on the back, paint it in using Winsor Red. Take Winsor Green (70%) and mix it with Neutral Tint (30%) on your palette. Use this dark green mixture to add details on the Vespa.

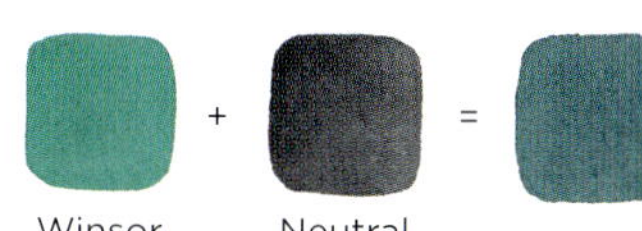

Winsor + Neutral =
Green (70%)   Tint (30%)

STEP 5: Paint the small light above the back tire with Cadmium Orange. Use Neutral Tint for the tires; this is very **saturated**, so don't mix a lot of water.

STEP 6: Paint the ground using a watered-down Neutral Tint. Use a **dry brush** technique to create **texture** on the bottom edging of the road.

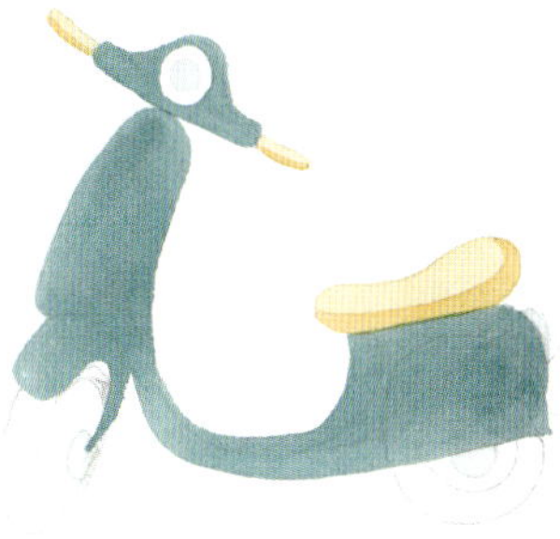

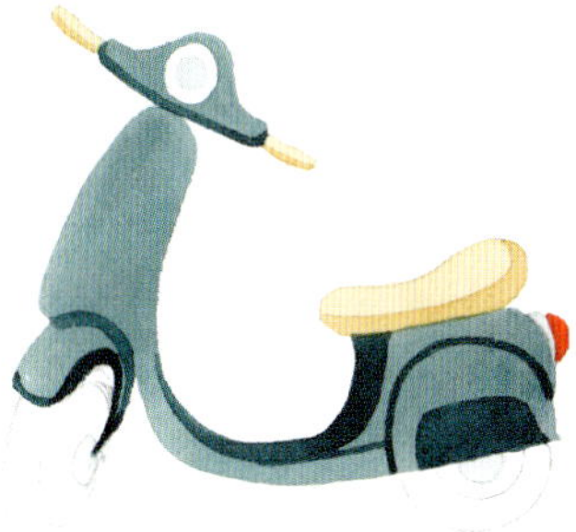

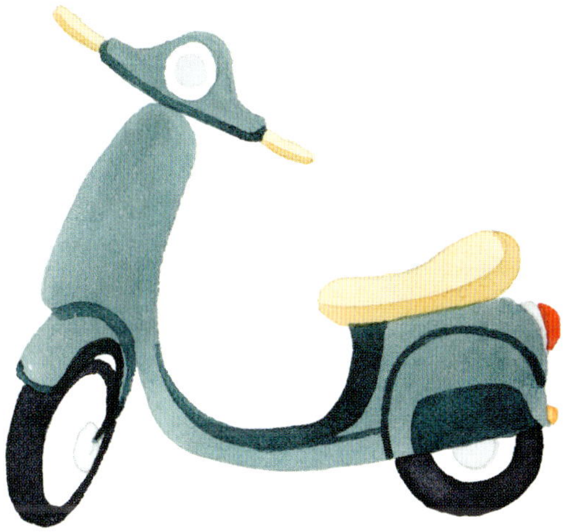

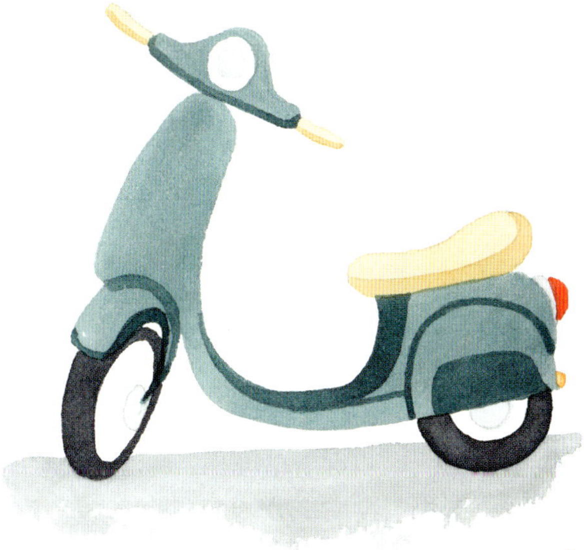

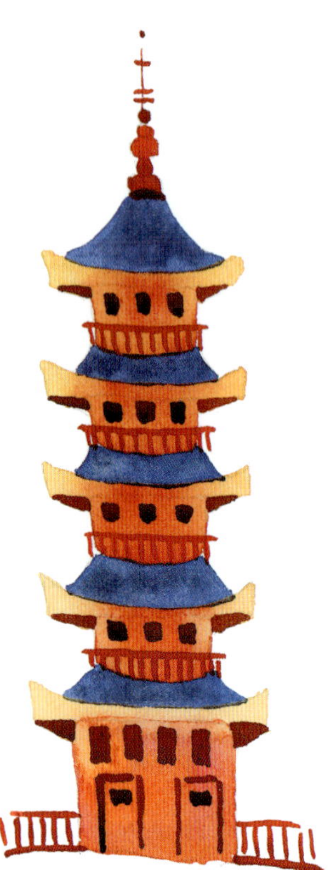

JAPANESE PAGODA

To create unity in your **subject**, try to use a limited palette of three to seven colors. The more you can mix the same colors within your piece, the more color harmony you will create. You'll notice in this Japanese Pagoda painting, there is a small number of colors used, but Alizarin Crimson is the dominate color throughout it. That one dominant color helps create a sense of unity throughout all the features and ultimately lends itself to a harmonious composition.

MATERIALS

Pencil

Watercolor paper

Size 8 round brush

Size 4 or 2 round brush (optional)

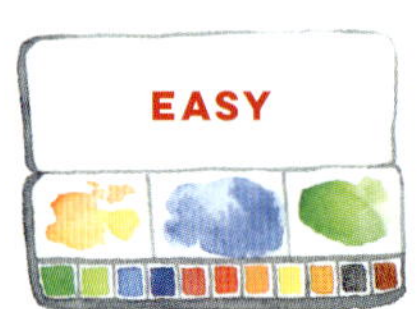

COLORS

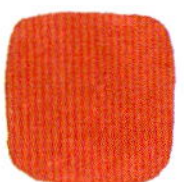  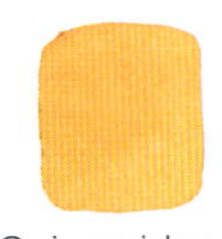 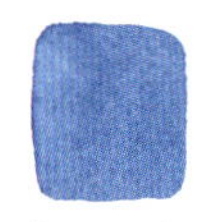 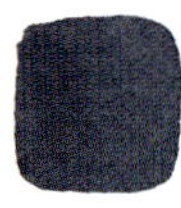

| Alizarin Crimson | Cadmium Orange | Quinacridone Gold | Ultramarine Blue | Indigo |

STEP 1: Take a pencil and lightly trace (page 237) or sketch the Japanese pagoda onto your watercolor paper.

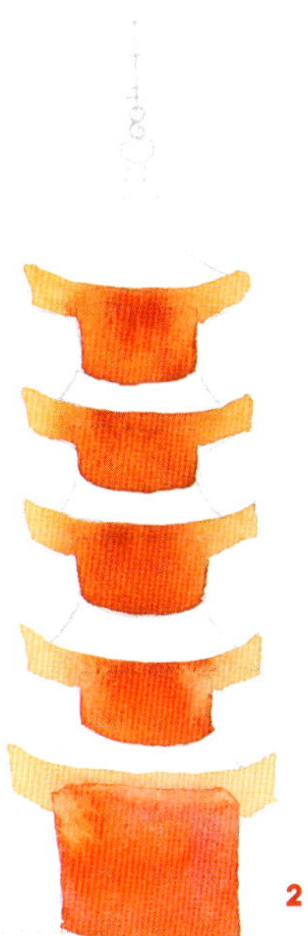

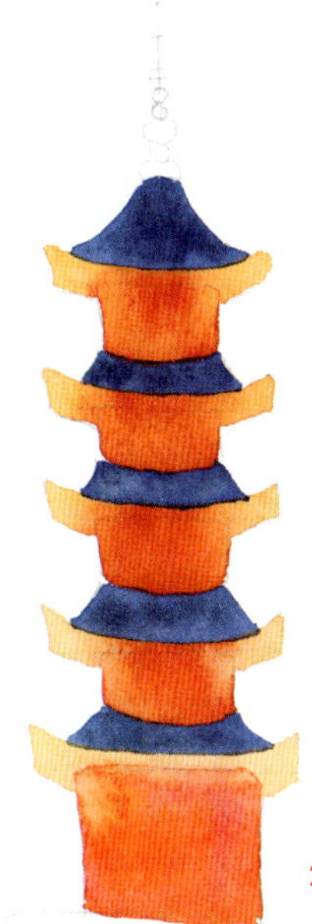

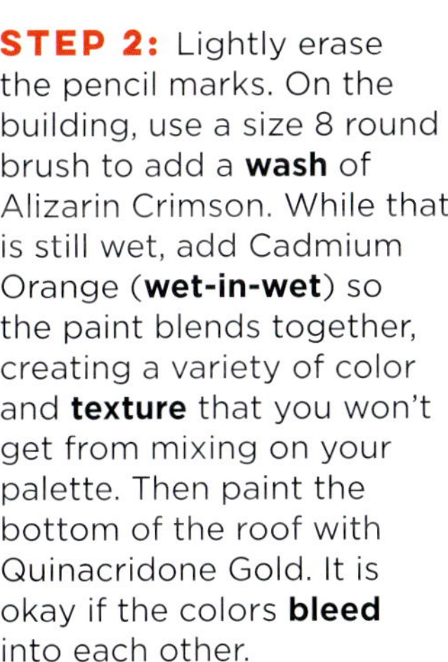

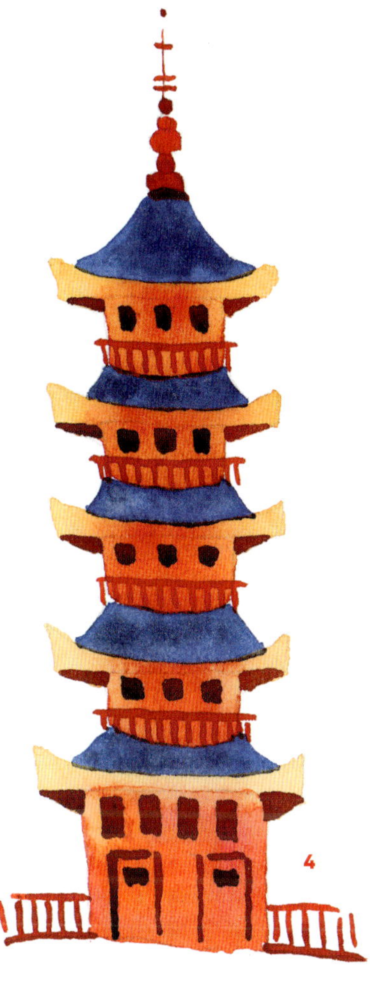

STEP 2: Lightly erase the pencil marks. On the building, use a size 8 round brush to add a **wash** of Alizarin Crimson. While that is still wet, add Cadmium Orange (**wet-in-wet**) so the paint blends together, creating a variety of color and **texture** that you won't get from mixing on your palette. Then paint the bottom of the roof with Quinacridone Gold. It is okay if the colors **bleed** into each other.

STEP 3: Start with one roof at a time because you will use the **wet-in-wet** technique and don't want to run out of time. Paint the roofs with Ultramarine Blue and then lay in Indigo. Repeat this process until all the roofs are done.

STEP 4: Windows and doors will be added in loosely. Just like in the Leaning Tower of Pisa (page 66), they don't need to be perfect rectangles. On your palette, combine Alizarin Crimson (80%) with a touch of Ultramarine Blue (20%) and use this color to add in the windows and the doors. Use this same mixture on the left and right sides of each roof for the **shadow**, painting in little triangular shapes.

On your palette, mix Cadmium Orange (60%) with Alizarin Crimson (40%) and paint the top spires and the railings (if needed, switch to a size 4 or 2 round brush).

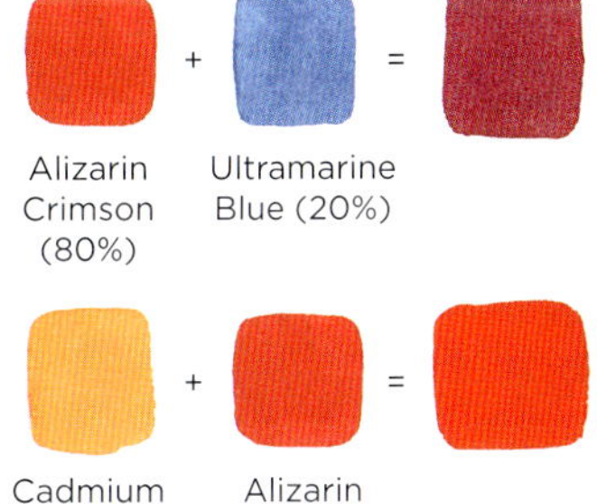

Alizarin Crimson (80%) + Ultramarine Blue (20%) =

Cadmium Orange (60%) + Alizarin Crimson (40%) =

NORTHERN LIGHTS

With stunning, bright, bold colors that we usually don't see in the sky, the northern lights are iconic! The most challenging part of painting with so many colors is not accidentally ending up with a muddy sky. Care must be taken with choosing which colors go next to each other to create beautiful **washes** when they mix on the paper. When doing a **wash** like this Northern Lights painting, it is essential to have your paper on a tilted surface. Tilting your paper allows gravity to do much of the work because the paint will naturally flow downward and mix instead of sitting on top of a flat paper.

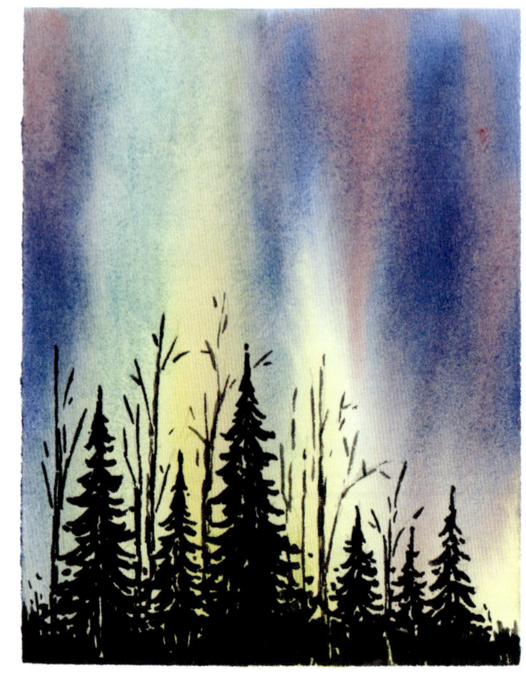

MATERIALS

Watercolor paper

Pencil

Painter's tape

Size 8 round brush

COLORS

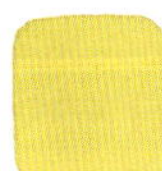
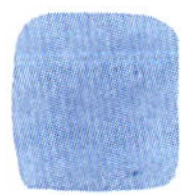
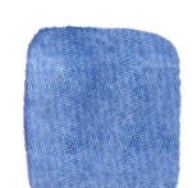
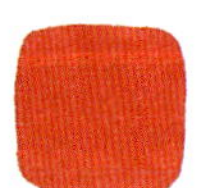
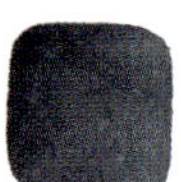

Green Gold   Cobalt Blue   Ultramarine Blue   Alizarin Crimson   Neutral Tint

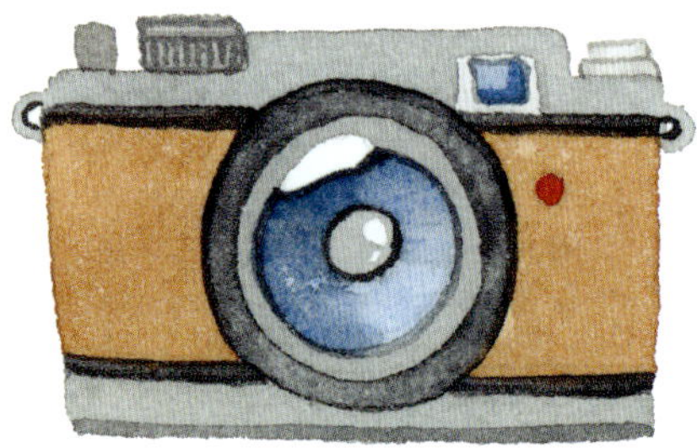

STEP 1: On your water-color paper, trace (page 235) or lightly sketch the northern lights landscape in pencil. For clean edges, tape the border of your painting. It is okay if the colors go down into the trees because they will be silhouetted (painted dark).

STEP 2: Use the **wet-in-wet** technique for this step. Starting with the sky, use your size 8 round brush to apply Green Gold in thick vertical lines. There will be two prominent lines of Green Gold, one main line off the center and one to the right of this. Paint Cobalt Blue between the Green Gold. Drop in Ultra-marine Blue from the top of the paper. Avoid dropping into the Green Gold as much as possible. Add Alizarin Crimson into the Ultramarine Blue. Try not to let Green Gold and Alizarin Crimson touch, or it will turn a brown color. You want the Ultramarine Blue and Alizarin Crimson to mix to create a beautiful purple. Have fun practicing with just this step over and over on a smaller scale.

STEP 3: Paint the silhou-ette of the tree line using Neutral Tint. If it needs to be darker, let it dry and then add another layer. As you paint in the Neutral Tint, leave pieces of the sky to poke through gaps in the trees. Let that dry, then remove the tape.

1

2

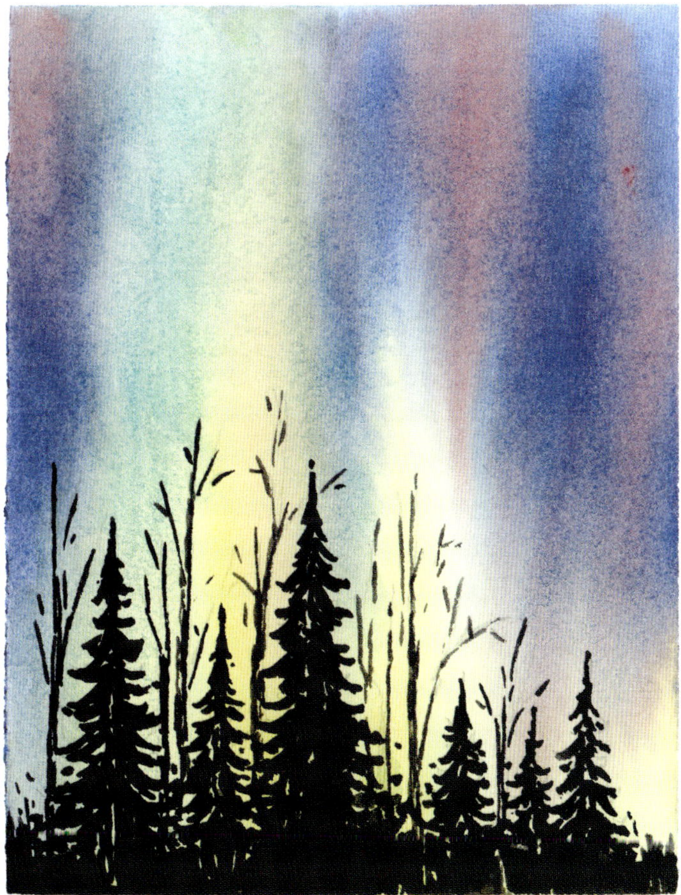

3

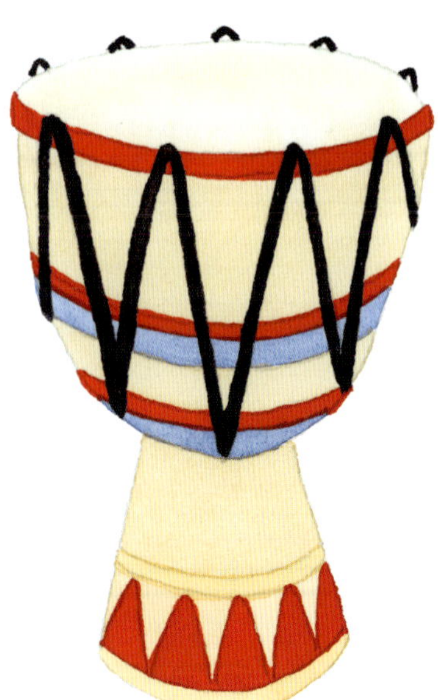

AFRICAN DRUM

This African Drum painting is a perfect example of how the **value** changes depending on whether we wet the paper first or paint on dry paper. When using the same color with **wet-in-wet**, our color will be lighter versus that same color in **wet-on-dry**, where it will be darker.

MATERIALS

Pencil
Watercolor paper
Size 8 round brush
Paper towel

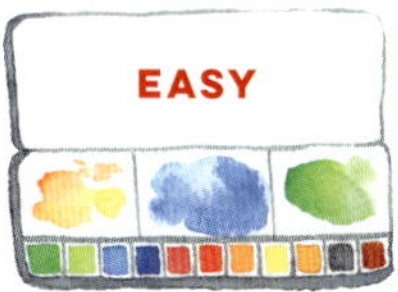

COLORS

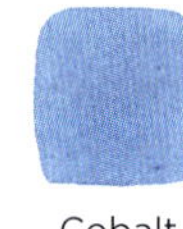
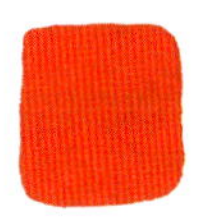
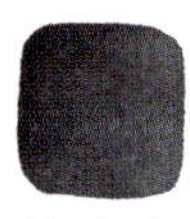

Yellow Ochre

Cobalt Blue

Winsor Red

Neutral Tint

STEP 1: With a pencil, trace (page 237) or sketch the African drum on your watercolor paper.

STEP 2: With a size 8 round brush, paint a **clear water wash** on the top of the drum. Use the **wet-in-wet** technique by laying Yellow Ochre into the **clear water wash**. If the color seems too dark, you can use the **lifting** technique to take away some of that color. Then paint in the four other areas on the side of the drum using a Yellow Ochre **wash**. For the sides, you don't need to lay down a **clear water wash** first; just paint in the Yellow Ochre **wet-on-dry**.

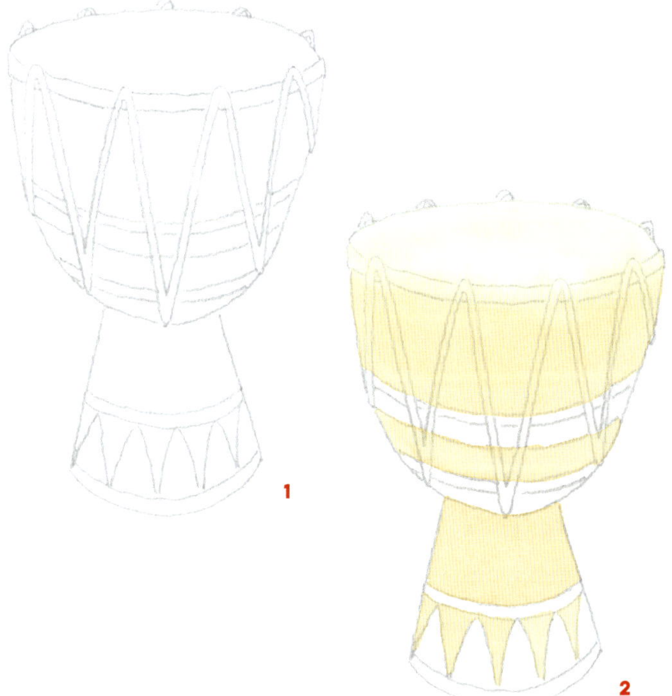

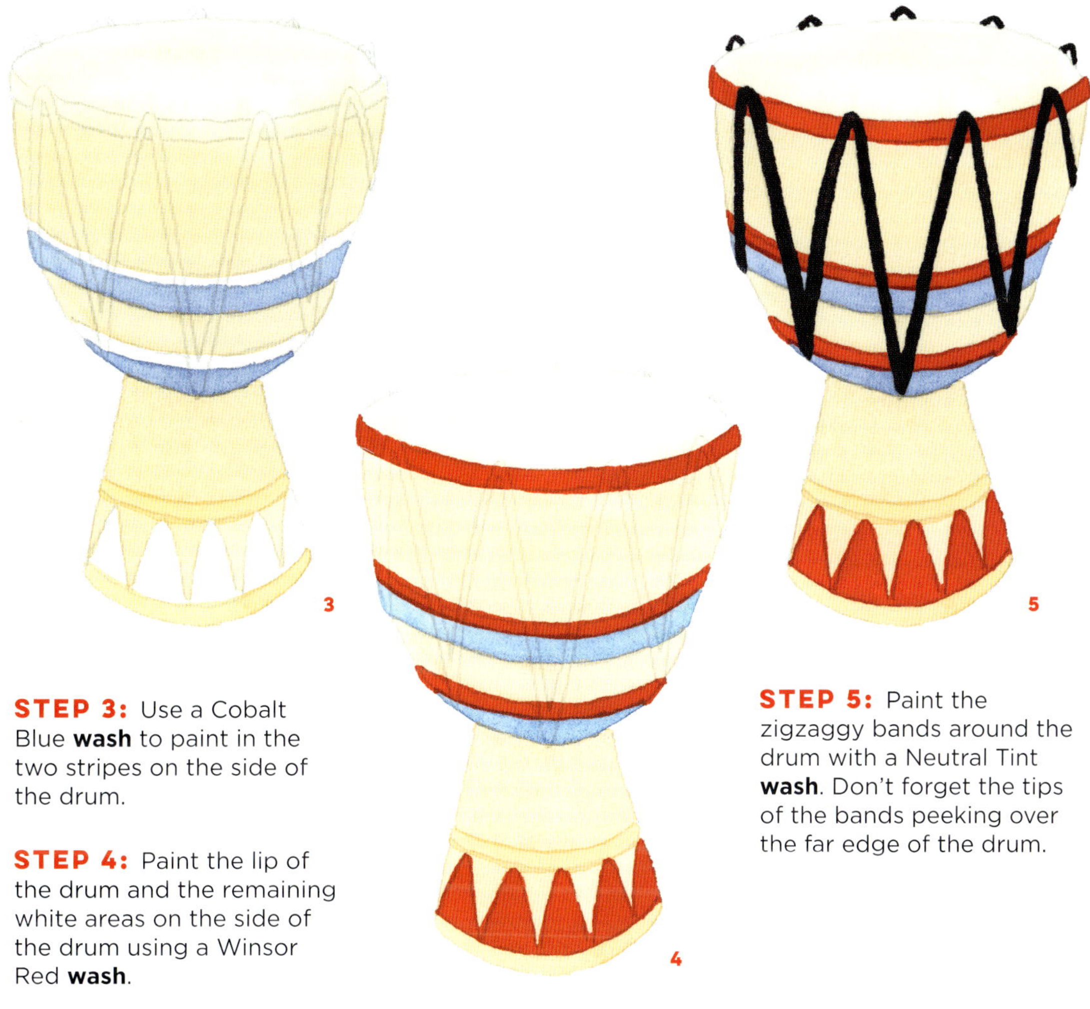

STEP 3: Use a Cobalt Blue **wash** to paint in the two stripes on the side of the drum.

STEP 4: Paint the lip of the drum and the remaining white areas on the side of the drum using a Winsor Red **wash**.

STEP 5: Paint the zigzaggy bands around the drum with a Neutral Tint **wash**. Don't forget the tips of the bands peeking over the far edge of the drum.

DAY OF THE DEAD

One way to unify a painting with many objects is to apply a **background**. In this Day of the Dead painting, there are five skulls that seem to be floating at the beginning until the **background** and border are added to unify them.

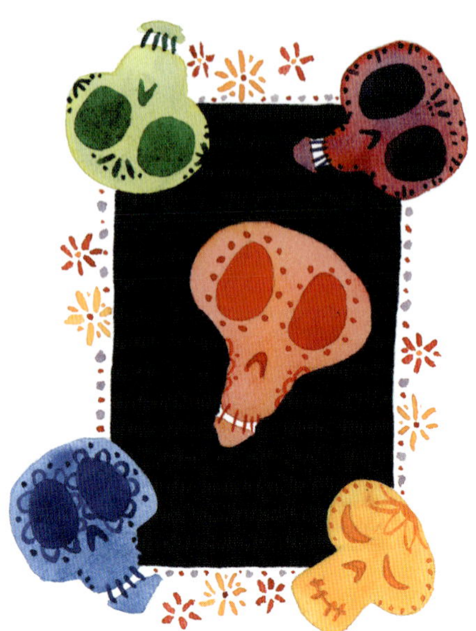

MATERIALS

Watercolor paper

Pencil

Size 8 round brush

Size 2 or 4 round brush (optional)

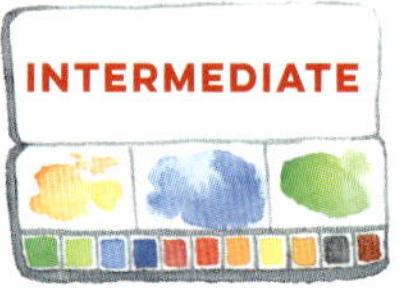

COLORS

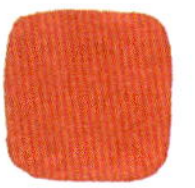 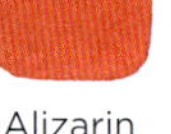 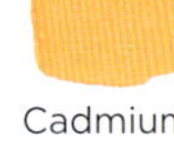 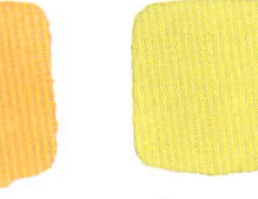 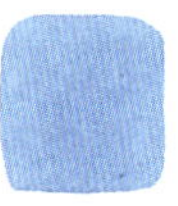 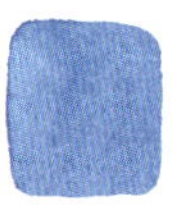 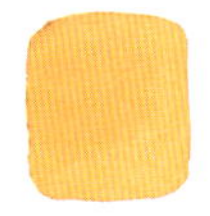 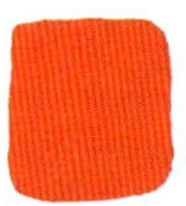  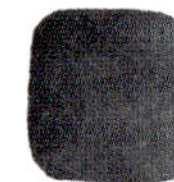

| Alizarin Crimson | Cadmium Orange | Green Gold | Cobalt Blue | Ultramarine Blue | Quinacridone Gold | Winsor Red | Winsor Green | Neutral Tint |

STEP 1: On your watercolor paper, trace (page 239) or sketch the Day of the Dead project in pencil.

STEP 2: The color choices are up to you for this project, but here is what I did. Everything in this step uses the **wet-in-wet** technique.

Start with the skull in the middle and, with your size 8 round brush, paint it with Alizarin Crimson. Then lay in Cadmium Orange while that is still wet. Then dab in some additional Alizarin Crimson until you feel like the colors blend together nicely.

Use Green Gold to fill in the skull on the top left corner. While that is wet, lay in a little Cobalt Blue.

Paint the top right skull with Alizarin Crimson. Add Ultramarine Blue into the Alizarin Crimson while it is still wet.

Take Cobalt Blue and add it to the bottom left skull. While that is still wet, paint in Ultramarine Blue.

For the bottom right skull, use Quinacridone Gold. While that is still wet, add in Cadmium Orange.

STEP 3: In this step, add the eyes, nose, teeth and decorative markings to each skull. Feel free to size down to a size 2 or 4 round brush for these details if you prefer. For the decorative designs, use dots, lines, half circles and flowers. Feel free to create your own fun patterns.

If you followed my color sequence in Step 2, then for the middle skull, use Winsor Red. For the top left corner skull, use Winsor Green. For the top right skull, use this mixture from your palette: Alizarin Crimson (50%) and Ultramarine Blue (50%). On the bottom left skull, use Ultramarine Blue, and for the bottom right skull, use Cadmium Orange.

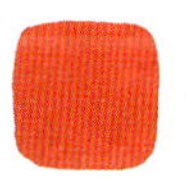 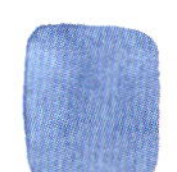 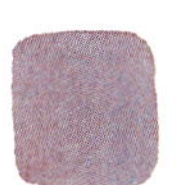

Alizarin Crimson (50%) + Ultramarine Blue (50%) =

STEP 4: Use Neutral Tint for the **background**. If it isn't dark enough, add a second layer. For the middle and top right skulls, don't apply Neutral Tint in their mouths.

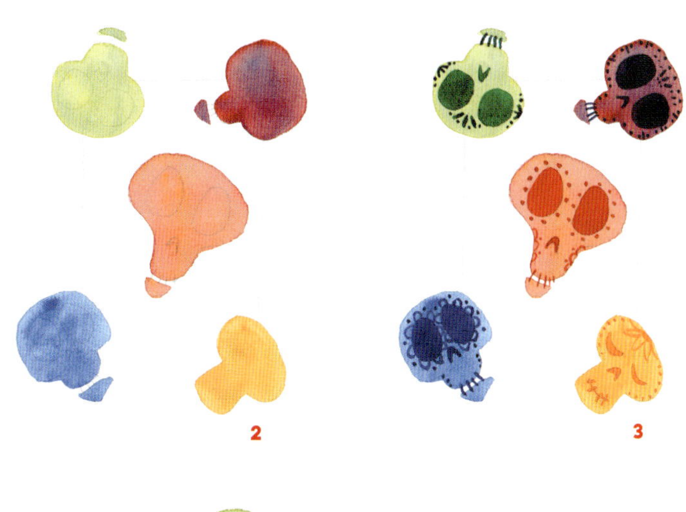

2   3

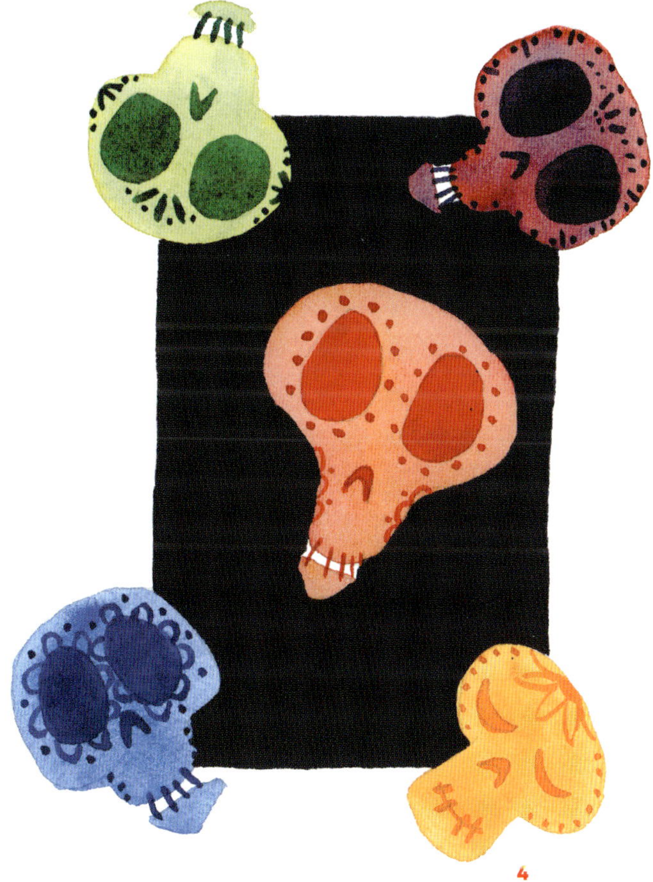

4

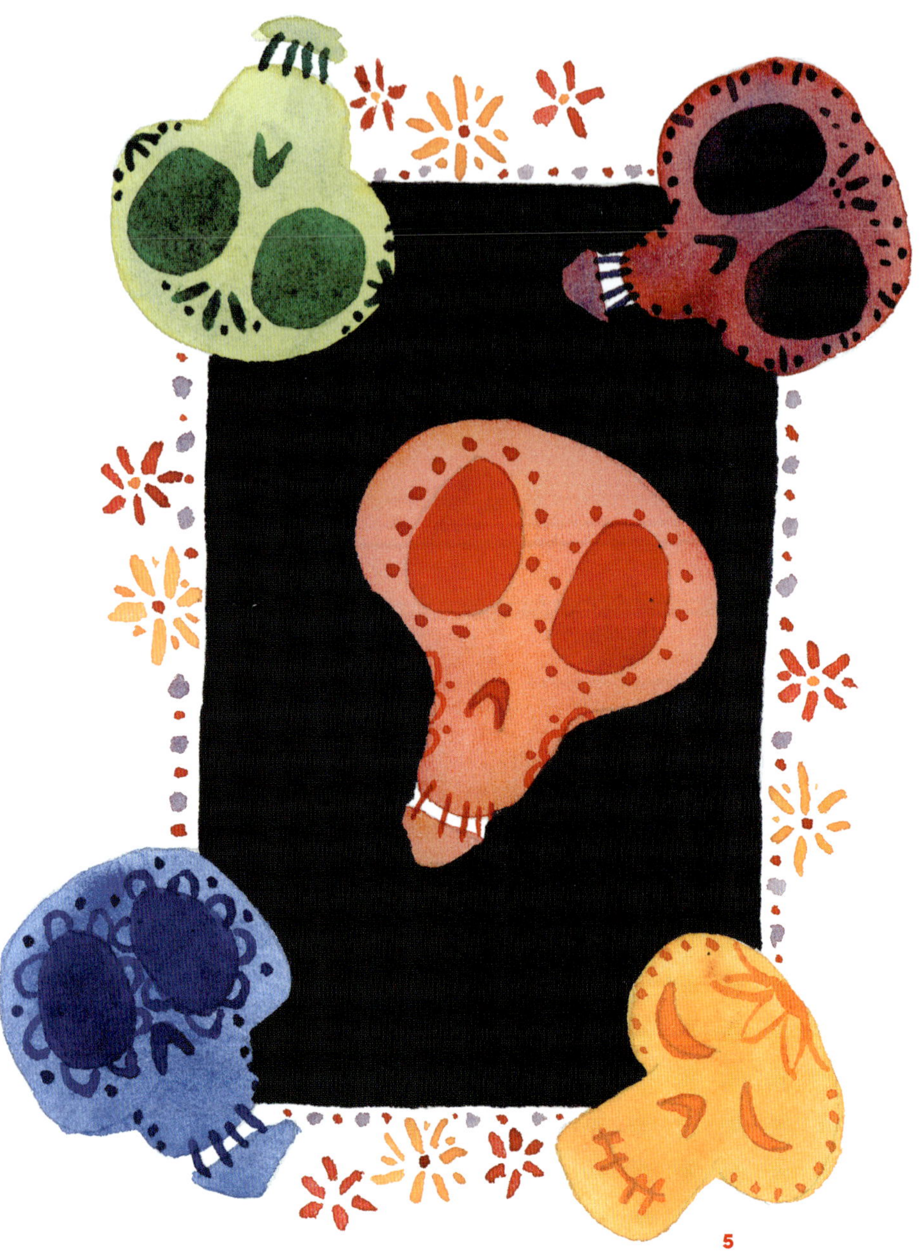

STEP 5: For the final details, you can switch to a size 2 or 4 round brush as needed. Using Cadmium Orange and Alizarin Crimson, add decorative flowers anywhere outside the black box between the skulls. If you aren't comfortable freehanding these flowers, you can pencil them in first before painting. No need to make sure they are perfect; this is a good place to be very loose with your paint and to have them all be different and messy. Finish the border using different sizes of dots. Painted in any colors you wish, these dots should line the black border between the skulls, avoiding the flowers.

EIFFEL TOWER

Few monuments are as instantly recogniz-
able as the Eiffel Tower surrounded by a
brilliant sky or the stars at night. In this
painting, we'll capture this iconic silhou-
ette while playing with negative space.
Every time we paint a positive shape, we
are also creating a negative shape. A fun
way to create clouds is to paint the sky
(positive shape) while leaving sections of
your paper white to create the cloud
formations (negative shapes).

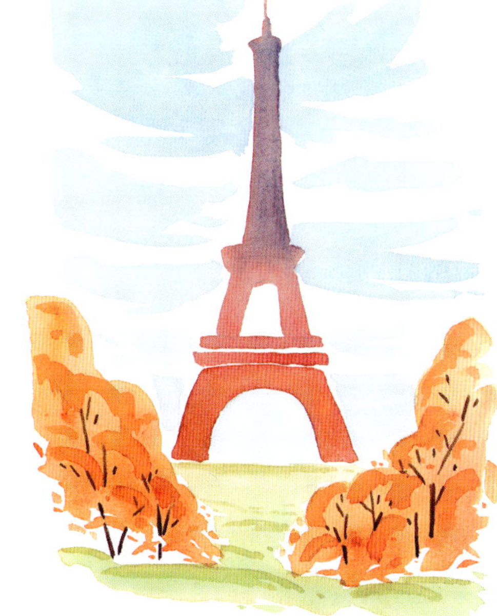

MATERIALS

Watercolor paper

Pencil

Size 8 round brush

Size 2 mop brush (optional)

COLORS

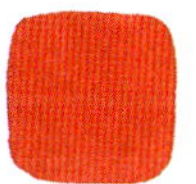 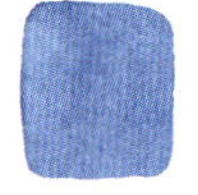 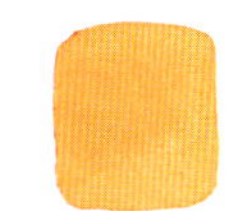 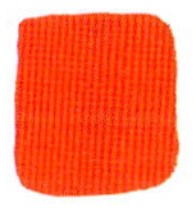 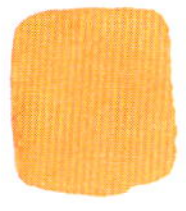 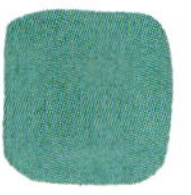 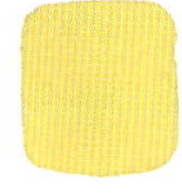  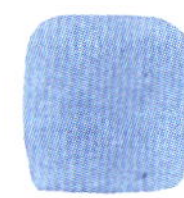

Alizarin Crimson	Ultramarine Blue	Quinacridone Gold	Winsor Red	Cadmium Orange	Winsor Green	Green Gold	Yellow Ochre	Cobalt Blue

STEP 1: On your watercolor paper, trace (page 241)
or lightly sketch the Eiffel
Tower in pencil.

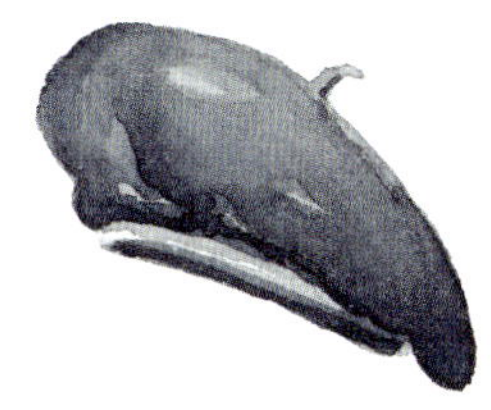

1

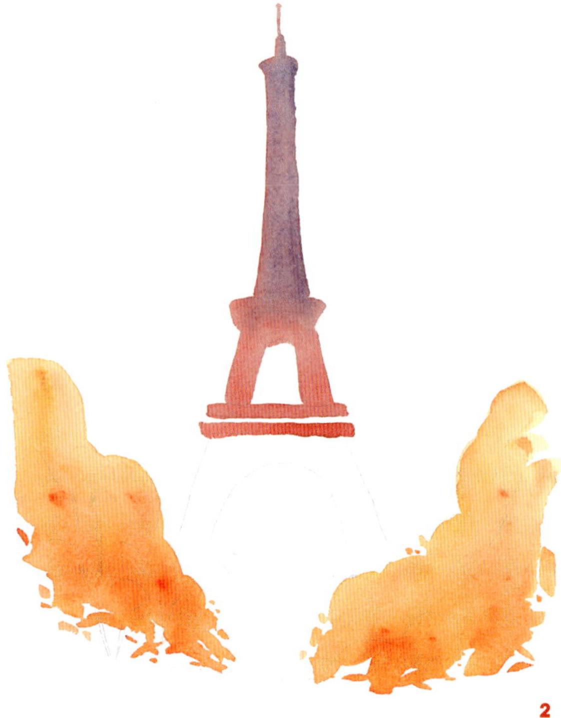

2

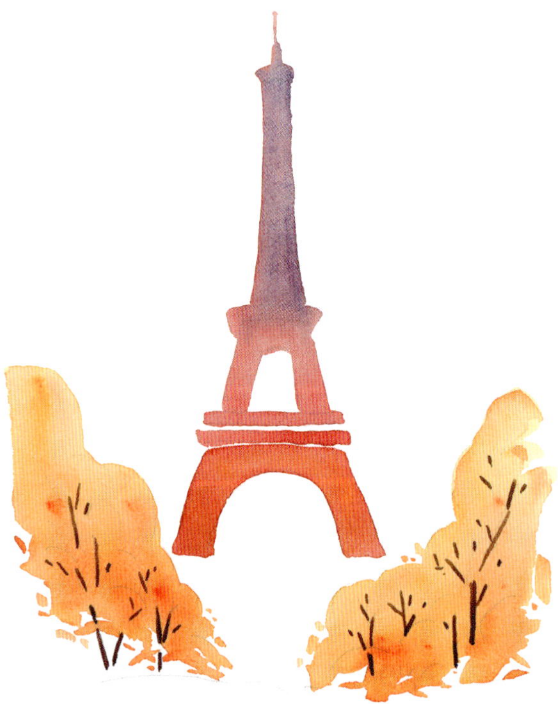

3

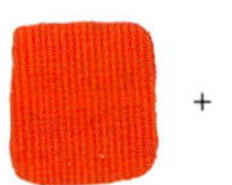

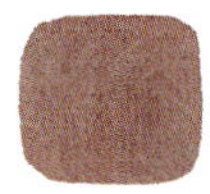

STEP 2: Lightly erase your pencil marks. Use the **wet-in-wet** technique for the tower and for the trees. First, use your size 8 round brush to paint the top half of the tower with Alizarin Crimson. While that is still wet, lay in Ultramarine Blue starting at the top and let it fade before you get to the middle.

Second, focus on the trees. If you want to use a mop brush (or larger round brush) to cover the large area, here would be a great spot to swap it out. Start with the trees on the left side and paint them in Quinacridone Gold. Once you lay in the Quinacridone Gold, dab in Winsor Red and Cadmium Orange throughout those trees. Then move on to the next set of trees on the right side and follow the same **wet-in-wet** paint sequence you used for the trees on the left side. Let the trees end with choppy, organic brushstrokes. In this composition, we are utilizing the white paper as part of the painting; this helps create unity between the art and the white of the paper.

STEP 3: For the base of the tower, use your size 8 round brush and paint with Alizarin Crimson. While that is still wet, lay in Cadmium Orange. The Cadmium Orange can be added to the whole base of the tower.

For the tree trunks, take Winsor Red (70%) and mix it with Winsor Green (30%) on your palette. Add in a variety of trunks and branches.

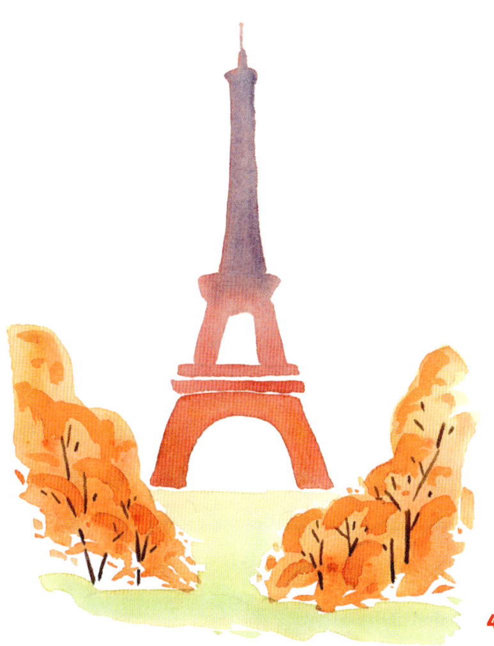

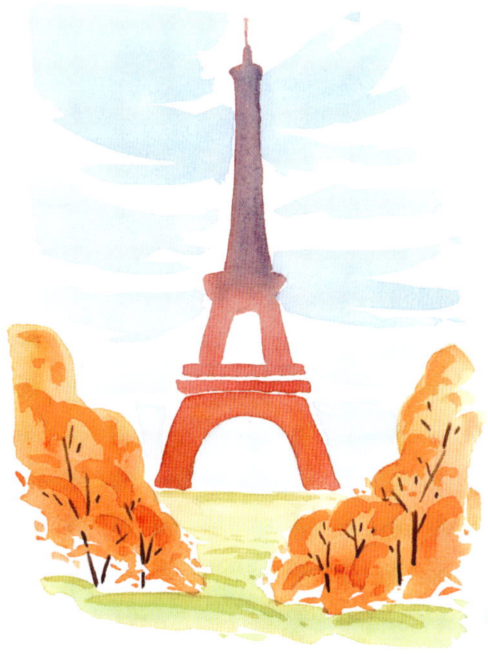

STEP 4: Premix Green Gold (60%) with Winsor Green (40%) on your palette. Clean off the brush and lay Yellow Ochre in the grass area. While that is wet, take the green mixture from your palette and add it in to the area that is located underneath the trees. Fade from Yellow Ochre near the base of the tower down to your green mixture at the base of the trees. As you lay in the grass, leave little areas of the paper white near the base of the trees.

Take Quinacridone Gold (70%) and combine it with Winsor Red (30%) to add a darker layer into your trees. Paint it using arch or rainbow shapes in the trees.

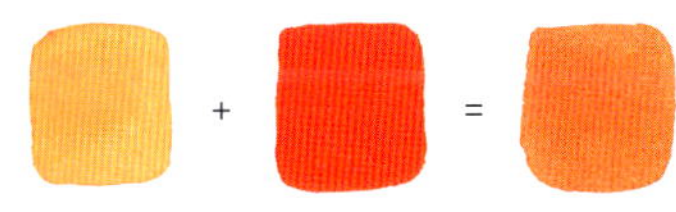

Quinacridone Gold (70%) + Winsor Red (30%) =

STEP 5: For the sky, paint in sections of Cobalt Blue, leaving gaps of your white paper in between to create the cloud formations. The sky is your positive space, and the clouds will be your negative space. To finish off your painting, add Yellow Ochre on the grass line to add **shadows**.

Green Gold (60%) + Winsor Green (40%) =

TAJ MAHAL

One way to be looser with watercolor paintings is to use a bigger brush or a mop brush. Staying loose with a painting like the Taj Mahal can help simplify such a complex **subject** because you end up focusing on the big shapes of the buildings and windows, with minimal detailing. For this project, I recommend using a mop brush to help cover these larger shapes quicker, allowing the colors to mix faster before drying on your paper. However, if this does happen, you end up with a **bloom**, which I think adds a beautiful little imperfection/**texture** to the buildings. If you don't like the look of a **bloom**, make sure to work fast while everything is still wet.

MATERIALS

Watercolor paper
Pencil
Size 2 mop brush
Size 8 round brush

COLORS

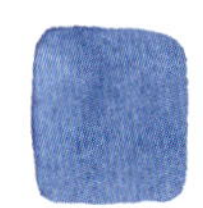 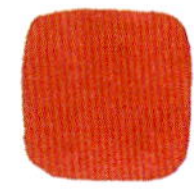 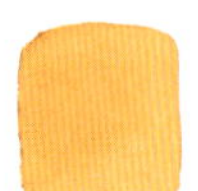

Ultramarine Blue · Alizarin Crimson · Quinacridone Gold

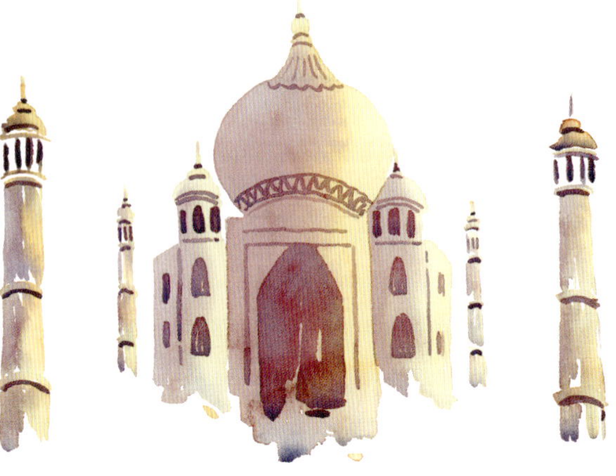

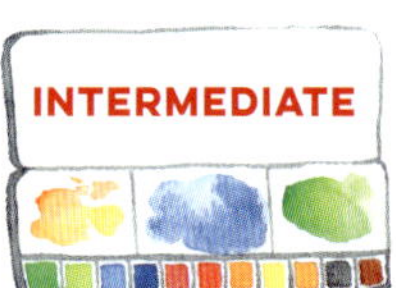
INTERMEDIATE

STEP 1: On your watercolor paper, trace (page 243) or lightly sketch the Taj Mahal in pencil.

STEP 2: You will be working with the **wet-in-wet** technique because we want the colors to **bleed** on the paper. On your palette, mix Ultramarine Blue (50%) and Alizarin Crimson (50%). I highly recommend using a mop brush, so that you can hold enough water in your brush. Clean your brush and **load** it with Quinacridone Gold.

1

2A

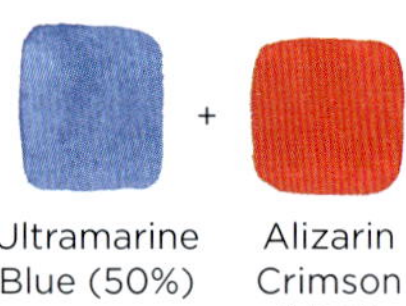

Ultramarine Blue (50%) + Alizarin Crimson (50%) =

2B

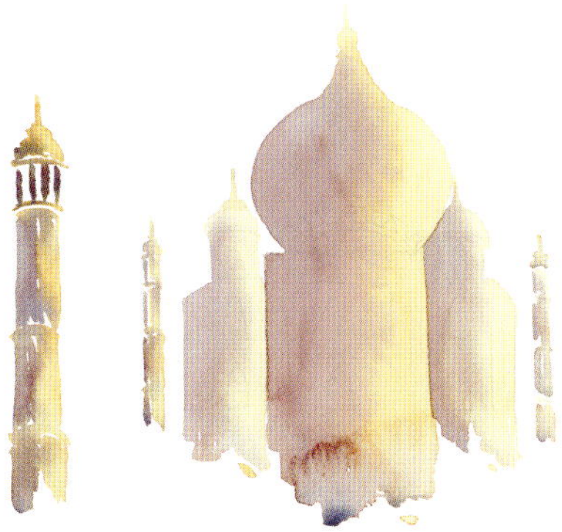

3A

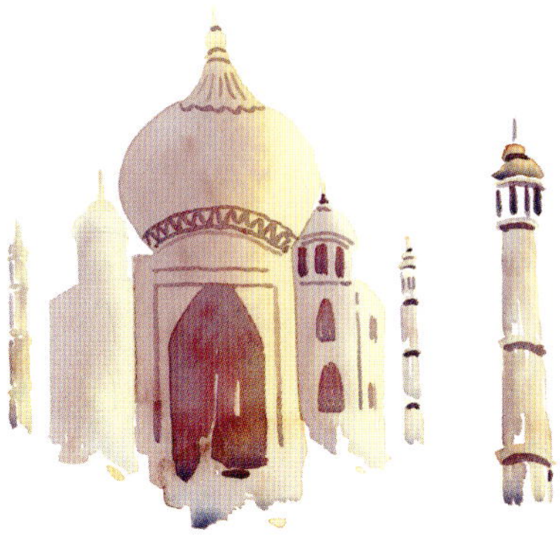

3B

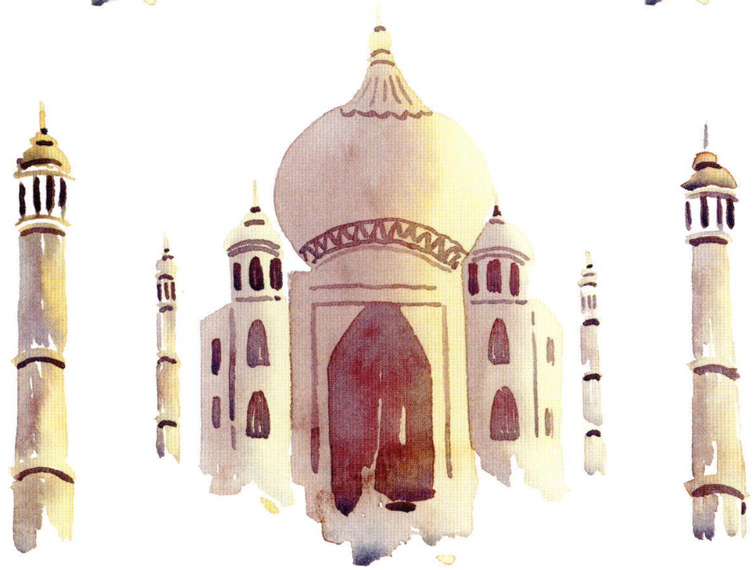

Take the buildings one section at a time. With the Quinacridone Gold, focus the color on the right side as you paint your chosen building section. You can pull the gold a little past the middle, but don't bring it all the way to the left side of the building. While the paint is wet, grab the Ultramarine Blue and Alizarin Crimson mixture from your palette. Paint the left side of the building and let it slowly mix with the Quinacridone

Gold in the center. Do this with each of the building sections. You may want to let each section dry in between so you don't accidentally touch them while wet. For this painting, be loose with your water-color; it is okay if you have **blooms** in some areas and not in others.

Then, take the same Ultra-marine Blue and Alizarin Crimson mixture from your palette and paint thin vertical stripes at the tops of the two front towers.

STEP 3: Take the same mixture of Ultramarine Blue (50%) and Alizarin Crimson (50%) on your palette and add the windows, door, detailing along the roof and **shadows** under the three rims around each column. If you want to do the detailing with a smaller brush, switch to the size 8 round brush.

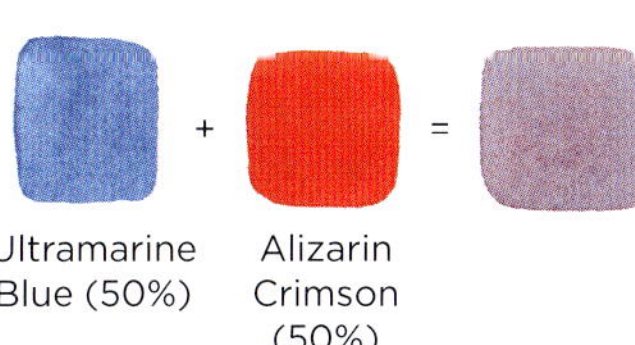

Ultramarine Blue (50%)

Alizarin Crimson (50%)

THAILAND LANTERNS

One of the scariest parts of painting can be adding **splatters** or a **background** to your object at the end. It also can make your painting go from good to mesmerizing, so the risk is worth it when it pays off! When painting these lanterns, I got to the end of painting them and felt like something was missing. I wanted more of a glowing effect. I decided to take a risk and paint around the lanterns in an edgy/rough way with **splatters**. The result was, luckily, precisely what I was hoping for: It suddenly illuminated the lanterns! Other times, I've taken that risk, and it has failed miserably, and I have to start all over; however, when it does turn out, you can see the difference it makes, so remember to be brave and take risks!

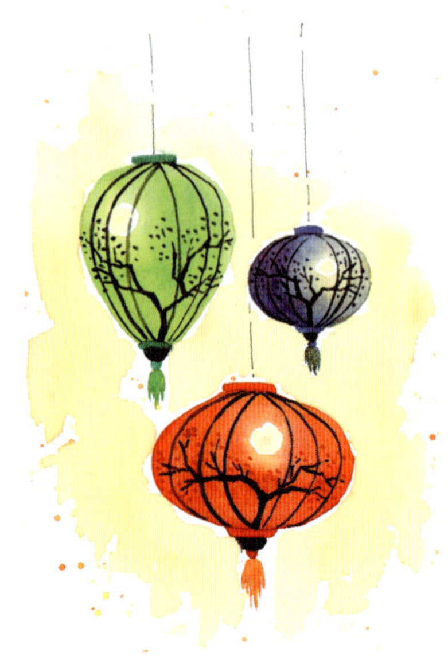

MATERIALS

Pencil

Watercolor paper

Old brush or a Q-tips cotton swab

Drawing gum paste

Size 8 round brush

Rubber cement eraser

Size 2 round brush

Sharpie felt-tip pen

Scrap paper

COLORS

Quinacridone Gold

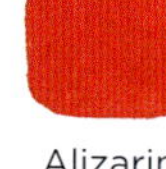

Alizarin Crimson

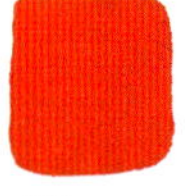

Winsor Red

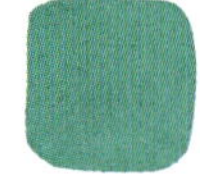

Winsor Green

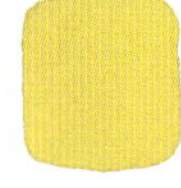

Green Gold

Ultramarine Blue

Cadmium Orange

Neutral Tint

Lemon Yellow

1

2

STEP 1: Use your pencil to lightly trace (page 235) or sketch the Thailand lanterns on your watercolor paper.

STEP 2: With an old brush or Q-tips cotton swab, add a dot of drawing gum paste on each of the lanterns. This will save the **highlights** on the painting.

 Work **wet-in-wet** on this step, so paint one lantern at a time with a size 8 round brush.

For the bottom lantern, paint Quinacridone Gold over and around the drawing gum paste area. While that is still wet, lay Alizarin Crimson into the lantern and add touches of Winsor Red into that as well. These red colors will **bleed**, but try to leave some Quinacridone Gold showing through because that is representing the light escaping the lantern. Let this lantern dry.

For your next lantern on the left, start by painting in Quinacridone Gold over and around the drawing gum paste area. While that is wet, use Winsor Green to paint the lantern and add touches of Green Gold into the color, allowing the greens to **bleed**. Don't completely cover the Quinacridone Gold color. Let this lantern dry.

Lastly, for the lantern on the right, paint Quinacridone Gold over and around the drawing gum paste area. While that is wet, add Ultramarine Blue to the lantern. As the colors mix, try to keep some of the Quinacridone Gold color so you can still see each color individually.

STEP 4: Apply a Cadmium Orange **glaze** to the red lantern. Then use a Green Gold **glaze** for the green lantern. For the blue lantern, use an Alizarin Crimson **glaze** (for this, keep the **glaze** mostly on the left side). Let those dry.

Again, make sure your painting is completely dry! Then remove the gum paste using a rubber cement eraser. Take a size 2 round brush and **load** it with Neutral Tint. Paint in the detail lines on the lanterns. Use this color to also paint in the black base at the bottom of the lanterns.

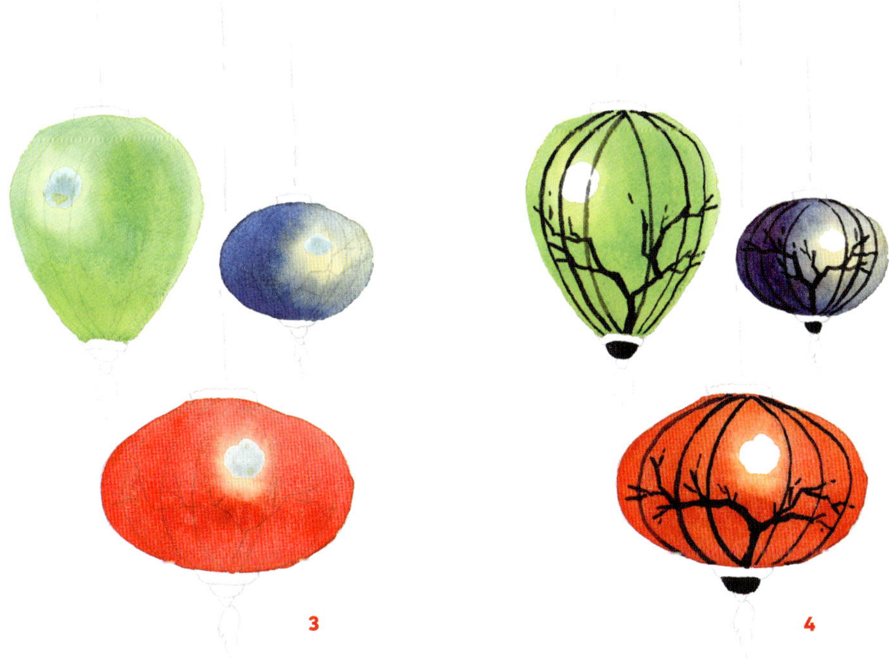

3

4

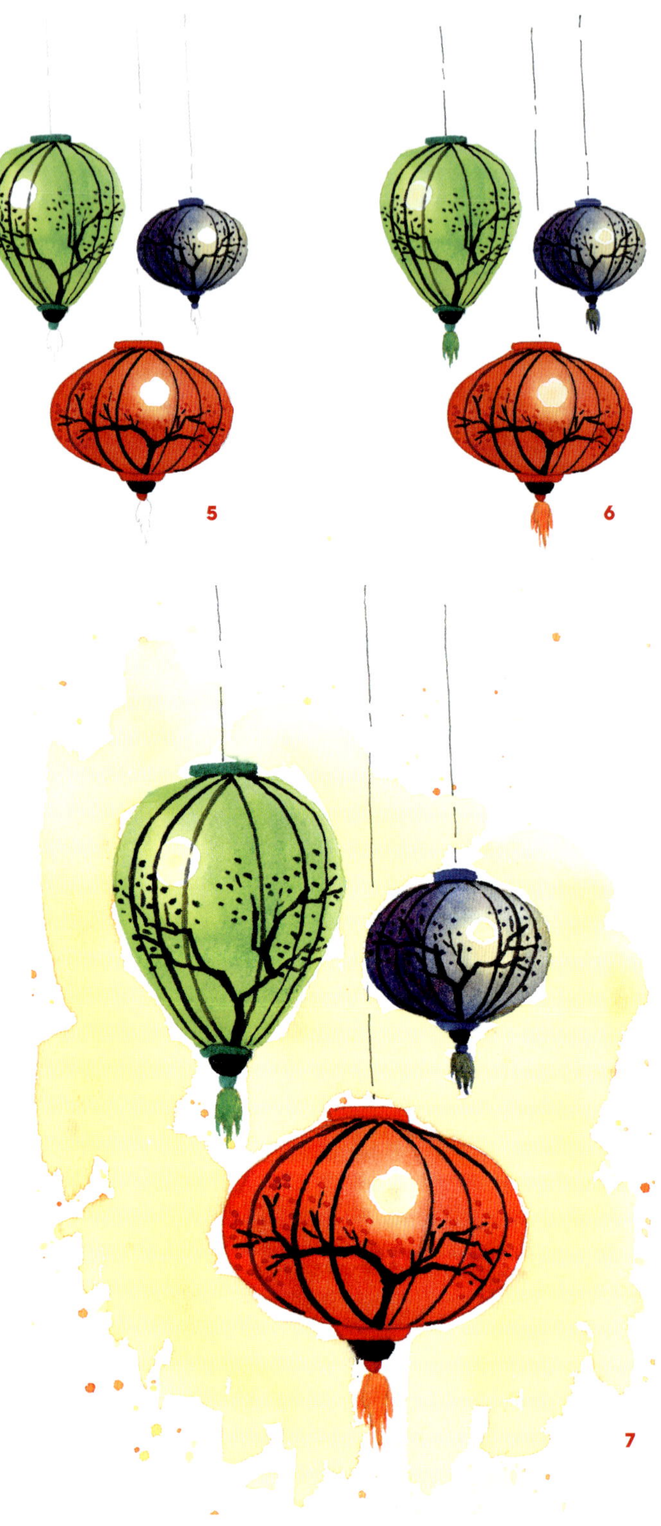

STEP 5: For the bottom lantern, take Winsor Red and paint the top and bottom of the lantern and add dots on the trees.

For the left lantern, use Winsor Green to paint the top and bottom and to add dots for leaves in the trees.

For the right lantern, use Ultramarine Blue to paint the top and bottom and add dots for leaves in the trees.

STEP 6: Drop Lemon Yellow into the center of the white **highlight** area on each of the lanterns. **Load** your brush with Cadmium Orange and add a dot of it into the center of that Lemon Yellow while it is still wet.

Use Quinacridone Gold for the tassels at the bottom of each lantern. While the tassels are wet, drop in the color of each lantern: Winsor Green for the green lantern, Ultramarine Blue for the blue lantern and Winsor Red for the red lantern. Once dry, use your waterproof Sharpie to draw the strings that are coming down.

STEP 7: Cover your lanterns with scrap paper. Using one color at a time, **splatter** (page 19) Lemon Yellow and Cadmium Orange on the painting. To make the lanterns seem illuminated, paint Lemon Yellow around each lantern. While that is still wet, drop Quinacridone Gold into areas of the Lemon Yellow.

GOLDEN GATE BRIDGE

As an artist, you have the artistic license to decide what to leave out, what to put in, what to alter and what to create for each painting you make. That is part of the fun of being an artist: You are the composer of each piece! With this San Francisco Golden Gate Bridge painting, I specifically chose to leave out the sky because I wanted the focus to be on the bridge. I felt like the bridge jumped out more without the sky. However, it is within your power to change the artwork how you want. If you think this piece needs a sky, experiment by adding a sky of your choosing (perhaps a negative space sky like the one in the Eiffel Tower painting on page 79 or a **gradient wash** sky like the one in the Southwest painting on page 154).

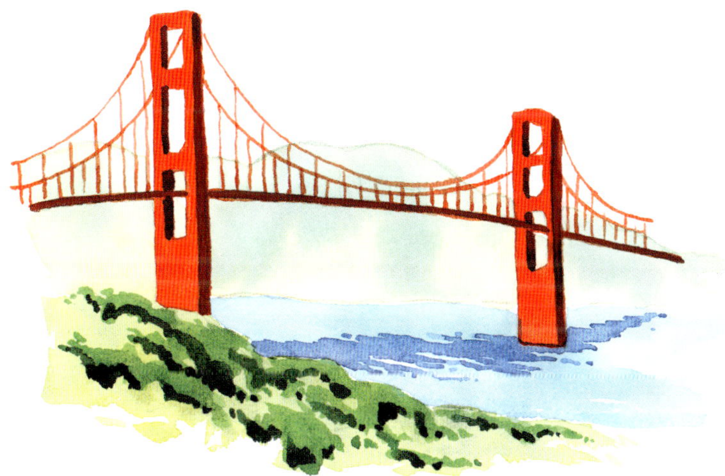

MATERIALS

Watercolor paper

Pencil

Size 8 round brush

Size 4 or 2 round brush (optional)

COLORS

 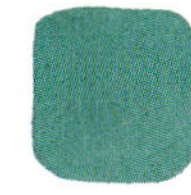 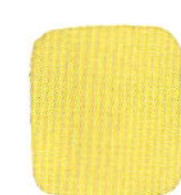

Yellow Ochre   Winsor Green   Green Gold

 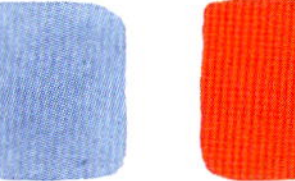 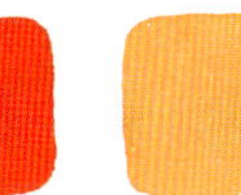

Cobalt Blue   Winsor Red   Cadmium Orange

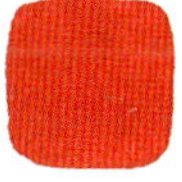 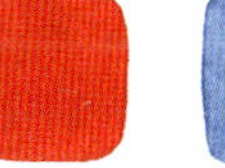 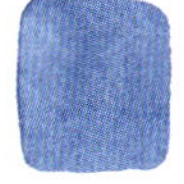

Alizarin Crimson   Ultramarine Blue

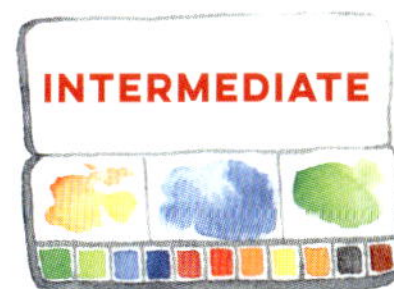

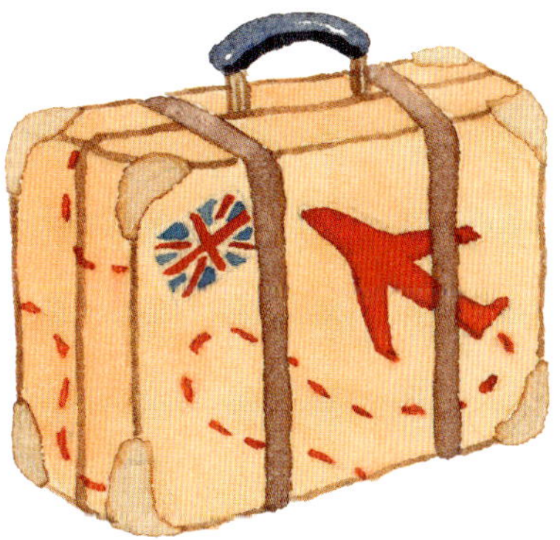

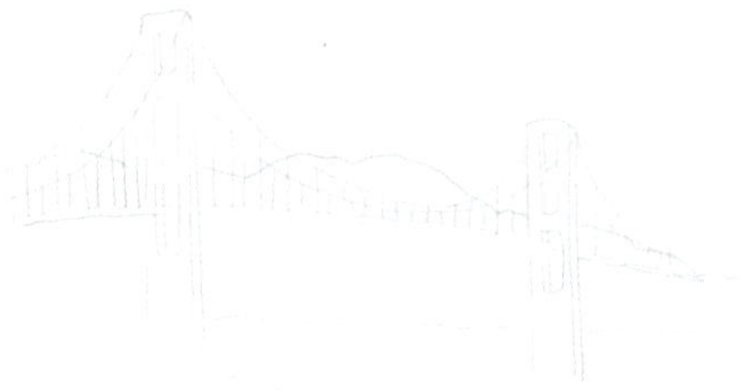

The numbered step illustrations (1, 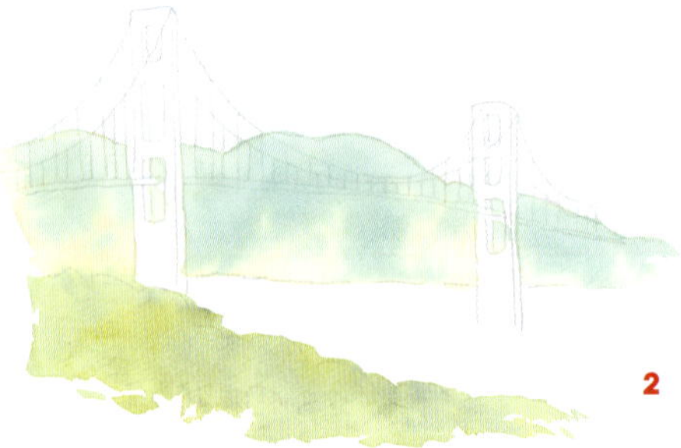 2, 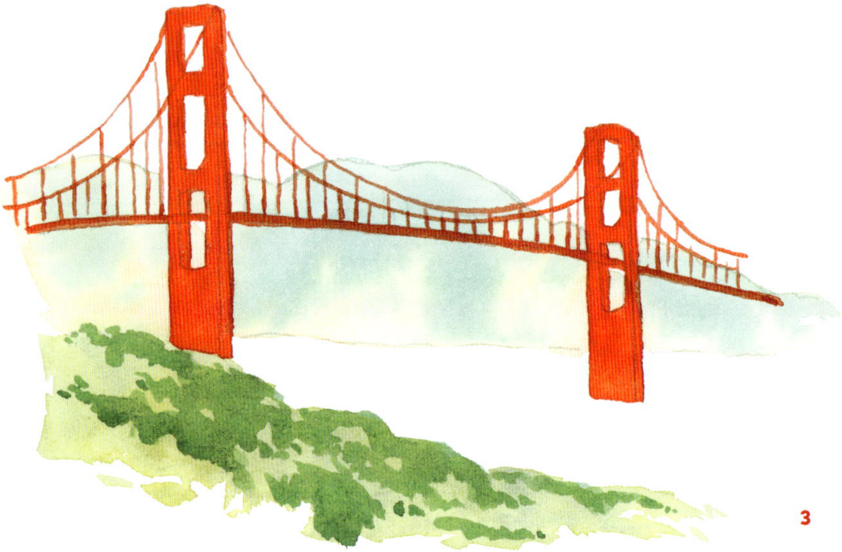 3) show the progression of painting the Golden Gate Bridge.

STEP 1: On your water-color paper, trace (page 245) or lightly sketch the Golden Gate Bridge in pencil.

STEP 2: Lightly erase your pencil marks. Use the **wet-in-wet** technique for this step. First, use a size 8 round brush to paint a light **value** of Yellow Ochre behind the bridge. Because the **value** is so light, don't worry if you accidentally paint a little of the bridge. While it is wet, lay in a light **value** of Winsor Green.

Second, take Green Gold and paint that into the bushes in the **foreground**. While those bushes are still wet, dab in Cobalt Blue.

STEP 3: Mix on your palette Winsor Red (60%) and Cadmium Orange (40%) to create the color for the bridge. Paint the bridge using this color. If you need to size down your brush to paint in the red cables, go down to a size 4 or 2 round brush. Next, mix Yellow Ochre (50%) with

Winsor Green (50%) to add more details to the **foreground** shrubs by making curved shapes on the tops of the shrubs with little gaps where the first layer shows through.

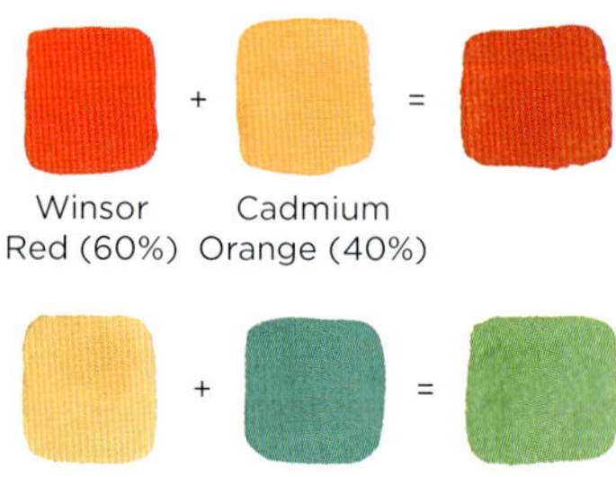

Winsor Red (60%) + Cadmium Orange (40%) =

Yellow Ochre (50%) + Winsor Green (50%) =

STEP 4: Take Cobalt Blue and add that to the water under the bridge (leave white spaces for the **highlights** on the water). While it is still wet, mix in a little Winsor Green. Let that dry.

Add the **shadows** on the bridge. Mix Alizarin Crimson (60%) with Ultramarine Blue (40%) on your palette. When adding these **shadows**, don't be afraid to rotate your paper to reach those difficult spots. Paint the **shadows** on the sides of the two bridge towers and the **shadow** all the way across the road of the bridge.

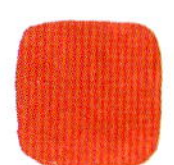 + 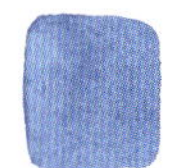 = 

Alizarin Crimson (60%) Ultramarine Blue (40%)

STEP 5: Use Ultramarine Blue to add the bridge's **shadow** on the water. We want to create the effect of ripples in the water. Lay the paint in a zigzag fashion, leaving little gaps in between where the white of the page peeks through.

Combine Winsor Green (60%) and Alizarin Crimson (40%) on your palette, then use the mixture to add additional **shadows** in the bushes.

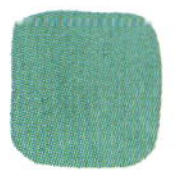 + 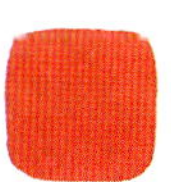 = 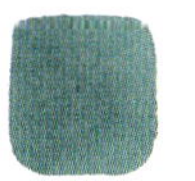

Winsor Green (60%) Alizarin Crimson (40%)

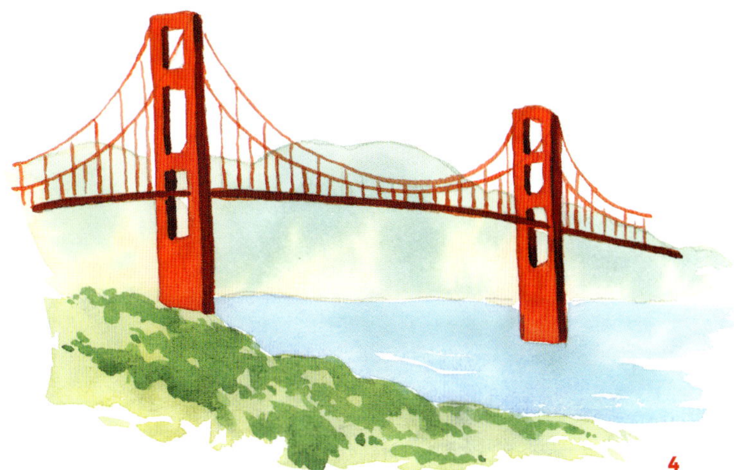

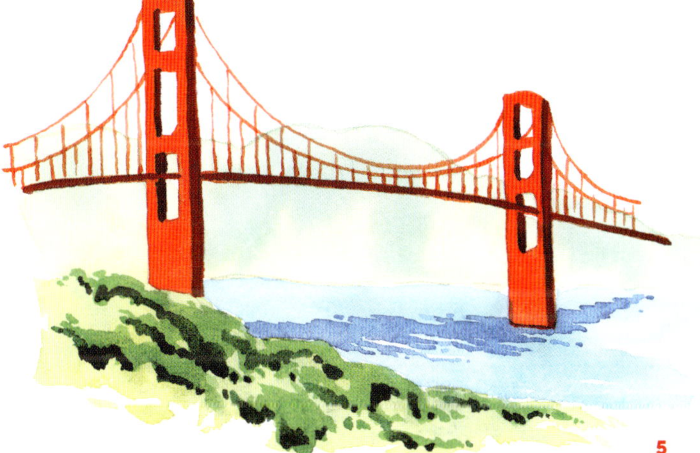

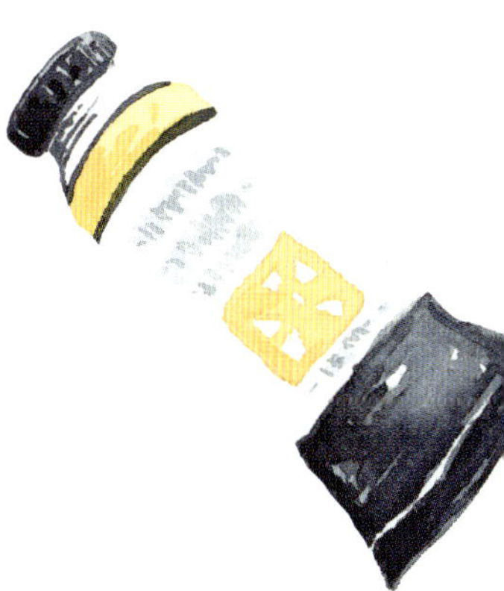

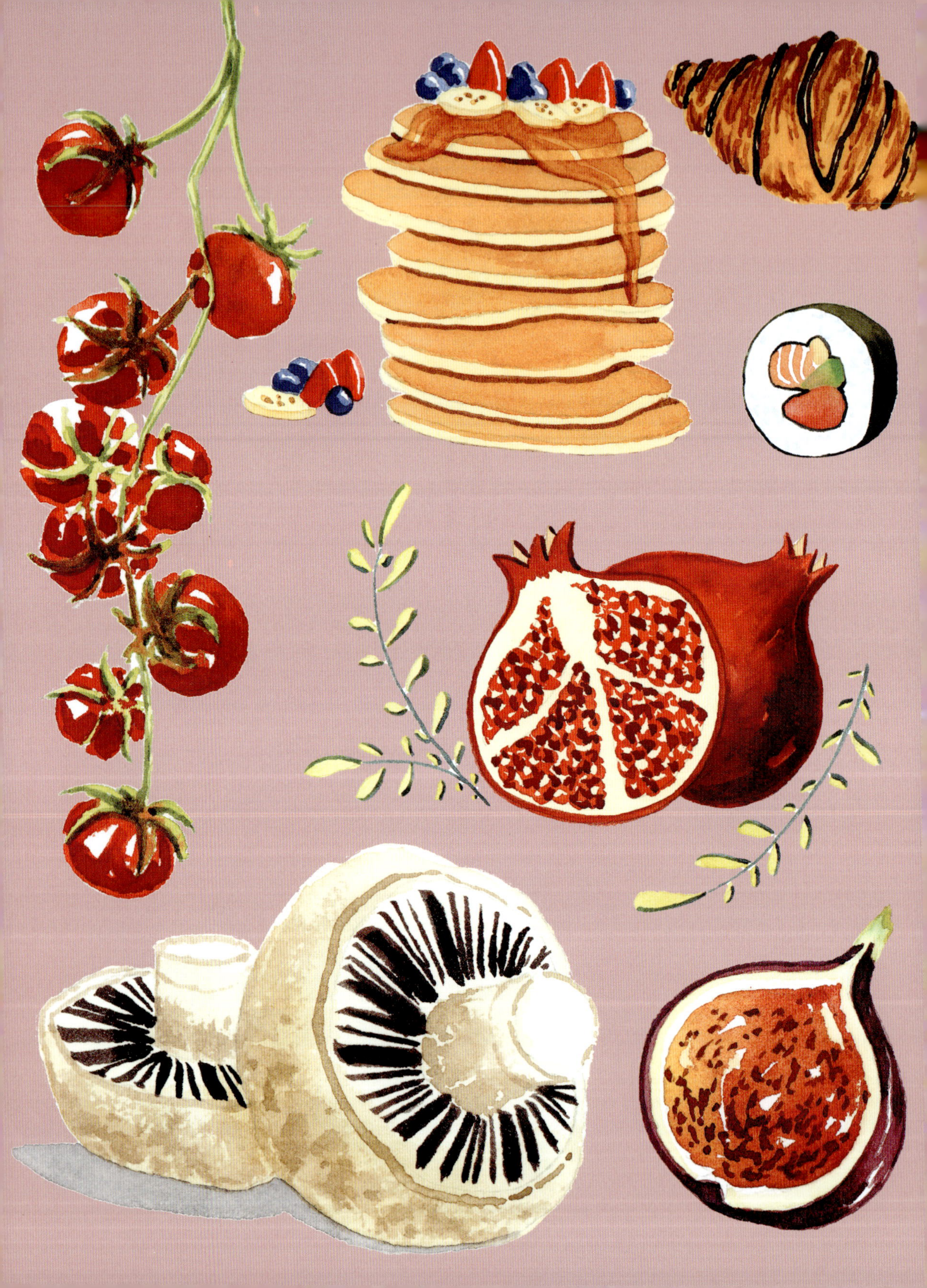

FOR THE **LOVE OF FOOD**

WARNING: Ensure you have eaten before jumping into this section, or you will be starving! After creating each food painting, I craved to eat it in real life, and I would have to jump in the car and drive to get it. Maybe this is why I wasn't fond of doing still-life paintings in college; I was probably always starving during those three-hour classes! Ten years later, food has become one of my favorite items to paint. I love the simplicity of the shapes and colors that allow a beginner painter to succeed. Food shapes also make an excellent subject for practicing curving your brushstrokes.

RIPE FIG

A common question in art is "How do I find my style?" One of the best ways to explore and find your style is to experiment with everything. For example, with this fig, I decided to leave little markings of white showing through. These markings are different than adding **highlights** because I chose to add them all over in random spots. I love the look, but feel free to experiment and test out different iterations of the same subject.

MATERIALS

Pencil
Watercolor paper
Size 8 round brush

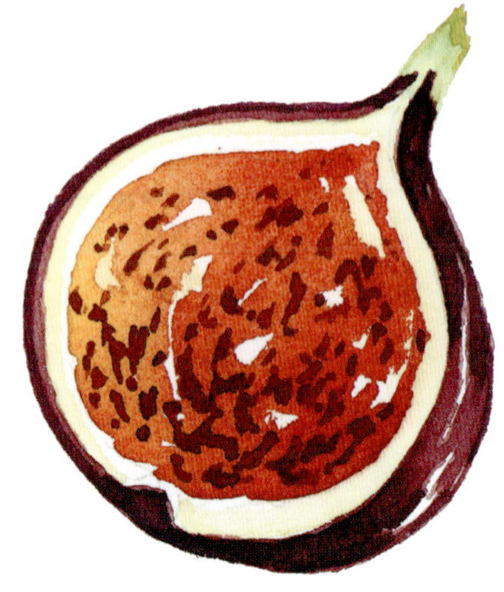

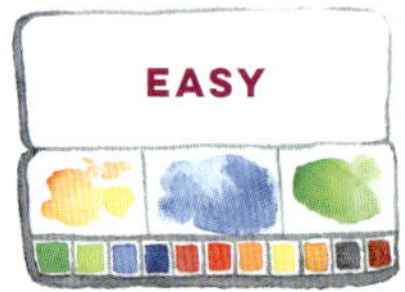

COLORS

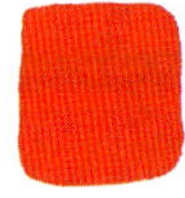
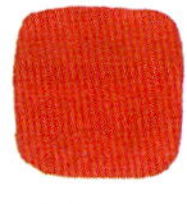
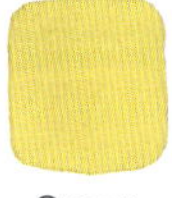
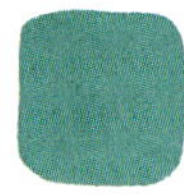

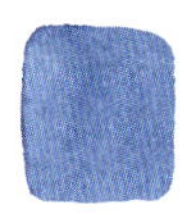

Quinacridone Gold	Winsor Red	Alizarin Crimson	Green Gold	Winsor Green	Cadmium Orange	Ultramarine Blue

STEP 1: Use your pencil to lightly trace (page 247) or sketch the fig on your watercolor paper.

STEP 2: Start by painting the center portion of the fig with a size 8 round brush. Paint the center with Quinacridone Gold, leaving white spaces for an added **texture**. While the color is still wet (**wet-in-wet**), place in Winsor Red and touches of Alizarin Crimson by only dabbing in a few drops. This will allow the Quinacridone Gold to show through and not be covered up.

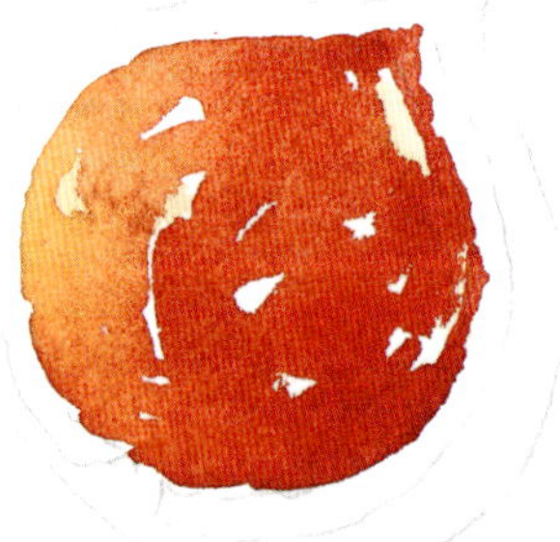

STEP 3: Using lots of water to create a **light value**, take Green Gold and paint the outside edging of the fig.

On your palette, mix Winsor Green (50%) with Cadmium Orange (50%). Set that mixture aside and clean your brush. Use Green Gold to paint the stem, then use the **wet-in-wet** technique to paint in the mixture of Winsor Green and Cadmium Orange that is on your palette. When you lay that mixture in, add it to the very top of the stem and let it **bleed** with the Green Gold. **Soften** the color at the end of the stem with a little water on your brush.

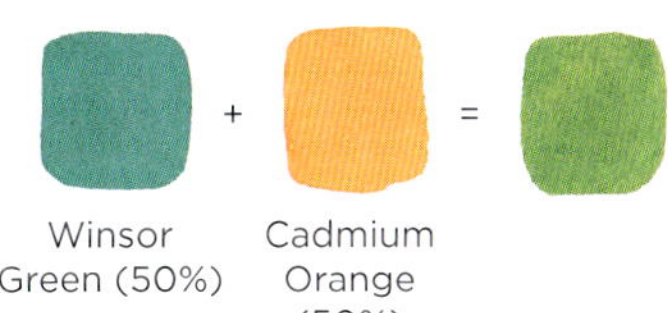

Winsor Green (50%) + Cadmium Orange (50%) =

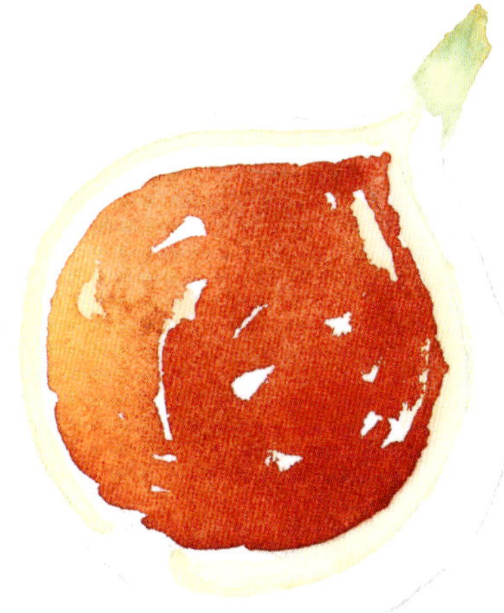

STEP 4: Mix Alizarin Crimson (60%) with Ultramarine Blue (40%) on your palette. Paint the outer layer of the fig in this color. (I chose to make a stylistic choice by leaving a few small stripes of white on the outside edge. This is optional.)

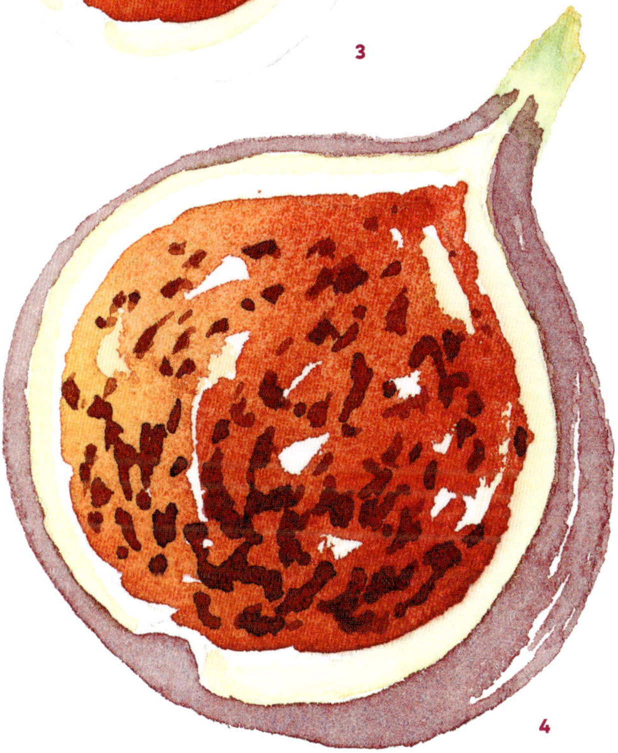

Take Alizarin Crimson (80%) and combine it with Winsor Green (20%) on your palette. Use this mixture in a dotting motion to apply seeds in the center of your fig. Add more seeds to the base of the fig and lessen the amount as you get closer to the top.

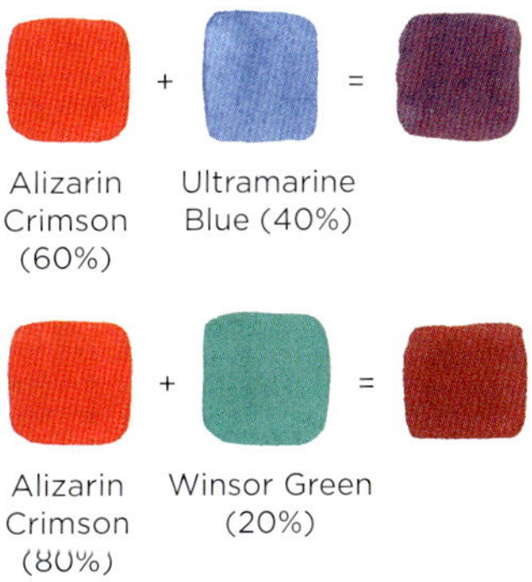

Alizarin Crimson (60%) + Ultramarine Blue (40%) =

Alizarin Crimson (80%) + Winsor Green (20%) =

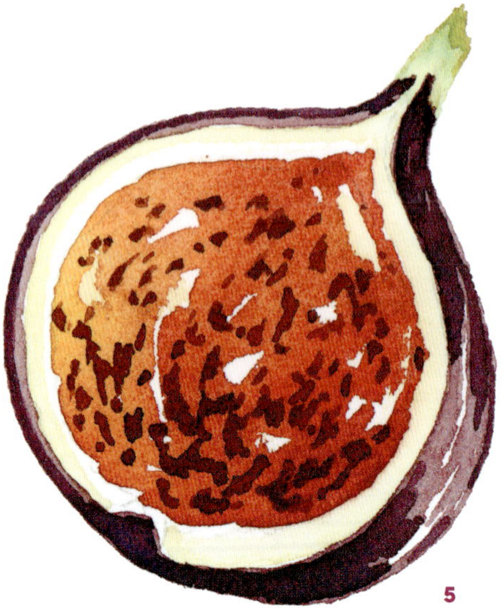

STEP 5: On your palette, mix Alizarin Crimson (60%) with Ultramarine Blue (40%). Use this color to add a darker layer on the outside of the fig. Make sure to not cover up the entire first layer; leave a small portion showing through on the middle of the side.

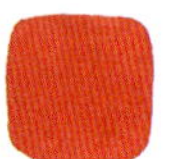 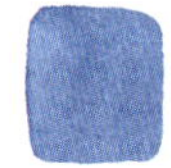 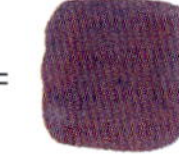

Alizarin Crimson (60%)   Ultramarine Blue (40%)

Combine Cadmium Orange (80%) and Winsor Green (20%) on your palette. Use the mixture to darken the top of the stem.

  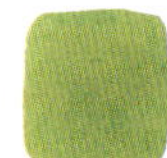

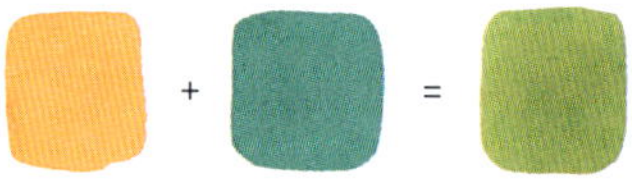

Cadmium Orange (80%)   Winsor Green (20%)

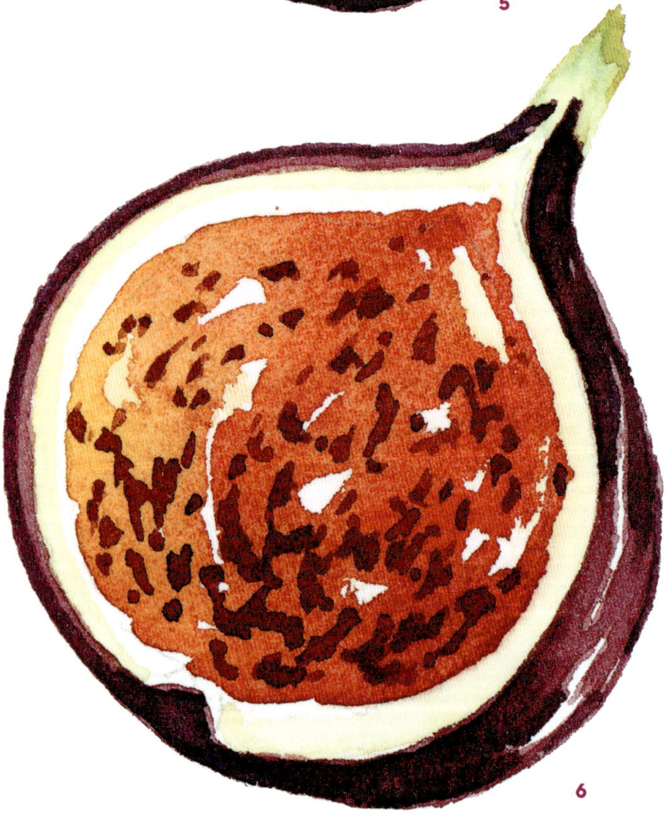

STEP 6: Use a **glaze** on the outer layer of the fig to warm the purple color. Take Alizarin Crimson (80%) and mix it with Ultramarine Blue (20%) on your palette. Apply the **glaze** by painting over the outside purple layer of the fig, avoiding all white areas. This helps unify the two layers of your purple and also changes your purple from being a cool **tone** to a warm one.

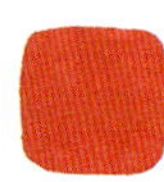 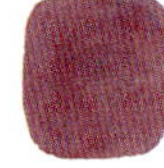

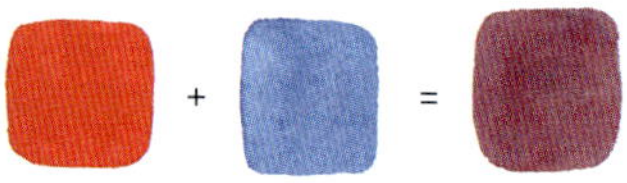

Alizarin Crimson (80%)   Ultramarine Blue (20%)

SYRUPY PANCAKES

Watercolor is semitransparent, so it allows the paper to show through the paint. Semitransparent can be difficult if you accidentally mess up and wish you could cover it up with paint. However, semitransparent paint can be beneficial when creating something like syrup, where the object is meant to be see-through. The syrup on your pancake is a great way to see the translucent quality of watercolor.

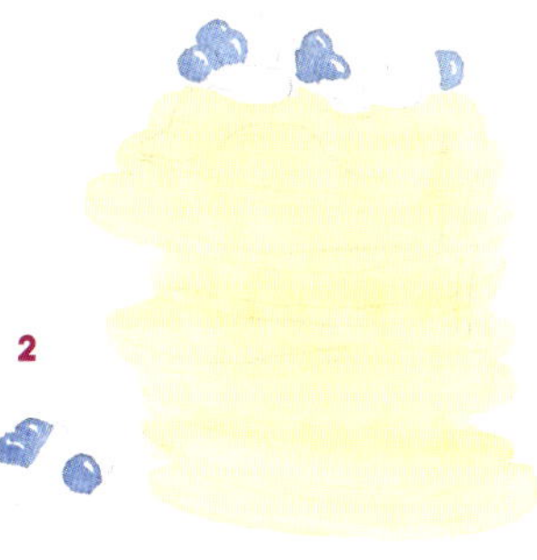

MATERIALS

Watercolor paper

Pencil

Size 8 round brush

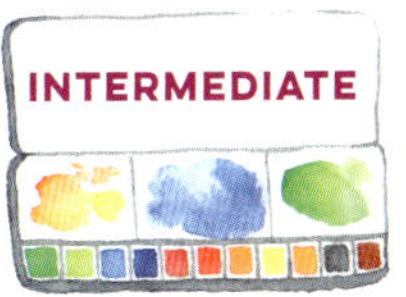

COLORS

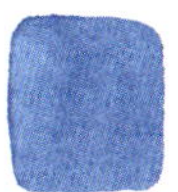

Yellow Ochre

Lemon Yellow

Ultramarine Blue

Quinacridone Gold

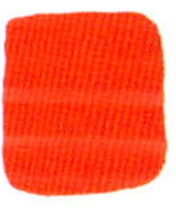
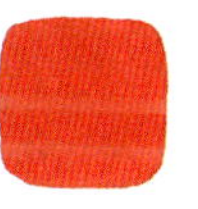

Winsor Red

Alizarin Crimson

Cadmium Orange

STEP 2: On your palette, combine Yellow Ochre (70%) and Lemon Yellow (30%). Use a size 8 round brush to paint the pancakes with the mixture. Once that is dry, paint in the blueberries using Ultramarine Blue. Leave a little white spot for the **highlight** on each blueberry.

STEP 1: On your water-color paper, use a pencil to trace (page 247) or sketch the syrupy pancakes.

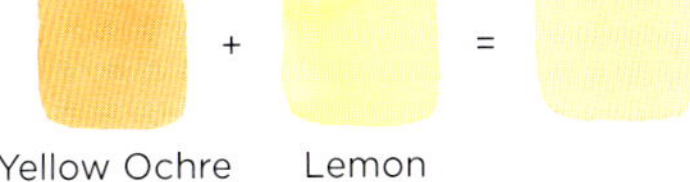

Yellow Ochre (70%)

Lemon Yellow (30%)

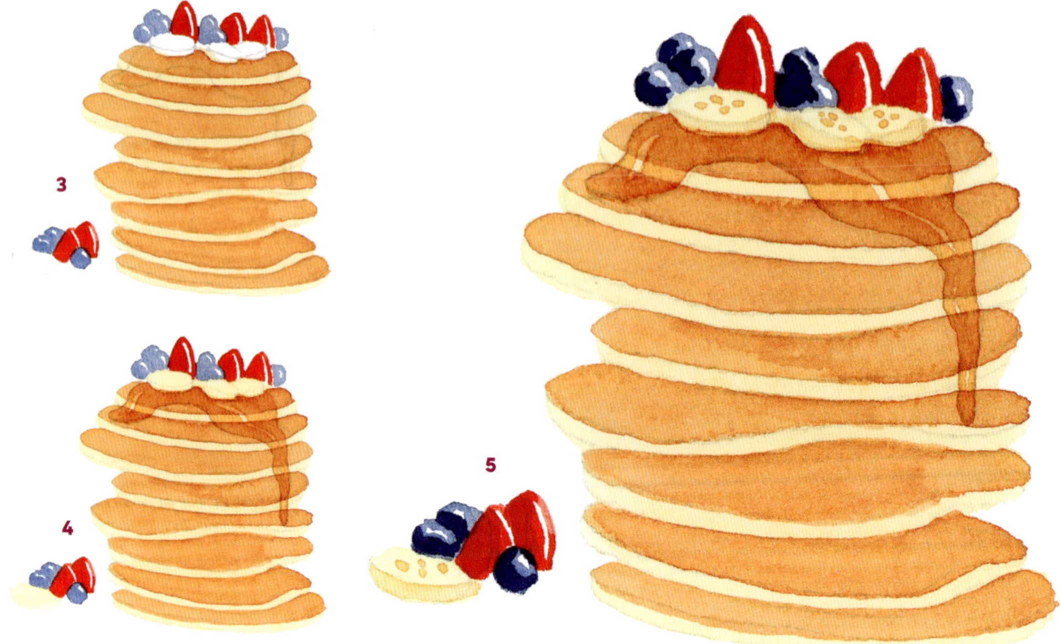

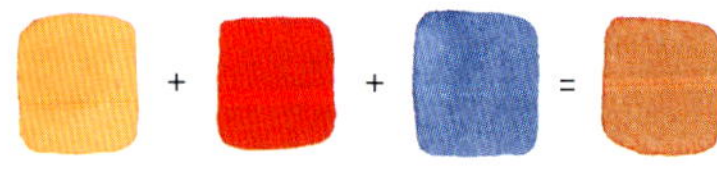

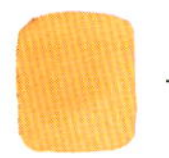

STEP 3: Mix Quinacridone Gold (60%), Winsor Red (30%) and Ultramarine Blue (10%) on your palette. Use this color mixture to create the look of cooked sides on each pancake.

Quinacridone Gold (60%) + Winsor Red (30%) + Ultramarine Blue (10%) =

Let that dry, then paint in the strawberries using Winsor Red.

STEP 4: Paint in the banana slices using Lemon Yellow. Let them dry.

On your palette, mix Quinacridone Gold (40%), Alizarin Crimson (30%), Lemon Yellow (20%) and Ultramarine Blue (10%). Water it down a lot. Use this color mixture as the syrup. Leave a thin **highlight** on the left and right side by not painting the syrup over those areas.

Quinacridone Gold (40%) + Alizarin Crimson (30%) + Lemon Yellow (20%) + Ultramarine Blue (10%) =

STEP 5: Add a **shadow** to the blueberries with another layer of Ultramarine Blue on the left sides to make them slightly darker. Wait for it to dry. Using Winsor Red, darken the strawberries. Wait for it to dry. With Yellow Ochre, darken the edge of each banana slice and add a few dots on the top for the seeds.

STEP 6: Combine Cadmium Orange (50%), Ultramarine Blue (30%) and Alizarin Crimson (20%) on your palette. Add a **shadow** directly under each pancake. Follow the shape of the pancake line. Don't add the pancake **shadow** where the syrup lays. Use that same **shadow** mixture to add a small dot inside each of the already dark dots of the bananas.

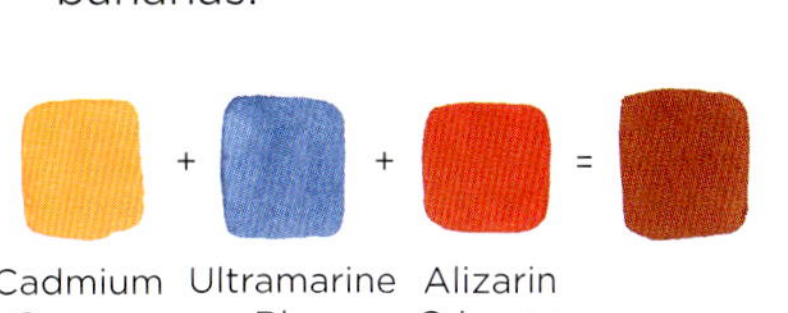

Cadmium Orange (50%) + Ultramarine Blue (30%) + Alizarin Crimson (20%) =

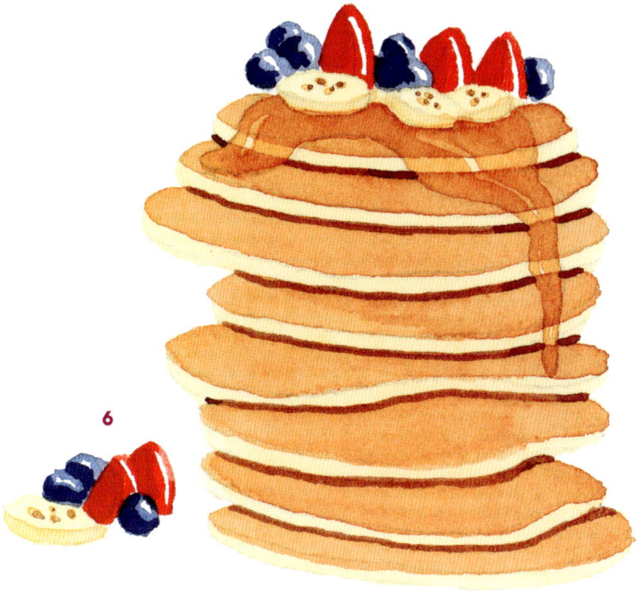

STEP 7: On your palette, mix Alizarin Crimson (50%) and Ultramarine Blue (50%). Use the mixture to add a **shadow** under the bottom pancake and under the fruit. As an optional last step, darken the syrup by using a very watered-down mixture of Quinacridone Gold (40%), Alizarin Crimson (30%), Lemon Yellow (20%) and Ultramarine Blue (10%).

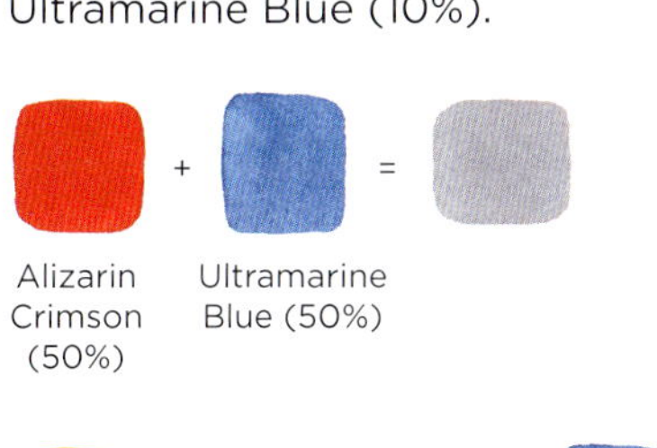

Alizarin Crimson (50%) + Ultramarine Blue (50%) =

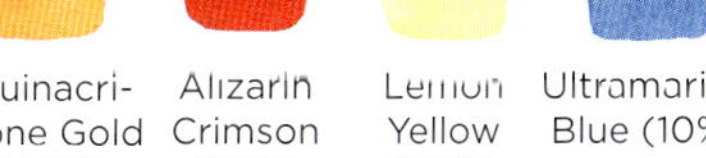

Quinacridone Gold (40%) + Alizarin Crimson (30%) + Lemon Yellow (20%) + Ultramarine Blue (10%) =

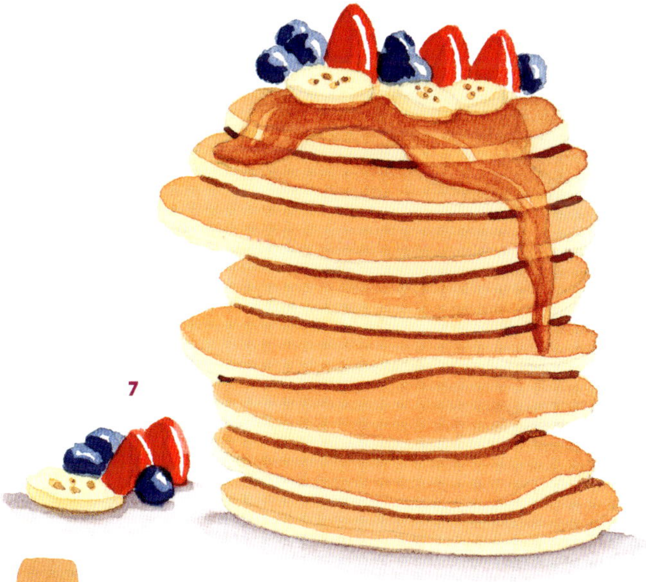

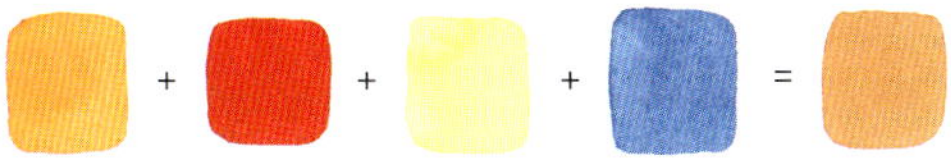

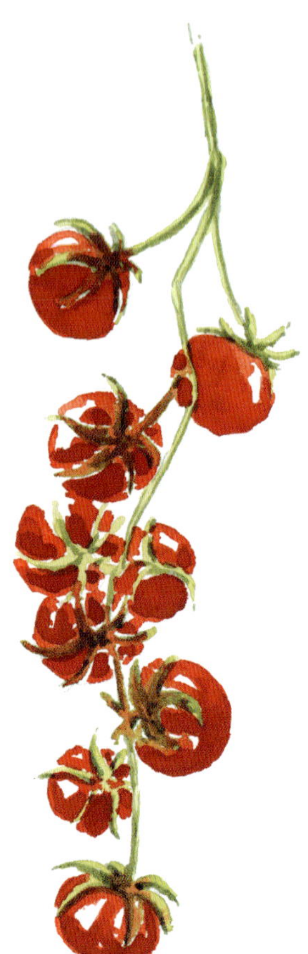

CHERRY TOMATOES

In this Cherry Tomatoes painting, let your green mixture **bleed** into your red. You get a loose, unpredictable effect when you allow your watercolors to **bleed** together. While it can be frustrating when you didn't mean to let the colors **bleed**, allowing your colors to **bleed** intentionally will help force you to be loose with watercolor and enjoy the beauty of the medium! Sometimes, we must trust in the process and let the paint be in control.

MATERIALS

Watercolor paper

Pencil

Size 8 round brush

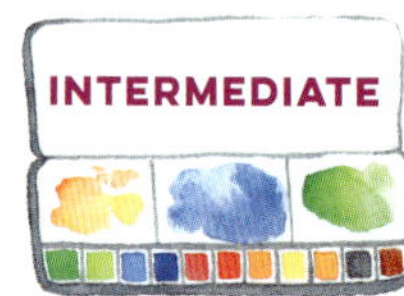

COLORS

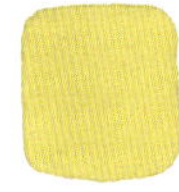
Green
Gold

Winsor
Red

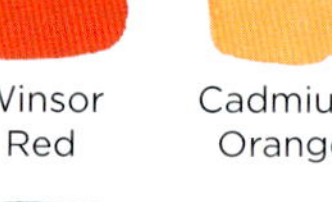
Cadmium
Orange

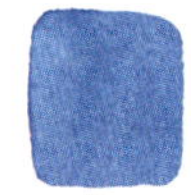
Ultramarine
Blue

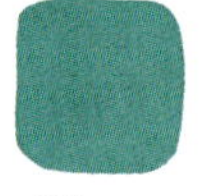
Winsor
Green

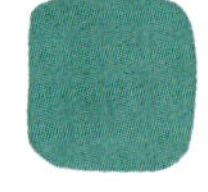

STEP 1: On your watercolor paper, trace (page 249) or lightly sketch the cherry tomatoes in pencil.

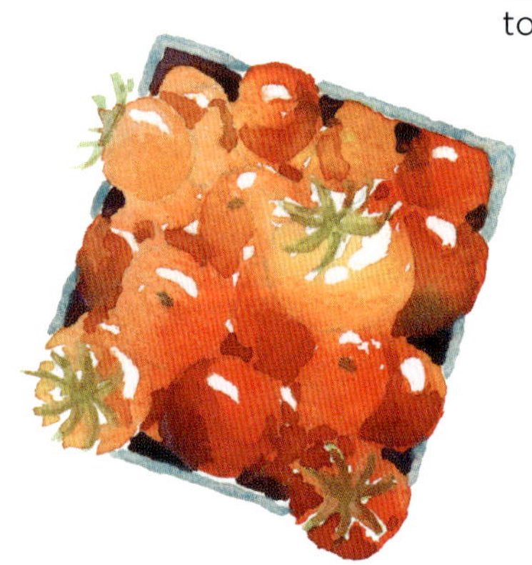

STEP 2: Lightly erase the pencil markings. In this step, focus on letting the colors **bleed** together without letting them dry (**wet-in-wet**). Use a size 8 round brush to paint the vine and stems in Green Gold. On your palette, combine Winsor Red (70%) and Cadmium Orange (30%). Go in while some of the stems are still wet because you will want some of the red of the tomatoes to **bleed** into the stems. Leave some of the white paper coming through on parts of the tomatoes to act as a **highlight**.

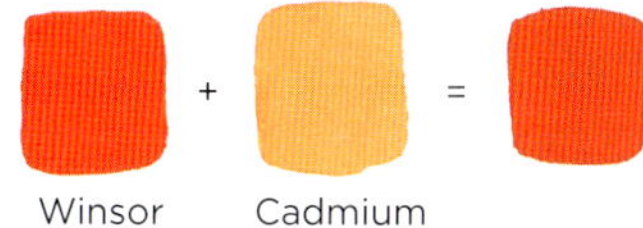

Winsor Red (70%) Cadmium Orange (30%)

STEP 3: Mix Winsor Red (50%), Cadmium Orange (30%) and Ultramarine Blue (20%) on your palette. Paint this into the tomatoes, leaving some of the first layer showing through.

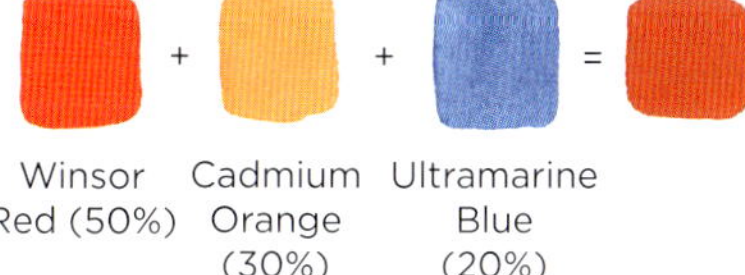

Winsor Red (50%) Cadmium Orange (30%) Ultramarine Blue (20%)

STEP 4: Combine Green Gold (50%), Winsor Green (40%) and Winsor Red (10%) on your palette. Apply this mixture to the stem and vine to add a darker **value** of green.

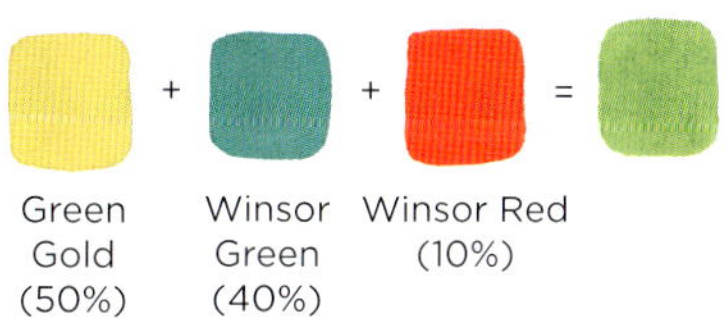

Green Gold (50%) Winsor Green (40%) Winsor Red (10%)

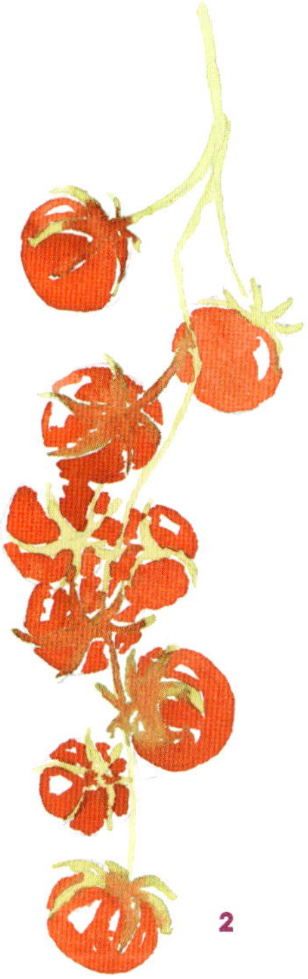

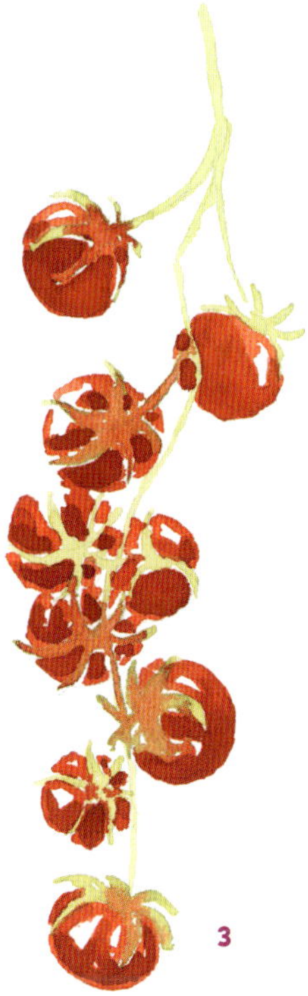

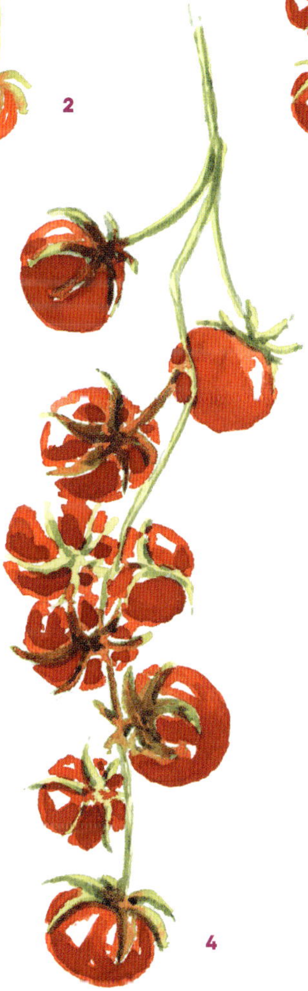

SUSHI TIME

Inside the sushi roll, this painting starts with a layer of warm colors for the fish and avocado. These warm **tones** enhance the color of the avocado when the green is layered on top at the end, giving the color more dimension. Plus, the more the colors blend and layer, the more unified the painting will be!

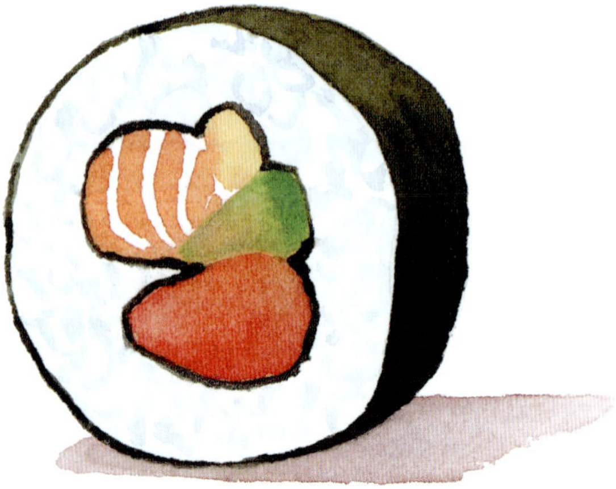

MATERIALS

Pencil
Watercolor paper
Size 8 round brush
Paper towel

COLORS

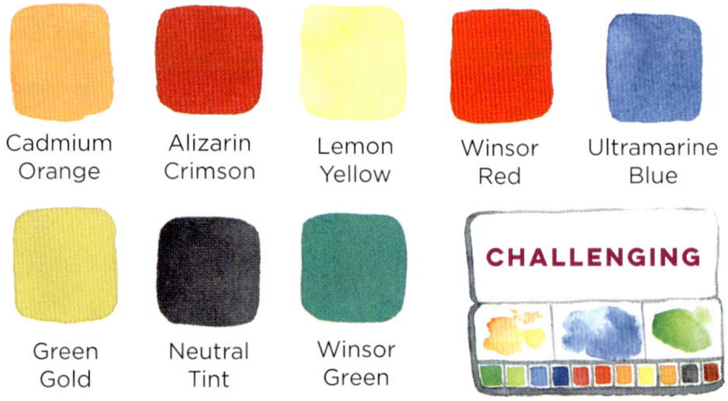

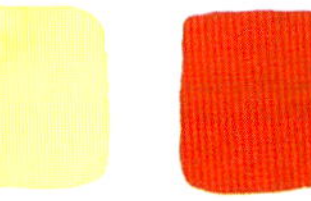

Cadmium Orange

Alizarin Crimson

Lemon Yellow

Winsor Red

Ultramarine Blue

Green Gold

Neutral Tint

Winsor Green

CHALLENGING

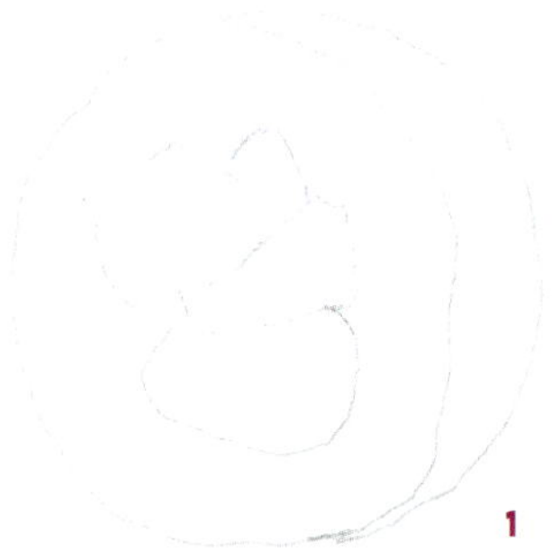

1

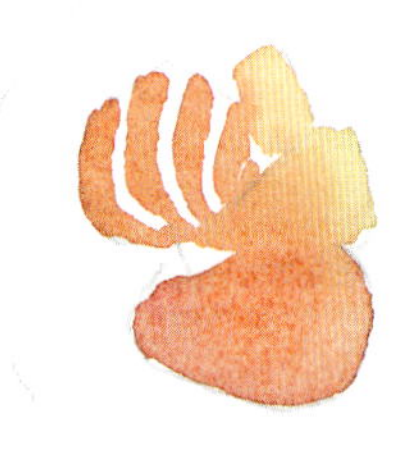

2

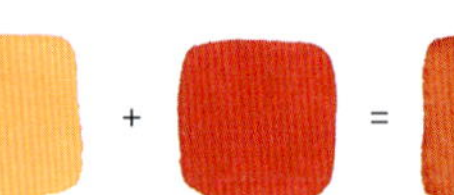

Cadmium Orange (70%)   +   Alizarin Crimson (30%)   =

STEP 1: In pencil, trace (page 247) or sketch your sushi on your watercolor paper.

STEP 2: Lightly erase your pencil marks. Use the **wet-in-wet** technique for this step.

On your palette, mix Cadmium Orange (70%) and Alizarin Crimson (30%). With a size 8 round brush, use this color to paint in four stripes for the salmon and leave white gaps in between.

Paint in the shrimp (located on the top right) using Cadmium Orange. Do this by blocking it in as a small square.

Paint in the light area of the avocado, on the right side in the middle, with Lemon Yellow.

On your palette, combine Winsor Red (50%) and Alizarin Crimson (50%). Take this color and apply it to the tuna area located on the bottom right side.

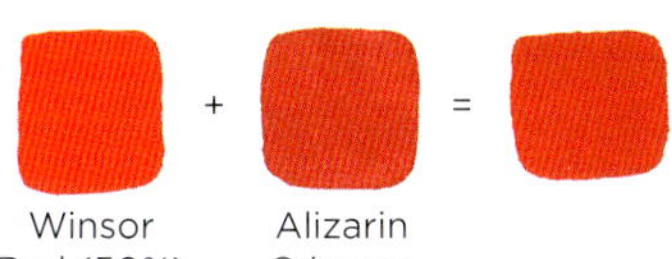

Winsor Red (50%) + Alizarin Crimson (50%) =

STEP 3: Mix Ultramarine Blue (80%) with a smidge of Alizarin Crimson (20%) on your palette. You will want it to be a very light **value**, so make sure to add more water than paint to your mixture. Use this color to paint in the rice by dabbing in little dot marks in the shape of rice. If you get it too dark, you can always **blot** it with a paper towel to keep it light.

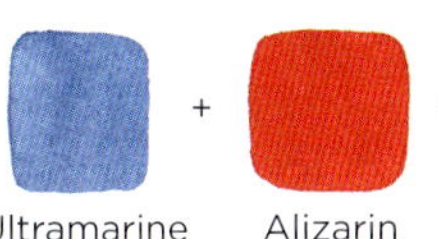

Ultramarine Blue (80%) + Alizarin Crimson (20%) =

STEP 4: For the seaweed, start painting at the top of the seaweed roll with Green Gold. As you move down the roll, add more and more Neutral Tint into that Green Gold paint. You don't need to mix the Neutral Tint into the palette; add it directly onto the paper.

STEP 5: Mix Neutral Tint (70%) and Green Gold (30%) on your palette. Around each of the food items inside the sushi roll, add a thin border of seaweed using this mixture.

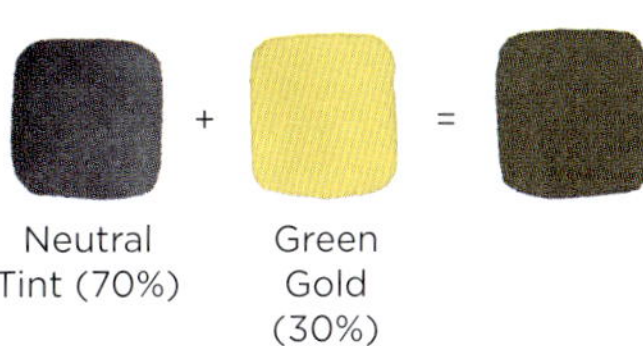

Neutral Tint (70%) + Green Gold (30%) =

On your palette, mix Alizarin Crimson (70%) and Ultramarine Blue (30%). Paint the **cast shadow** on the ground by pulling it to the right side. The edge of the **shadow** ends in a diagonal motion to provide dimension for the sushi roll.

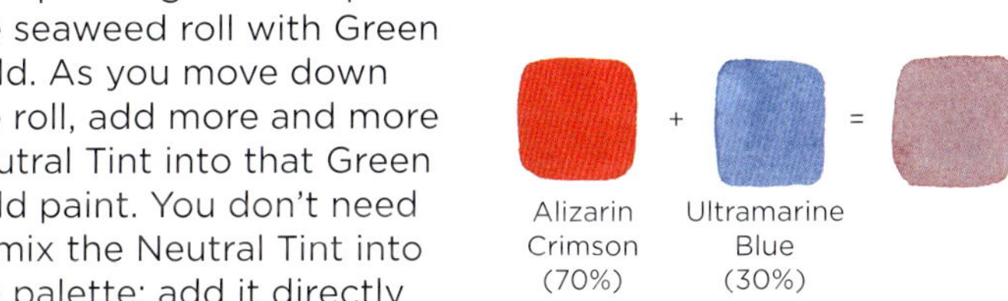

Alizarin Crimson (70%) + Ultramarine Blue (30%) =

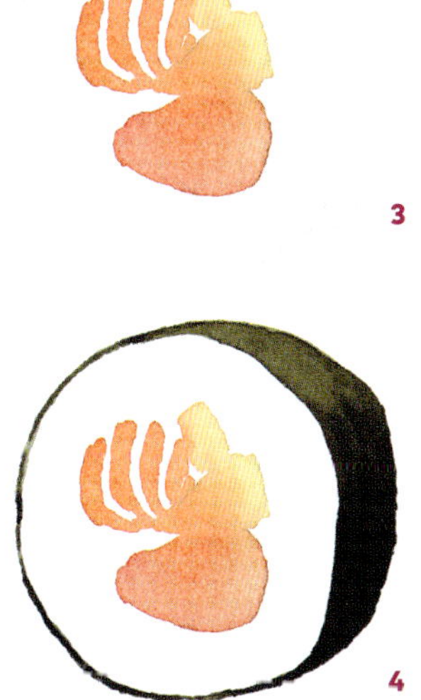

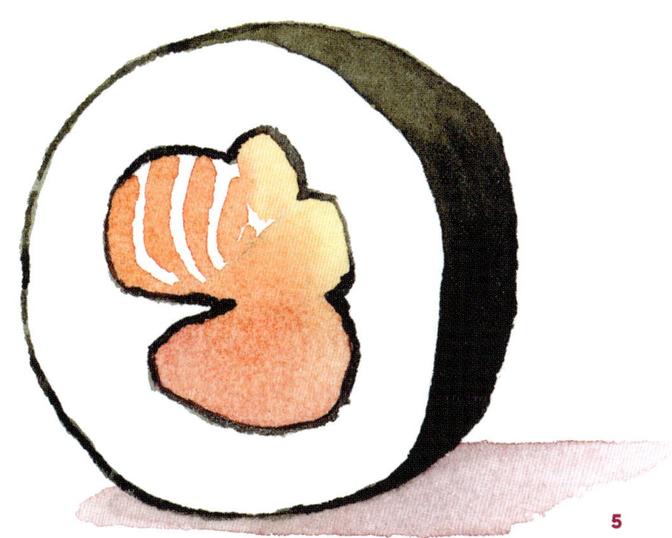

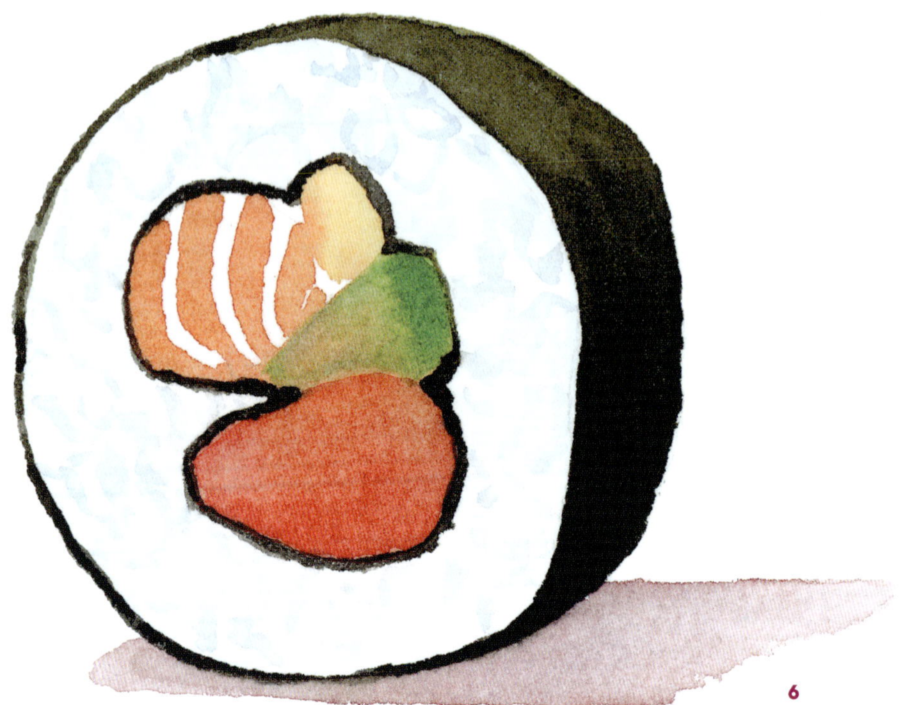

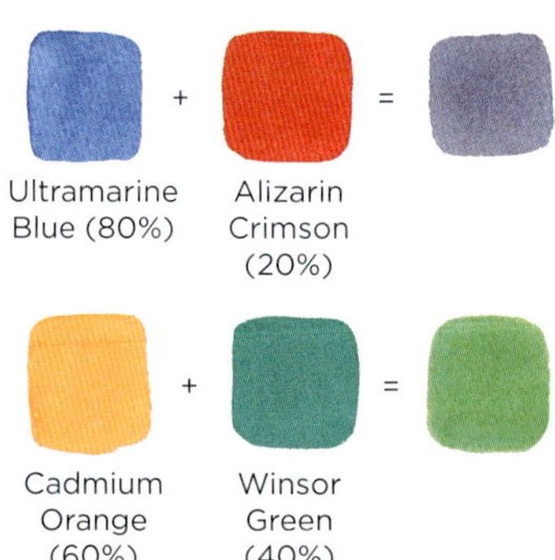

STEP 6: Add definition to the rice by using a light **value** of this color mixture, prepared on your palette: Ultramarine Blue (80%) with Alizarin Crimson (20%). When applying this on the rice, paint little smiley and frowny face shapes.

Darken the tuna with Alizarin Crimson. Layering this on top of your first layer will help give the tuna a warm glow. Let this dry before proceeding.

For the avocado, combine Cadmium Orange (60%) with Winsor Green (40%) on your palette. Paint this over the avocado. Let that dry. Then come back with the same mixture of Cadmium Orange and Winsor Green to paint in the darker part on the avocado.

POMEGRANATE

When painting fruit, adding little blemishes can really make your fruit come to life and look more realistic. In this Pomegranate painting, add small blemishes and spots by layering and allowing the first lighter layers to show through as those beautiful imperfections.

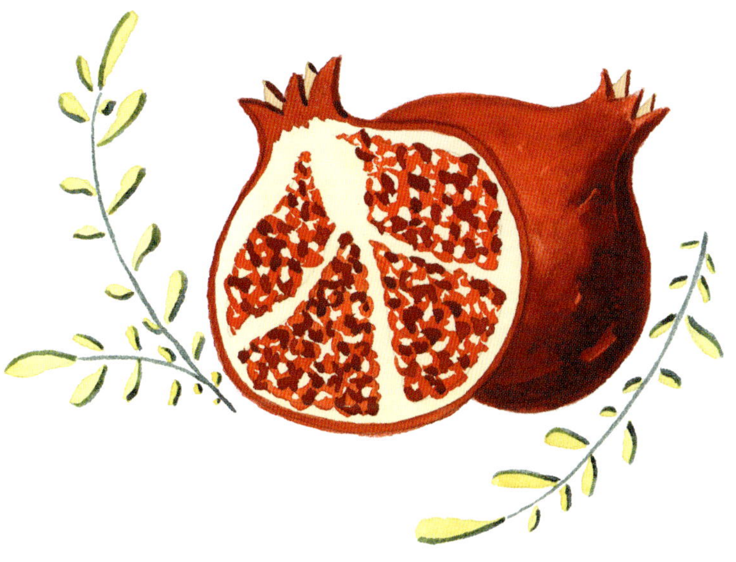

MATERIALS

Pencil

Watercolor paper

Size 8 round brush

COLORS

Yellow Ochre

Lemon Yellow

Green Gold

Winsor Red

Cadmium Orange

Ultramarine Blue

Winsor Green

Alizarin Crimson

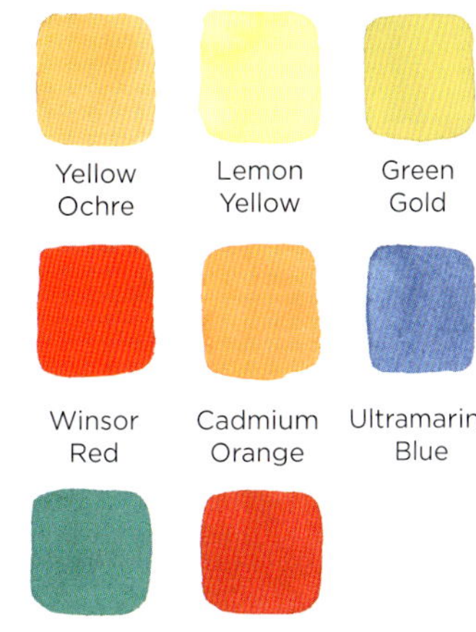

STEP 1: Trace (page 249) or lightly sketch the pomegranates in pencil on your watercolor paper.

STEP 2: On your palette, mix Yellow Ochre (50%) with Lemon Yellow (50%). Make this color a light **value** by adding lots of water. Use this mixture and a size 8 round brush to paint the inside of the pomegranate that is cut open. Let that dry.

Paint the leaves with Green Gold. Don't be afraid to rotate your paper to get to all the little spots.

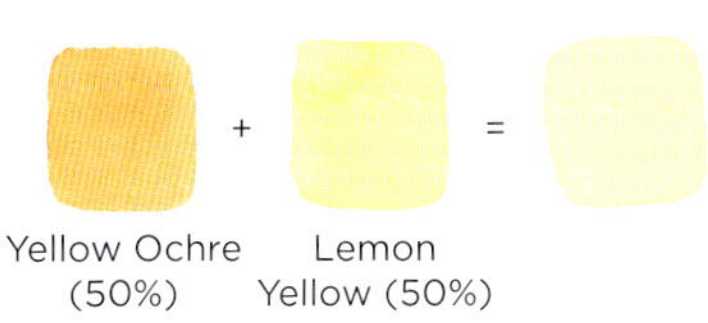

Yellow Ochre (50%)   Lemon Yellow (50%)

STEP 3: Combine Winsor Red (80%) with Cadmium Orange (20%) on your palette. Use this color for the seeds by painting circle shapes with holes in the middle. With this same color, fill in the pomegranate in the **background**.

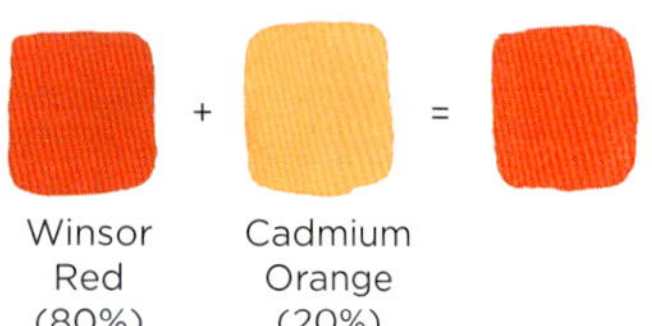

Winsor Red (80%) + Cadmium Orange (20%) =

STEP 4: On your palette, combine Winsor Red (50%), Cadmium Orange (30%) and Ultramarine Blue (20%). Use this mixture to outline the pomegranate that is cut in half. Also fill in the three calyxes at the top of the pomegranate. With this same color mixture, add little dabs into the seeded area.

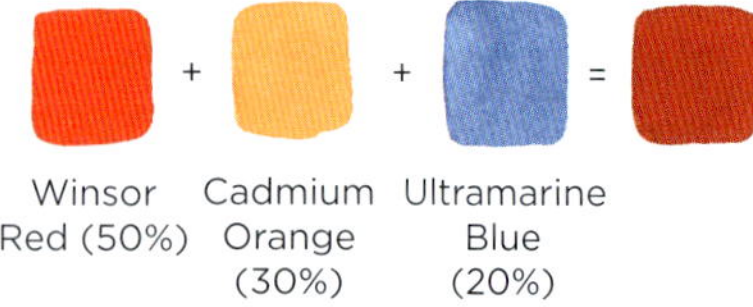

Winsor Red (50%) + Cadmium Orange (30%) + Ultramarine Blue (20%) =

Using this same color, paint the **background** pomegranate. Start painting on the bottom right corner, and as you pull the color toward the middle, add more water to lighten the color. The border of the pomegranate should be darker than the center. Make sure to leave little markings of the first layer showing through to act as blemishes on the pomegranate.

STEP 5: Combine Cadmium Orange (90%) with Ultramarine Blue (10%) on your palette. With this golden mixture, fill in the two **background** calyx on each pomegranate.

On your palette, mix Winsor Red (50%), Cadmium Orange (30%) and Ultramarine Blue (20%). Darken the pomegranate in the **background** by applying the paint only on the right side. Make sure to leave those blemish markings and feel free to add more for the final layer.

Load your brush with Winsor Red and outline the calyx on the pomegranates. Make sure that it is dry before you place the color on it.

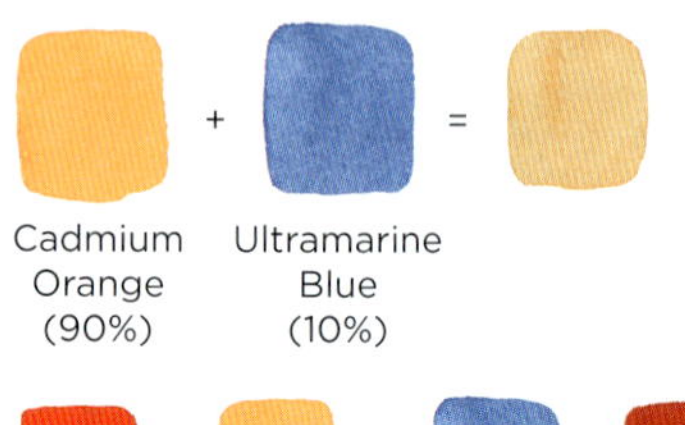

Cadmium Orange (90%) + Ultramarine Blue (10%) =

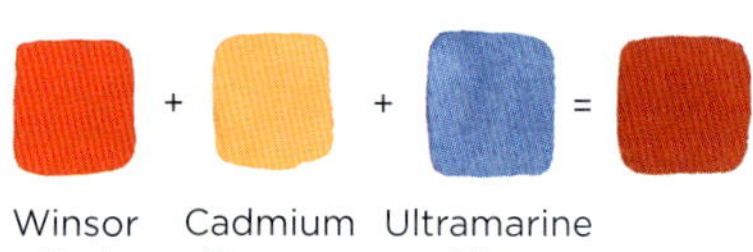

Winsor Red (50%) + Cadmium Orange (30%) + Ultramarine Blue (20%) =

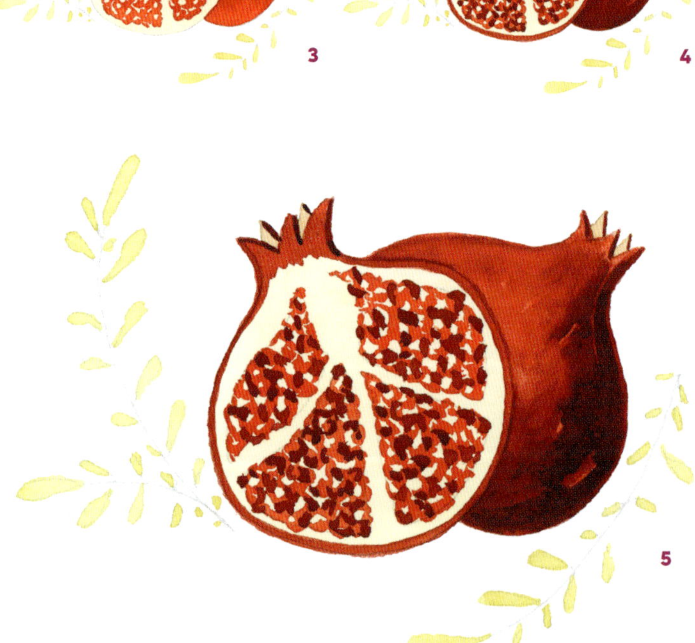

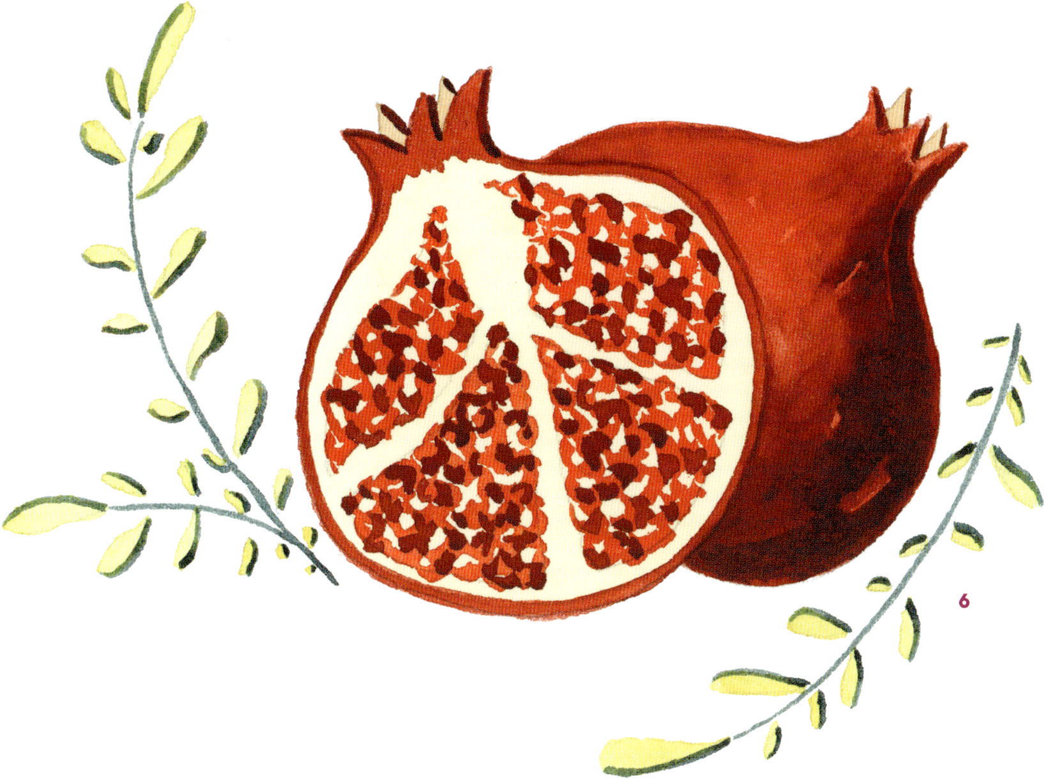

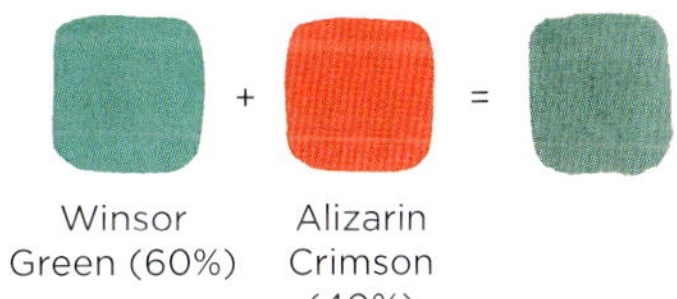

STEP 6: Mix Winsor Green (60%) with Alizarin Crimson (40%) on your palette. Paint a thin line for the stems and then paint a thin line on the bottom of each leaf.

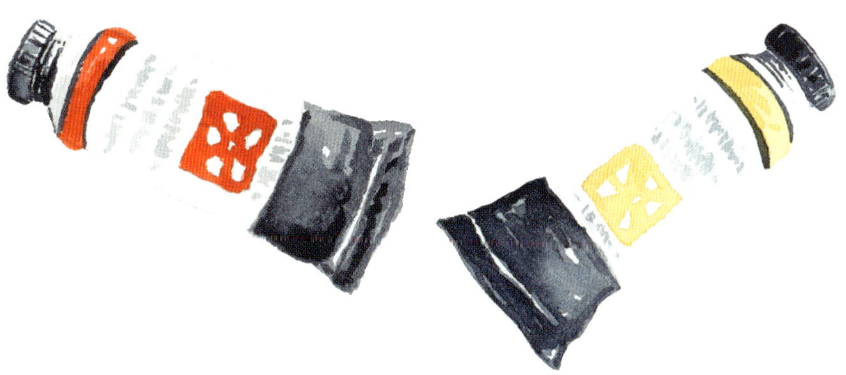

MUSHROOMS

There can be many sources of light that present themselves in a variety of ways. For instance, we don't just have outdoor lighting direct from the midday sun. We also have twilight, golden hour, dusk, light filtered through clouds, etc. Inside lighting can vary from warm or cool lightbulbs to fluorescent or candle lighting. All of this affects the colors in our object, including our **shadow** color. If you are painting an object without a reference photo, and aren't sure what colors to use for your **shadow**, try pulling a **complementary color** from your object for the **shadow**. For this project, we use a purplish **shadow** because the mushroom has yellowish/tan colors.

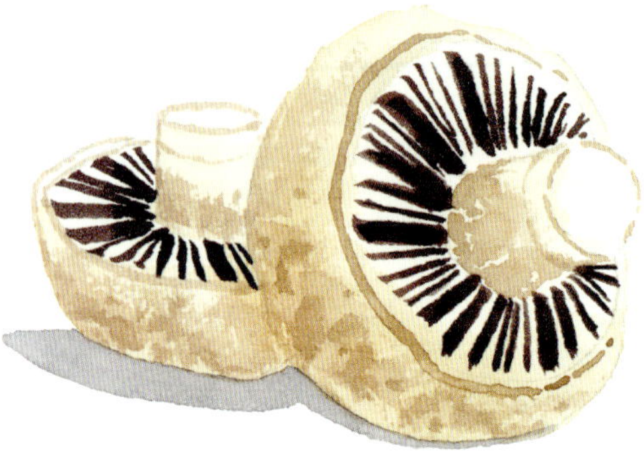

MATERIALS

Watercolor paper
Pencil
Size 8 round brush

COLORS

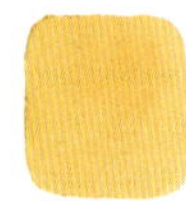 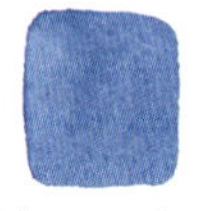 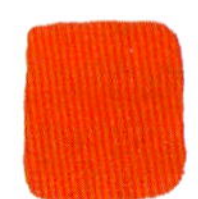

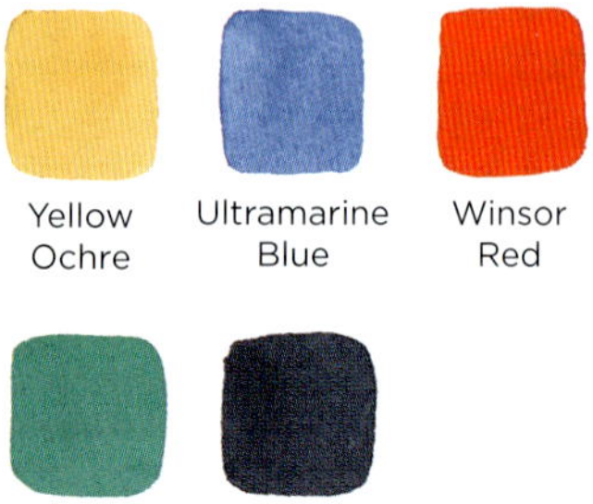

Yellow Ochre   Ultramarine Blue   Winsor Red

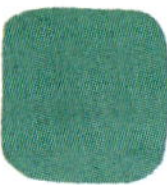 

Winsor Green   Indigo

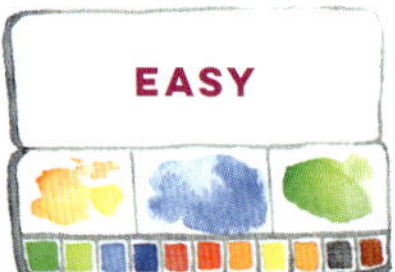

1

2

STEP 1: On your watercolor paper, lightly trace (page 249) or sketch the mushrooms in pencil.

STEP 2: Lightly erase your pencil markings. With a size 8 round brush, paint Yellow Ochre over the mushrooms. While it is still wet, mix Yellow Ochre (80%) with Ultramarine Blue (20%) on your palette, then lay it on the cap (dome) and stalk (stem) of the mushrooms (**wet-in-wet**).

 + 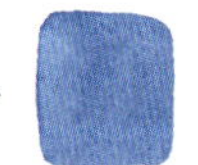 = 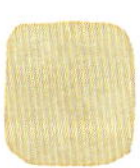

Yellow Ochre (80%)   Ultramarine Blue (20%)

STEP 3: To create the color for the gills (dark interior) of the mushroom, combine these colors on your palette: Winsor Red (60%) and Winsor Green (40%). When you paint the gills of the mushroom, apply the mixture using thick and thin strokes. Let that dry.

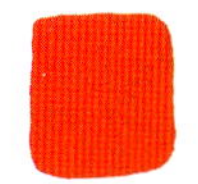 + 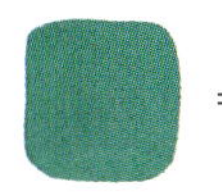 = 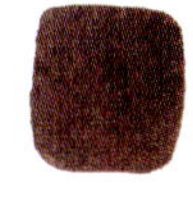

Winsor Red (60%)   Winsor Green (40%)

Add the **shadow** using a mix of Indigo (80%) and Winsor Red (20%). The **shadows** will be behind the mushrooms on the left side.

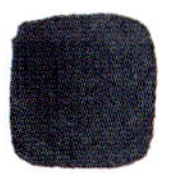 + 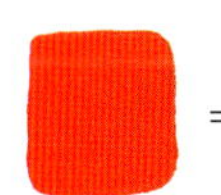 = 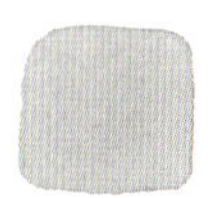

Indigo (80%)   Winsor Red (20%)

STEP 4: Take Yellow Ochre (60%) and mix it with Ultramarine Blue (20%) and Winsor Red (20%) on your palette. Using this mixture, paint in a line around the cap and the stalk of the mushroom. Then speckle the color on the cap with the **dry brush** technique for **texture**. After you apply the **dry brush**, go back in and add a few dots with the same color mixture to add another **texture** layer.

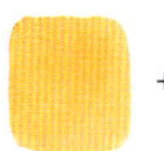 + 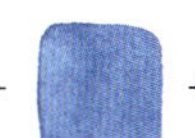 + 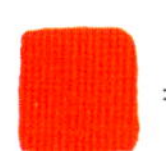 = 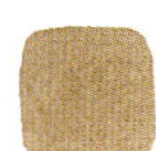

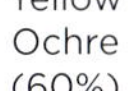

Yellow Ochre (60%)   Ultramarine Blue (20%)   Winsor Red (20%)

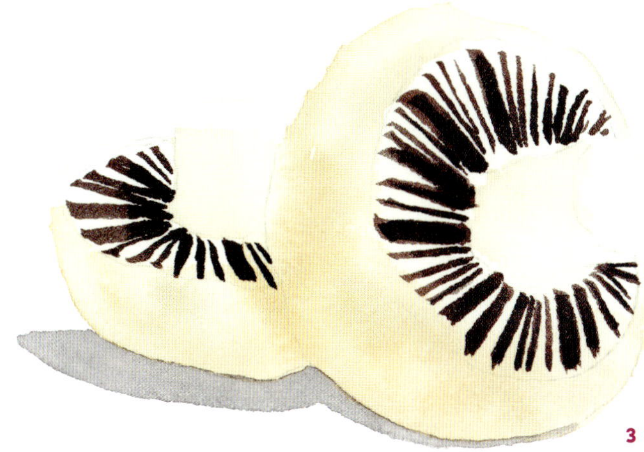

3

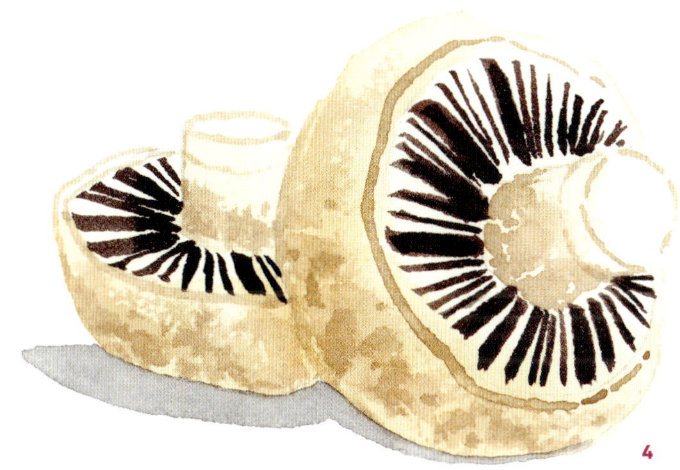

4

HAPPY BIRTHDAY CAKE

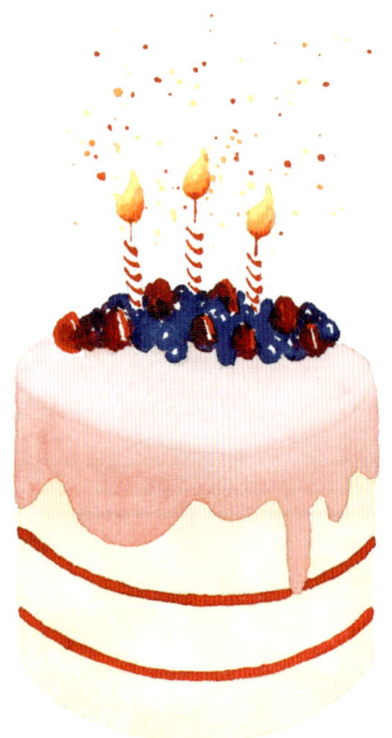

When painting multiple sides of an object, like in this project, one of the sides must be darker than the others to create dimension. The **light source** on this birthday cake painting is coming from the top, so the top frosting is painted lighter than the side frosting. If the top and side frosting were painted the same **value**, the cake would appear flatter. And who wants a flat cake?

MATERIALS

Pencil

Watercolor paper

Size 8 round brush

Paper towel

Scrap paper

COLORS

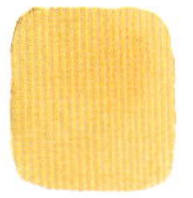
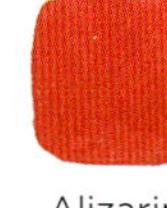

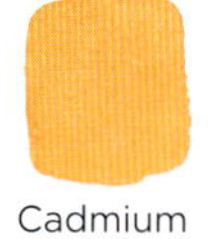
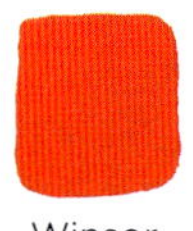
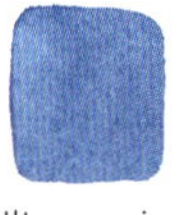

| Yellow Ochre | Alizarin Crimson | Lemon Yellow | Cadmium Orange | Winsor Red | Ultramarine Blue |

STEP 1: Use a pencil to trace (page 247) or sketch the birthday cake onto your watercolor paper.

STEP 2: Lightly erase your pencil markings. With a size 8 round brush, use a light **value** of Yellow Ochre to paint the body of the cake. While the cake is still wet, **blot** out some areas on the yellow cake by using a paper towel in light dabbing motions. This will create different **values** and **texture**. Let this dry before moving on to the frosting.

Clean your brush, then apply a **clear water wash** onto the frosting on top of the cake. Avoid adding it to the frosting dripping over the side of the cake. Use the **wet-in-wet** technique to add a light **value** of Alizarin Crimson into the **clear water wash**. While the paint is still wet, rinse out your brush and **lift** the paint from the frosting on the top of the cake. You don't need to **lift** the paint where the berries will go; it's okay if it is darker in that area. The top of the cake is **highlighted**, which is why you are only **lifting** the paint color from the top frosting and not the frosting dripping down.

Load your brush with a light **value** of Alizarin Crimson and paint a **wash** on the frosting dripping down the side of the cake. This will be darker in **value** than the frosting on the top of the cake. Let the frosting dry.

Paint the tip of the flame with Lemon Yellow. While this is wet, add Cadmium Orange to the base of the flame (**wet-in-wet**). These two colors should **bleed** together in the middle.

STEP 3: Take a dark **value** of Alizarin Crimson and paint it into the sections of jelly filling between the yellow cake layers. It is easier to paint in the jelly filling if you turn your paper sideways. Let that dry.

Paint the strawberries using Winsor Red. For the blueberries, use Ultramarine Blue. For the berries, you don't need to dry in between, so you can have a fun **bleed** effect. On a few berries, leave a little mark of the white paper showing through to be a **highlight**; use straight lines for the straw-berries and curved shapes or dots for the blueberries.

Use Winsor Red to paint in the stripes on the candles.

At the base of the flame, add a little Winsor Red. Lightly drag a vertical line down to represent the wick of the candle.

STEP 4: Cover the cake with a scrap piece of paper. One at a time, **load** a clean brush with these colors: Lemon Yellow, Cadmium Orange and Winsor Red. **Splatter** (page 19) with one color at a time to create a fun effect that makes the birthday candles look magical.

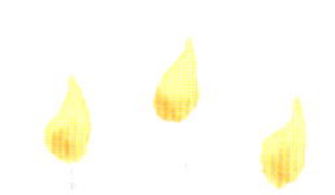

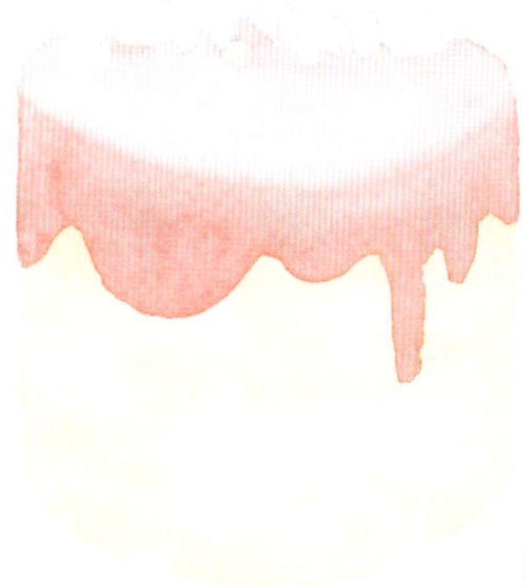

2

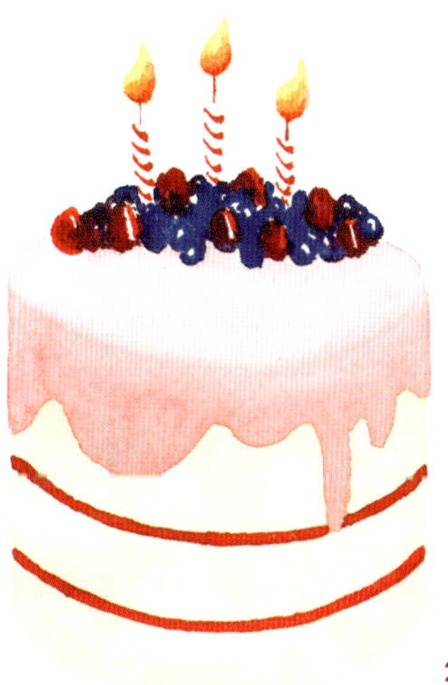

3

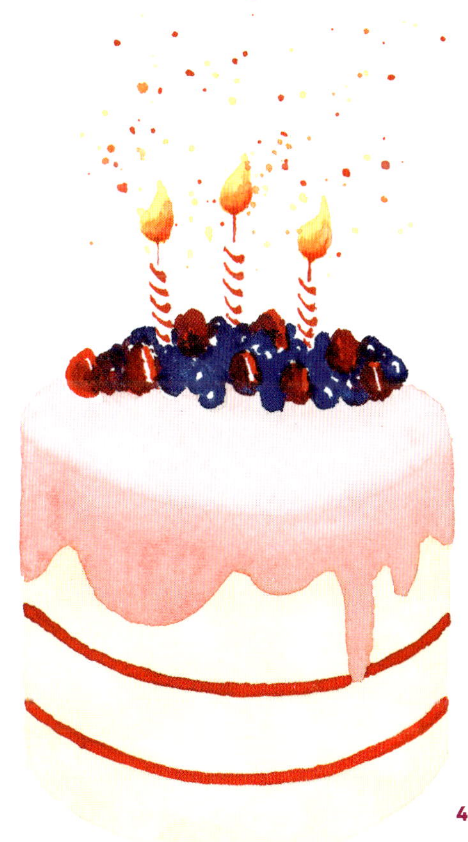

4

BOXED DONUTS

This Boxed Donuts painting is an excellent example of how adding a **shadow** can make a massive difference to the overall painting. Suddenly, the painting went from flat to having dimension! I like to call this the power of adding a **cast shadow**. Other great examples of this are the Mushrooms (page 106) and Candy Cane (page 176) paintings. Feel free to be creative with this painting by adding different kinds of donuts with your own creative sprinkles, glazes and flavors!

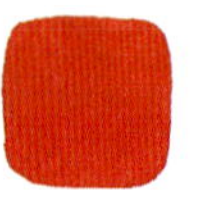
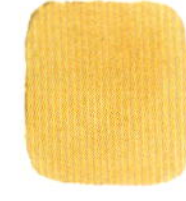

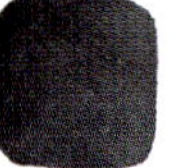
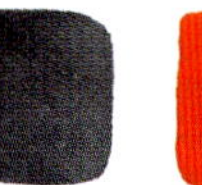
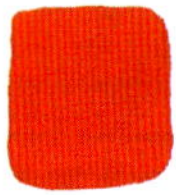
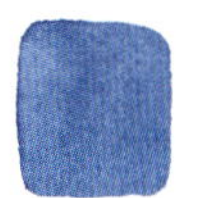
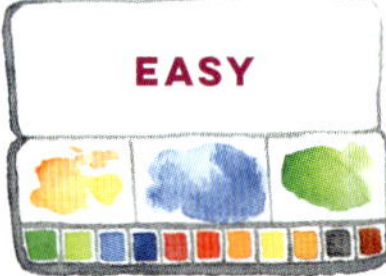

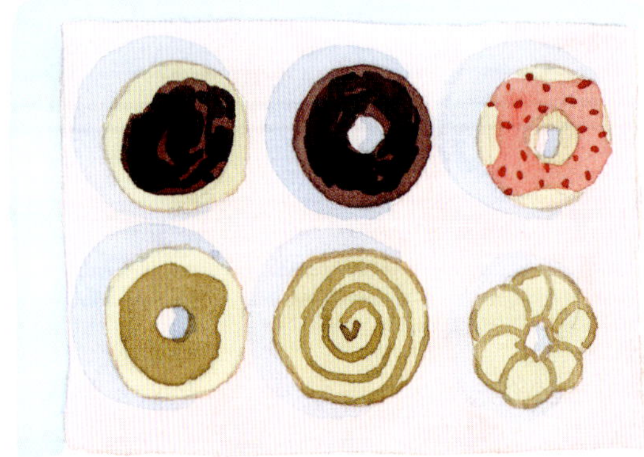

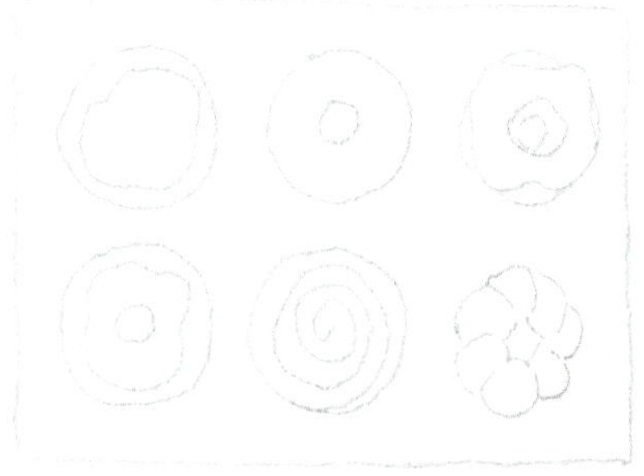

1

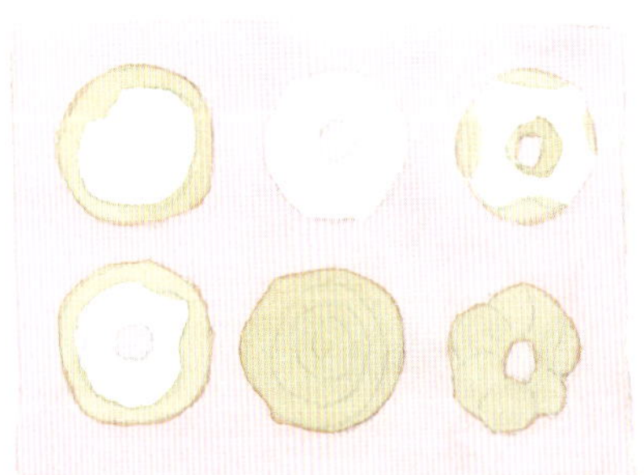

2

STEP 1: Use a pencil to trace (page 249) or sketch the donuts and donut box on your watercolor paper.

STEP 2: Take Alizarin Crimson and make it a light **value** before using a size 8 round brush to paint the donut box. Let that dry.

Next, add the base color for each donut. Mix Yellow Ochre (90%) and Indigo (10%) on your palette. Add a lot of water to lighten the **value**, then apply the mixture to five of the donuts. (I made my sixth donut a chocolate base, shown in Step 3.)

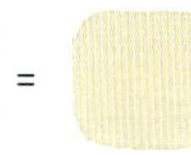

Yellow Ochre (90%) + Indigo (10%) =

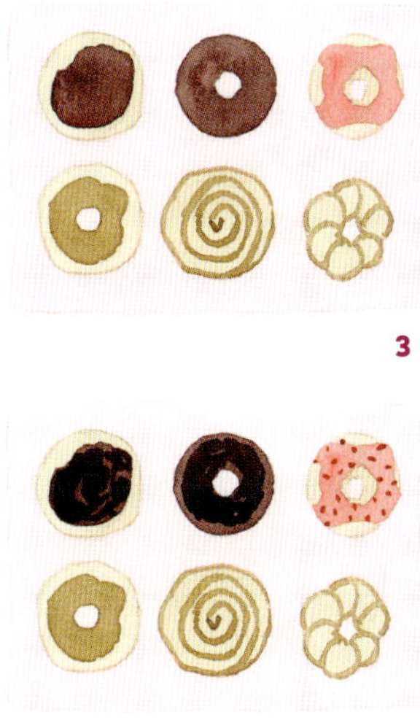

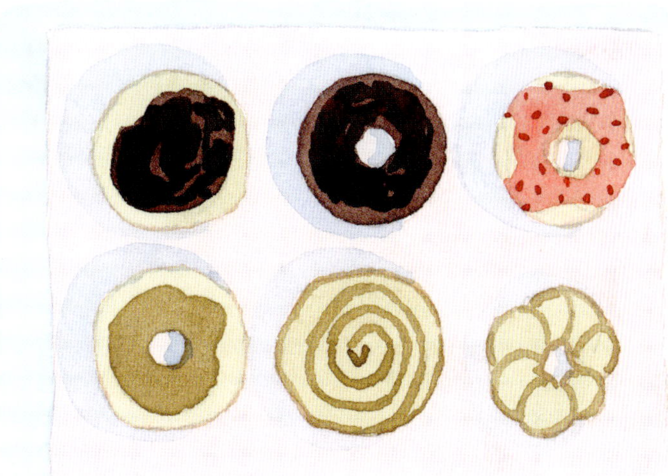

3

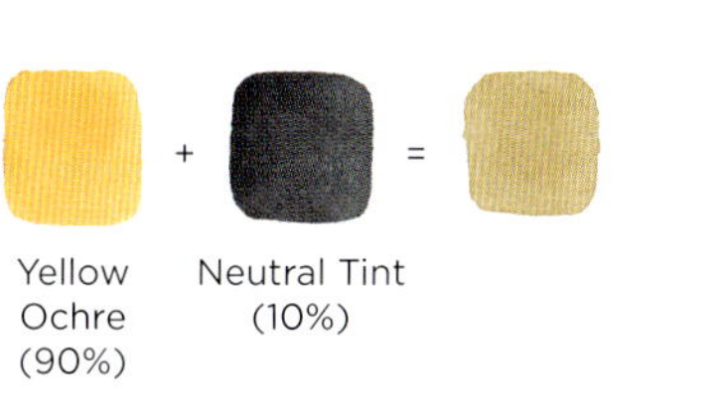

4

5

STEP 3: For the maple frosting on the bottom left donut, mix Yellow Ochre (90%) with a touch of Neutral Tint (10%) on your palette. Paint in the maple frosting using this mixture. Apply the same color on the detailing for the cinnamon swirl donut and puffy circular donut. For the pink frosting, use a watered-down Alizarin Crimson (lighter **value**). Combine Yellow Ochre (40%), Winsor Red (40%) and Indigo (20%) to use for the chocolate-based donut and chocolate frosting.

STEP 4: Make that same chocolate mixture of Yellow Ochre (40%), Winsor Red (40%) and Indigo (20%). This time you don't want to add as much water so that it is a darker **value**. Paint another layer on the top of the chocolate frosting donut, and then use this paint to add chocolate frosting on the chocolate donut. Leave some areas of the first layer showing through. To add some sprinkles to the top of the pink frosting donut, use Alizarin Crimson.

STEP 5: Time to add **shadows**. Use a light **value** of Ultramarine Blue to paint around the left side of the donuts and the left and top side of the box. Don't forget to add the **shadow** inside the four donuts with holes. The **shadow** should be painted against the right side of each hole.

Yellow Ochre (90%)   +   Neutral Tint (10%)   =

Yellow Ochre (40%)   +   Winsor Red (40%)   +   Indigo (20%)   =

Yellow Ochre (40%)   +   Winsor Red (40%)   +   Indigo (20%)   =

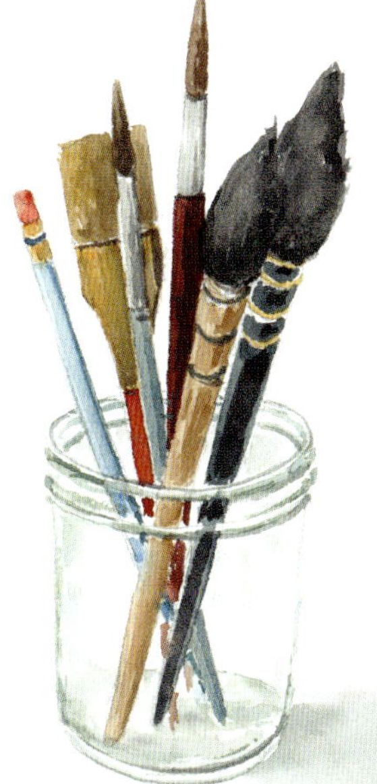

STRAWBERRY PICKING

When starting a painting, one of the biggest challenges is knowing which color to paint first. One way to determine which color to start with is to look for the lightest color/**value** in the painting and work from light to dark. In this Strawberry Picking painting, we paint the entire strawberry yellow at the beginning because the seeds need to be yellow at the end and it is the lightest color. Since watercolor is semi-transparent, we can't paint yellow on top of a darker color like red; hence, we need to start with yellow.

MATERIALS

Watercolor paper
Pencil
Size 8 round brush
Old brush
Drawing gum paste
Rubber cement eraser
Paper towel

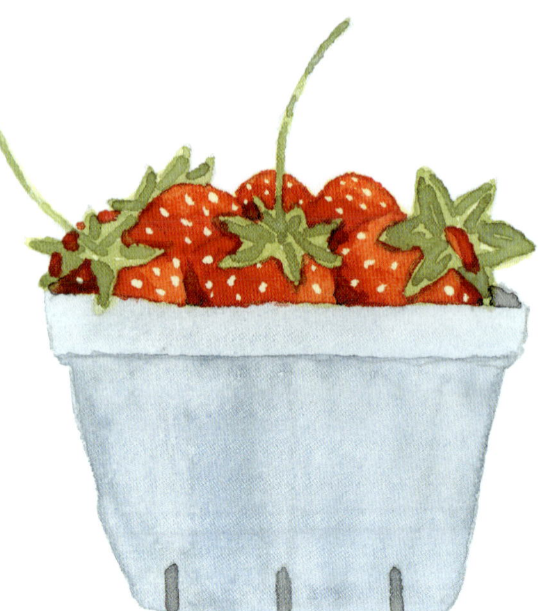

COLORS

Lemon
Yellow

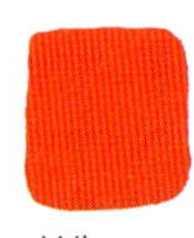

Cobalt
Blue

Winsor
Red

Neutral
Tint

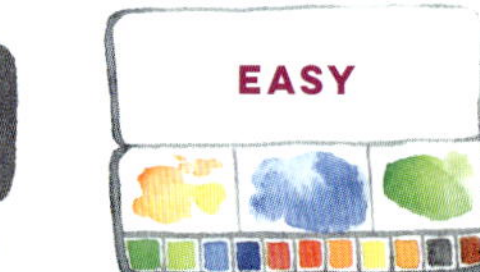

STEP 1: On your water-color paper, trace (page 247) or lightly sketch the Strawberry Picking composition in pencil.

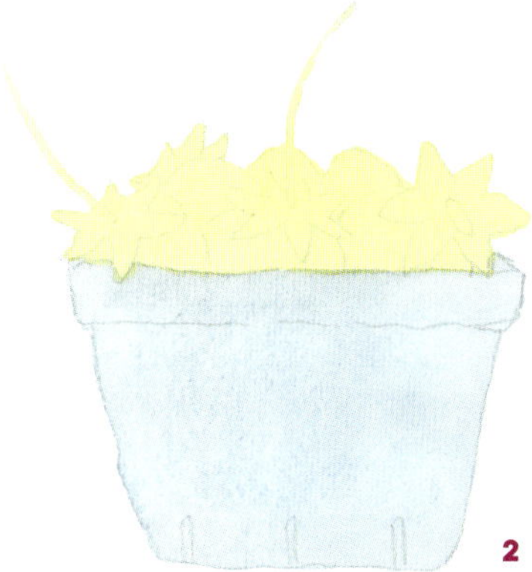

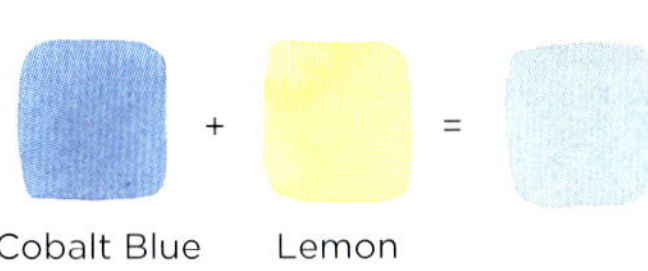

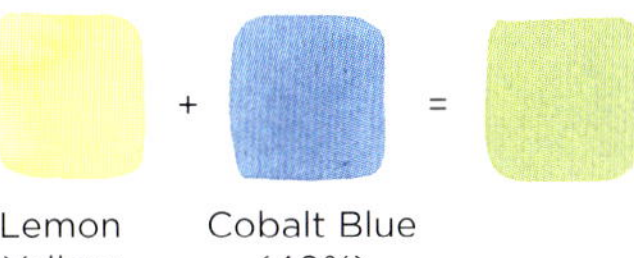

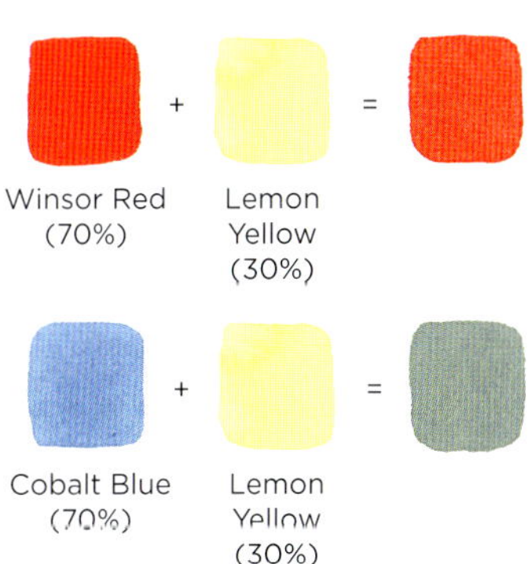

STEP 2: With your size 8 round brush, paint a Lemon Yellow **wash** over all the strawberries, stems and leaves. Let that dry.

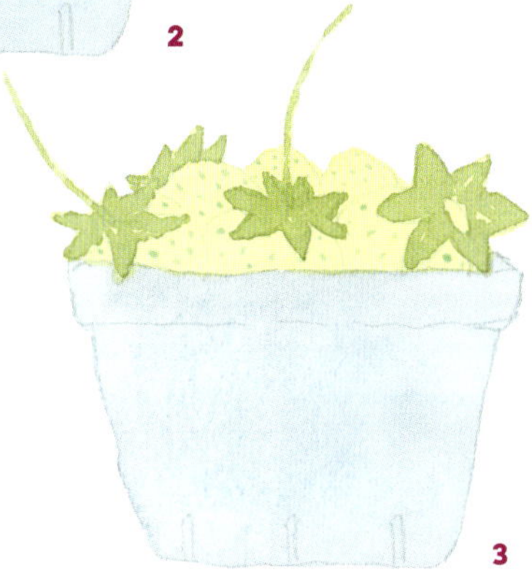

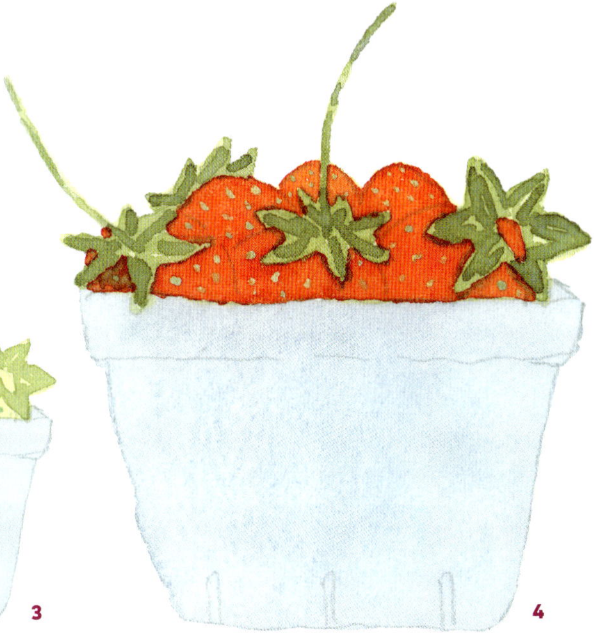

On your palette, combine Cobalt Blue (90%) with Lemon Yellow (10%). Take this mixture and make it a light **value** by adding water, then paint it onto the strawberry carton.

Cobalt Blue (90%) + Lemon Yellow (10%) =

STEP 3: With an old brush, apply your drawing gum paste to paint in little seeds onto the strawberries. Let that dry.

Mix Lemon Yellow (60%) and Cobalt Blue (40%) on your palette. Take this mixture and paint in the stems and leaves on the strawberries.

Lemon Yellow (60%) + Cobalt Blue (40%) =

STEP 4: Take Winsor Red (70%) and mix it with Lemon Yellow (30%) on your palette. Take that color and paint it on the strawberries. Make sure to let this dry before moving forward (I didn't and green bled into my red strawberries a bit). Use Cobalt Blue (70%) and Lemon Yellow (30%) mixed on your palette to paint over the leaves and stems. Don't completely cover over your first layer of green.

Winsor Red (70%) + Lemon Yellow (30%) =

Cobalt Blue (70%) + Lemon Yellow (30%) =

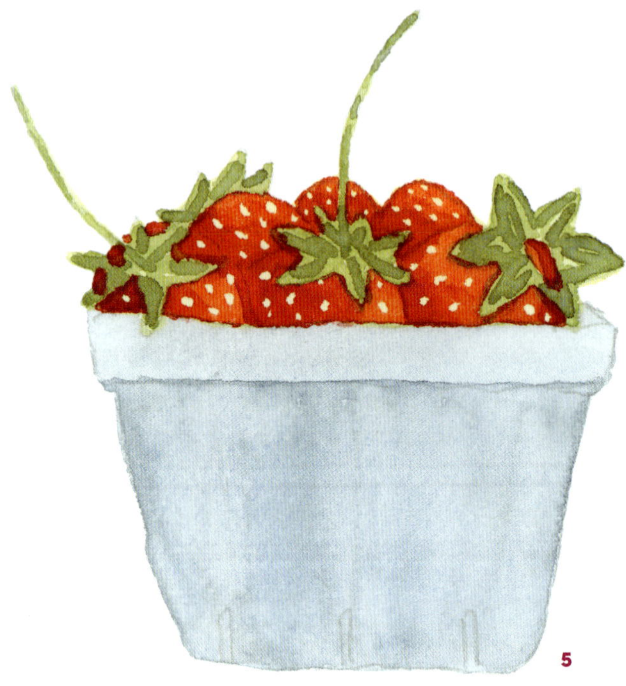

5

STEP 5: Take Winsor Red (80%) and Cobalt Blue (20%) and mix that on your palette. Add this mixture near the edges of the strawberries. If there are any **hard edges**, make them more blended by creating **soft edges**.

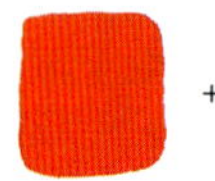 + 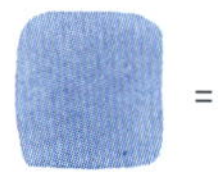 = 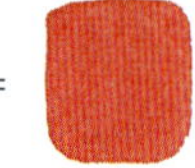

Winsor Red (80%)   Cobalt Blue (20%)

Make sure everything dries before you use the rubber cement eraser to remove the drawing gum paste!

Then, take the mixture from Step 2, Cobalt Blue (90%) with Lemon Yellow (10%), to paint in **shadow** detailing on the carton. Also use this color to darken the bottom half and under the lip of the carton. When painting it on, you will want to create a **texture** by **lifting** it off in some areas of the carton so that it isn't a solid **value**. You can also **lift** it using a paper towel.

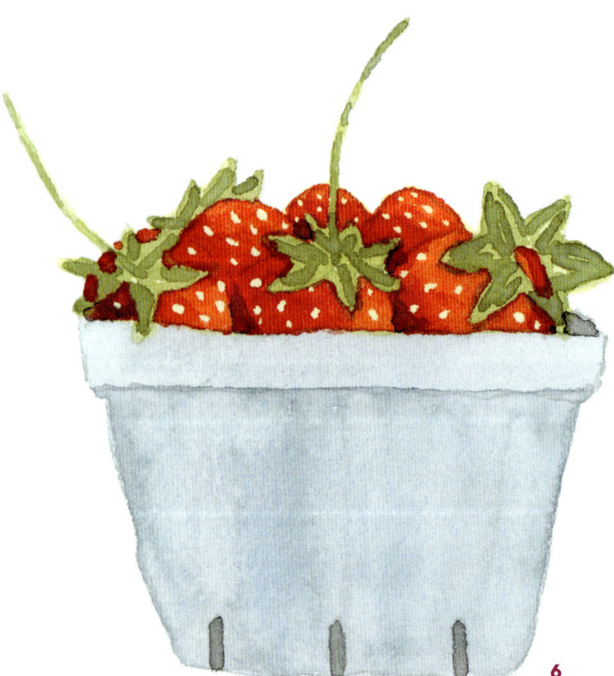

Cobalt Blue (90%)   Lemon Yellow (10%)

STEP 6: Take a medium **value** of Neutral Tint and paint in the three vertical lines at the bottom of the carton. Then paint this same color between the strawberries and in the carton corner.

CHOCOLATE CROISSANT

When adding a **highlight** to your object, it doesn't necessarily have to be the white of your paper that acts as the **highlight**. In this Chocolate Croissant painting, we add a light **value** in our first layer that will become the **highlight** on the chocolate at the end. This light **value** will still act as the **highlight** because it is the lightest **value** in the entire painting and will stand out; however, it will be slightly softer and not pop as much as having the white of the paper. A softer **highlight** can come in handy when the object isn't as shiny as candy; for example, look at the Candy Cane project (page 176).

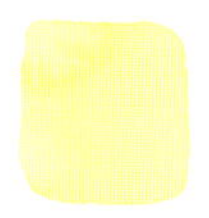

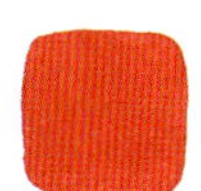

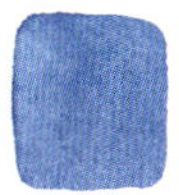

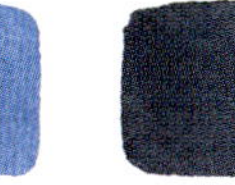

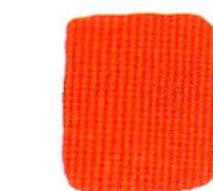

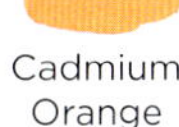

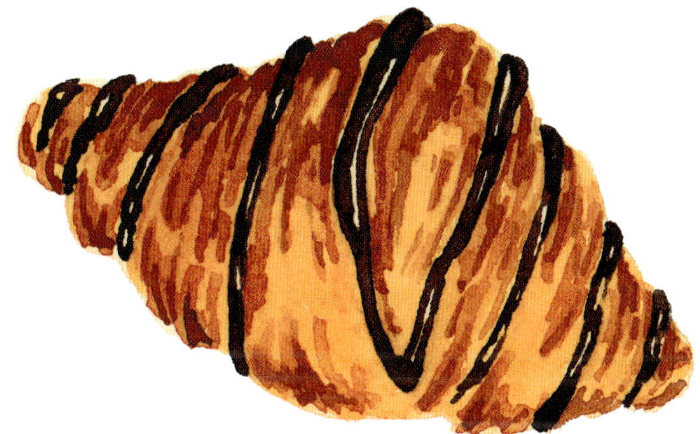

STEP 1: Take your pencil and lightly trace (page 249) or sketch the chocolate croissant on your watercolor paper.

1

STEP 2: Lightly erase your pencil markings. On your palette, combine Lemon Yellow (50%), Quinacridone Gold (30%) and Alizarin Crimson (20%). Use this color and a size 8 round brush to paint a **wash** over your croissant.

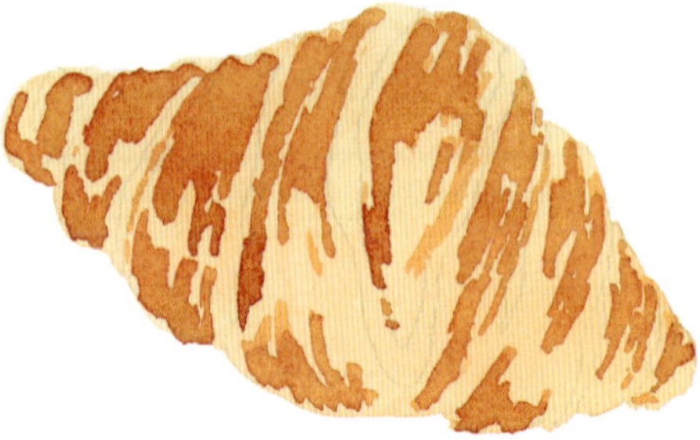

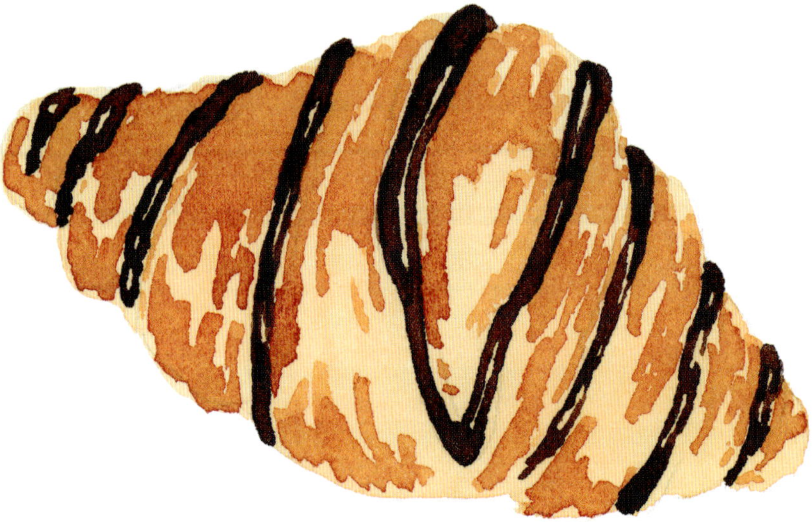

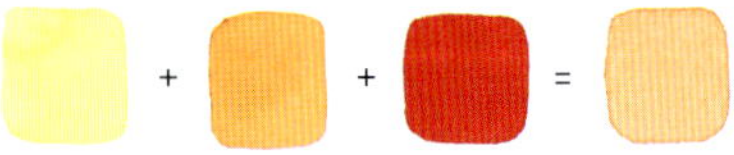

STEP 3: Darken areas of the croissant using this mixture on your palette: Quinacridone Gold (60%), Alizarin Crimson (30%) and a touch of Ultramarine Blue (10%). Apply it as if you were adding stripes on a tiger. Don't paint the areas that you will add chocolate on in Step 4.

STEP 4: Mix Winsor Red (40%), Indigo (30%) and Cadmium Orange (30%) on your palette. Using this color, paint on the chocolate. Add a **highlight** by leaving little slivers of your first layer showing through.

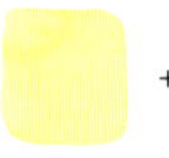 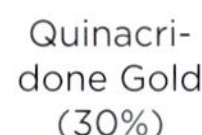 

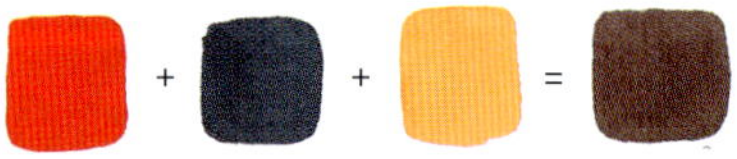

Lemon Yellow (50%) + Quinacridone Gold (30%) + Alizarin Crimson (20%) =

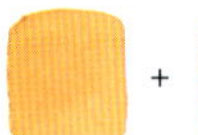 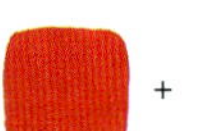 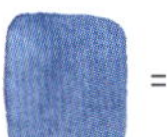 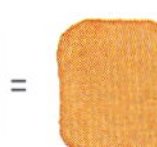 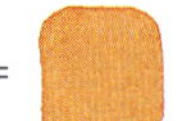

Quinacridone Gold (60%) + Alizarin Crimson (30%) + Ultramarine Blue (10%) =

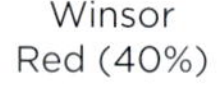 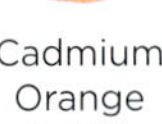 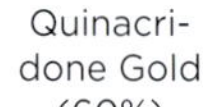

Winsor Red (40%) + Indigo (30%) + Cadmium Orange (30%) =

STEP 5: Add a darker layer on the croissant by using a mixture of Quinacridone Gold (50%), Alizarin Crimson (30%) and Ultramarine Blue (20%) that you combine on your palette. You want to place this dark color on top of the already darkened layer from before. Don't completely cover the layer you made in Step 3; allow some areas of that layer to show through.

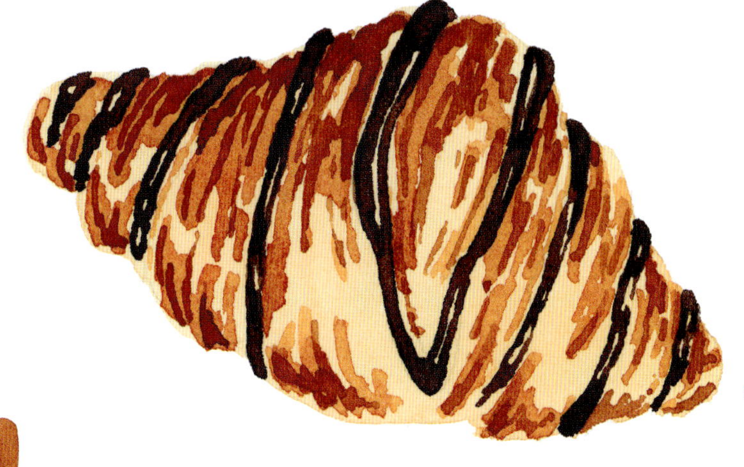

 + 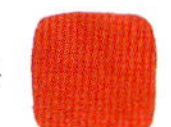 + 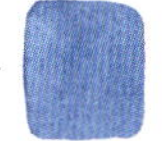 = 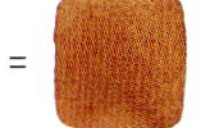

Quinacri-
done Gold
(50%)

Alizarin
Crimson
(30%)

Ultramarine
Blue (20%)

STEP 6: To warm up and unify the whole croissant, paint a Quinacridone Gold **glaze** over the croissant. When applying the **glaze**, avoid painting over the chocolate.

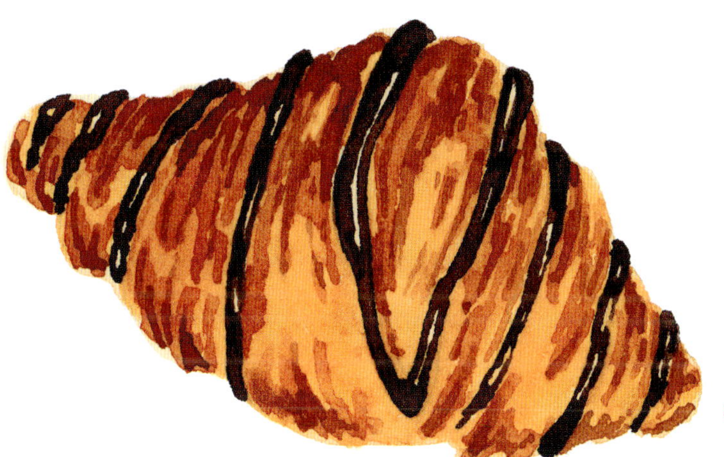

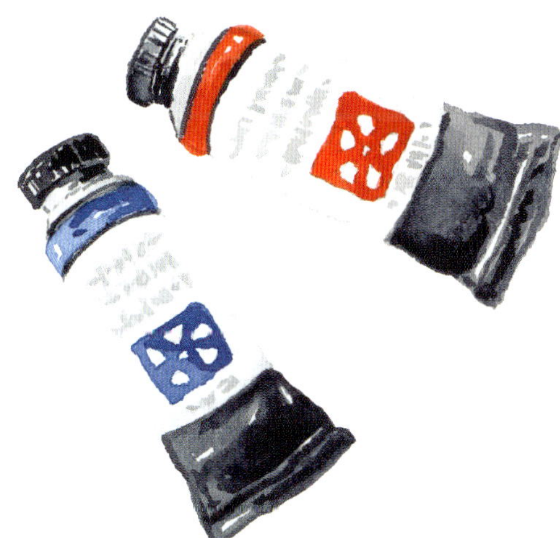

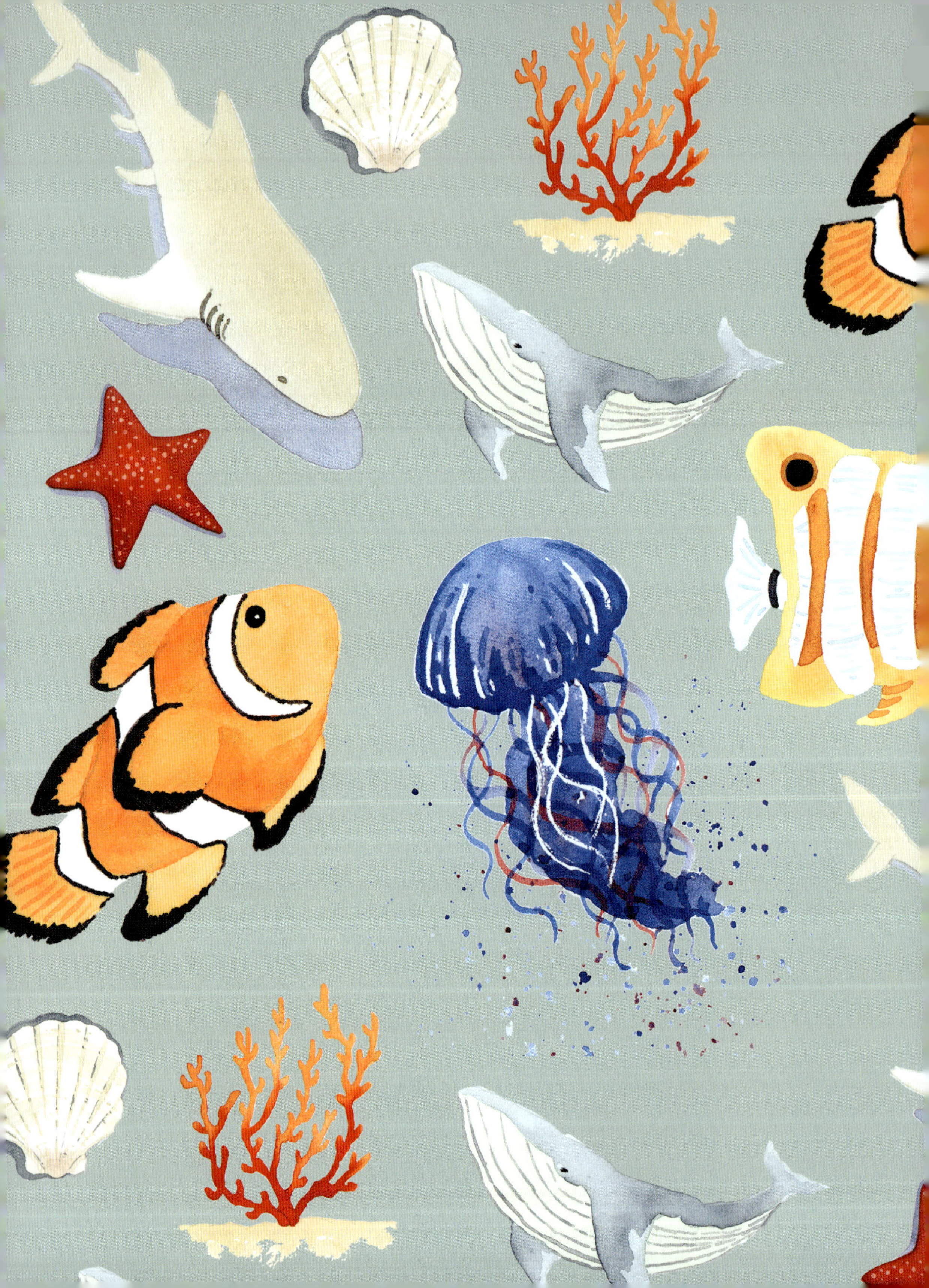

UNDER THE SEA

In this chapter, we dive into painting all the beautiful colors we find in our oceans! I am always amazed at how bright and vibrant ocean life is. The **saturated** colors we find in the ocean are perfect for **wet-in-wet** blending, so really lean into this fun technique. We play with color in many of these paintings by adding **glazes** and letting colors **bleed** together on the paper to create different effects. The more we can understand how to use color, the more control we have over our paintings!

COLORFUL CORAL

The highest **saturation** you can get is when you take the color directly from your paint palette. The moment you start mixing into those colors, you lessen the **saturation**, making the color less vibrant. For this Colorful Coral painting, there is no color mixing, in order to maintain that vibrancy.

MATERIALS

Pencil

Watercolor paper

Size 8 round brush (or smaller)

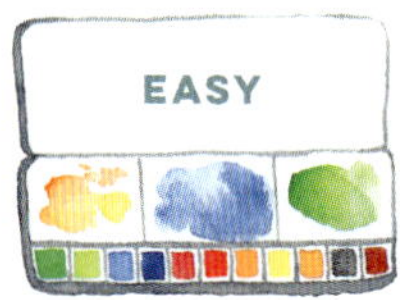

COLORS

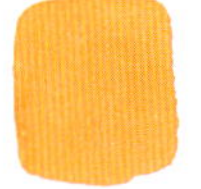

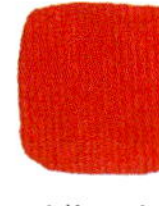

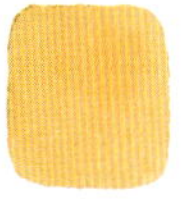

Cadmium Orange

Alizarin Crimson

Yellow Ochre

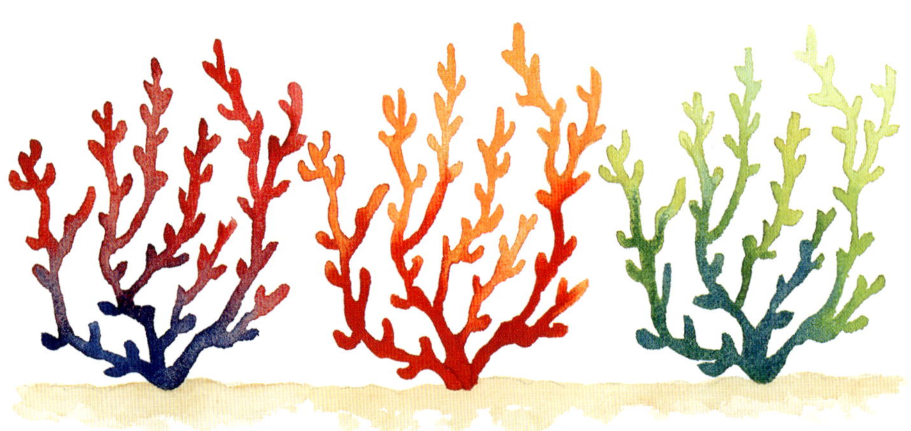

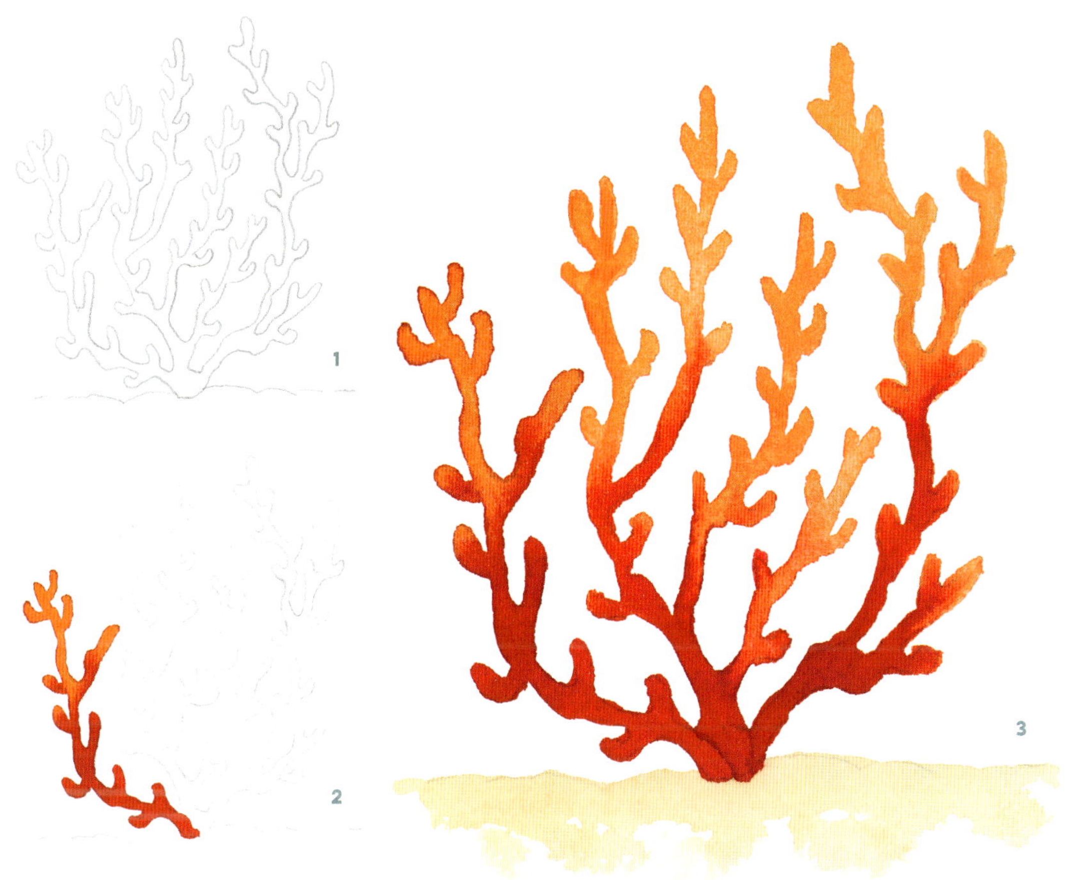

STEP 1: Use your pencil to lightly trace (page 251) or sketch the Colorful Coral composition onto your watercolor paper.

STEP 2: Lightly erase your pencil marks. Using a size 8 round brush, paint one coral branch at a time. Use a Cadmium Orange **wash** to paint the top half of a coral branch. Then lay Alizarin Crimson in starting at the base and painting up until you reach the Cadmium Orange; allow the two colors to **bleed** together (**wet-in-wet**).

Repeat this process with all the branches of coral.

STEP 3: Use the **dry brush** technique (page 16) to paint in Yellow Ochre for the sand.

CLOWN FISH

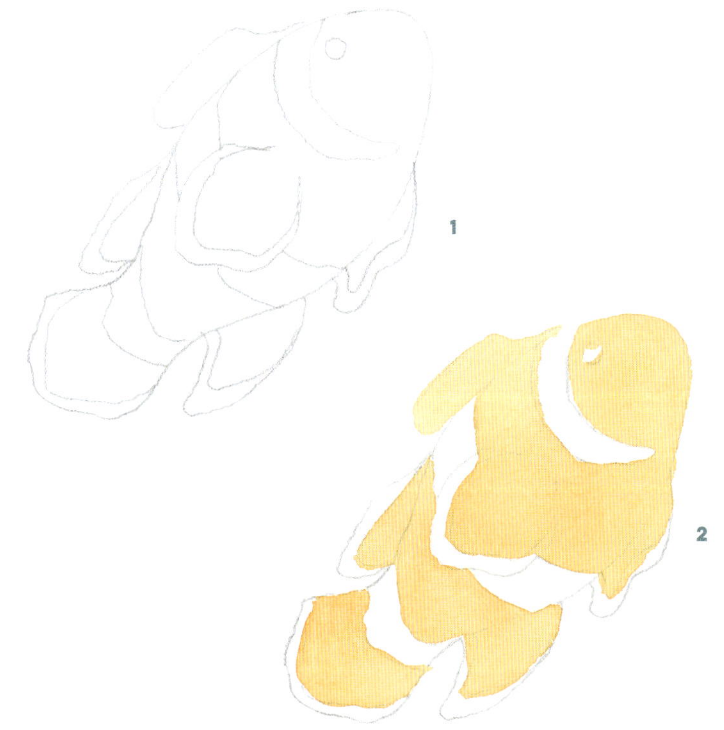

Throughout this book, we use **glazes** frequently.
A **glaze** can be applied in any color over a layer
of paint. For this Clown Fish painting, you'll apply
the same color **glaze** multiple times to achieve a
darker **value**.

MATERIALS

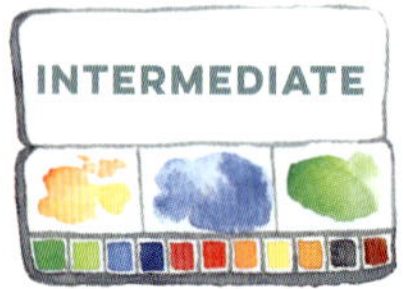

Pencil
Watercolor paper
Size 8 round brush

COLORS

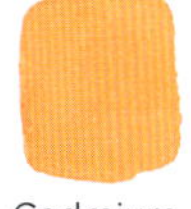
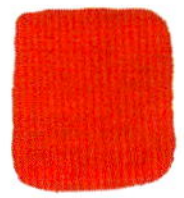
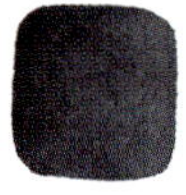
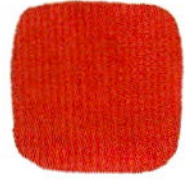

Quinacridone Gold · Cadmium Orange · Winsor Red · Neutral Tint · Alizarin Crimson

STEP 1: Trace (page 251) or lightly sketch the clown fish in pencil on your watercolor paper.

STEP 2: Lightly erase the pencil marks. **Load** your size 8 round brush with Quinacridone Gold and paint the clown fish's body. Avoid the white striped areas. Make sure you leave a white space for the eye.

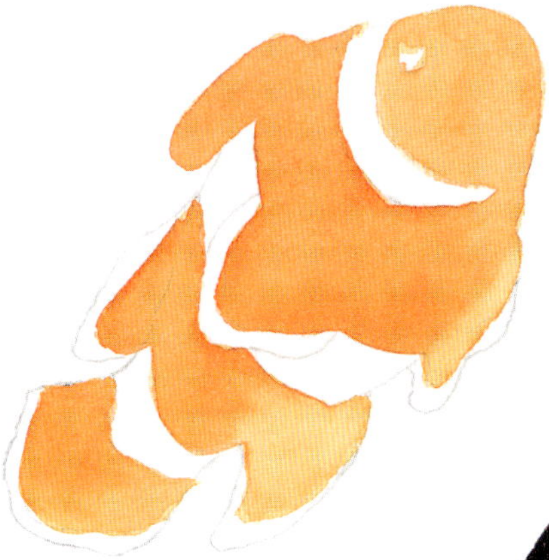

STEP 3: Mix Cadmium Orange (70%) and Winsor Red (30%) together on your palette. Apply this color as a **glaze** over the color used in Step 1. Focus the **glaze** more on the top and sides of the fish, and don't apply the **glaze** on the bottom two fins.

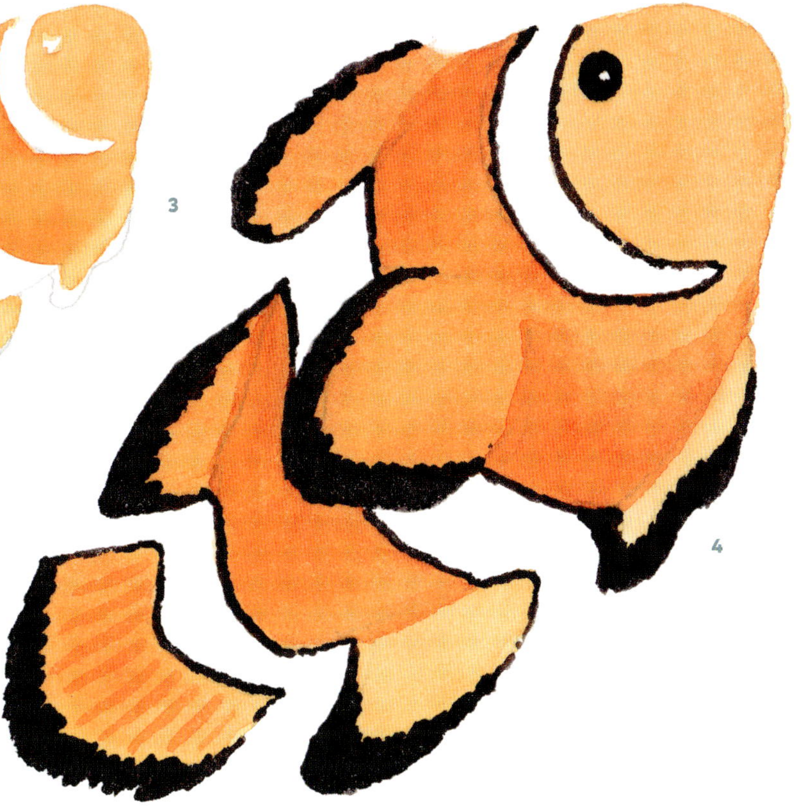

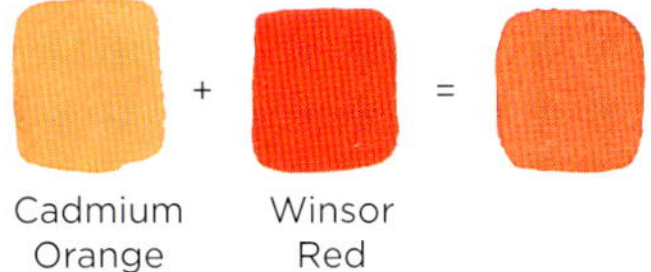

Cadmium Orange (70%) + Winsor Red (30%) =

STEP 4: Use the same mixture of Cadmium Orange (70%) and Winsor Red (30%) from the previous step to add a second **glaze** on the main body of the clown fish to separate the fins from the body. Avoid adding the **glaze** on all the fins and the face. With the same mixture, add lines to create stripes on the back fin.

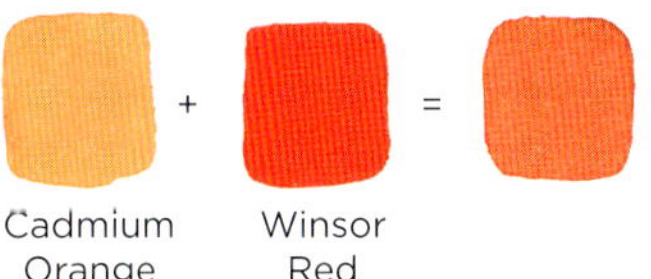

Cadmium Orange (70%) + Winsor Red (30%) =

To paint on the black detailing, mix Neutral Tint (60%) with Alizarin Crimson (40%) on your palette. Apply the black detailing on the fins in a jagged motion with this mixture. When painting the black border around the white stripes, use a thin line. This same color mixture is also used for the eye, but leave a white dot in the middle. Feel free to use the same black mixture to close off the white stripes; I chose to leave mine open as a stylistic preference.

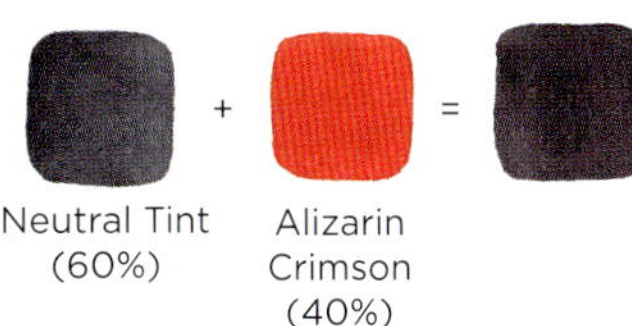

Neutral Tint (60%) + Alizarin Crimson (40%) =

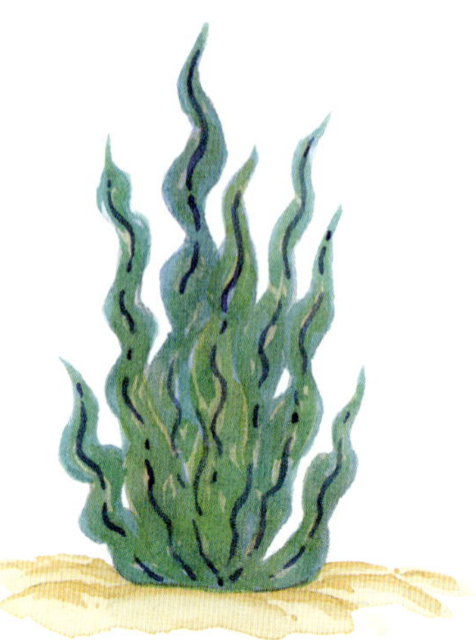

SEAWEED

When painting objects underwater, like seaweed, one way to help convey the colors beneath the ocean is to start with a layer of blues and purples. The actual color of the seaweed is then applied on top with a **glaze**. Notice how we cover up a portion of the first layer but can still see little glimmers of blue and purple poking through, giving the appearance of being deep under the ocean.

MATERIALS

Pencil

Watercolor paper

Size 8 round brush

COLORS

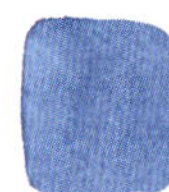 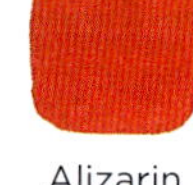  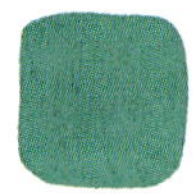 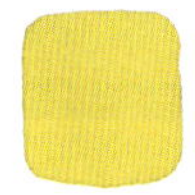

Ultramarine Blue · Alizarin Crimson · Yellow Ochre · Winsor Green · Green Gold (optional)

STEP 1: Take your pencil and lightly trace (page 251) or sketch the seaweed on your watercolor paper.

STEP 2: Lightly erase the pencil marks. Using the **wet-in-wet** technique, lay in a **wash** of Ultramarine Blue over all the seaweed with a size 8 round brush before dropping in Alizarin Crimson in a few areas. Let this dry. Then add Yellow Ochre to the sand.

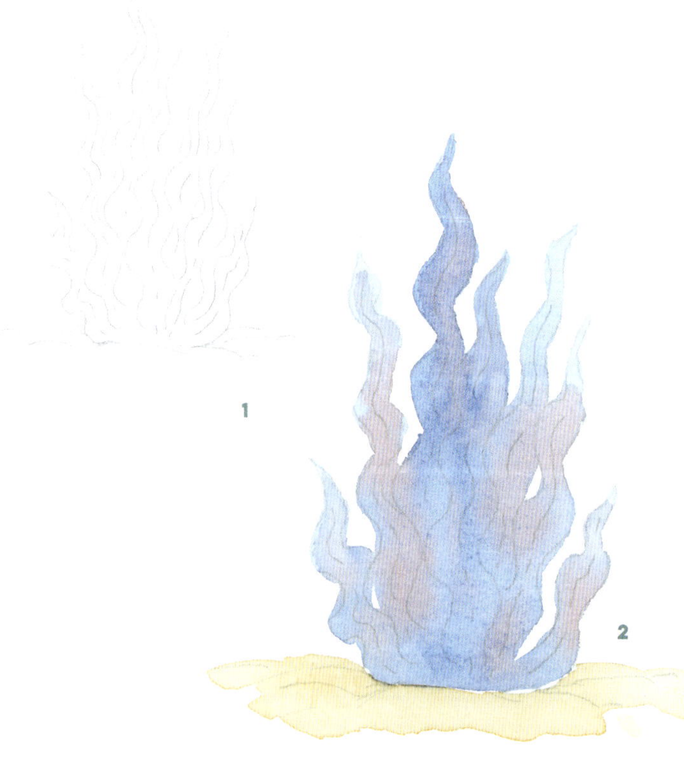

STEP 3: Apply a Winsor Green **glaze** over the seaweed. Make sure to leave little gaps so those colors from Step 2 are visible.

STEP 4: Use Ultramarine Blue to paint dark detailing on the seaweed. Do this by painting wavey thin lines down the center of each seaweed leaf. For a more effective look, break up the lines so they aren't continuous. Then add a darker **shadow** to the top layer of sand by painting on a Yellow Ochre **glaze**.

STEP 5: This step is optional. If you want your seaweed to be greener, add a Green Gold **glaze** over the entire seaweed.

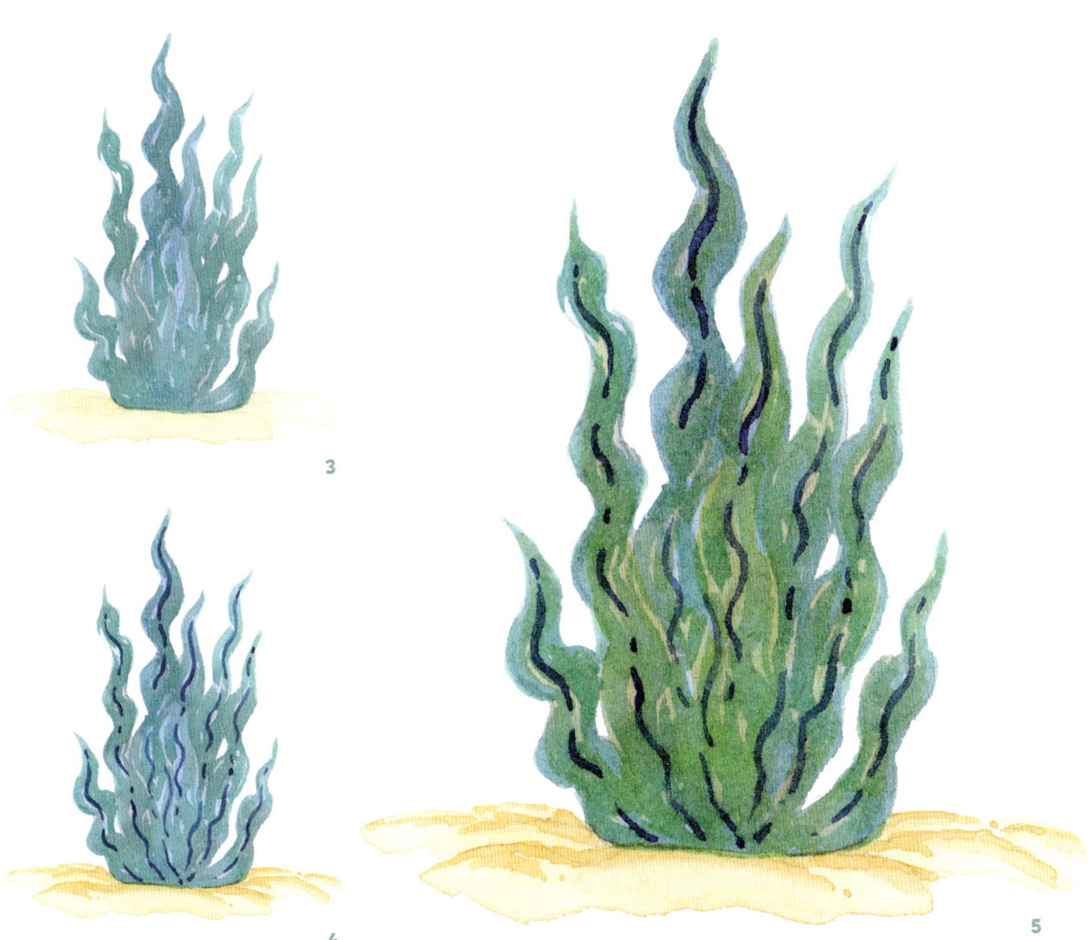

QUIRKY STARFISH

Drawing gum paste doesn't always have to be used at the beginning of a painting to preserve the white of your paper. You can use it throughout your paintings to save layers. With this Quirky Starfish project, we want to use the drawing gum paste to keep our first paint layer showing through at the end.

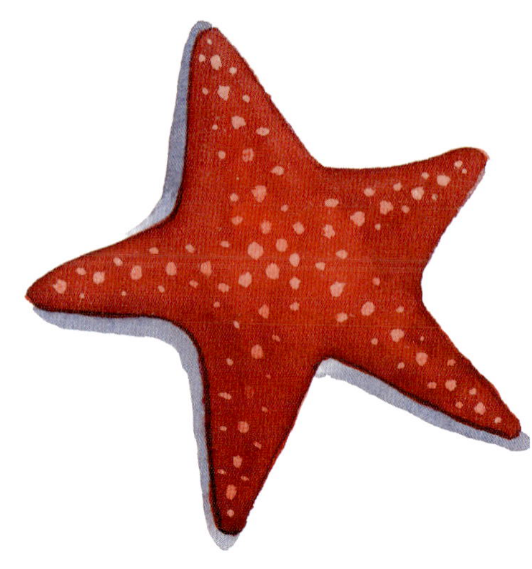

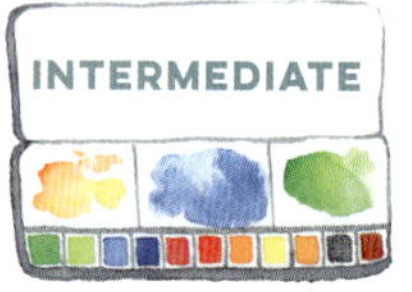

MATERIALS

Pencil

Watercolor paper

Size 8 round brush

Old brush or Q-tips cotton swab

Drawing gum paste

Rubber cement eraser

COLORS

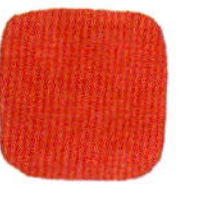
Alizarin Crimson

Cadmium Orange

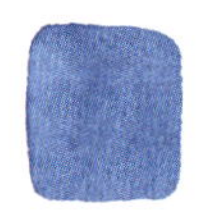
Ultramarine Blue

STEP 1: With a pencil, trace (page 251) or sketch the starfish on your watercolor paper.

STEP 2: Lightly erase the pencil marks. On your palette, combine Alizarin Crimson (60%) with Cadmium Orange (40%). You want the color to be a light **value**, so add a lot of water to the color mixture. Use your mixture and a size 8 round brush to paint a **wash** over the starfish.

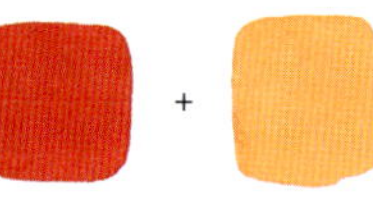

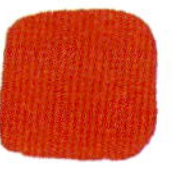

Alizarin Crimson (60%)   Cadmium Orange (40%)

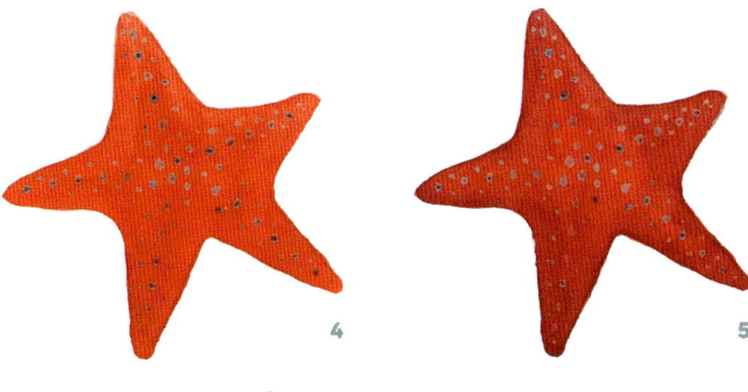

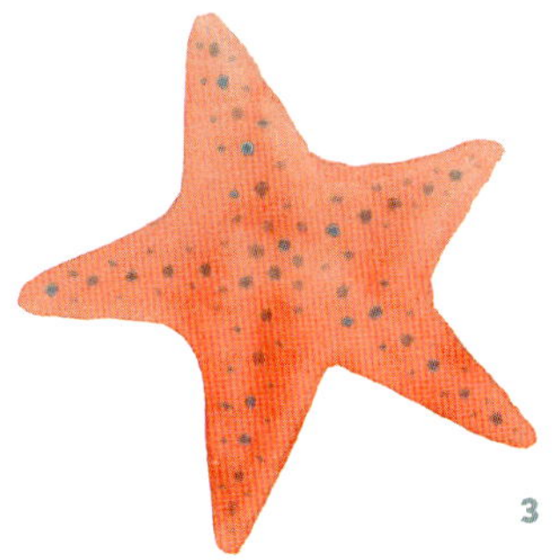

3

4

5

STEP 3: With an old brush or a Q-tips cotton swab, apply the drawing gum paste in a fun pattern of circular marks on the top of the starfish. This will help you preserve the color you laid in Step 2.

STEP 4: Add another layer of the Alizarin Crimson (60%) and Cadmium Orange (40%) mixture to the whole starfish.

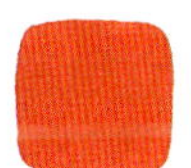 + 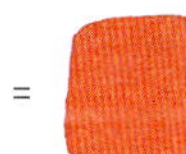 =

Alizarin Crimson (60%)   Cadmium Orange (40%)

STEP 5: On your palette, mix Alizarin Crimson (70%) with Ultramarine Blue (30%). Apply this mixture to the inside edges of the starfish. You aren't pulling the paint to the center of the starfish. Keep this color to the interior border. If you have a **hard edge**, take a little bit of water (no paint) and follow along the **hard edge** to achieve a blended look (**soft edge**).

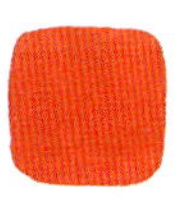 + 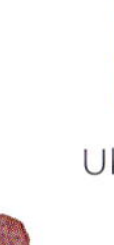 =

Alizarin Crimson (70%)   Ultramarine Blue (30%)

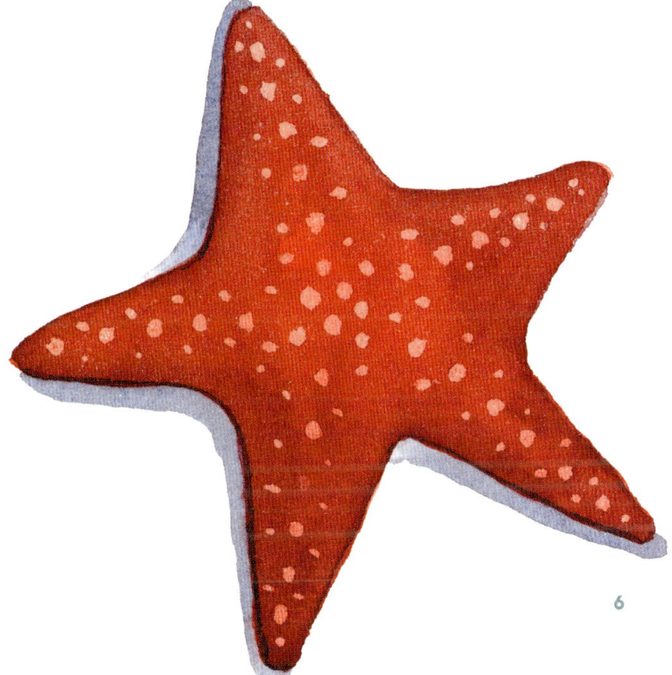

6

STEP 6: Before moving forward, make sure your painting is completely dry! Use a rubber cement eraser to remove the gum paste. After combining Ultramarine Blue (60%) and Alizarin Crimson (40%) on your palette, add the **shadows** under the starfish and to the left side of your starfish.

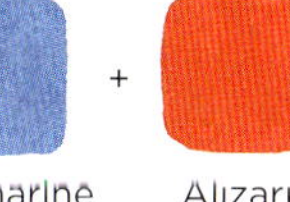 + 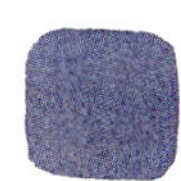 =

Ultramarine Blue (60%)   Alizarin Crimson (40%)

SEASHELL

When making a lot of similar markings on an object, you want to make sure you have a variety of strokes. A seashell is imperfect. To convey this, we use lots of different markings. It will also get the viewer to be more interested in the **subject** because the eyes will focus on something with variety for longer but pass over something that's uniform more quickly.

MATERIALS

Pencil
Watercolor paper
Size 8 round brush
Paper towel

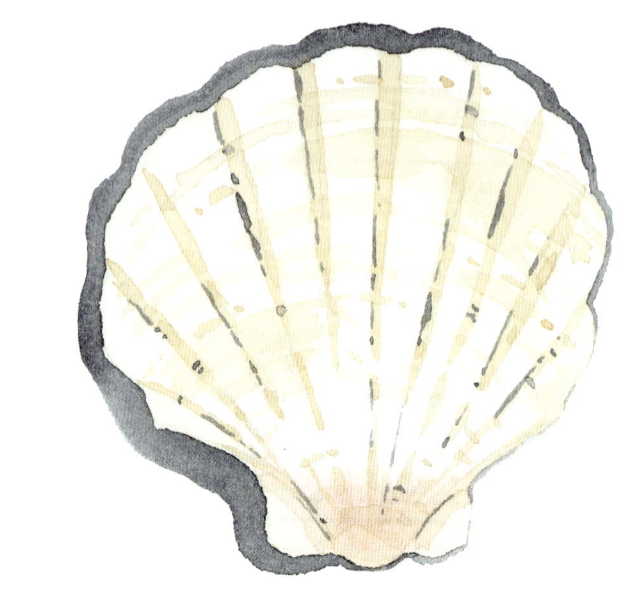

COLORS

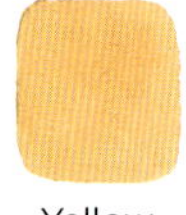

Yellow Ochre

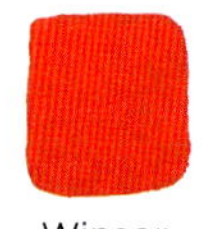

Winsor Red

Indigo

Neutral Tint

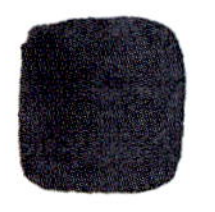

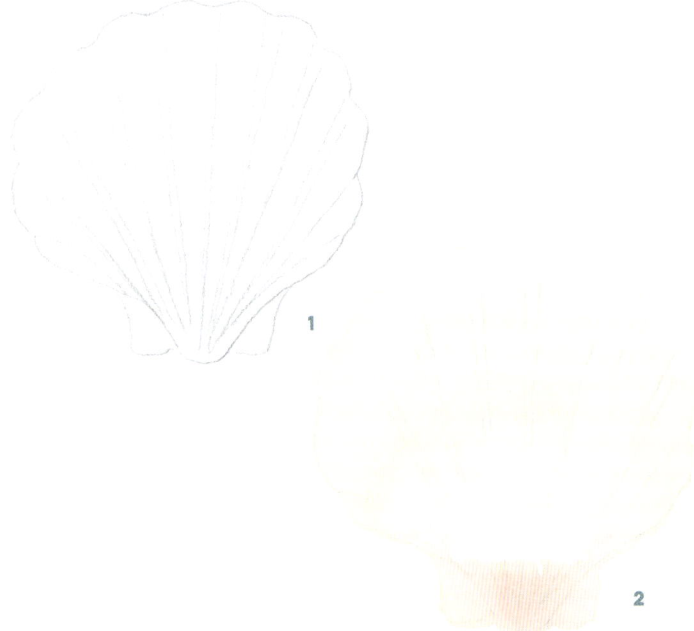

STEP 1: With a pencil, trace (page 255) or sketch the seashell on your watercolor paper.

STEP 2: Erase the pencil marks. With a size 8 round brush, apply a light **wash** of Yellow Ochre, mixed with a lot of water for a light **value**, over the whole shell. Leave a white area near the base of the shell for a **highlight**. While this is still wet, drop a watered-down Winsor Red into the base of the seashell (**wet-in-wet**).

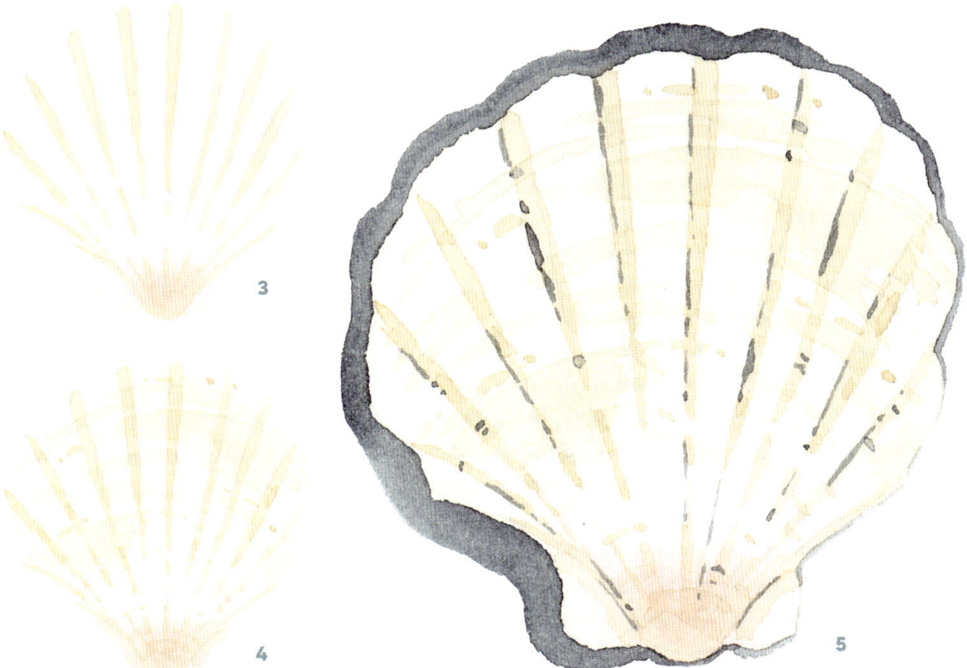

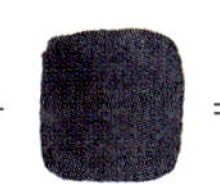

STEP 3: Paint Yellow Ochre in vertical lines along the seashell to create a grooved **texture** on the shell. Near the **highlight**, leave little gaps with no color.

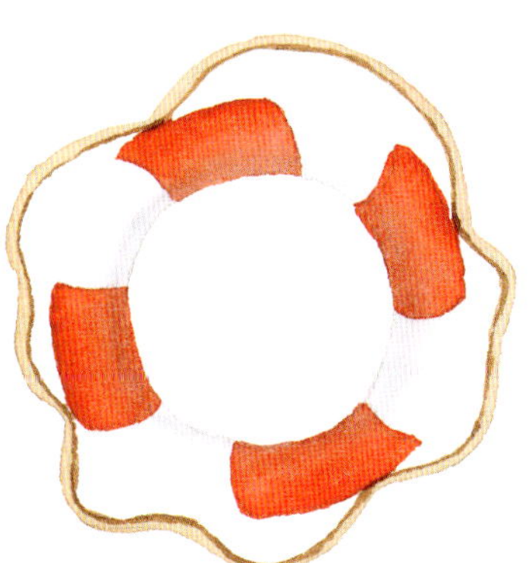

STEP 4: On your palette, take Yellow Ochre (80%) and mix it with Indigo (20%) for the arched lines going across the seashell. To create visual variety, apply thin, medium and thick curved strokes. If you get too dark with the mixture when adding it to the shell, you can always **blot** it with a paper towel.

Yellow Ochre (80%) + Indigo (20%) =

STEP 5: Combine Indigo (60%) and Neutral Tint (40%) on your palette. Lighten the **value** by adding more water, then paint thin lines and tiny marks vertically on the seashell to create darker spots. With the same color mixture, add a **shadow** under the shell. You are adding such a dark **shadow** because the object is closer to the ground with a tiny gap, which creates a stronger **shadow** than an object that is more raised, as in the Mushrooms painting (page 106). Apply the **shadow** following the curvature of the seashell on the top and left side.

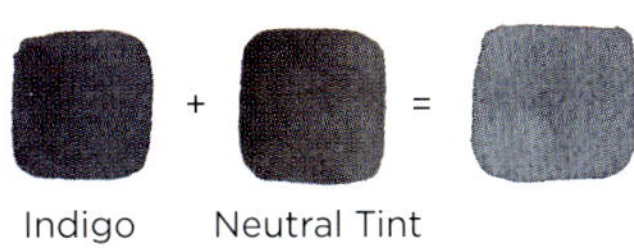

Indigo (60%) + Neutral Tint (40%) =

HUMPBACK WHALE

In the first mixture for this project, we use White Gouache to achieve a creamier color for the whale's underbelly. Gouache is a water-based, paint-like watercolor with similar ingredients; hence, you can mix it with watercolor. Gouache, however, can be opaque, unlike see-through watercolor. When combining the two, you'll get a semi-opaque medium. Make sure to rinse your brush and palette after using them together to avoid tainting the rest of your mixtures.

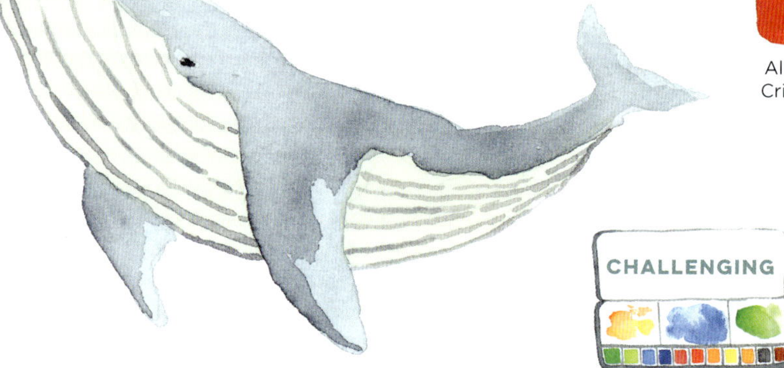

MATERIALS

Pencil
Watercolor paper
Size 8 round brush

COLORS

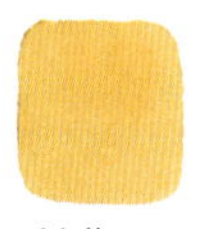

White Gouache · Yellow Ochre · Indigo

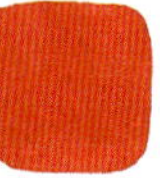

Alizarin Crimson · Neutral Tint

1

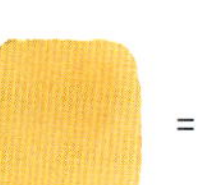

2

STEP 1: Use a pencil to lightly trace (page 255) or sketch the humpback whale on your watercolor paper.

STEP 2: Lightly erase the pencil marks. On your palette, mix White Gouache (70%) with Yellow Ochre (30%). **Load** your size 8 round brush with this color and start applying it to the whale's underbelly.

White Gouache (70%) + Yellow Ochre (30%) =

STEP 3: **Load** your brush with Indigo (20%) and a lot of water (80%) to achieve a lighter **value**. Paint this on the body of the whale.

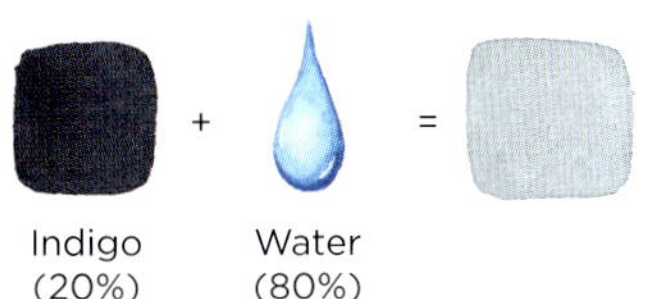

Indigo (20%) Water (80%)

STEP 4: Take Indigo (70%) and mix it with Alizarin Crimson (30%) on your palette. Apply this mixture on the edging of the body, starting at the bottom of the eye down to the tail (fluke). For the main body, make sure your paint is all **soft edges**. To do this, add water to your brush and pull into the body to **soften** the color over the whale. On the two flippers, leave your paint stroke as a **hard edge**.

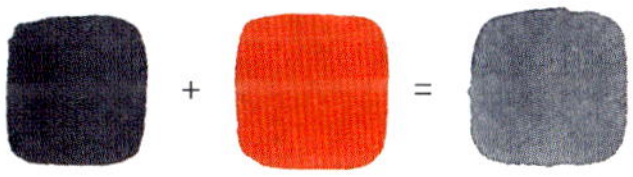

Indigo (70%) Alizarin Crimson (30%)

STEP 5: **Load** your brush with the Indigo (70%) and Alizarin Crimson (30%) mixture from Step 4. Lay in thin lines on the belly.

Take Neutral Tint and paint in your humpback whale's eye.

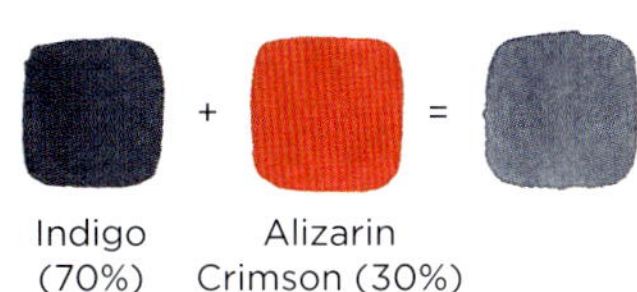

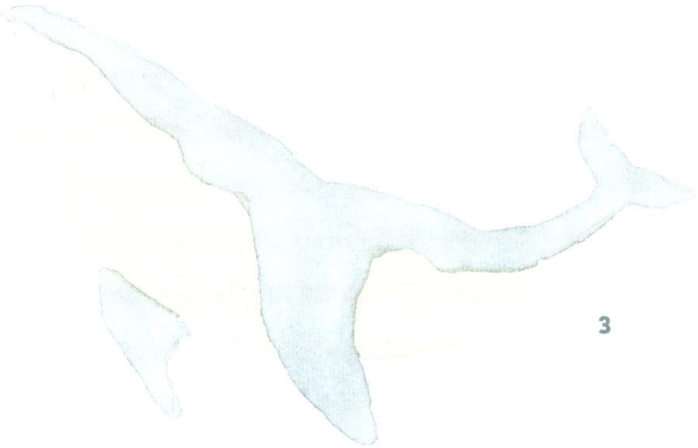

Indigo (70%) Alizarin Crimson (30%)

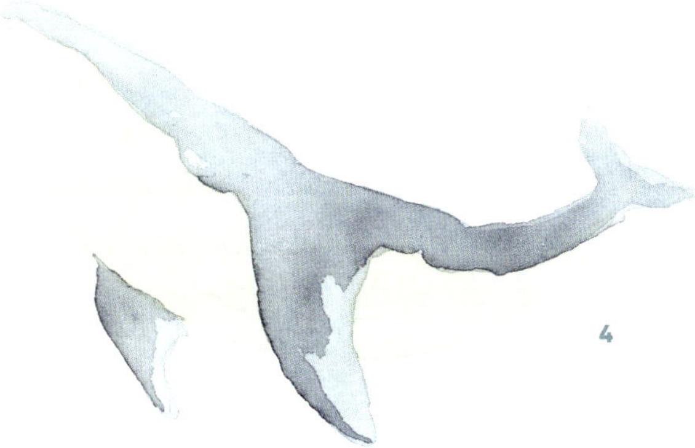

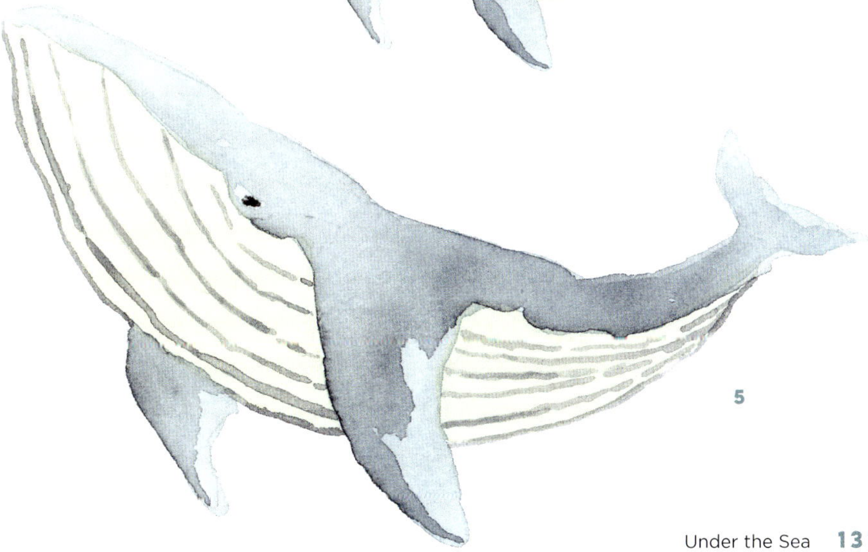

FUNKY CRAB

Watercolor dries lighter than when you first apply it because when it is wet, it has a darker **value**. A great example of this would be when you get your hair wet; it appears a few shades darker than when it is dry. We want the color to be extra **saturated** for this crab, so we add excess pigment into our **wet-in-wet** steps by adding more Cadmium Orange. Adding more pigment can ensure the **value** will be darker, even when it dries.

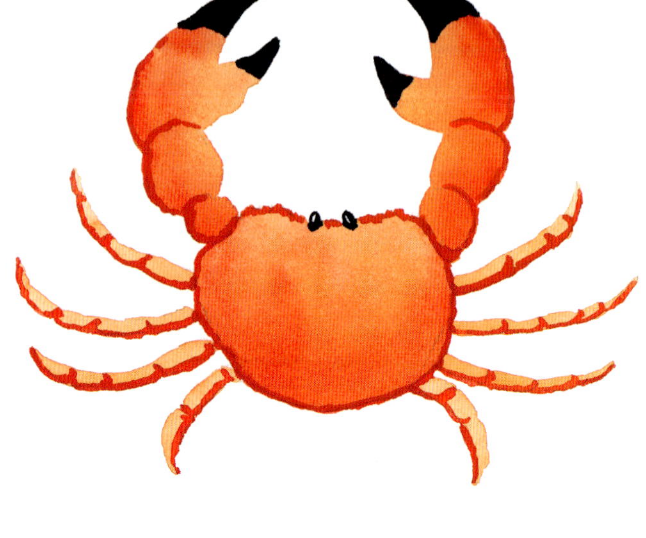

MATERIALS

Watercolor paper
Pencil
Size 8 round brush

COLORS

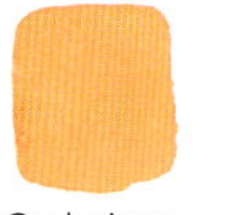

Cadmium
Orange

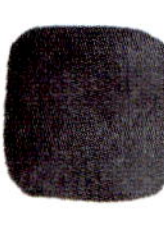

Winsor
Red

Neutral
Tint

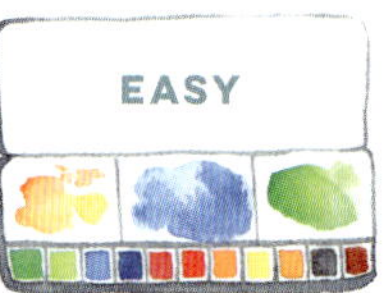

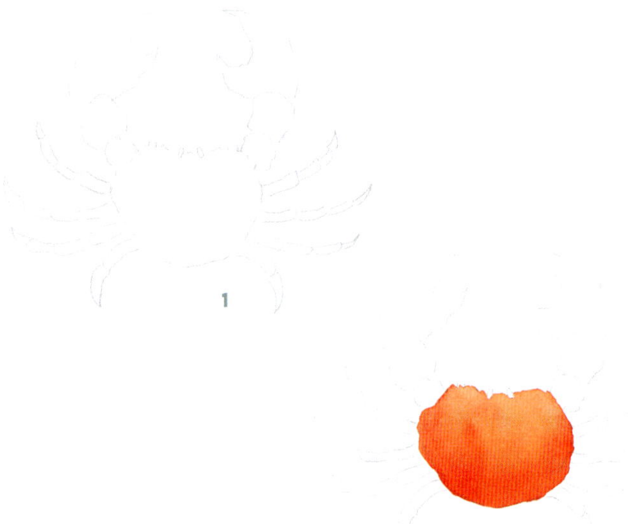

1

2

STEP 1: Trace (page 253) or sketch the crab onto your watercolor paper using a pencil.

STEP 2: Lightly erase your pencil marks. Start by using the **wet-in-wet** technique for the main body of the crab. With a size 8 round brush, paint in Cadmium Orange. While that is still wet, apply Winsor Red. To intensify the color, add a second pass of Cadmium Orange (while still wet).

STEP 3: For the legs, paint them using Cadmium Orange.

STEP 4: To the bottom half of the crab legs, add a Winsor Red **glaze** to help define where the legs have joints.

STEP 5: Begin working on the crab's claws. This is the same **wet-in-wet** process as in Step 2. Lay Cadmium Orange in first, then come in with Winsor Red, dropping it at the outer edges of each claw. If you need to, add another layer of Cadmium Orange to intensify the **saturation**.

STEP 6: Add a layer of Winsor Red to the outside layer of each claw. Outline the crab's body with Winsor Red in a jagged motion. To add the final details to the eyes and claw tips, use Neutral Tint.

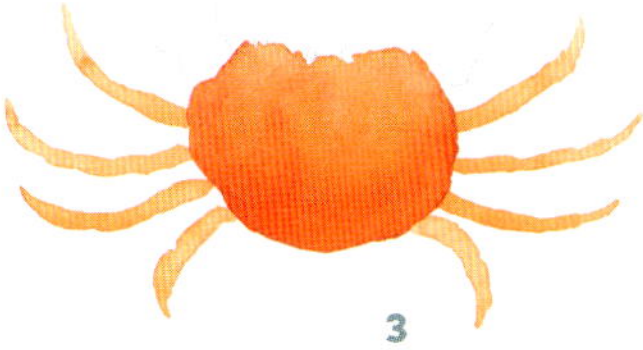

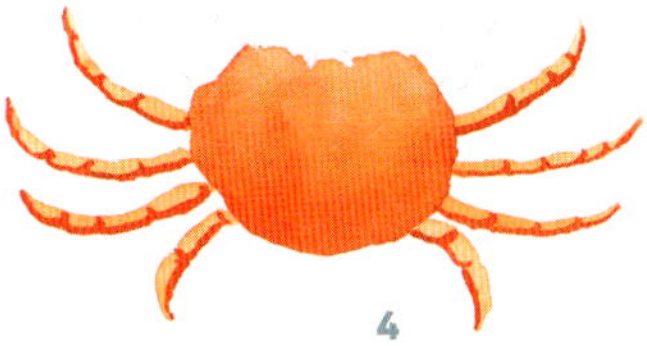

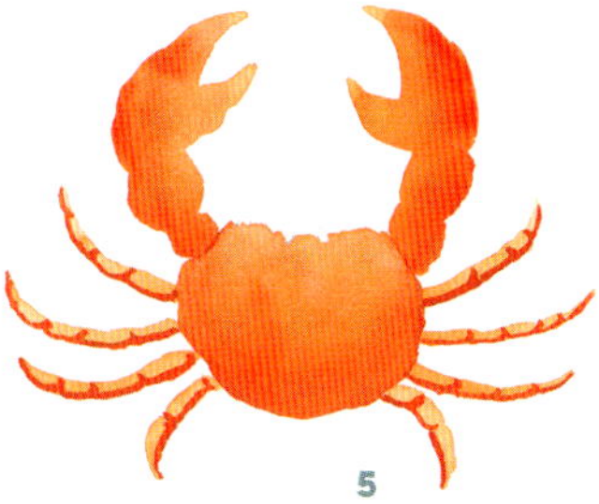

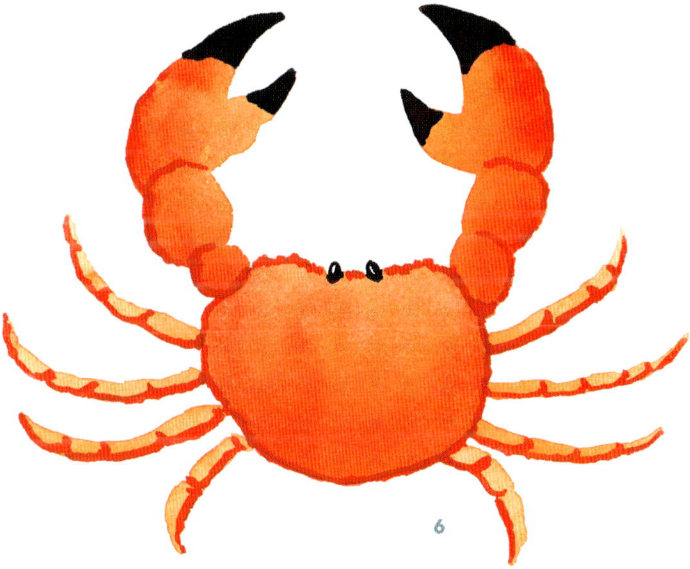

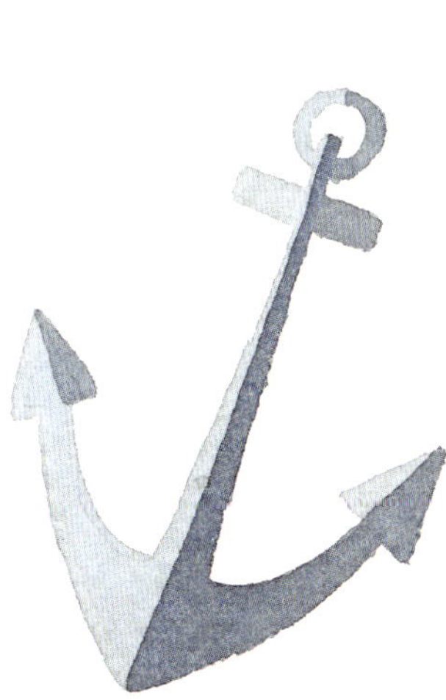

BUTTERFLY FISH

With watercolor, you must move fast before it dries on your paper. No need to waste time painting around something that will be a darker **value** later. I suggest thinking about the order of the colors before jumping into a painting. If you have a dark color, you can paint this at the end on top of other colors because it will cover up anything underneath. For this Butterfly Fish painting, you will see firsthand the importance of working smarter, not harder, by adding your darkest **values** on top of your painting last.

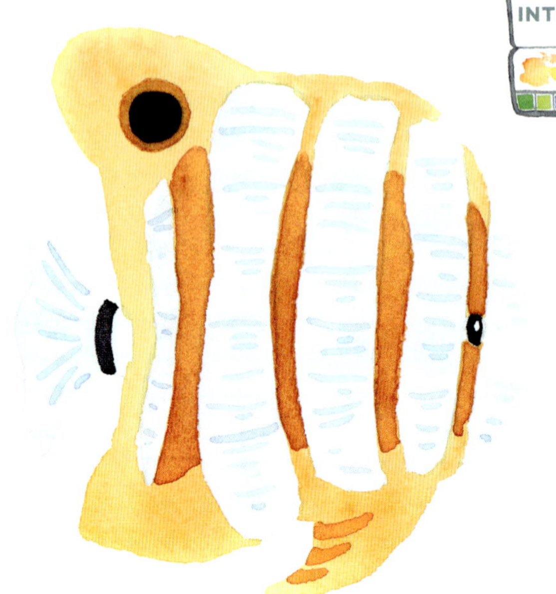

MATERIALS

Pencil

Watercolor paper

Size 8 round brush

Paper towel

COLORS

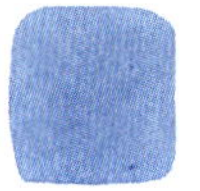

Cobalt Blue

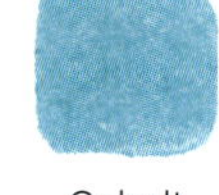

Cobalt Teal Blue

Lemon Yellow

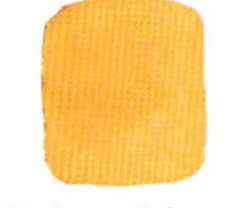

Quinacridone Gold

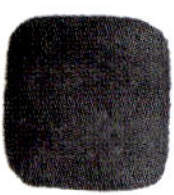

Neutral Tint

STEP 1: Use a pencil to trace (page 255) or sketch the butterfly fish on your watercolor paper.

STEP 2: Lightly erase your pencil marks. With a size 8 round brush, apply a light Cobalt Blue **wash** onto the thicker stripes of the fish. Using the **wet-in-wet** technique, dab in Cobalt Teal Blue while the first color is still wet. Take a scrunched paper towel and **blot** it on the wet paint to create a fun **texture** and look.

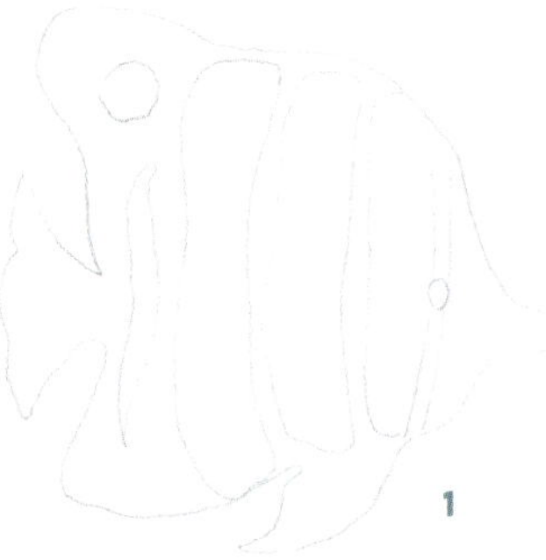

STEP 3: Lay in Lemon Yellow in the areas around the fish, avoiding the stripes you painted in Step 2. While that is still wet, apply Quinacridone Gold right on top of the Lemon Yellow (**wet-in-wet**). Don't waste your time going around the circle on the top back of the fish; you can paint right over it. The circle will be dark, so your paint will cover it in the next step. However, don't paint through the eye because you want some of the white of the paper to show.

STEP 4: Use Neutral Tint on the back stripe, the back circle and the eyeball, but leave the white of the paper in the center of the eye.

STEP 5: Go around the back circle with Quinacridone Gold and add more to the middle stripes of the fish to make that layer darker. Using the same color, add three lines on the bottom fin.

STEP 6: To add **texture**, make scales on the body by adding a light **value** of Cobalt Blue in little horizontal lines with varying lengths.

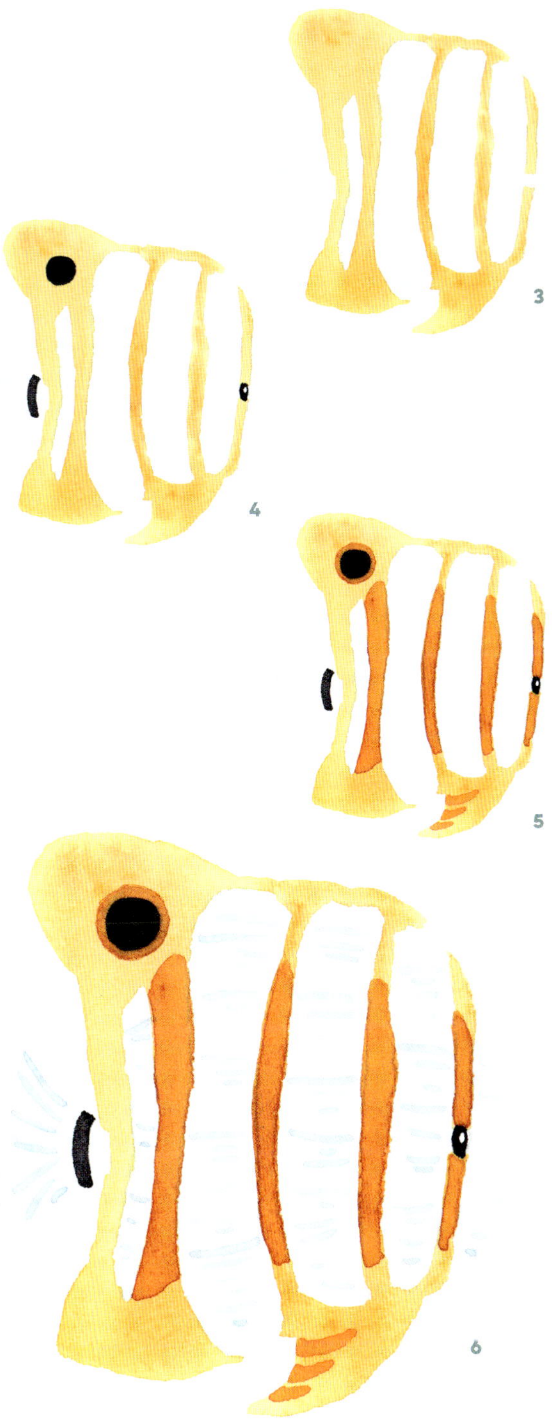

JELLYFISH

Splattering is a technique that adds a fun flair to any painting. In the final step of this Jellyfish painting, we apply a **splatter**. This effect adds movement to the jellyfish so it looks as if it is swimming through the water. The **splattering** technique is also used for the candles in the Happy Birthday Cake project (page 108) to help signify flickering coming from the flame, and in the Thailand Lanterns painting (page 84).

MATERIALS

Watercolor paper

Pencil

Old brush

Drawing gum paste

Size 8 round brush

Scrap paper

Rubber cement eraser

COLORS

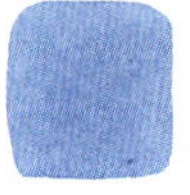
Cobalt
Blue

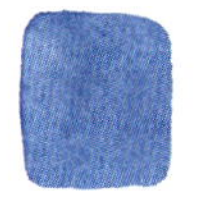
Ultramarine
Blue

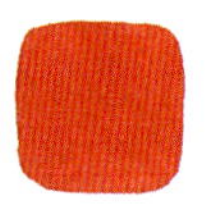
Alizarin
Crimson

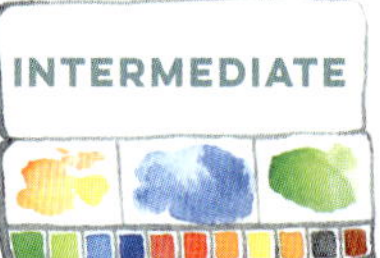

STEP 1: On your water-color paper, trace (page 253) or sketch your jellyfish in pencil.

STEP 2: Lightly erase your pencil marks. Using an old brush for the drawing gum paste, freehand a few jellyfish tentacles and a few vertical arched lines on the bell-shaped body.

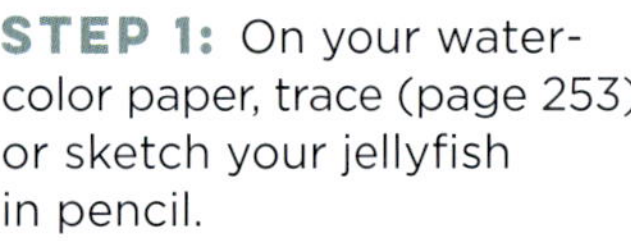

1

2

STEP 3: Use the **wet-in-wet** technique for the bell of the jellyfish and down to the bottom of the tentacles. Start by painting Cobalt Blue with a size 8 round brush. While that is still wet, dab in Ultramarine Blue and some Alizarin Crimson throughout.

STEP 4: Add about eight tentacles by painting them with Ultramarine Blue. Let those dry.

Load your brush with Alizarin Crimson and add four more tentacles. Let that dry.

Mix Alizarin Crimson (50%) and Ultramarine Blue (50%) on your palette, then add three tentacles with that color mixture.

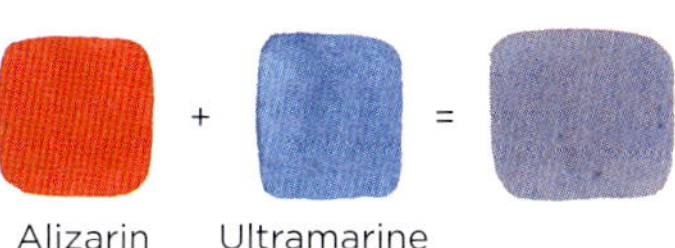

Alizarin Crimson (50%) + Ultramarine Blue (50%) =

Use Ultramarine Blue and outline the base of the bell. Don't bring the outside edges to the top of the bell. Then use Ultramarine Blue to paint vertical arched lines starting at the middle of the bell and carrying it down to the base of the bell.

STEP 5: With a scrap piece of paper, cover up the bell of the jellyfish. Using one color at a time, **splatter** (page 19) paint using these three colors: Cobalt Blue, Ultramarine Blue and Alizarin Crimson. Make sure you let this dry completely before removing the gum paste using the rubber cement eraser.

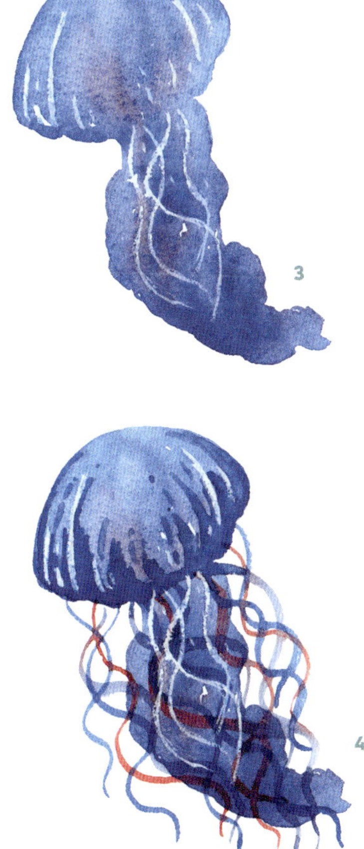

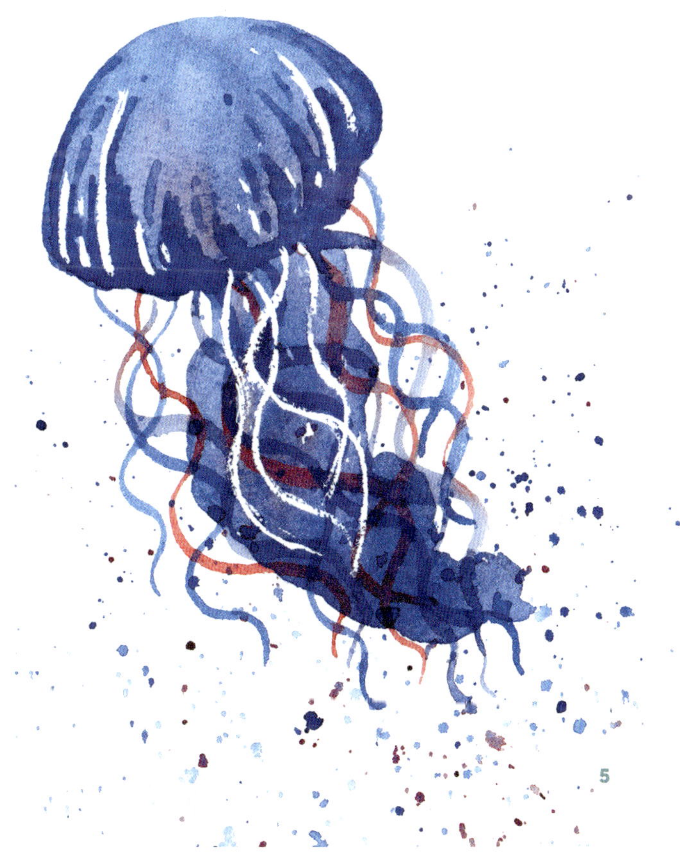

LEMON SHARK

In this Lemon Shark project, we paint the **cast shadow** a purple color because purple is yellow's **complementary color**, and yellow is the primary color for the shark. **Complementary colors** can create a lot of contrast, making this simple shark pop! (For more on Basic Color Theory, see page 22.)

MATERIALS

Watercolor paper

Pencil

Size 8 round brush

Size 2 round brush (optional)

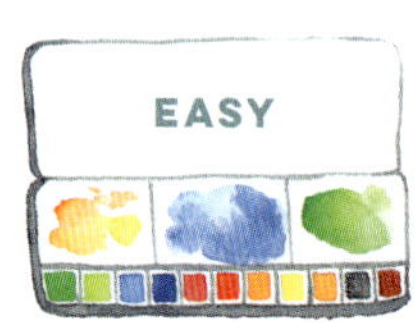

COLORS

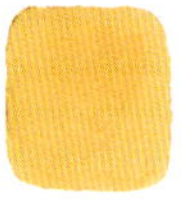
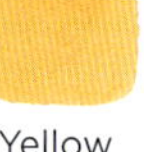

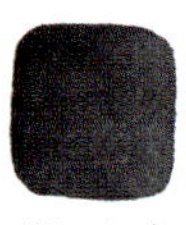
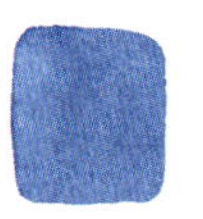
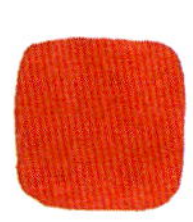

Yellow Ochre   Indigo   Neutral Tint   Ultramarine Blue   Alizarin Crimson

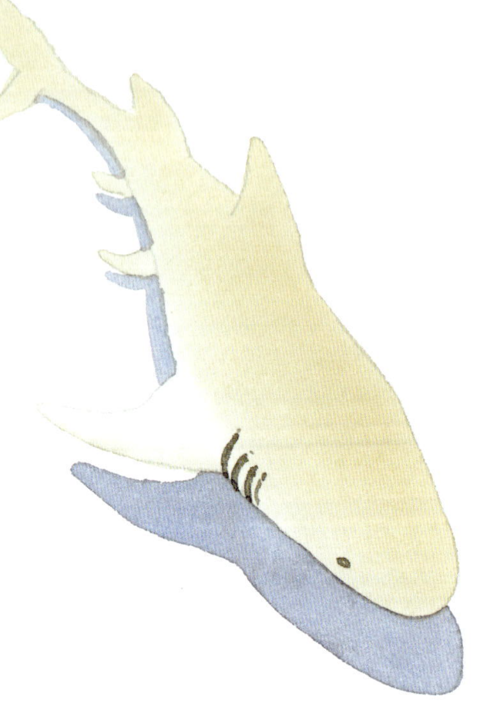

STEP 1: On your watercolor paper, trace (page 253) or lightly sketch the lemon shark in pencil.

STEP 2: On your palette, mix Yellow Ochre (80%) and Indigo (20%) with a size 8 round brush. Clean off your brush and **load** it with water, then apply a **clear water wash** over the entire shark. Using the **wet-in-wet** technique, **load** your brush with the mixture from your palette and paint it into your **clear water wash**, avoiding the space between the large left fin and the shark's gill area.

1

2

Yellow Ochre (80%)   +   Indigo (20%)   =

STEP 3: If you would like, use a smaller brush (size 2) to paint in the finer details. Mix Neutral Tint (70%) with Yellow Ochre (30%) on your palette. Use this mixture to paint in the gills and the eye.

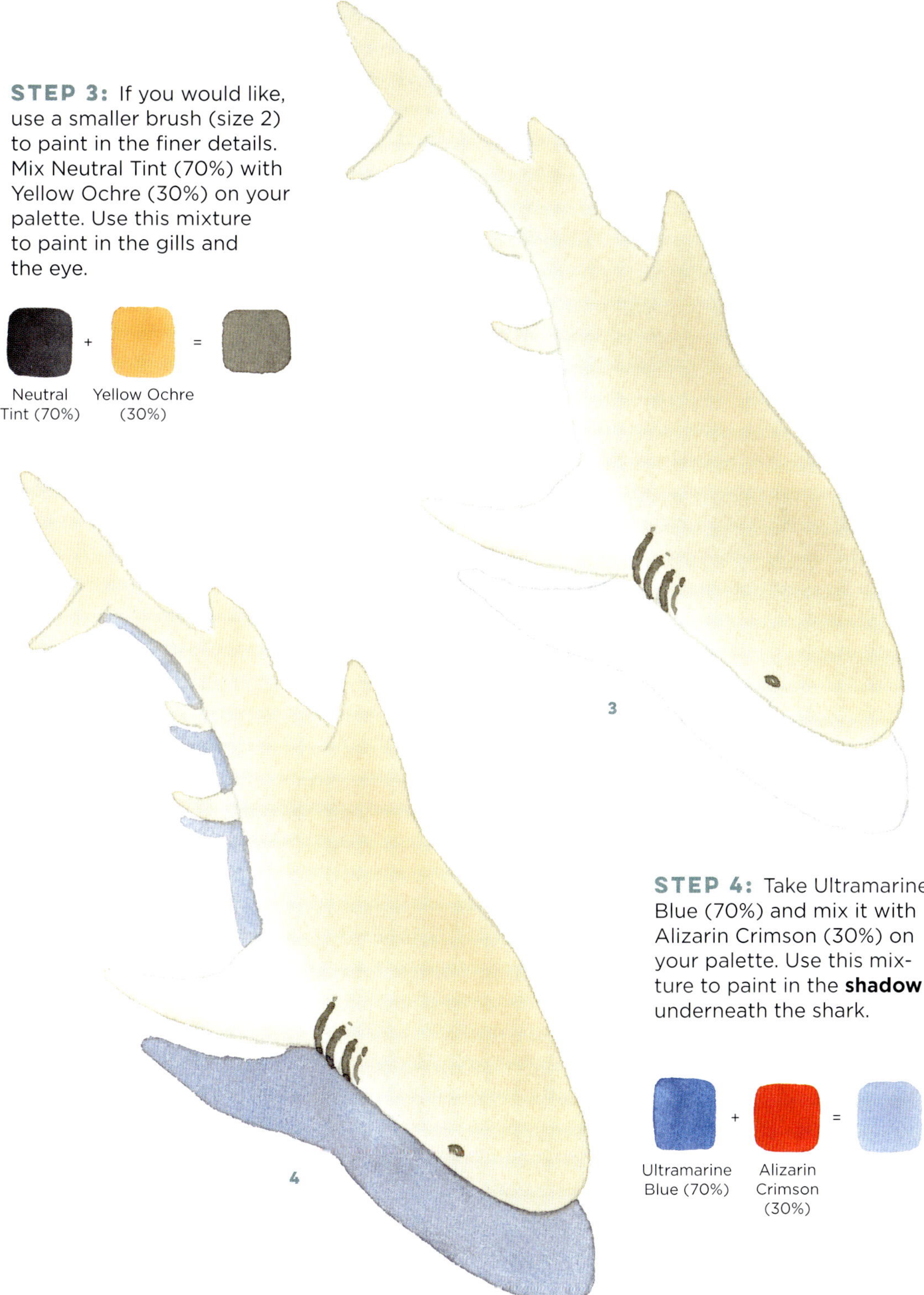

Neutral Tint (70%) + Yellow Ochre (30%) =

3

STEP 4: Take Ultramarine Blue (70%) and mix it with Alizarin Crimson (30%) on your palette. Use this mixture to paint in the **shadow** underneath the shark.

Ultramarine Blue (70%) + Alizarin Crimson (30%) =

4

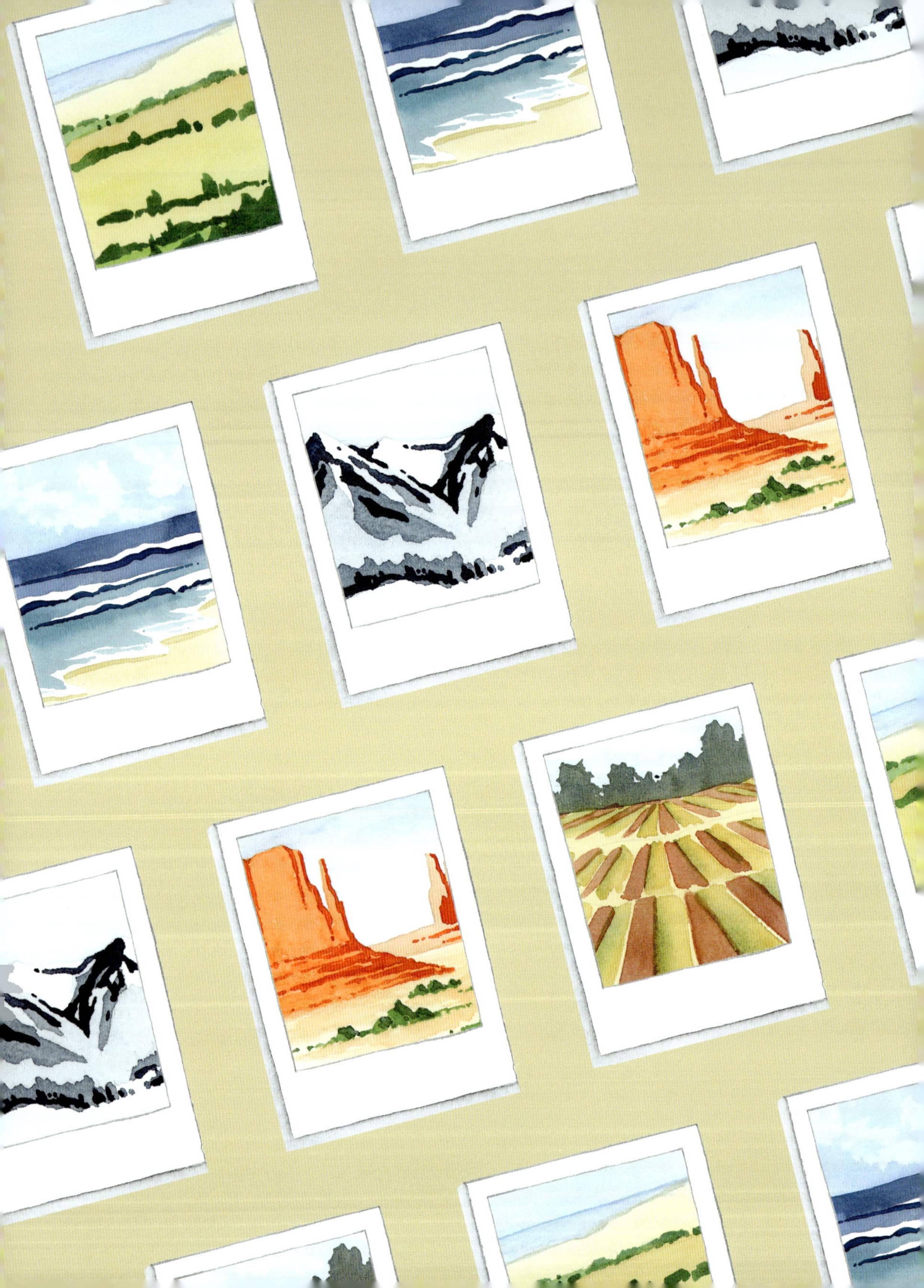

TRAVELING
THROUGH
LANDSCAPES

Painting landscapes can be overwhelming because the **subject** is much more complex than when we paint a single object, like a piece of fruit or a seashell. One of the biggest tips when painting a landscape is to simplify, simplify, simplify! The landscapes in this chapter are broken down into simple steps with minimal details, focusing on each place's overall feeling. When deciding what to prioritize in a landscape, ask yourself what jumps out to you in the scene: the trees, rolling hills, ocean waves, the sky, etc. In the Snowy Mountain painting (page 156), the trees are kept extremely simple because the focus is on the mountain, not the trees. Even though the tree lines are extremely simple, little zigzag lines, they still convey trees to our viewers and keep them from getting lost in an area of the painting that isn't the primary focus. Whatever your main focus is, try to simplify the other elements in the painting with fewer details.

BEACH TIME

No beach day is complete without a brilliant sky filled with fluffy clouds. To create those clouds for this Beach Time painting, you'll use a common tool you probably already have in your cupboard or under your sink. Paper towels can create some of the best cloud formations! To get an assortment of cloud shapes, make sure you twist your paper towel, wrinkle it or ball it up differently each time you **blot** off the paint, to create unique shapes. You can also angle the paper towel in a diagonal direction; the cloud varieties are endless!

MATERIALS

Watercolor paper

Pencil

Painter's tape (optional)

Size 14 round brush

Paper towel

Size 8 round brush

COLORS

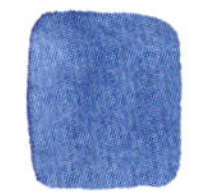

Ultramarine Blue

Yellow Ochre

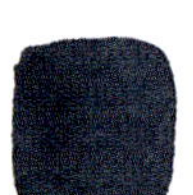

Indigo

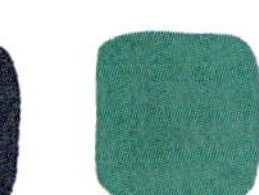

Winsor Green

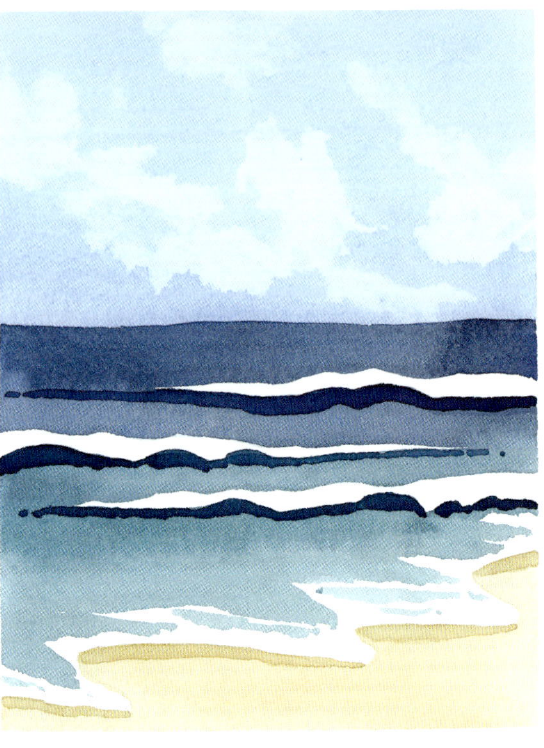

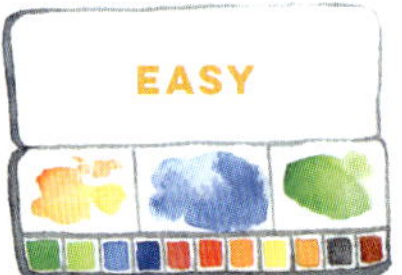

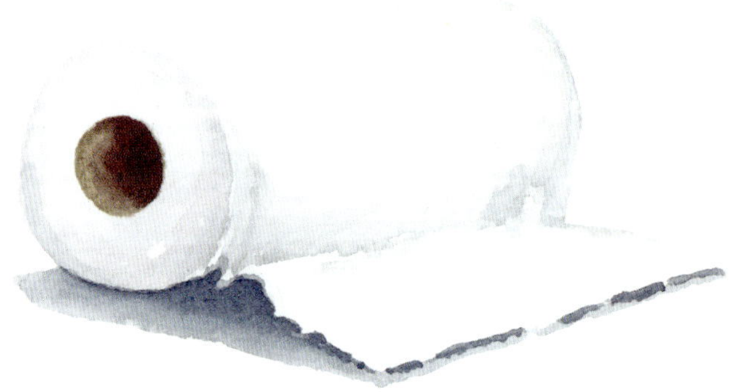

STEP 1: On your water-color paper, trace (page 257) or sketch the Beach Time landscape. If you want crisp edges, use painter's tape to create a border.

STEP 2: Lightly erase the pencil marks. Using a size 14 round brush, paint the sky with Ultramarine Blue. Use a paper towel to **blot** off the color to create the clouds. (For my cloud shapes, I angled my paper towel in a diagonal direction.)

For the remainder of the painting, switch to a size 8 round brush. **Load** your brush with Yellow Ochre and apply that to the entire sand area at the bottom.

STEP 3: The ocean gets darker closer to the horizon line. Start painting the ocean near the horizon line by **loading** your brush with a mixture of Indigo (60%) and Ultramarine Blue (40%). Once you reach the closest wave, add water to your mixture to lighten the ocean color. When you reach the next wave, add Winsor Green (50%) to that blue mixture. Pull that mixture toward the beach, leaving some white spaces.

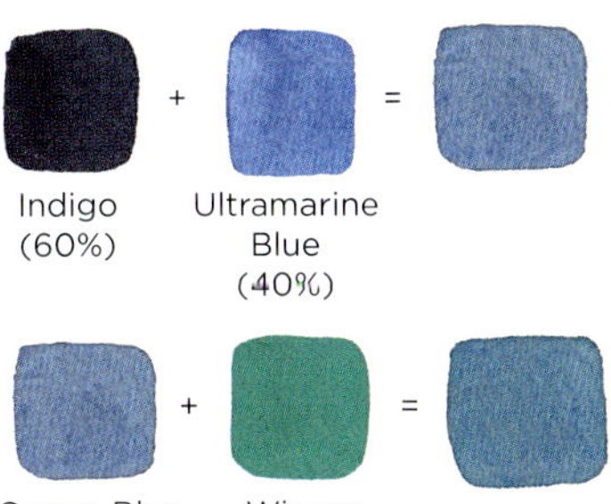

Indigo (60%) + Ultramarine Blue (40%) = Ocean-Blue Color (50%) + Winsor Green (50%) =

1

2

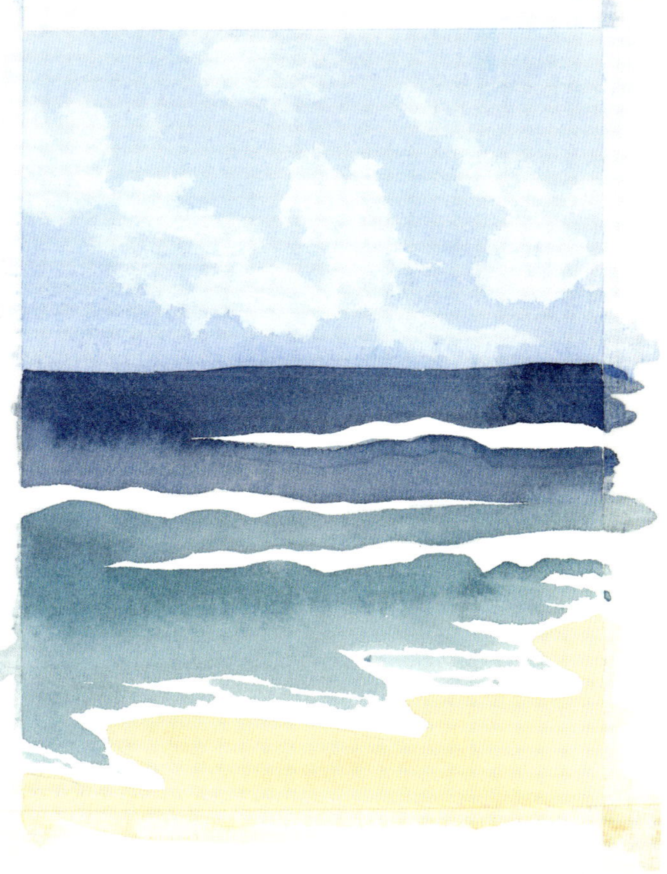

3

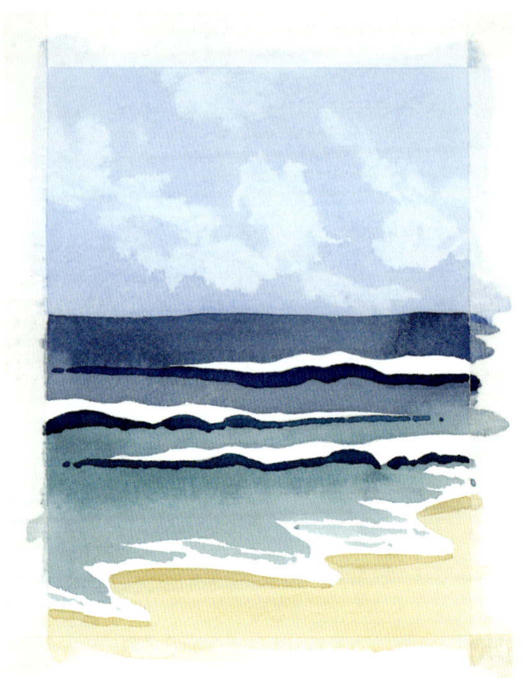

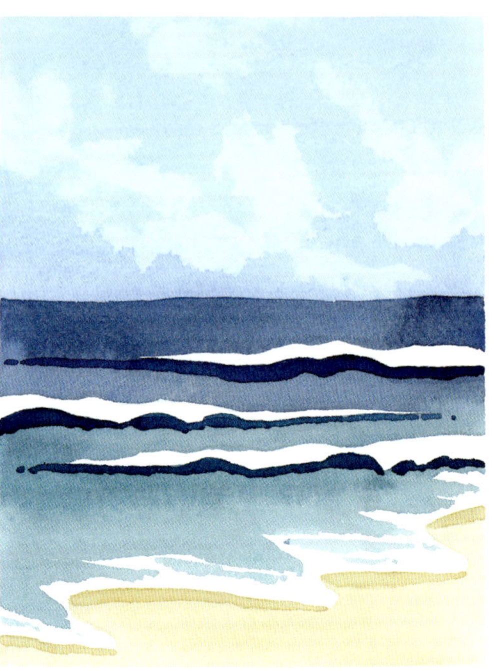

4A   4B

STEP 4: Make a **shadow** underneath all the waves. For the farthest wave back, mix Indigo (60%) and Ultramarine Blue (40%) on your palette. Using this mixture, paint a thin line underneath the white part of the wave farthest away. Add Winsor Green (50%) to the ocean-blue mixture you have on your palette and apply the **shadow** under the two waves closest to the shoreline (because these waves are closer, they will have a greener wave coloring). The last **shadow** is for the sand. For this **shadow**, mix Yellow Ochre (80%) with Indigo (20%) on your palette. Paint this mixture under the left side of the shoreline wave.

Once the paint is dry, remove the tape.

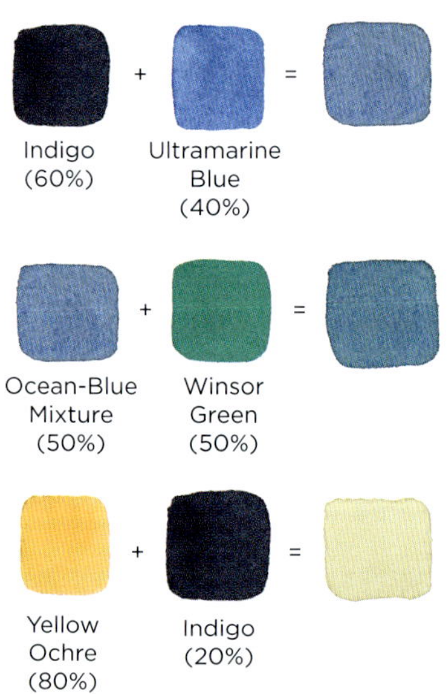

MATERIALS

Pencil

Watercolor paper

Painter's tape (optional)

Old brush

Drawing gum paste

Size 2 mop brush

Size 8 round brush

Rubber cement eraser

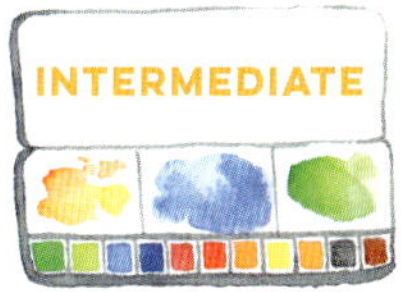

COLORS

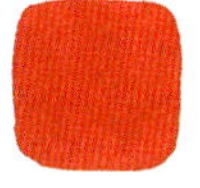

Alizarin
Crimson

Cadmium
Orange

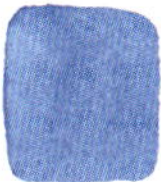

Lemon
Yellow

Ultramarine
Blue

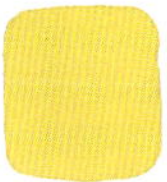
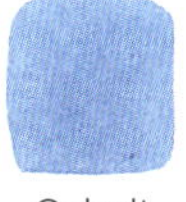

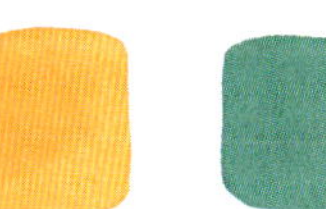
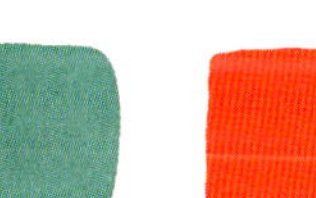

Green
Gold

Cobalt
Blue

Quinacridone
Gold

Winsor
Green

Winsor
Red

LOST IN THE DESERT

For this Lost in the Desert painting, we use a **variegated wash**. While a **variegated wash** can be done on dry or wet paper, for this landscape, a dry paper **variegated wash** is used in order to get high **saturation** more easily. Try experimenting with both ways of applying the **variegated wash** to see the difference and decide which method you prefer! A **variegated wash** for this project allows us to quickly achieve the blending of colors that appear in a sunset.

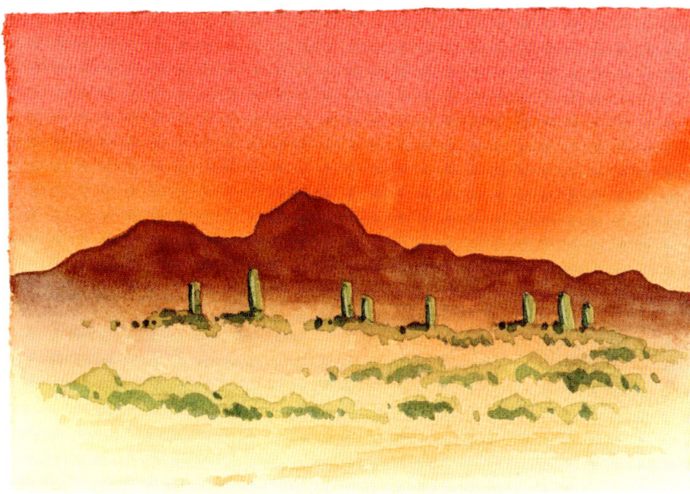

STEP 1: Take your pencil and trace (page 255) or sketch this Lost in the Desert landscape on your watercolor paper. Use painter's tape to apply a border around your painting for a clean cut edge. This is a stylistic choice and is optional.

STEP 2: Paint on drawing gum paste with an old brush over the eight cacti in the **background**. Use a mop brush to paint a **gradient wash** in the sky. Apply an Alizarin Crimson **wash** at the top, then switch to a Cadmium Orange **wash** in the middle. At the end, you will add a Lemon Yellow **wash**. Bring that Lemon Yellow all the way down to the bottom of the painting.

STEP 3: Switch to a size 8 round brush. On your palette, mix Alizarin Crimson (70%) with Ultramarine Blue (30%). Use this color to paint in the mountains. Once you reach where the mountain touches the desert, create a **soft edge**. You will do this by rinsing out your brush, putting just a bit of water on it, and using that brush to blend out the **hard edge** into the desert. Once that is completely dry, remove the drawing gum paste by using a rubber cement eraser.

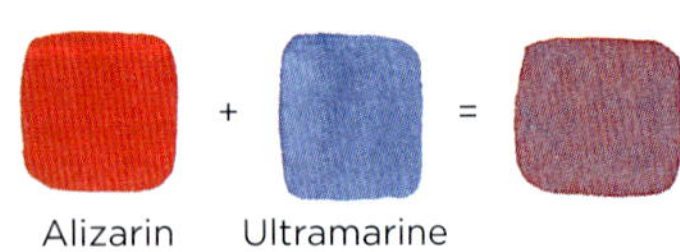

Alizarin Crimson (70%) + Ultramarine Blue (30%) =

STEP 4: Take Green Gold (50%) and mix it with Cobalt Blue (50%) on your palette. Paint in the cacti using this mixture.

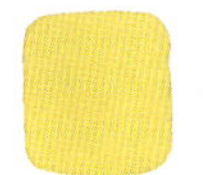 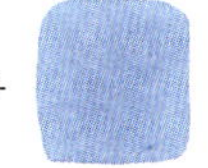 

Green Gold (50%)   Cobalt Blue (50%)

Create a new mixture of Green Gold (70%) and Cobalt Blue (30%) on your palette, and use this color for all the bushes.

  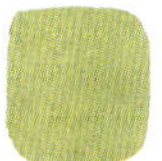

Green Gold (70%)   Cobalt Blue (30%)

Once that is dry, remove the painter's tape border.

STEP 5: Apply a Quinacridone Gold **wash** on the right side of each of the cacti to add a **highlight**. Let that dry.

Now, paint the **shadow** side, which is located on the left side. Use a mix of Winsor Green (70%) and Winsor Red (30%) from your palette. Also use this same mixture in a dotting motion on the bushes for a bit of **shadow**. Take Yellow Ochre and dot in, then drag some of those dots into strokes following the pencil lines in a diagonal manner on the desert **foreground**.

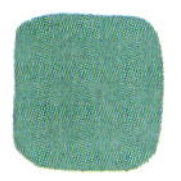 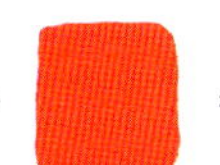 

Winsor Green (70%)   Winsor Red (30%)

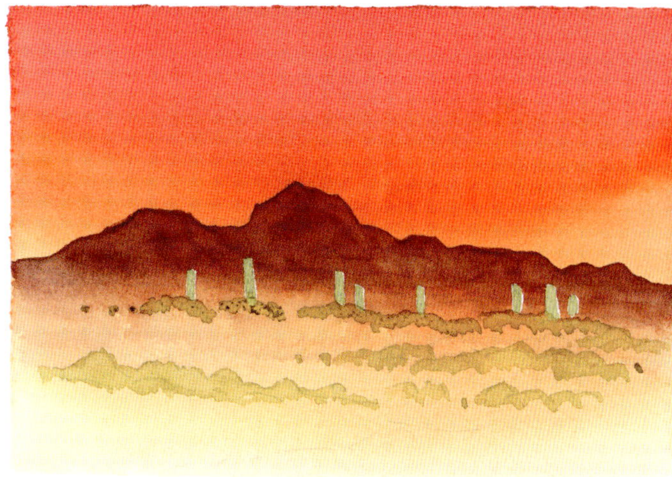

4

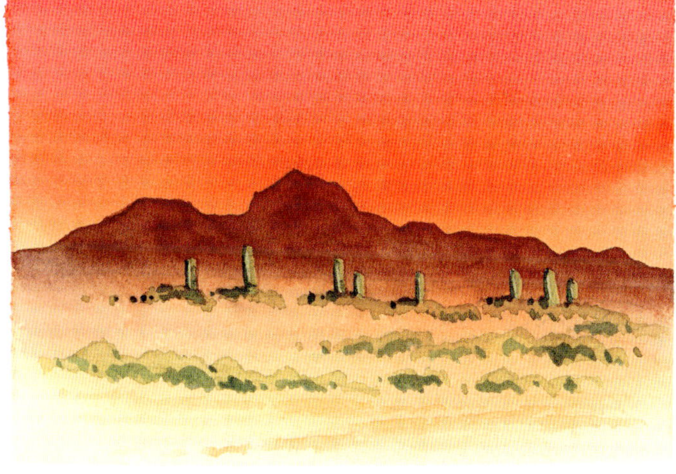

5

ENGLISH COUNTRYSIDE

Sometimes a painting doesn't come alive until the very last step when you get to add the last 10 to 20 percent of the detail. With this English Countryside painting, blocking in and laying the foundation takes up the first 80 percent of the project. Remember to not give up halfway through a painting because it often comes together on that final step.

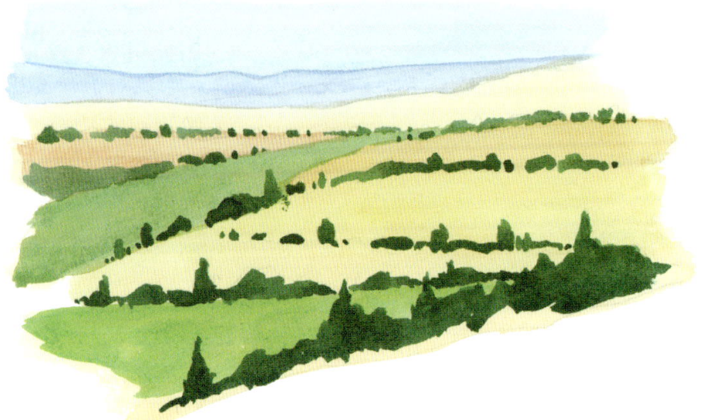

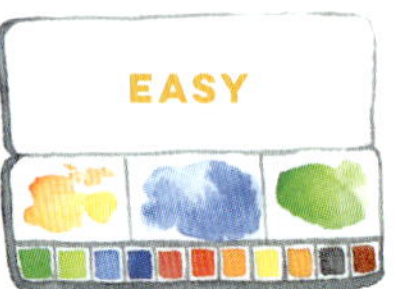

COLORS

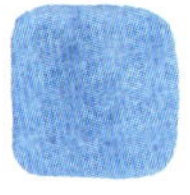 Cerulean Blue
 Quinacridone Gold
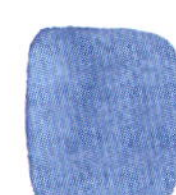 Ultramarine Blue
 Winsor Green
 Cadmium Orange
 Yellow Ochre
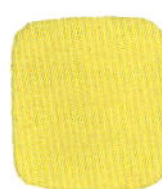 Green Gold
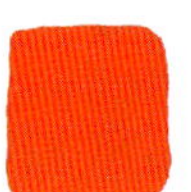 Winsor Red

STEP 1: On your watercolor paper, trace (page 259) or sketch the English Countryside landscape in pencil. To create a fun, edgy look, I chose to not tape my borders, but you can add painter's tape if you prefer.

STEP 2: Lightly erase the pencil markings. Using a size 14 round brush, paint the sky with Cerulean Blue. Clean and **load** your brush with Quinacridone Gold. Apply a **wash** over the bottom of the landscape.

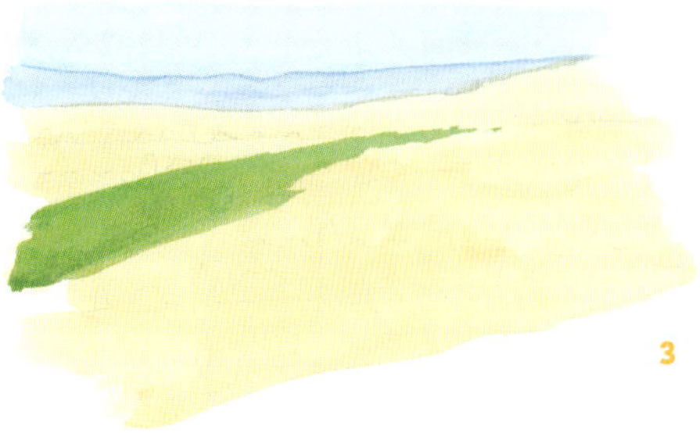

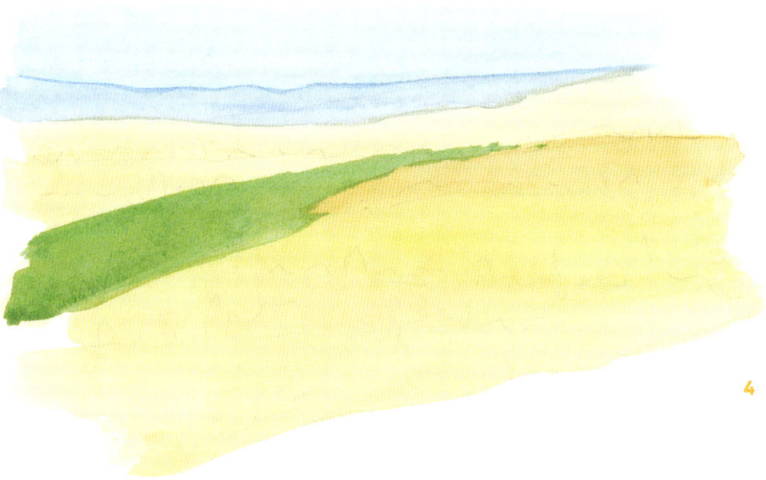

STEP 3: Moving forward, switch to the size 8 round brush. Using Ultramarine Blue, paint the mountain range in the **background**. With your brush, create little bumps at the top of the mountain range to signify peaks. On your palette, combine Winsor Green (50%) and Cadmium Orange (50%). Lay this green mixture in the middle of the countryside.

STEP 4: Apply a **glaze** in the **middle ground**. Start by painting in Yellow Ochre. This will be added farthest away. While that is still wet, paint Green Gold directly below it. If the two colors mix, that is okay.

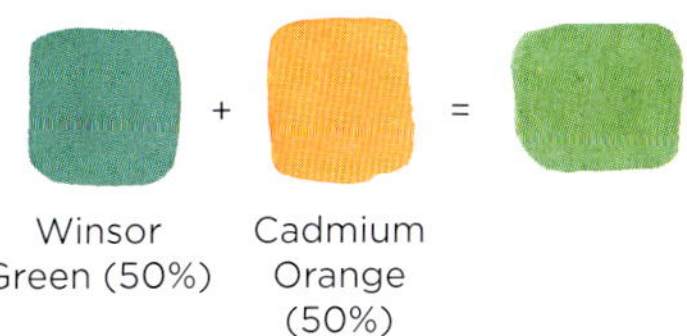

STEP 5: To add a bit more definition in the fields, add another **glaze** using a mix of Yellow Ochre (70%) and Winsor Red (30%). Create a light **value** by adding water into this mixture. Paint this **glaze** in the mid-**background**.

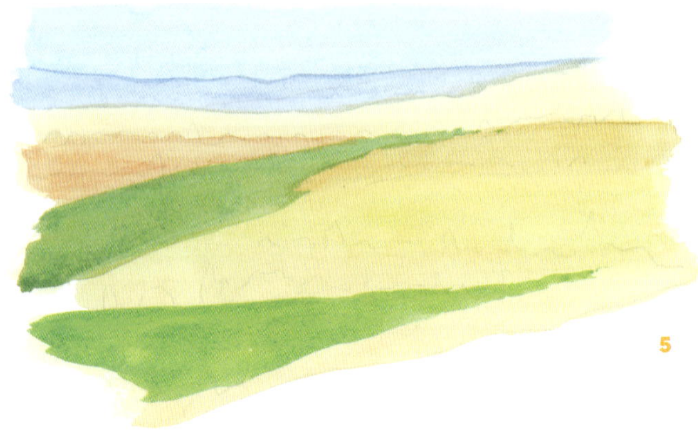

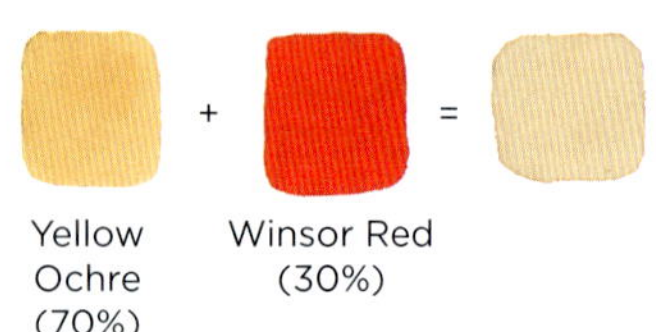

Yellow Ochre (70%) + Winsor Red (30%) =

Next, add a green **glaze** in the mid-**foreground**. Use Green Gold (70%) combined with Winsor Green (30%). Create a light **value** by adding water into this mixture.

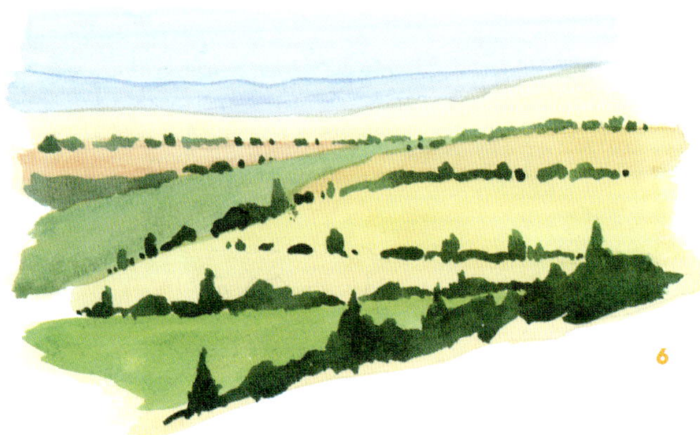

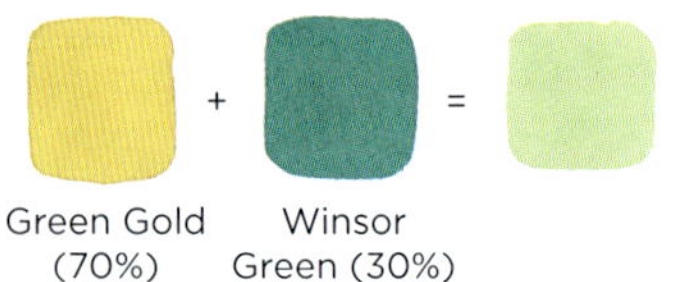

Green Gold (70%) + Winsor Green (30%) =

STEP 6: Time to add the trees! Mix Winsor Green (40%) with Cadmium Orange (30%) and a little bit of Ultramarine Blue (30%). Start by painting the trees in the **foreground** using a pointy jagged motion to make the illusion of a tree line. As you move deeper into the landscape, add more water to your mixture to lighten the **value**; this will make the trees less **saturated** and appear farther in the distance. You will also want to start turning your trees into little dots with less detail.

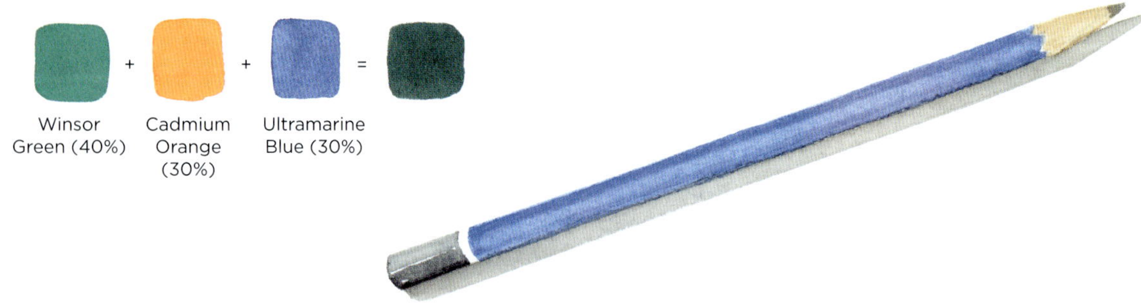

Winsor Green (40%) + Cadmium Orange (30%) + Ultramarine Blue (30%) =

SUNLIT FOREST

When painting something with thousands of the same object, like leaves on a tree, focus on groupings of light and dark shapes. You can put a single dot here or there to signify a leaf on the edges of those light and dark clusters. In this Sunlit Forest, we add large areas of shapes with layers of light, medium and dark greens to create foliage.

MATERIALS

Watercolor paper

Pencil

Painter's tape

Size 8 round brush

Size 2 round brush (optional)

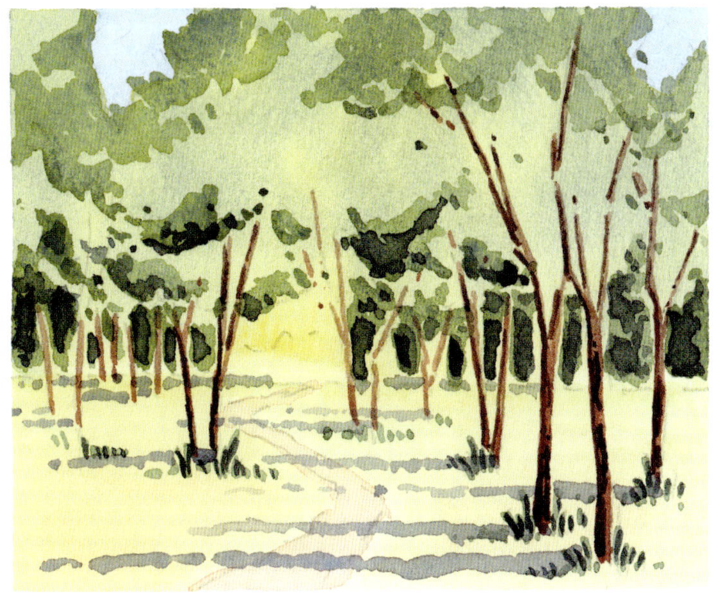

COLORS

Cobalt Blue

Lemon Yellow

Yellow Ochre

Green Gold

Winsor Red

Winsor Green

Ultramarine Blue

Alizarin Crimson

Indigo

STEP 1: On your watercolor paper, trace (page 261) or sketch the Sunlit Forest landscape in pencil. Apply painter's tape around the border of the painting.

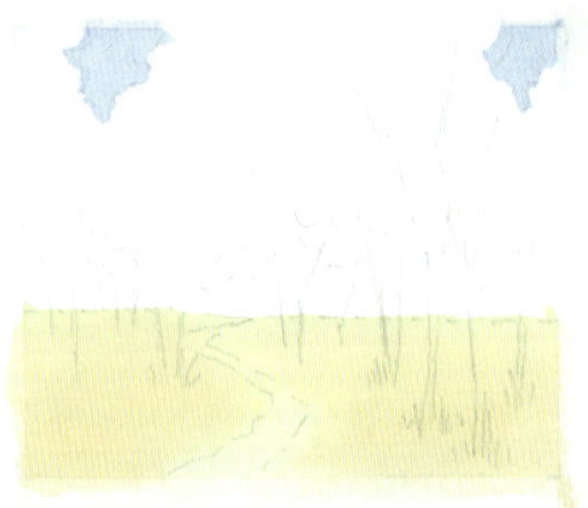

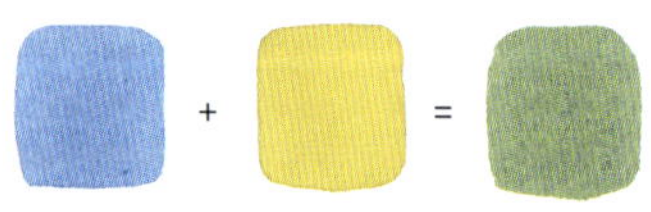

2

STEP 2: Lightly erase your pencil marks, but not too much because you need to be able to see the details. With a size 8 round brush, take Cobalt Blue and paint in the sky at the top. Paint Lemon Yellow on the bottom half of the landscape. While that is wet, lay Yellow Ochre over the Lemon Yellow everywhere except on the path (**wet-in-wet**).

STEP 3: On your palette, combine Cobalt Blue (50%) with Green Gold (50%). Clean your brush. Paint the top half of the landscape using Green Gold. Work **wet-in-wet** by taking the mixture from your palette and dotting it into the Green Gold in random spots; don't completely cover the Green Gold.

Cobalt Blue (50%) + Green Gold (50%) =

Add grass into the **fore-ground** and **middle ground** using the same mixture from your palette.

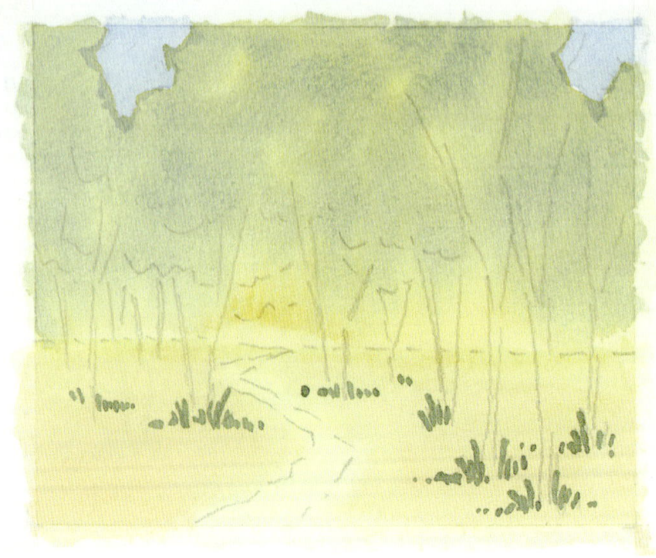

3

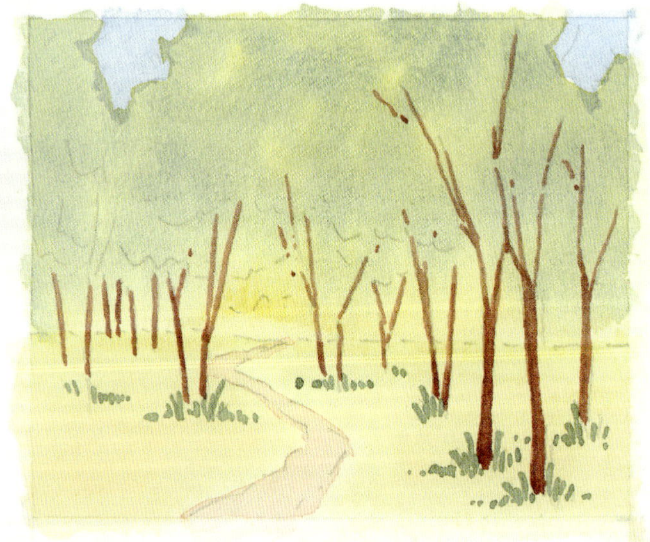

4

STEP 4: Paint a light **value** of Winsor Red along the path. Clean your brush and mix Winsor Red (70%) with Winsor Green (30%) on your palette. Use this mixture to paint in all the tree trunks. You can switch to a smaller brush (size 2) if you need to.

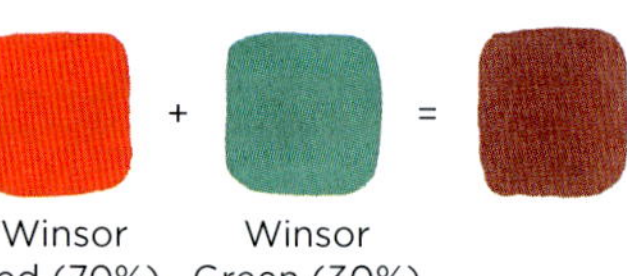

Winsor Red (70%) + Winsor Green (30%) =

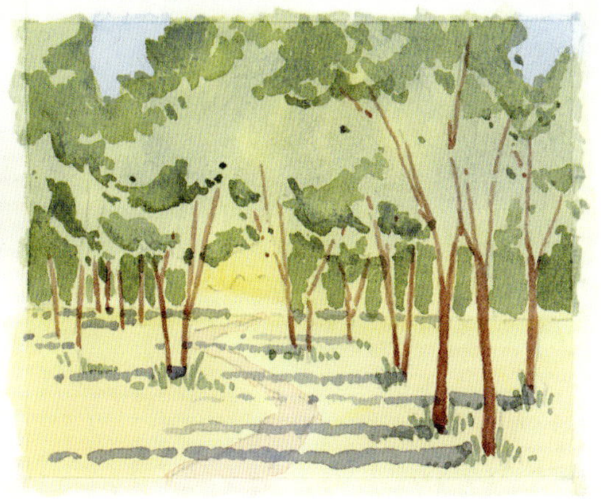

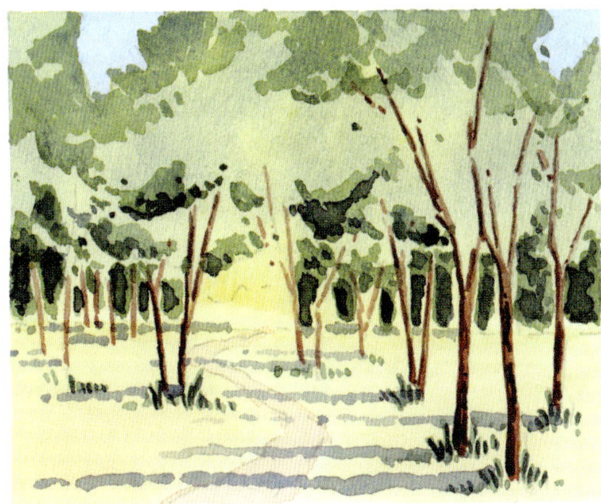

5

6

STEP 5: Combine Ultramarine Blue (70%) and Alizarin Crimson (30%) on your palette. Lighten the **value** of this mixture by adding water. Paint the **cast shadows** on the ground using this mixture. The **shadows** start on the left side of the tree trunks and continue in a line cast on the ground. If you want to lighten the **value** as you paint farther into the **background**, add more water into the mixture.

Paint a layer on your trees using this mixture from your palette: Cobalt Blue (50%) with Green Gold (50%). Use this color in between each of the trunks, avoiding the area where the path leads. Start shaping the foliage by applying this paint on the outer edges of the trees in a motion that starts with a dot, drags down and swoops in an arch in the direction the trees are facing.

STEP 6: Mix Winsor Red (70%) and Winsor Green (30%) on your palette, then paint in the **shadow** on the left side of the seven trunks in the **foreground**. You don't want to paint the trunks in completely; leave some of the first layer showing through.

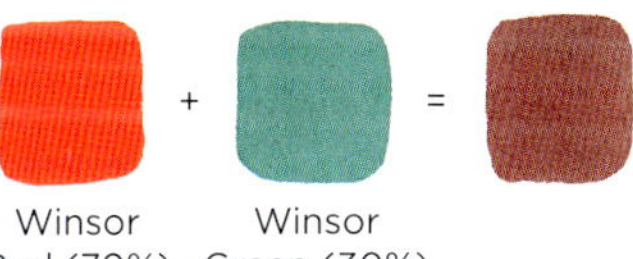

Winsor Red (70%)   Winsor Green (30%)

Use Indigo to darken the forest in the **middle ground**. Allow some of the other layers to show through. Also use Indigo to darken the blades of grass in the **foreground**.

Once your paint is dry, remove the painter's tape around the border.

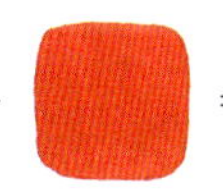 +  =

Ultramarine Blue (70%)   Alizarin Crimson (30%)

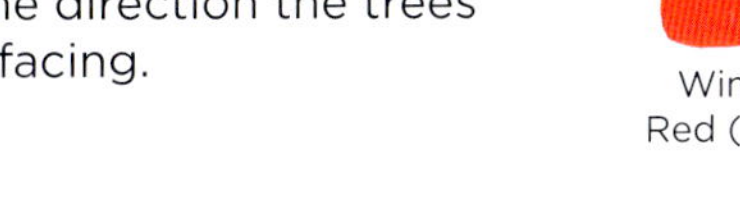

Cobalt Blue (50%)   Green Gold (50%)

SOUTHWEST

In this Southwest landscape, we paint a **gradient wash** in the sky. Using a **gradient wash** in the sky helps to naturally create the illusion of the atmosphere because the horizon is always lighter. A **gradient wash** against the orange rock formations also helps create depth. Creating a solid blue sky would make it appear flatter.

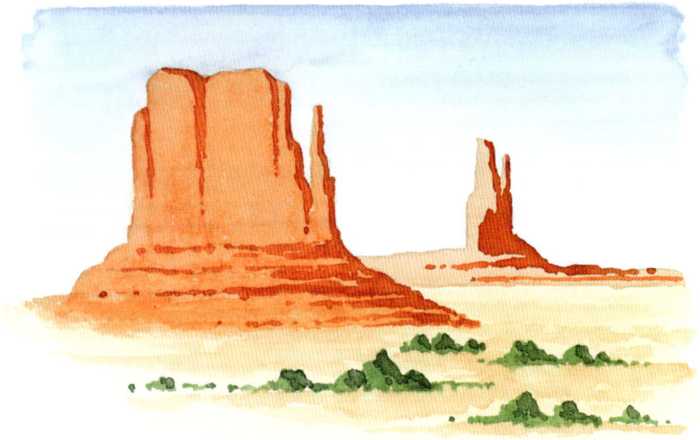

MATERIALS

Pencil

Watercolor paper

Size 2 mop brush

Size 8 round brush

COLORS

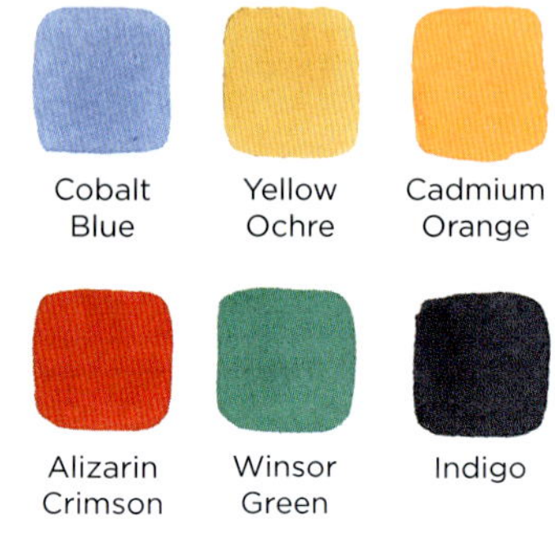

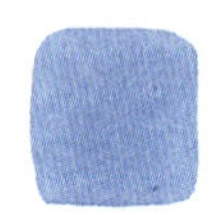

Cobalt Blue

Yellow Ochre

Cadmium Orange

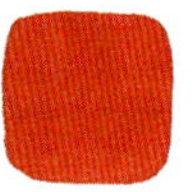

Alizarin Crimson

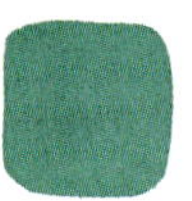

Winsor Green

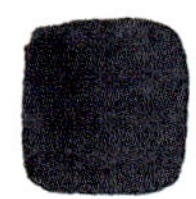

Indigo

Quinacridone Gold

1

2

STEP 1: Use a pencil to lightly trace (page 259) or sketch the Southwest landscape on your watercolor paper.

STEP 2: Create a **gradient wash** for the sky using Cobalt Blue and a size 2 mop brush. Let that dry.

Then take Yellow Ochre and paint the ground.

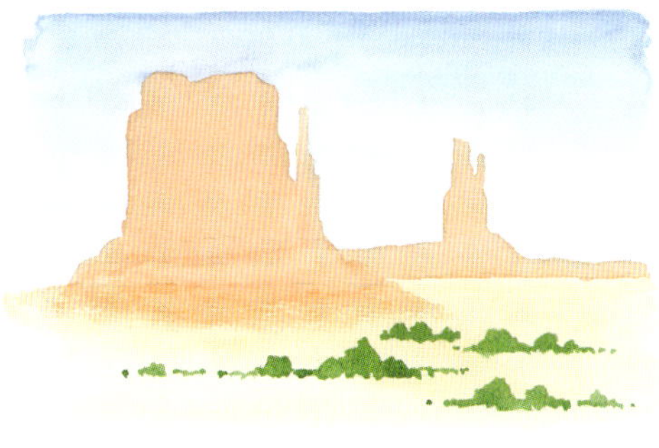

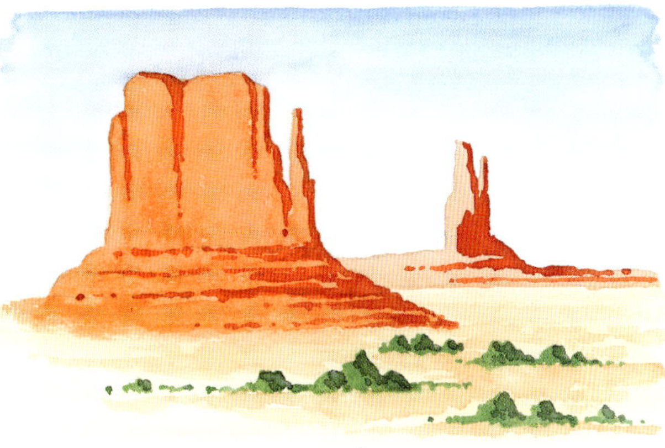

3

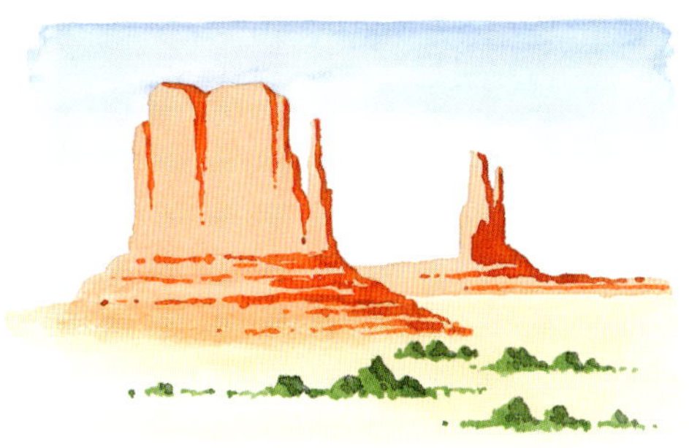

4

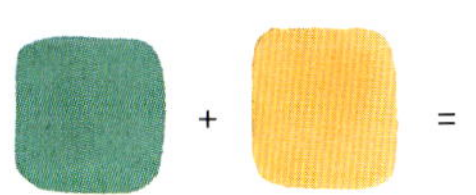

5

STEP 3: For the remainder of the painting, use your size 8 round brush. On your palette, combine Cadmium Orange (70%) with Alizarin Crimson (30%). **Load** your brush with this mixture and paint in the rock formation. As you get to the base of the mountain, don't reload your brush with paint; use the **dry brush** technique to taper the end to give the rock **texture**.

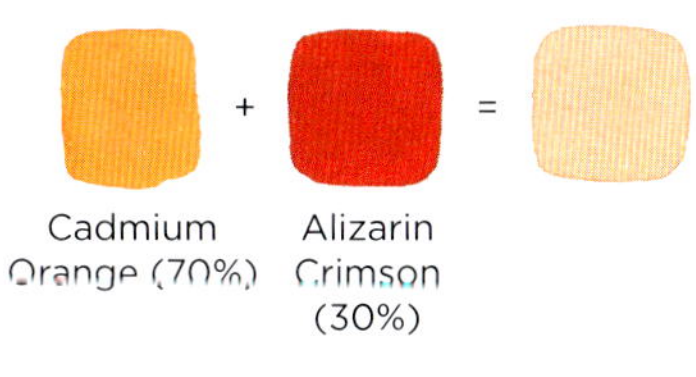

Cadmium Orange (70%) + Alizarin Crimson (30%)

Mix Winsor Green (60%) and Yellow Ochre (40%) on your palette. In a dotting motion, paint in the green shrubs using this mixture.

Winsor Green (60%) + Yellow Ochre (40%)

STEP 4: Mix Cadmium Orange (50%) with Alizarin Crimson (50%) on your palette. Paint the **shadows** on the right side of the rock formations using this color mixture.

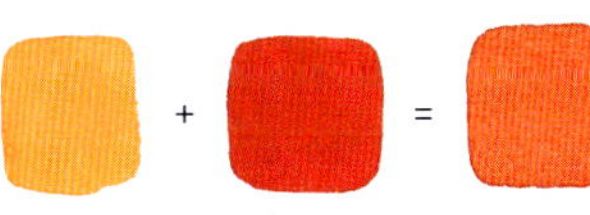

Cadmium Orange (50%) + Alizarin Crimson (50%)

Take Indigo and apply it as a **glaze** on the right side of the bushes for **shadows**.

STEP 5: Mix Quinacridone Gold (70%) with Alizarin Crimson (30%) on your palette. Use this mixture to apply a **glaze** on the **middle ground** rock formation. Once you finish painting the **glaze** on the **middle ground** rock formation, pull the **glaze** into the **foreground** underneath the bushes. Don't completely cover the initial Yellow Ochre layer.

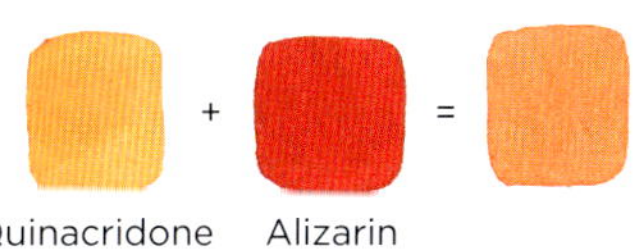

Quinacridone Gold (70%) + Alizarin Crimson (30%) =

SNOWY MOUNTAIN

To create a monochromatic painting in watercolor, only one color and water is used. Varying the **water-to-paint ratio** changes the **values** of the color. By only using Indigo and water, this Snowy Mountain landscape comes to life! In most of the paintings in this book, the **water-to-paint ratio** is only described; however, in this painting as well as the Humpback Whale (page 130) and Fishing Boat (page 207) paintings, the mixtures show a water droplet, visually representing the **water-to-paint ratio**.

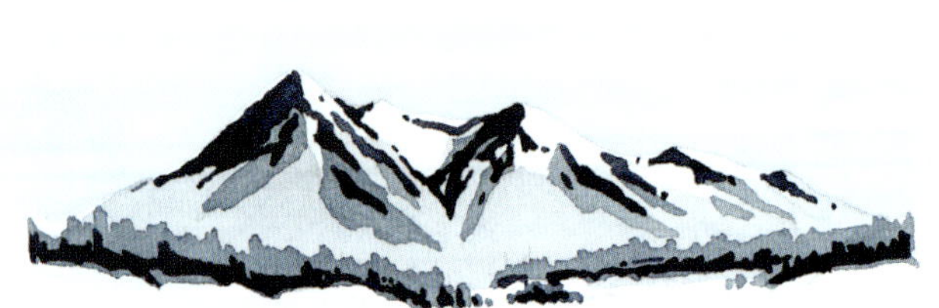

MATERIALS

Pencil
Watercolor paper
Size 8 round brush

COLORS

Indigo

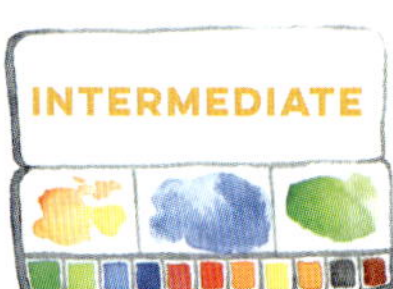

STEP 1: Take your pencil and lightly trace (page 257) or sketch the Snowy Mountain landscape on your watercolor paper.

STEP 2: Lightly erase the pencil marks. For the **fore-ground**, use your lightest **value** of Indigo, which is a mixture of mostly water (90%) with a little bit of Indigo (10%). With a size 8 round brush, loosely paint this into the **foreground,** leaving spaces of white showing through. To create a slightly darker **value** than what was used for the **foreground**, mix water (70%) and Indigo (30%). Use this darker **value** to paint the base of the mountain range, leaving the tips of the mountains white to signify snow.

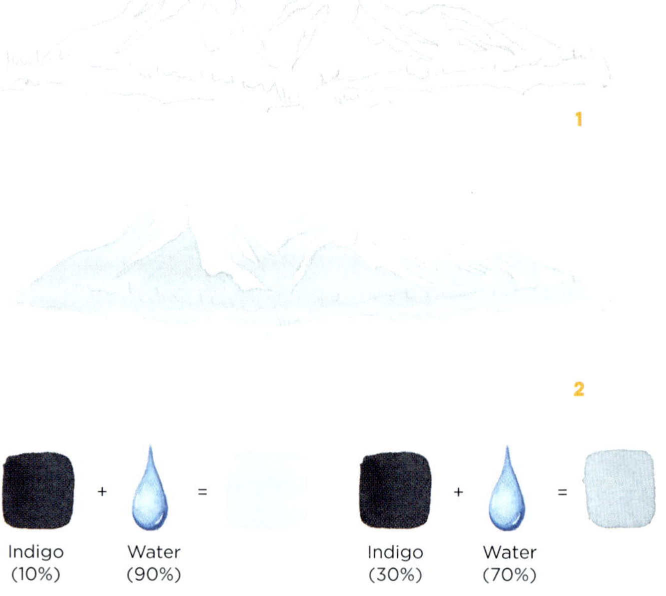

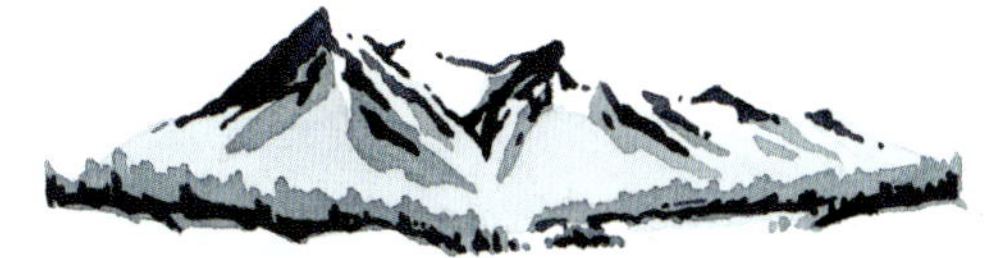

3

4

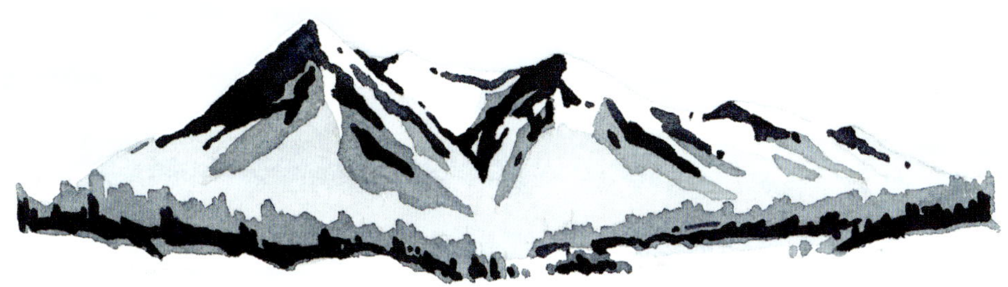

5

STEP 3: Paint the tree line and **shadows** on the mountain using your next, slightly darker, **value**: water (50%) and Indigo (50%). To paint the tree line, use little jagged strokes at the top to create the look of treetops in the distance. To apply the **shadows**, make sure to keep the shapes geometric (the shapes should have sharper characteristics to them).

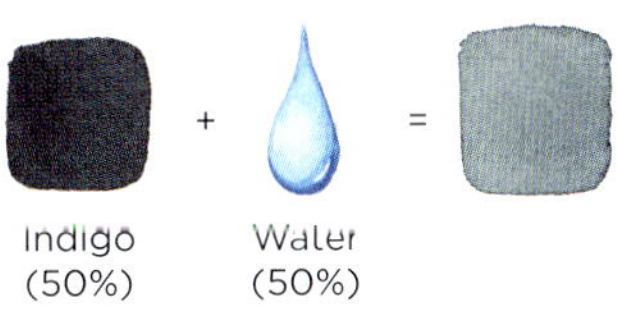

Indigo (50%) + Water (50%) =

STEP 4: The darkest **value** is for the detailing on the mountain and tree line. Mix Indigo (70%) with water (30%). When painting the tree line with this mixture, add small, jagged details to the base. For the mountain, start painting at the top and work your way down in a similar way to the geometric shapes used in Step 3. Remember to still leave some of the white showing for the snow.

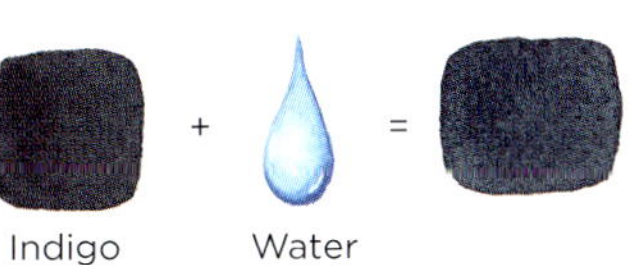

Indigo (70%) + Water (30%) =

STEP 5: For the final step, go back to your lightest **value** that you painted on the **foreground**: water (90%) and Indigo (10%). Apply this mixture to your sky. After you paint in the sky, all of a sudden, your snow pops! This is because the white of the snow is your lightest **value** in the **value scale**. For the brightest **highlights** in watercolor, you need to save the white of your paper because watercolor does not have white opaque paint.

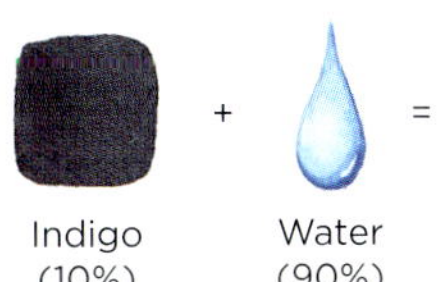

Indigo (10%) + Water (90%) =

ITALIAN LAKESIDE

One way to create depth in a landscape painting is to use atmospheric perspective. This is done by having light **values** in the **background** and darker **values** in the **foreground**. In this Italian Lakeside landscape, we add more water to the mixture for the houses farther away to create the illusion that they are in the distance. Atmospheric perspective is also used in the Golden Gate Bridge painting (page 87) and the English Countryside painting (page 148).

MATERIALS

Watercolor paper
Pencil
Painter's tape
Sharpie felt-tip pen
Size 8 round brush
Paper towel

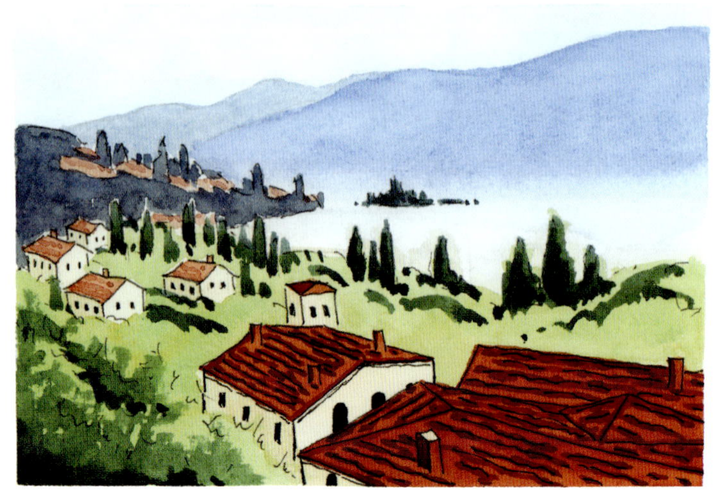

COLORS

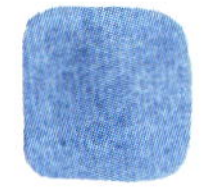
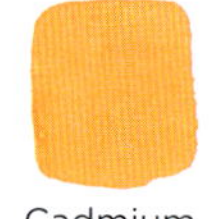
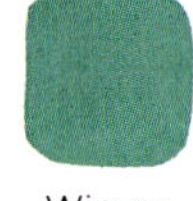
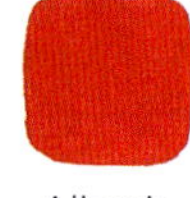

Cerulean Blue   Ultramarine Blue   Cadmium Orange   Winsor Green   Alizarin Crimson

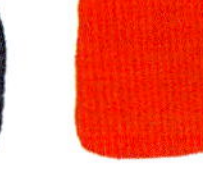
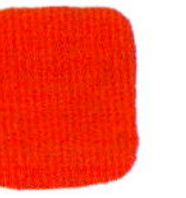
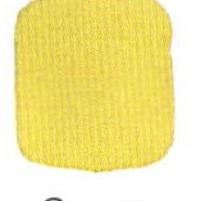
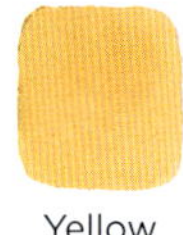

Indigo   Winsor Red   Green Gold   Yellow Ochre

STEP 1: Trace (page 261) or lightly sketch the Italian Lakeside landscape on your watercolor paper in pencil.

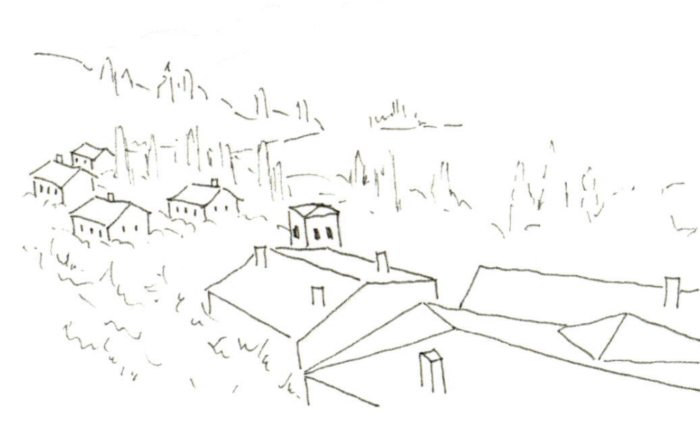

STEP 2: Very lightly erase the pencil markings; you still want to see the lines since this is a detailed landscape. Using painter's tape, add a border around your drawing. Now, use a Sharpie to add ink over the pencil lines, except for the two mountains in the **background** and the waterline that touches the **background** mountain.

STEP 3: On your palette, use your size 8 round brush to mix Cerulean Blue (80%) with a touch of Ultramarine Blue (20%). Clean your brush, then apply a **clear water wash** on the top half of your paper (sky, mountains and lake). Once you have added the clear water to the top half of the paper, use the **wet-in-wet** technique to add the blue mixture into the watered top half (sky, mountains and lake).

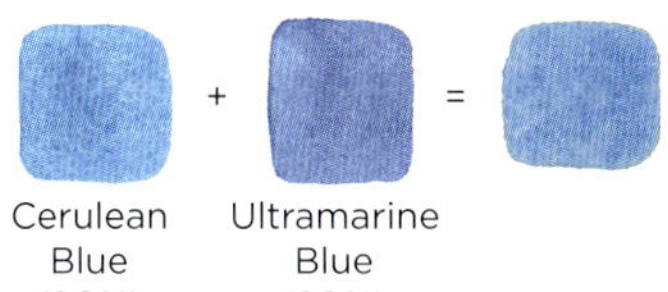

Cerulean Blue (80%) + Ultramarine Blue (20%) =

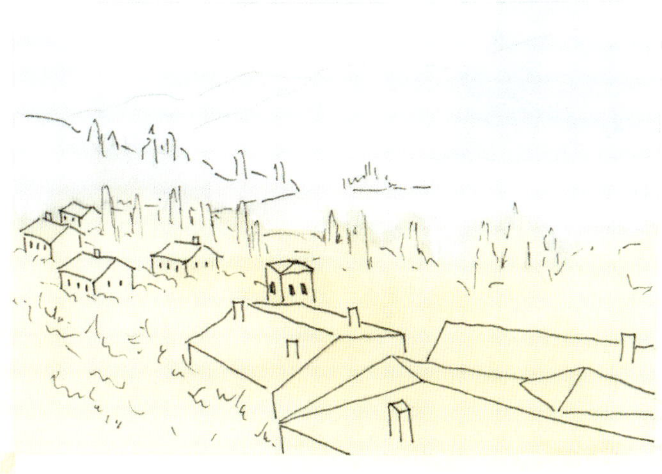

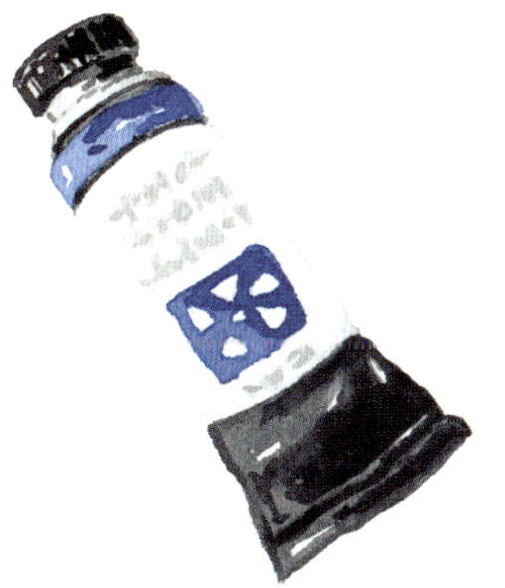

While the sky is still wet, **blot** out some clouds behind the mountain. To **blot**, use a paper towel in light dabbing motions to soak up the area.

On the bottom half of your painting, wet the paper with a **clear water wash**. Use a light **value** of Cadmium Orange to paint into the water (**wet-in-wet**).

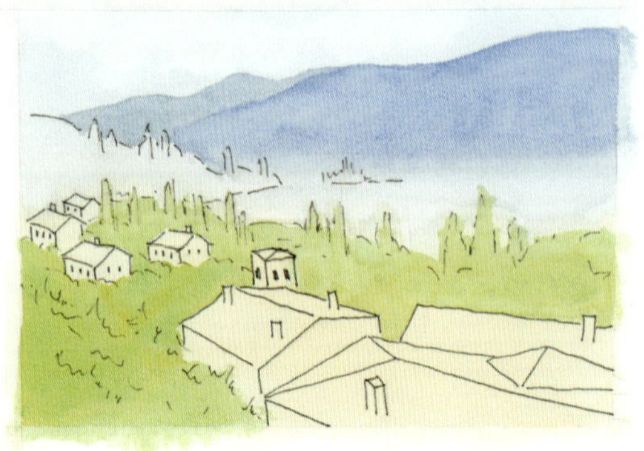 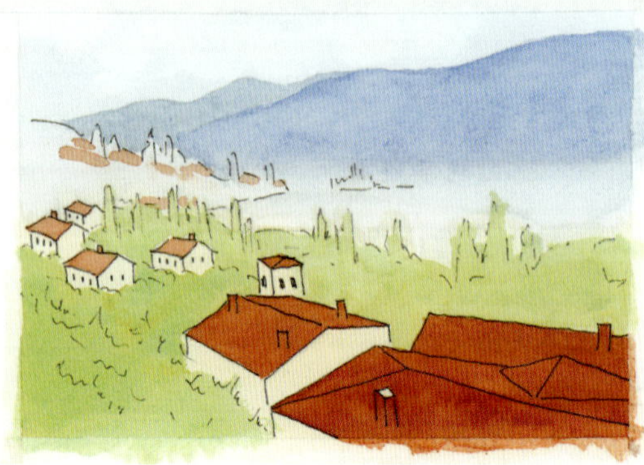

STEP 4: Combine Cerulean Blue (80%) with a touch of Ultramarine Blue (20%) on your palette. Make sure to lighten the **value** of the color mixture by adding water; in a landscape, mountains are lighter in color the farther back they go. Paint in the farthest mountain in the **background** of your painting using this color mixture.

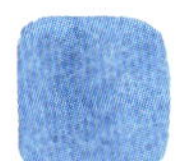 + 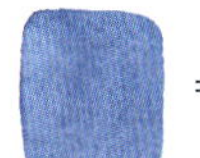 =

Cerulean Blue (80%)

Ultramarine Blue (20%)

Paint the **background** mountain that touches the lake using Cerulean Blue (70%) with a bit more Ultramarine Blue (30%). Lighten the **value** of that mixture by adding water. Use this mixture to paint in your biggest mountains.

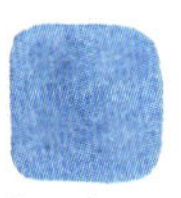 + =

Cerulean Blue (70%)

Ultramarine Blue (30%)

Where the mountain line reaches the lake, create a **soft edge**. Do this by adding a little water on your brush and slowly pulling the paint from the mountain down into the lake. Pull it until the color fades out.

On your palette, mix Cadmium Orange (70%) with Winsor Green (30%). **Load** your brush with this mixture and paint in the green **foreground**, avoiding the houses.

 + 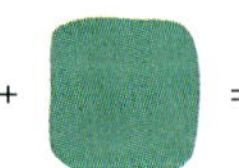 = 

Cadmium Orange (70%)

Winsor Green (30%)

STEP 5: Mix Cadmium Orange (50%), Alizarin Crimson (40%) and Ultramarine Blue (10%) on your palette. Lighten the **value** of this color mixture by adding a touch of water. Paint the roofs on the first three houses in the **foreground**. To paint the four roofs in the **middle ground**, take the color mixture and add more water to create a lighter **value**. Repeat this process of lightening the mixture's **value** one more time, then paint in the roofs in the **background**. We didn't draw in the houses in the **background**, so when you paint in the roofs, use slanted rectangular shapes to block them in on the paper (the slanted rectangular shapes help indicate that these houses are on a hillside).

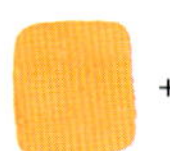 + 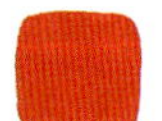 + 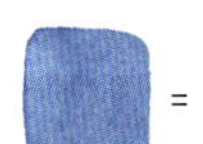 =

Cadmium Orange (50%)

Alizarin Crimson (40%)

Ultramarine Blue (10%)

STEP 6: On your palette, combine Cadmium Orange (50%), Alizarin Crimson (40%) and Ultramarine Blue (10%). Using this mixture, paint the roof shingles on the three houses in the **foreground**. Paint the roof shingles as a bumpy line across the roofs. For the four homes in the **middle ground**, lighten the **value** of the color mixture before painting the roof shingles. Lighten the **value** of your color mixture one last time. Use that lightened mixture to paint the roof shingles on the roofs in the **background**. This will be one bumpy line on top of the roofs.

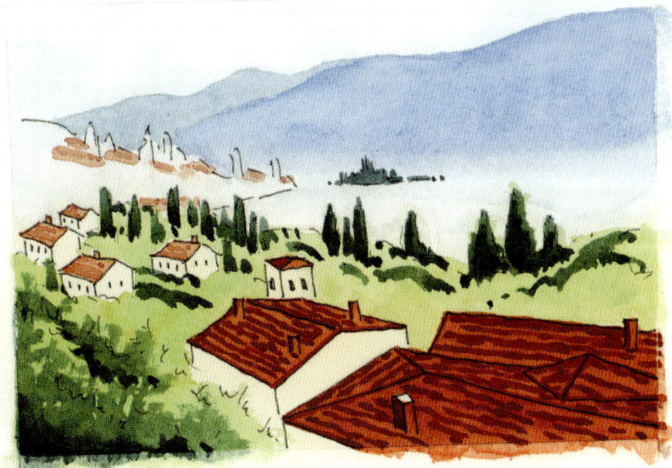

6

 + 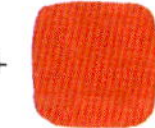 + 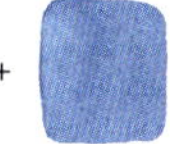 = 

Cadmium Orange (50%) Alizarin Crimson (40%) Ultramarine Blue (10%)

Combine Winsor Green (50%), Indigo (30%) and Winsor Red (20%) on your palette. Paint in the trees in the **foreground** and on the island in the lake. You will want these trees to be nice and dark, so you may need to go in with a second layer.

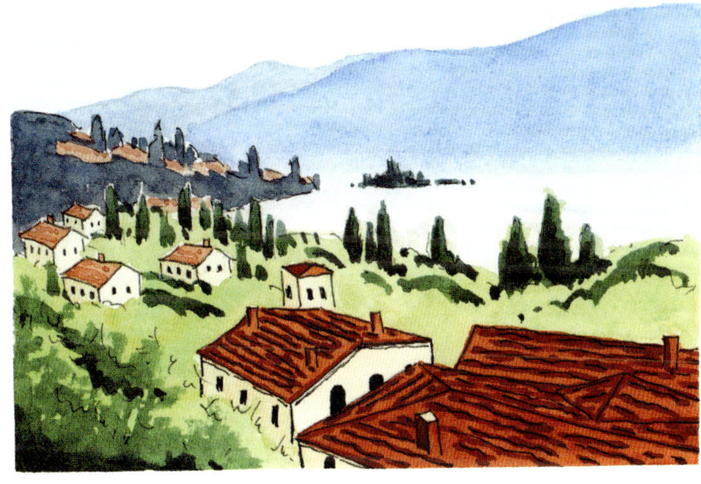

7

 + 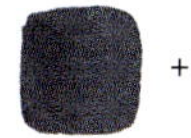 + 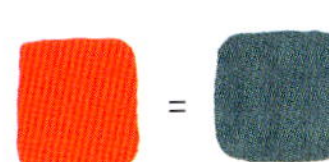 = 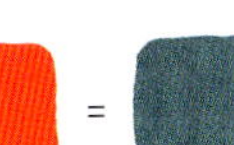

Winsor Green (50%) Indigo (30%) Winsor Red (20%)

STEP 7: Use Yellow Ochre to paint the left sides of the houses; this will darken them and act as the **shadow** side. Let this dry before moving forward.

Mix Ultramarine Blue (80%) and Green Gold (20%) on your palette. Take this mixture and paint in the mountain in the **middle ground**.

With your pen, add some black windows on the houses. Also, add a little ink to the roofs as well.

Once your painting is dry, remove the tape.

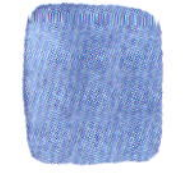 + 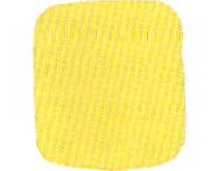 = 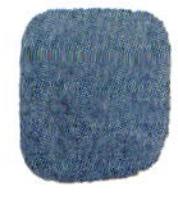

Ultramarine Blue (80%) Green Gold (20%)

IN THE FIELDS

It can be fun to draw outside the lines. For this landscape, I have a border framing where the painting should go. But to add a twist, I have drawn some of the landscape escaping the frame to add an "outside the box" effect.

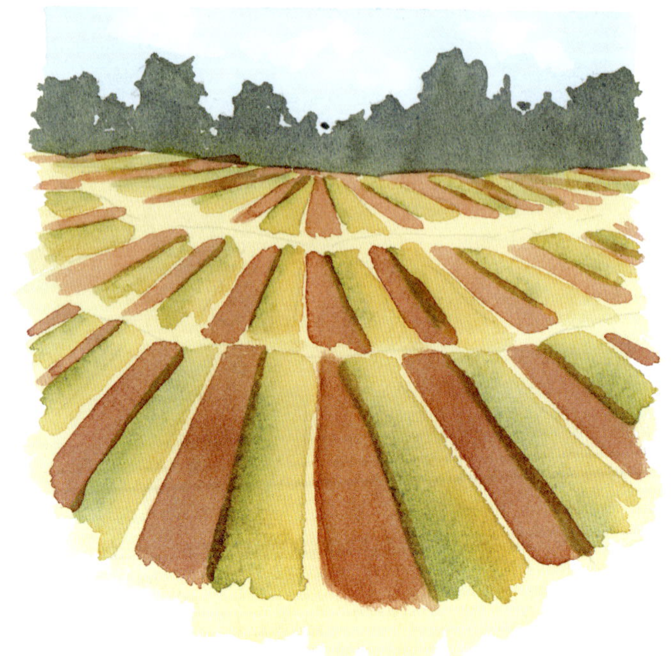

MATERIALS

Pencil

Watercolor paper

Painter's tape

Size 2 mop brush

Paper towel

Size 8 round brush

COLORS

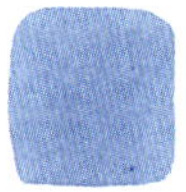
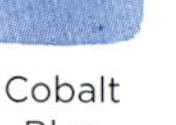
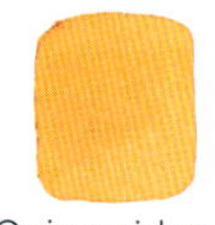
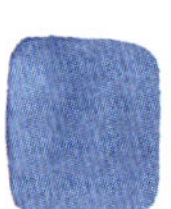
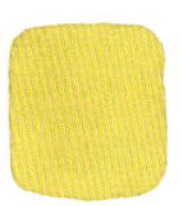
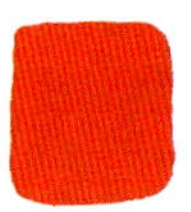
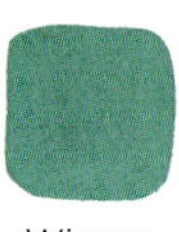
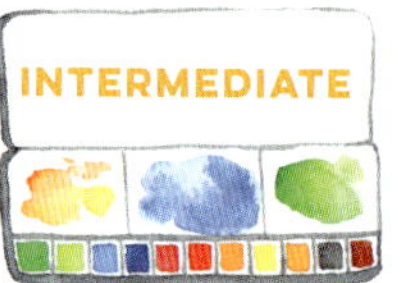

Cobalt Blue · Quinacridone Gold · Ultramarine Blue · Green Gold · Winsor Red · Winsor Green

STEP 1: Use your pencil to lightly trace (page 263) or sketch the In the Fields landscape on your watercolor paper. Use painter's tape on the top so you get a crisp edge at that end.

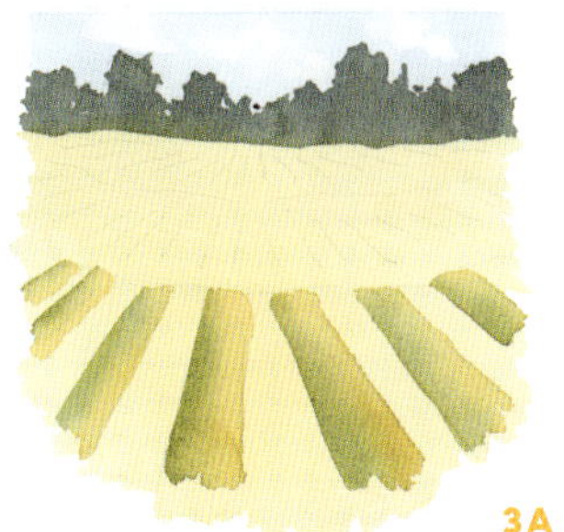

2

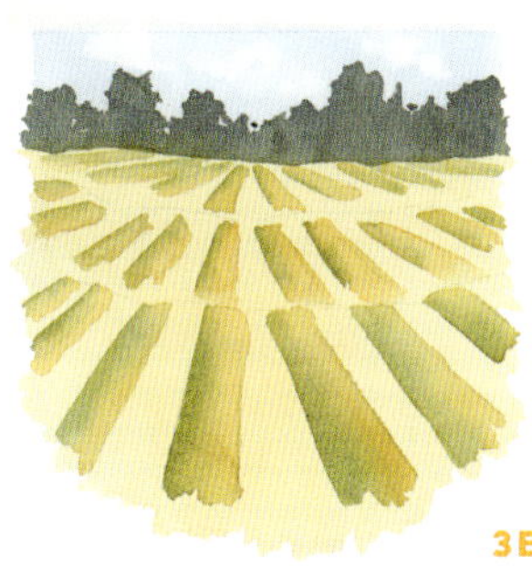

3A

3B

STEP 2: For the sky, use a mop brush to paint a Cobalt Blue **wash**. Carry this all the way down to the field line (it's okay to paint over the trees). While it is still wet, take a paper towel and **blot** out areas of the sky to create clouds. Rinse and **load** your brush with Quinacridone Gold, then use that color to paint a **wash** over the field. If your sky and field **bleed** a little, that is okay.

STEP 3: Take Ultramarine Blue (70%) and mix it with Green Gold (30%) on your palette. Switch to your size 8 round brush, then use this mixture to paint in the trees in the **background**, leaving some of the first layer of sky showing through. Let that dry.

On your palette, mix Green Gold (70%) with Cobalt Blue (30%). Use this to paint on the left side of every other column of field. While that is wet, lay Quinacridone Gold on the right side of every other column so this **bleeds** in with the mixture on the left.

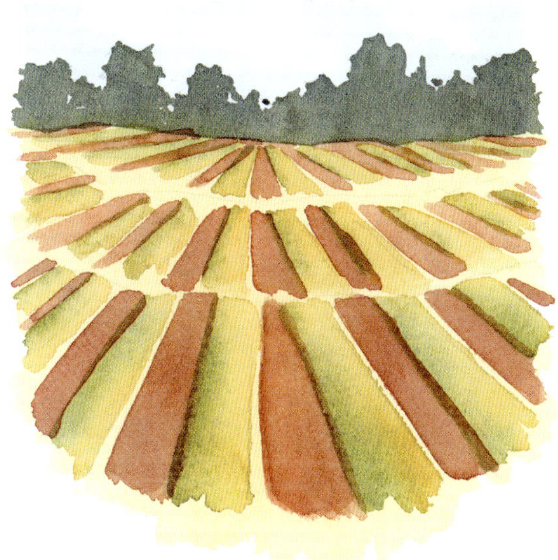

4

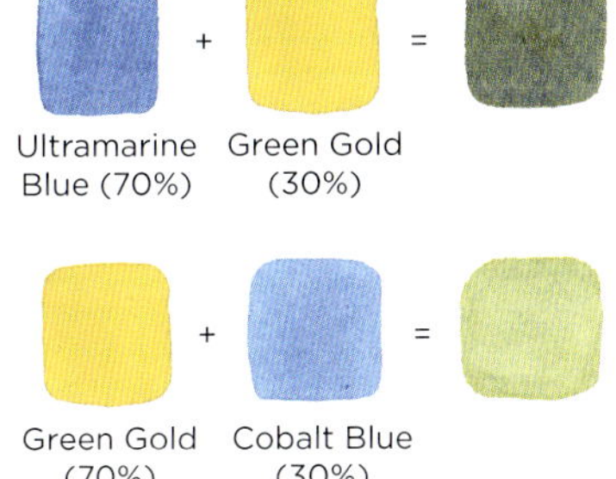

Ultramarine Blue (70%) + Green Gold (30%) =

Green Gold (70%) + Cobalt Blue (30%) =

STEP 4: Paint in the dirt in the fields with a Winsor Red (80%) and Winsor Green (20%) mixture from your palette. For a little **highlight** on the ground, don't paint the brown all the way to the left side; leave that yellow layer showing through. When painting the brown mixture, lay it over part of the green field so it acts as a **shadow**.

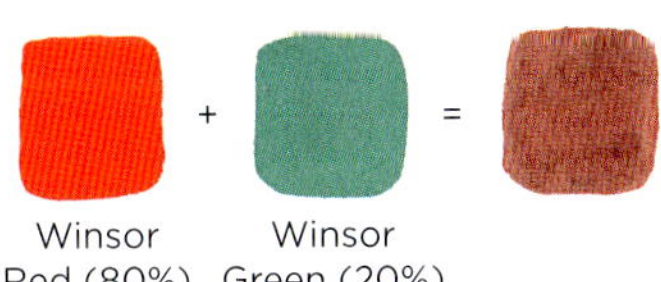

Winsor Red (80%) + Winsor Green (20%) =

'TIS THE SEASONS

When the seasons change, and the weather starts turning warmer or cooler, it always brings a sense of excitement for the traditions in each season. Even though I love fall, it wouldn't be as unique if it lasted half the year or even longer. Each season can only be enjoyed for a short while before it's time to change, making them so beautiful and cherished. Each time a new one comes around, it is like a breath of fresh air. As you go through these paintings, I hope you will feel the warmth of spring and summer and the coolness of fall and winter.

MAPLE LEAF

To get a beautiful, rich color for this Maple Leaf painting, we need to not only paint **wet-in-wet**, but we also need to have generous amounts of paint for high **saturation**, since watercolor dries into a lighter **value**. It may be tempting to think your color is perfect while it is wet, but once it dries, you'll quickly notice that it has become less **saturated**. To fix this problem, add extra pigment (paint) to the leaf.

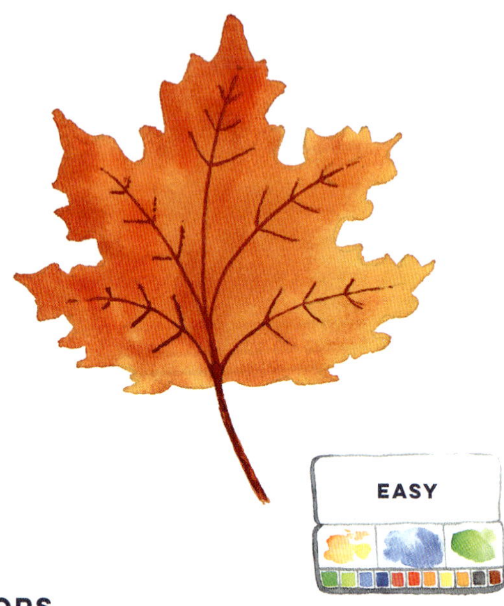

MATERIALS

Pencil

Watercolor paper

Size 8 round brush

Size 2 round brush (optional)

COLORS

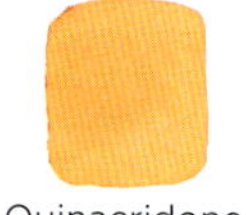 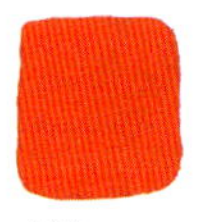 

| Quinacridone Gold | Cadmium Orange | Winsor Red | Alizarin Crimson | Winsor Green |

STEP 1: Trace (page 263) or lightly sketch the maple leaf in pencil on your watercolor paper.

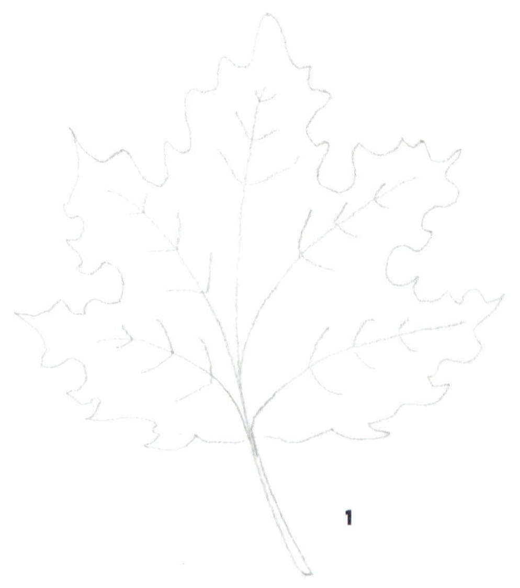

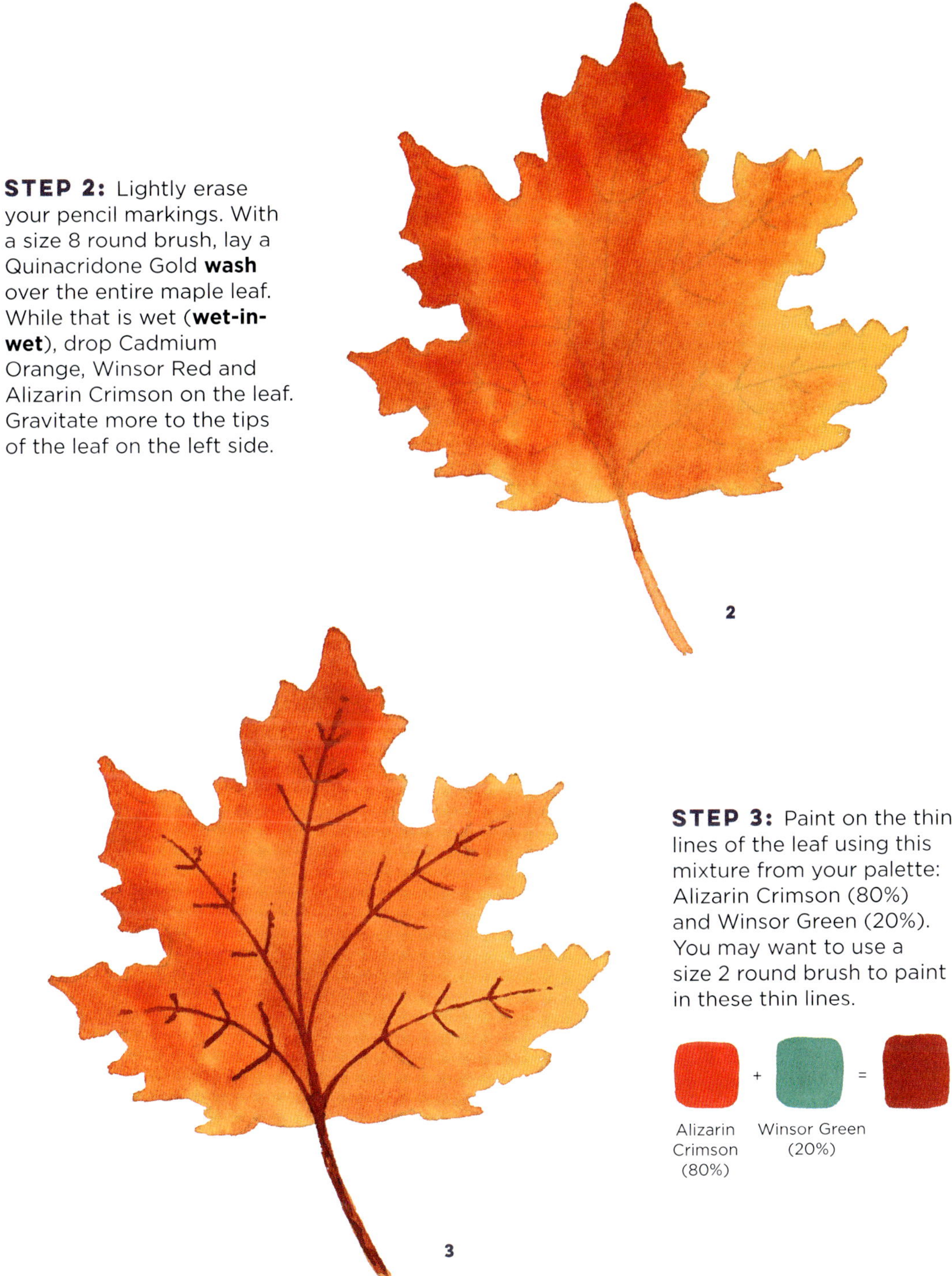

STEP 2: Lightly erase your pencil markings. With a size 8 round brush, lay a Quinacridone Gold **wash** over the entire maple leaf. While that is wet (**wet-in-wet**), drop Cadmium Orange, Winsor Red and Alizarin Crimson on the leaf. Gravitate more to the tips of the leaf on the left side.

STEP 3: Paint on the thin lines of the leaf using this mixture from your palette: Alizarin Crimson (80%) and Winsor Green (20%). You may want to use a size 2 round brush to paint in these thin lines.

SCARF

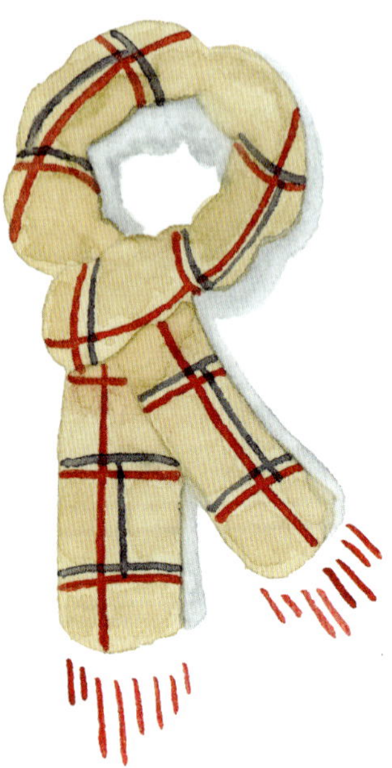

When trying to paint a **cast shadow**, you may wonder, as others commonly do, which color should you use? If you don't have a reference photo to look at to figure out the color of the **cast shadow**, use either a **complementary color** or a color in the object. Picking a color in the object for the **cast shadow** can add harmony and unity to the painting. For this Scarf painting, we use the same blue from the stripes for the **cast shadow**. For the placement of the **cast shadow**, follow along the right edge of the scarf and inside the loop.

MATERIALS

Pencil
Watercolor paper
Size 8 round brush
Size 2 round brush

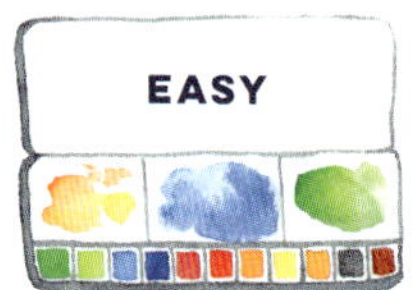

COLORS

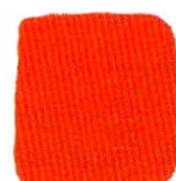

Yellow
Ochre

Indigo

Winsor
Red

STEP 1: Take your pencil and lightly trace (page 265) or sketch the scarf on your watercolor paper.

STEP 2: On your palette, mix Yellow Ochre (80%) and Indigo (20%). With a size 8 round brush, paint this mixture as a **wash** over the entire scarf.

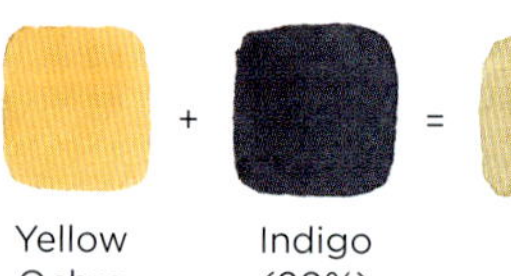

Yellow
Ochre
(80%)

+

Indigo
(20%)

=

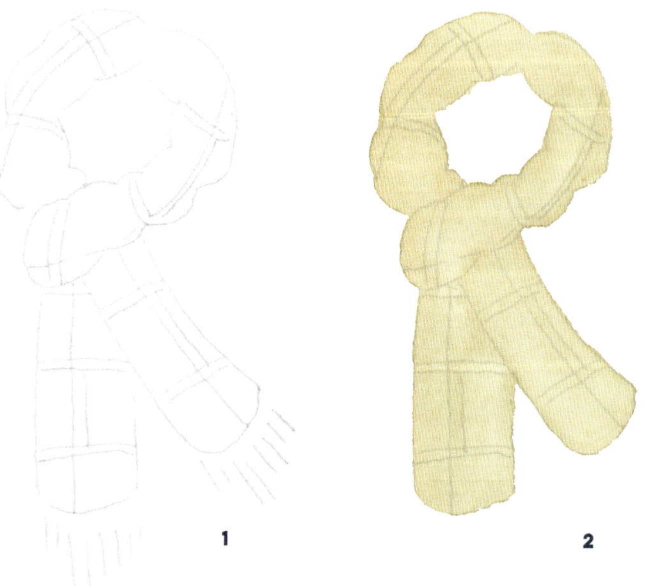

1

2

STEP 3: Take Winsor Red (80%) and mix it with Indigo (20%) on your palette. Use this mixture and a size 2 round brush to paint in the thin red lines of the scarf and the tassels.

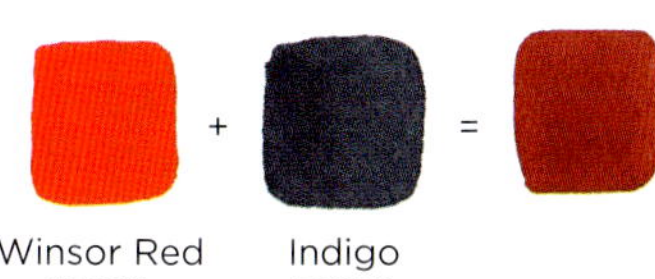

Winsor Red (80%) + Indigo (20%) =

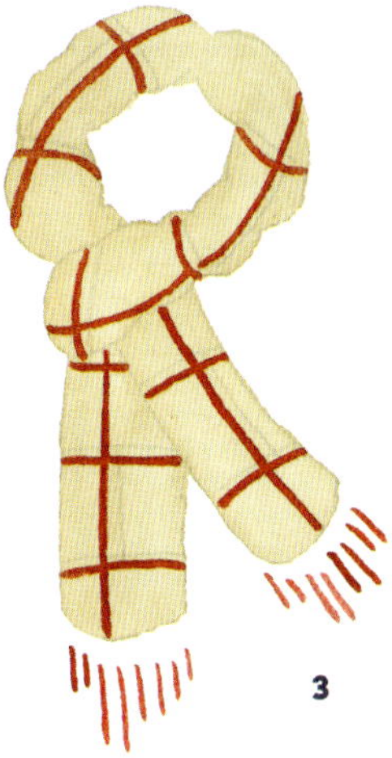

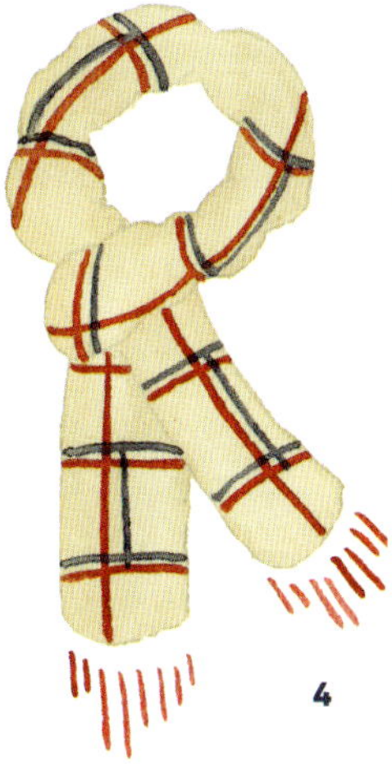

STEP 4: Use Indigo to paint the remaining thin lines on the scarf.

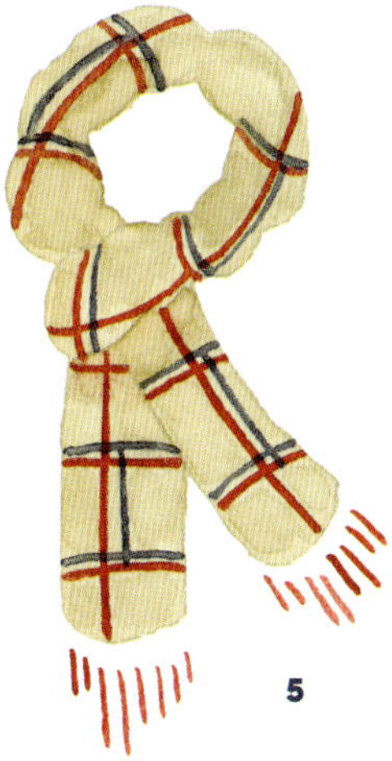

STEP 5: Take Yellow Ochre (80%) and mix it with Indigo (20%) on your palette. Add water to this mixture to get a light **value**. The goal is to achieve a cloth **texture**, so the scarf doesn't look flat. Do this by painting a **glaze** on all the dark yellow scarf areas, avoiding the red and indigo lines. Don't completely cover your first layer of yellow; it is okay if that layer shows through.

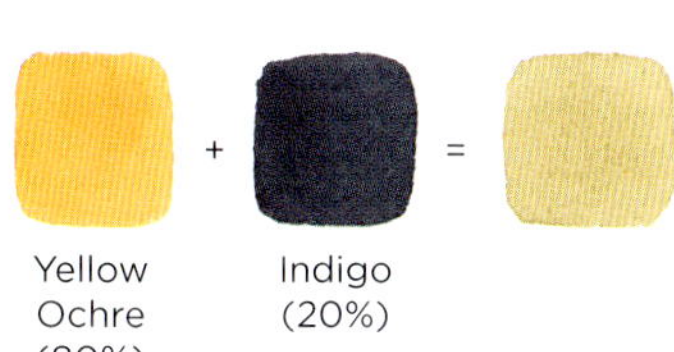

Yellow Ochre (80%) + Indigo (20%) =

STEP 6: Take a light **value** of Indigo and paint in the **shadow** on the ground to the right of the scarf.

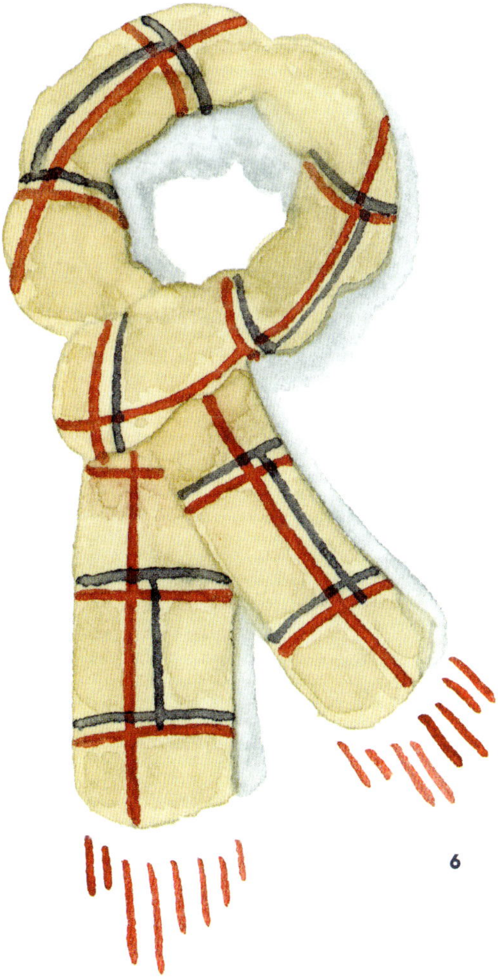

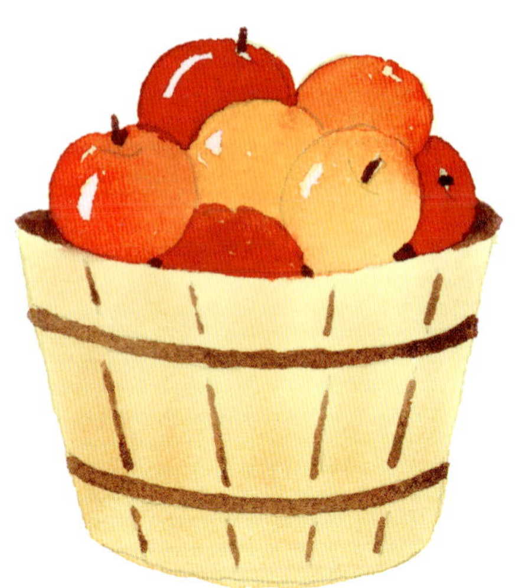

APPLE PICKING

When painting the apples and bucket, a layer of Lemon Yellow over our entire painting helps warm all the subsequent layers on top. Having the Lemon Yellow also helps unify the painting by having the same under-layer across the entire **subject**.

MATERIALS

Pencil
Watercolor paper
Size 8 round brush

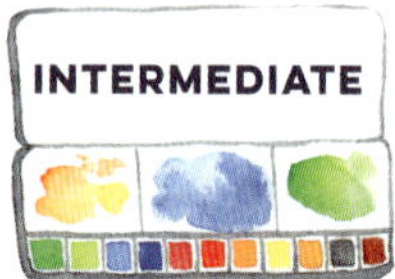

COLORS

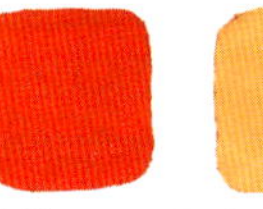
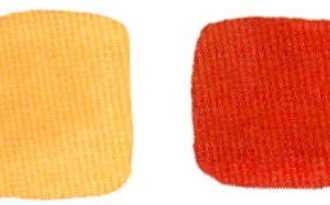
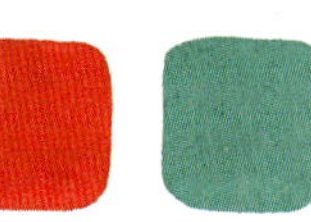

| Lemon Yellow | Yellow Ochre | Winsor Red | Quinacridone Gold | Alizarin Crimson | Winsor Green |

STEP 1: Use a pencil to lightly trace (page 263) or sketch the apples and bucket onto your watercolor paper.

STEP 2: Load your size 8 round brush with Lemon Yellow and paint a **wash** over the apples and the bucket. Leave a **highlight** on four of the apples. Using the **wet-in-wet** technique, dot Yellow Ochre into each rectangle on the bucket. You want the Yellow Ochre to **bleed** into the wet Lemon Yellow.

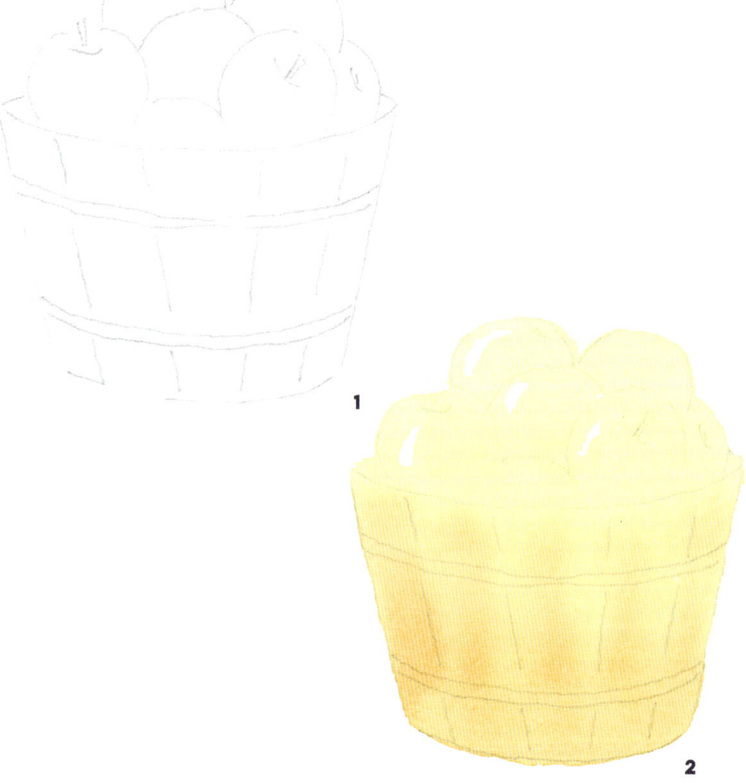

STEP 3: Use Winsor Red to paint the apple on the farthest left and the right apple on the top. Avoid painting in the **highlights** and apple stems. Clean and **load** your brush with Quinacridone Gold, and paint in the three middle apples. Because the paint is still wet, the Winsor Red and Quinacridone Gold apple colors will **bleed**, and you want that because it creates more than one color on the apples, which looks more realistic.

STEP 4: On your palette, mix Winsor Red (60%) and Alizarin Crimson (40%). Use this to paint the apple at the top, the apple on the bottom right, and the middle apple that's touching the bucket. Avoid painting the **highlights** and the apple stems.

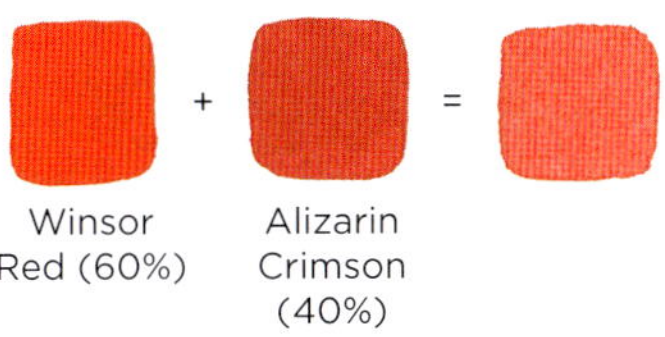

Winsor Red (60%) + Alizarin Crimson (40%) =

STEP 5: Combine Winsor Red (70%) with Winsor Green (30%) on your palette. Use this mixture to paint in the apple stems, the horizontal stripes and the vertical wood slats on the bucket. When you paint in the thin, vertical wood slats, don't make it a continuous line; leave gaps in between the vertical lines. Use this brown mixture to fill in the dark areas inside the bucket.

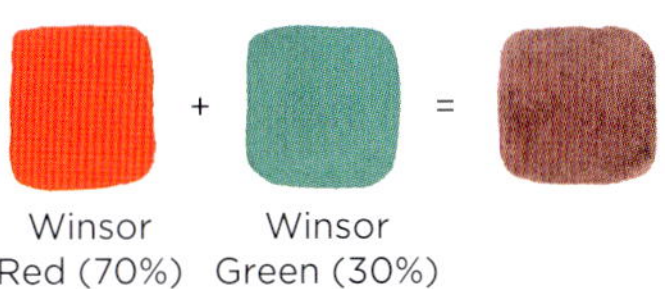

Winsor Red (70%) + Winsor Green (30%) =

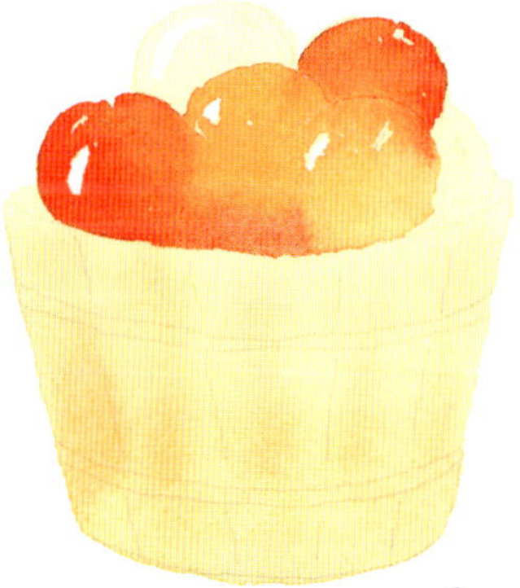

3

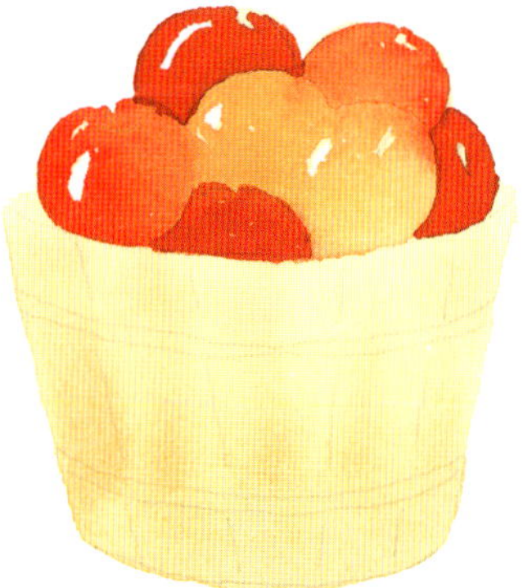

4

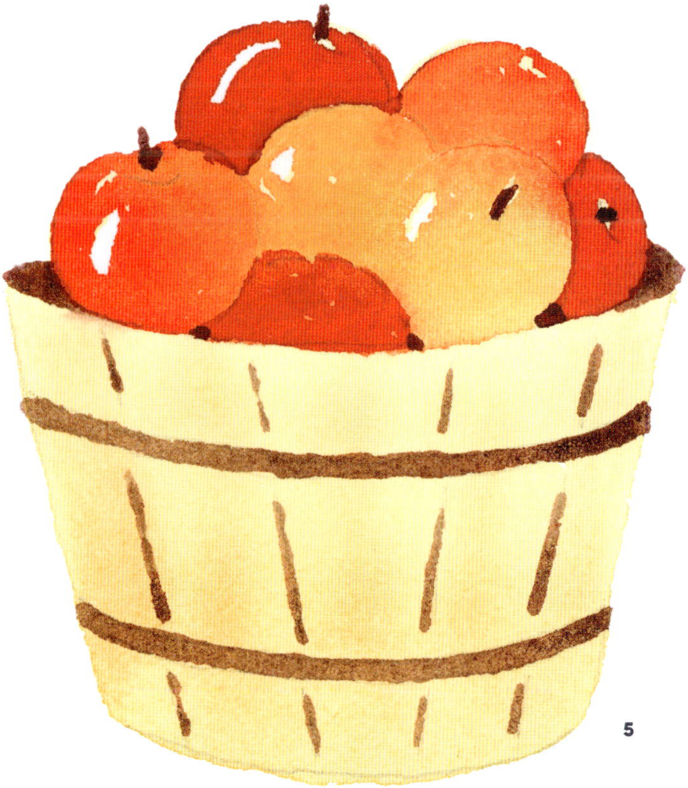

5

WITCH'S HAT

When you have an object that appears black, like a witch's hat, a great way to add dimension is to use other dark colors instead of black. Using black can sometimes make an object appear flat. When we use Indigo and Alizarin Crimson, we create warm and cool **tones** within the hat that we could never achieve by using black alone.

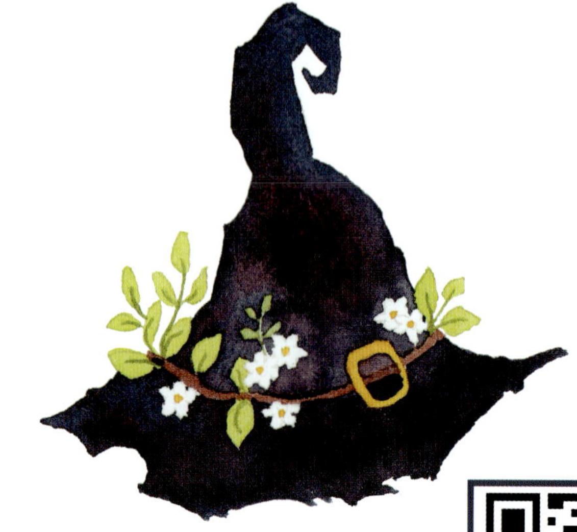

MATERIALS

Pencil

Watercolor paper

Old brush

Drawing gum paste

Size 8 round brush

Size 2 round brush

Q-tips cotton swab (optional)

Rubber cement eraser

COLORS

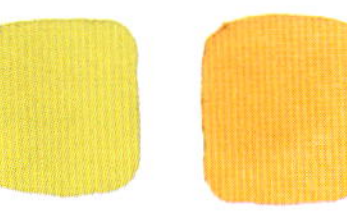

Green Gold

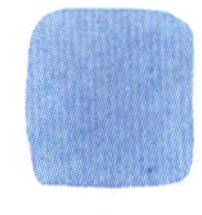

Quinacridone Gold

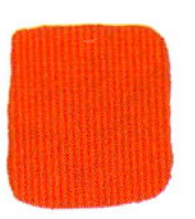

Cobalt Blue

Winsor Red

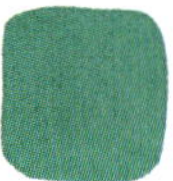

Winsor Green

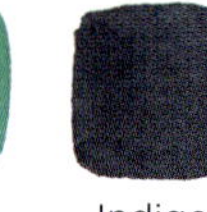

Indigo

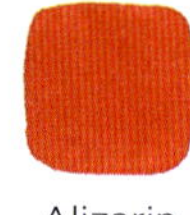

Alizarin Crimson

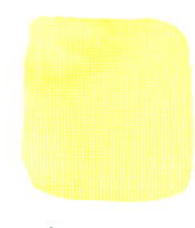

Lemon Yellow

CHALLENGING

STEP 1: With a pencil, trace (page 265) or sketch the witch's hat onto your watercolor paper.

STEP 2: Use an old brush to paint the drawing gum paste on the flowers. Once that is dry, use a size 8 round brush to paint the larger leaves using Green Gold. Paint the buckle on the hat with Quinacridone Gold.

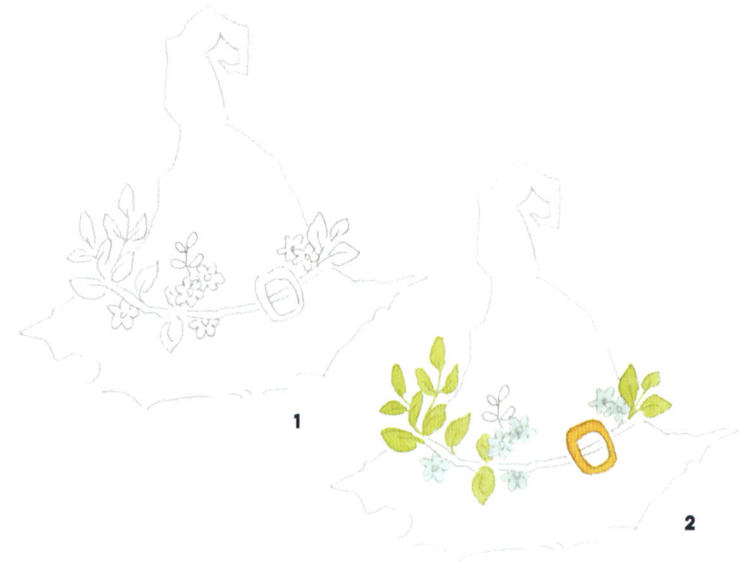

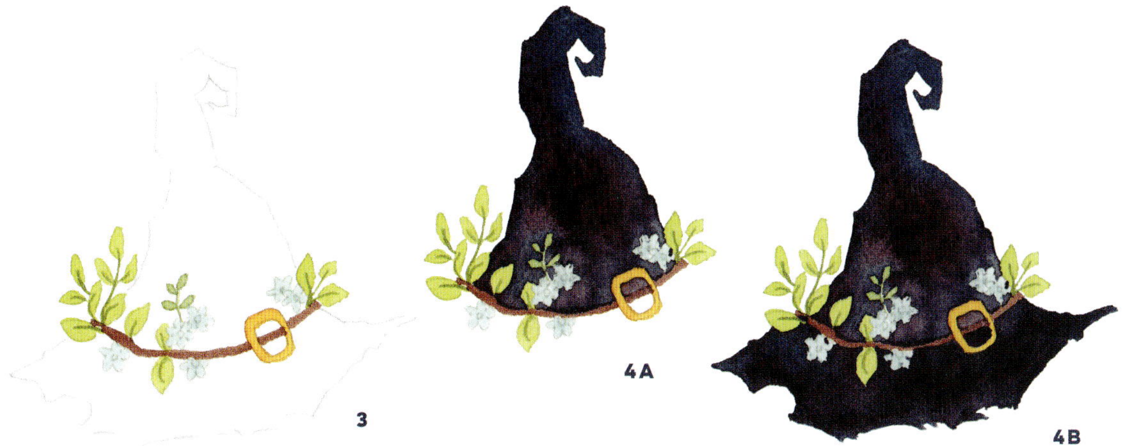

STEP 3: Paint the smaller leaves using this mixture from your palette: Green Gold (50%) and Cobalt Blue (50%). Use this mixture to paint in the stem and detailing on the other set of leaves that you painted in Step 2.

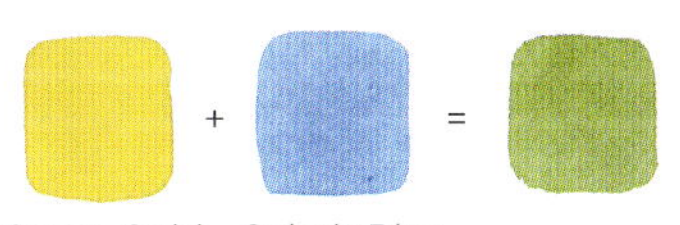
Green Gold (50%)   +   Cobalt Blue (50%)   =

On your palette mix Winsor Red (70%) and Winsor Green (30%). Use this mixture to paint in the rope around the hat.

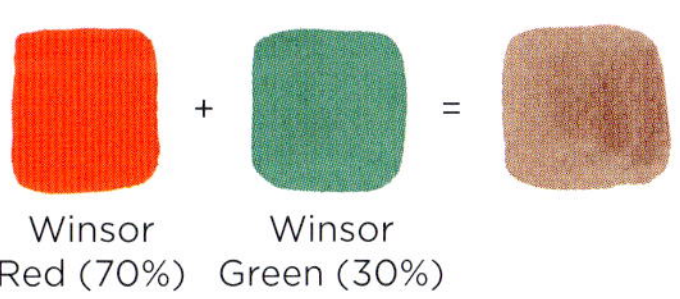
Winsor Red (70%)   +   Winsor Green (30%)   =

STEP 4: Paint in the top section of the hat by **loading** your brush with Indigo, painting the tip of the hat and bringing that down the right side. Then **load** your brush with Alizarin Crimson and paint in the middle of the hat, allowing the colors to **bleed** together (**wet-in-wet**). Once you get close to all the leaves and rope, switch to a size 2 round brush so you can paint around those fine details. If you get paint on the leaves or rope, you can try to remove it with a dry Q-tips cotton swab.

Paint the bottom half of the hat by starting at the bottom left corner with Indigo. Then begin dropping in Alizarin Crimson.

STEP 5: Make sure your painting is completely dry! Then take your rubber cement eraser and remove the drawing gum paste on the flowers. Paint in the center of the flowers using this yellow mixture: Lemon Yellow (60%) and Quinacridone Gold (40%).

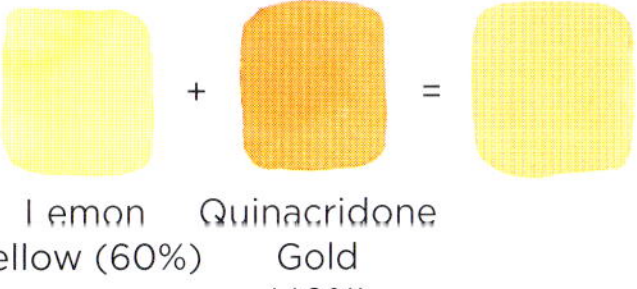
Lemon Yellow (60%)   +   Quinacridone Gold (40%)   =

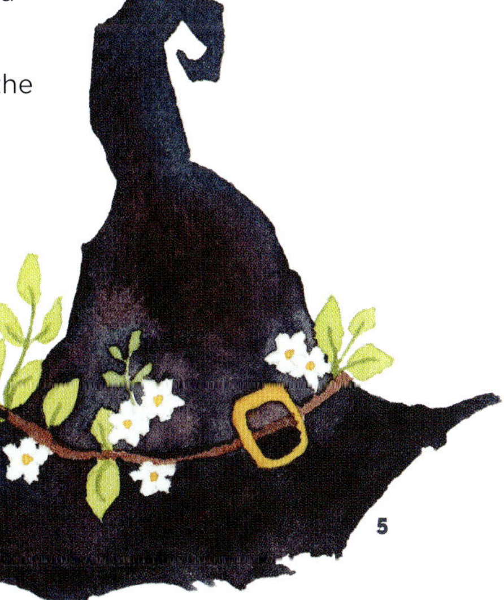

PUMPKIN

One way I like to use **complementary colors** is to layer them at the beginning where the **shadows** lie. We use orange and yellow's **complementary colors**—blue and purple—for the pumpkin, as well as red's **complementary color**—green—for the stem, creating a brown. Using **complementary colors** at the beginning can help create more depth and dimension within the layers.

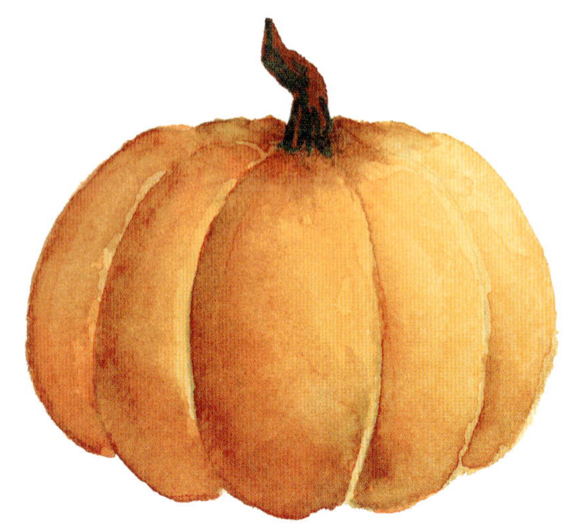

MATERIALS

Watercolor paper

Pencil

Size 8 round brush

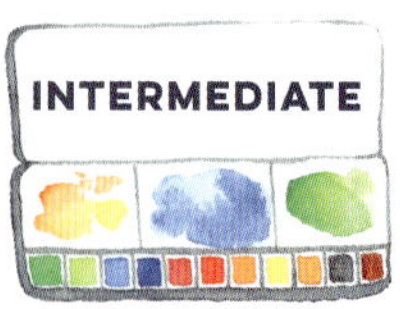

COLORS

Ultramarine Blue

Alizarin Crimson

Winsor Green

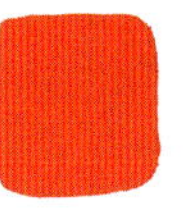

Quinacridone Gold

Winsor Red

Cadmium Orange

STEP 1: On your watercolor paper, trace (page 265) or lightly sketch the pumpkin in pencil.

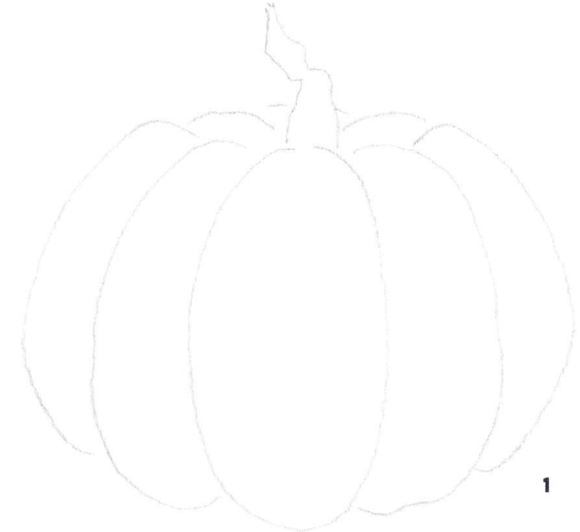

STEP 2: Lightly erase the pencil marks. With your size 8 round brush, paint a light **value** of Ultramarine Blue over the top of the pumpkin and on the left sides of each column. Add a light **value** of Alizarin Crimson on the Ultramarine Blue while it is still wet (**wet-in-wet**). Let that dry.

Paint the stem with Winsor Green using thin vertical lines gravitating to the left side. Leave white spaces on the stem.

STEP 3: Paint over the entire pumpkin using Quinacridone Gold. On your palette, mix Winsor Red (80%) with Winsor Green (20%), then use this mixture to paint in the stem. If the stem color **bleeds** in with the wet Quinacridone Gold color, that is okay and adds a fun look.

STEP 4: Take Cadmium Orange (80%) and combine it on your palette with Alizarin Crimson (20%). **Glaze** the **shadows** on the left edging of each pumpkin column with this mixture. Use water to **soften** the edges.

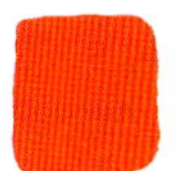 + 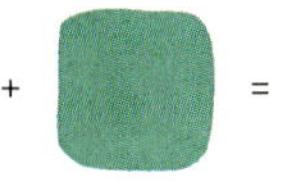 = 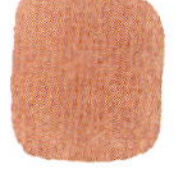    + 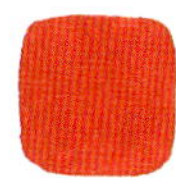 = 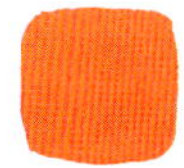

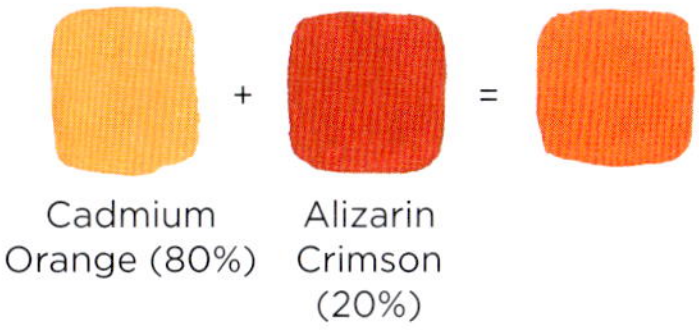

Winsor Red (80%) + Winsor Green (20%) =

Cadmium Orange (80%) + Alizarin Crimson (20%) =

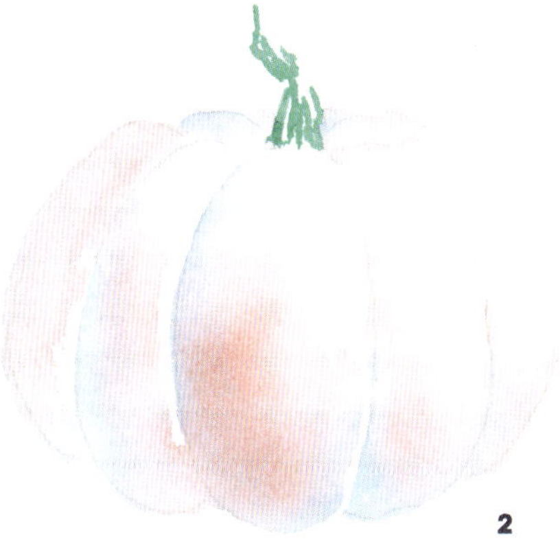

2

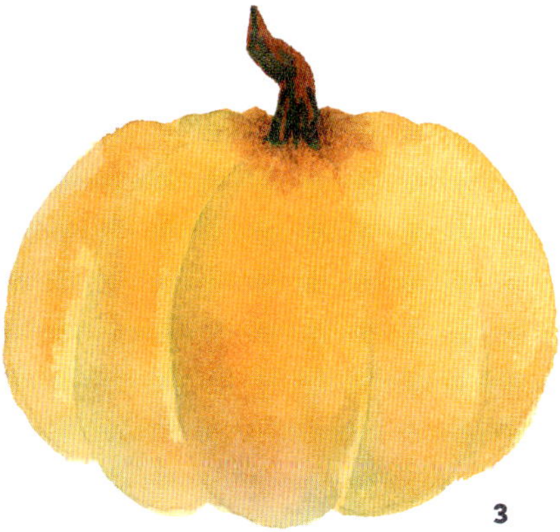

3

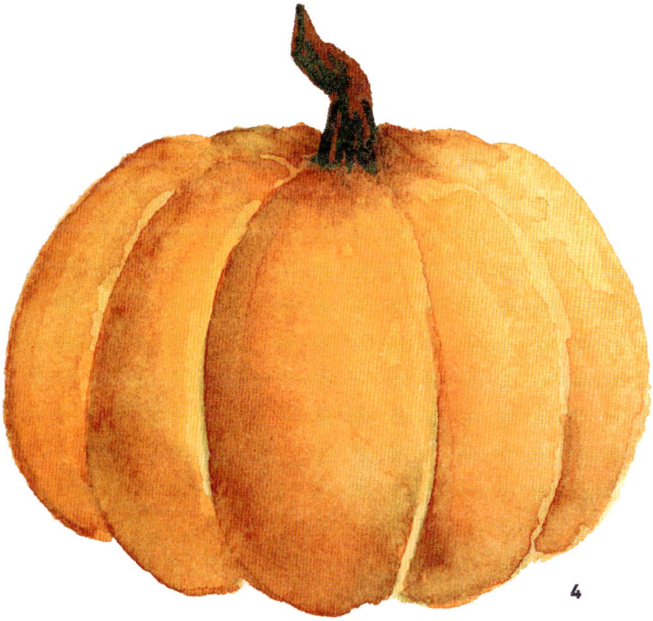

4

CANDY CANE

In this Candy Cane painting, start by blocking in the **shadow**. To help show that the candy cane is rounded, apply the **shadow** on the ground and on the inside edge of the candy cane. Leaving the outside edge of the candy cane as the white of the paper creates a **highlight** without adding any paint. All of a sudden, the candy cane now has dimension!

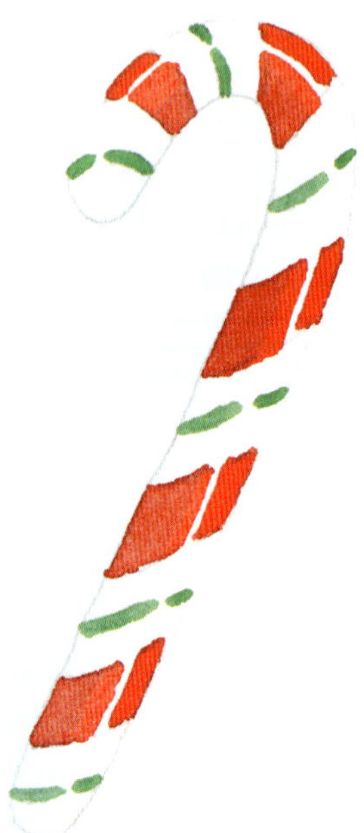

MATERIALS

Watercolor paper

Pencil

Size 4 round brush

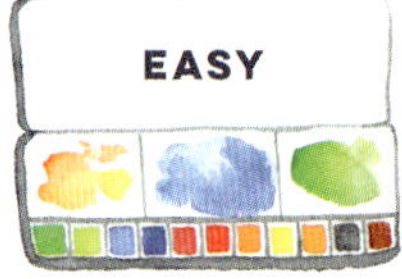

COLORS

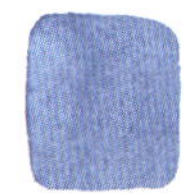
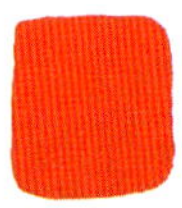

Ultramarine Blue Winsor Red Cadmium Orange

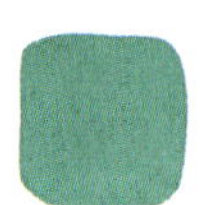
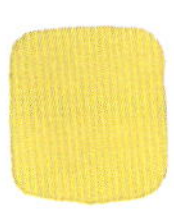

Winsor Green Green Gold

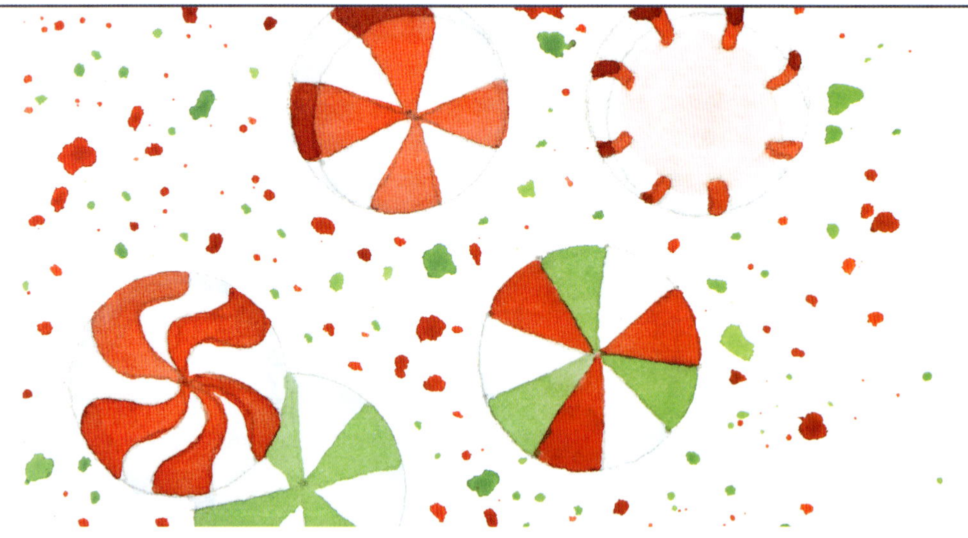

STEP 1: On your watercolor paper, trace (page 265) or sketch the candy cane in pencil.

STEP 2: Water down your Ultramarine Blue to get a light **value** and use that color to paint in the **shadow** with a size 4 round brush. When you paint in the **shadow**, half will be on the left side of the candy cane and the other half should be cast on the **background**.

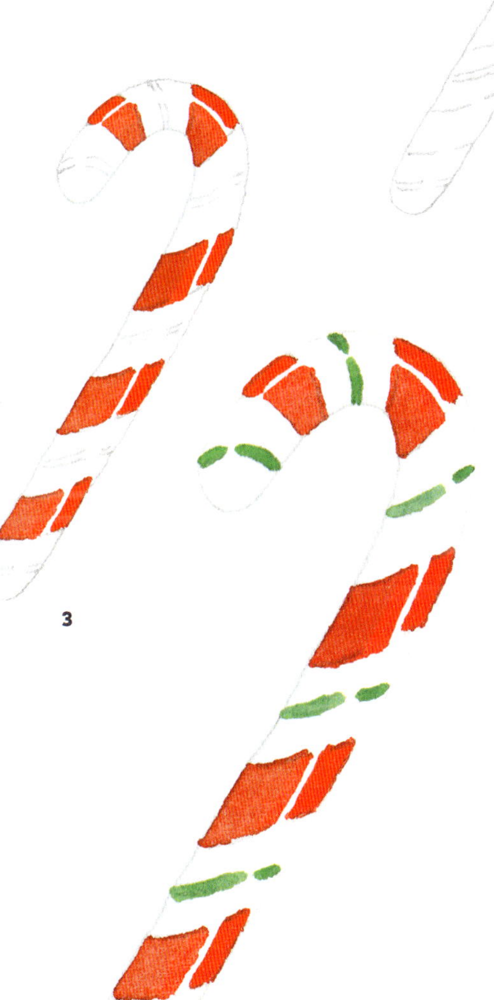

1

2

3

4

STEP 3: Paint in the red stripe on the candy cane using this color from your palette: Winsor Red (80%) and Cadmium Orange (20%). Leave the white paper as a **highlight** running up the candy cane; don't paint in that area on the red stripe.

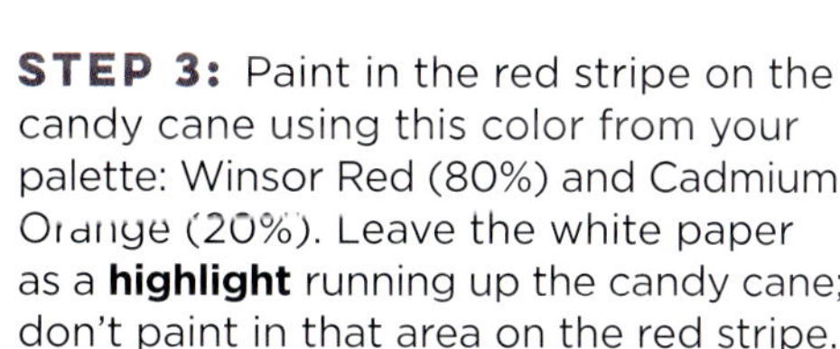

Winsor Red (80%)　+　Cadmium Orange (20%)　=

STEP 4: On your palette, mix Winsor Green (70%) with Green Gold (30%). Use this green mixture to paint on the green stripe around the candy cane. Avoid painting the white paper **highlight**.

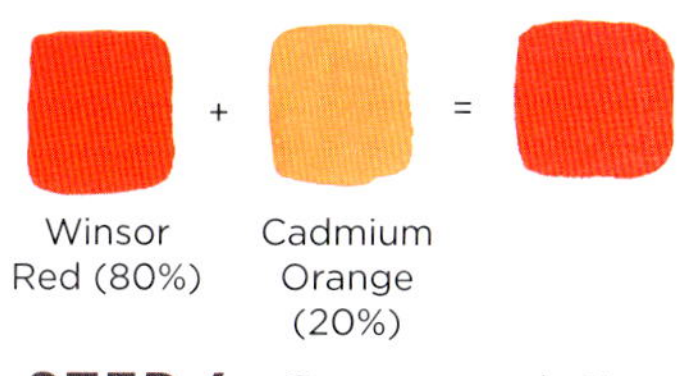

Winsor Green (70%)　+　Green Gold (30%)　=

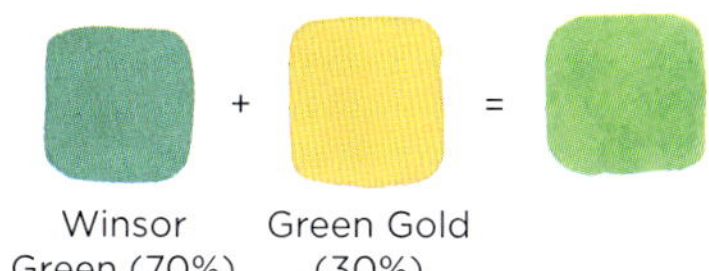

SNOWY PINE

In this Snowy Pine painting, we start with the light blues for the snow, which appears somewhat dark compared to the white of our paper. UNTIL, that is, we place the pine tree color next to it. Then the white of the paper and the snow look incredibly similar. This is part of the magic of color theory: Depending on their placement, colors can make each other appear darker or lighter.

MATERIALS

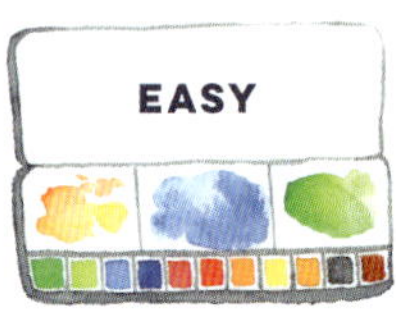

Pencil
Watercolor paper
Size 8 round brush
Paper towel

COLORS

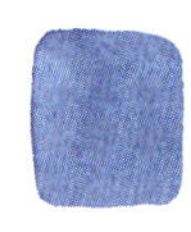
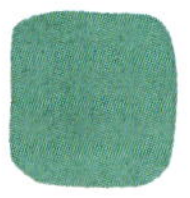

Cobalt
Blue

Ultramarine
Blue

Winsor
Green

STEP 1: With a pencil, lightly trace (page 267) or sketch the snowy pine on your watercolor paper.

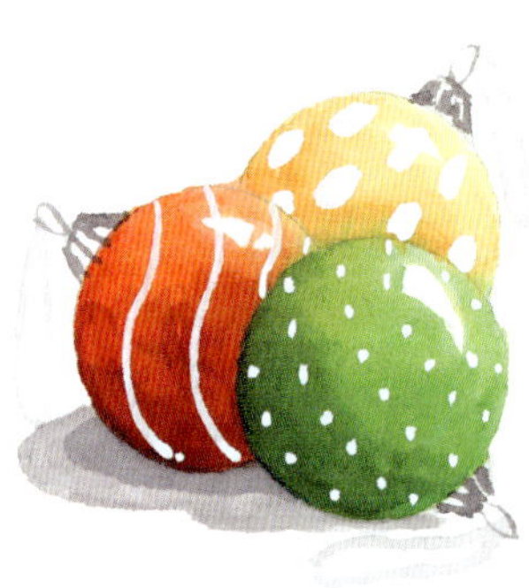

1

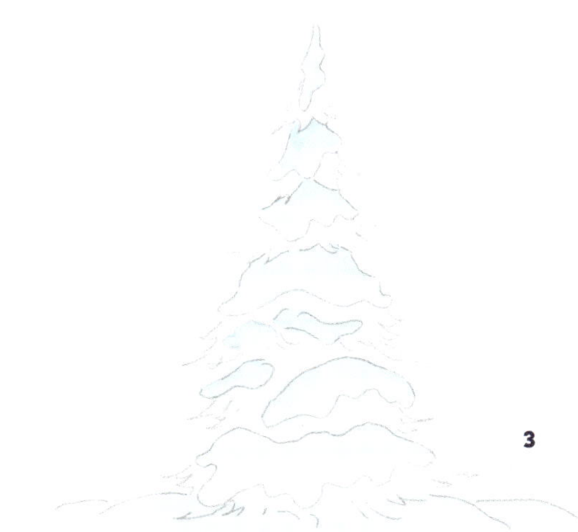

2

3

STEP 2: Make a light **value** of Cobalt Blue by adding lots of water. With a size 8 round brush, paint in the snow on the tree and on the ground. While that is wet, take a paper towel and **blot** the color.

STEP 3: Use a light **value** of Ultramarine Blue to paint a **shadow** on the snow under each tree branch and along the base of the tree.

STEP 4: Mix Ultramarine Blue (50%) and Winsor Green (50%) on your palette. Paint in the tree branches using this mixture and quick curved strokes.

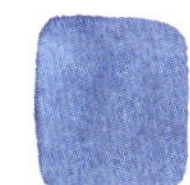 + 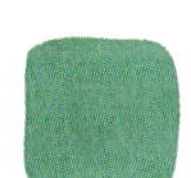 = 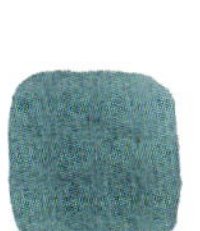

Ultramarine Blue (50%) Winsor Green (50%)

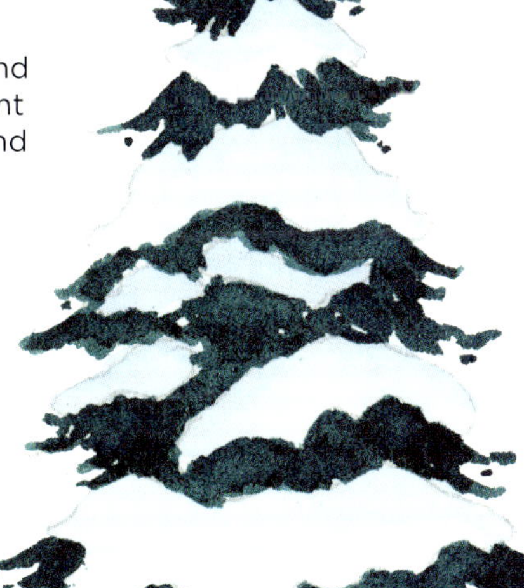

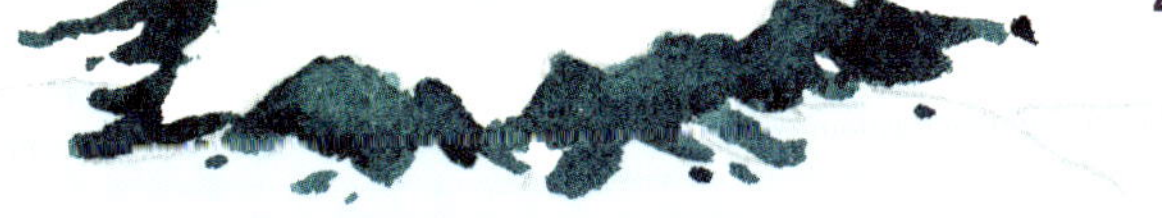

4

HOME FOR THE HOLIDAYS

In watercolor, we always want to save darker **values** for the end because we can always add layers to darken the painting, but we can't lighten a color if we go too dark. In this painting, you have the option at the end to darken the roof for more contrast or leave the roof as is for a more subtle look.

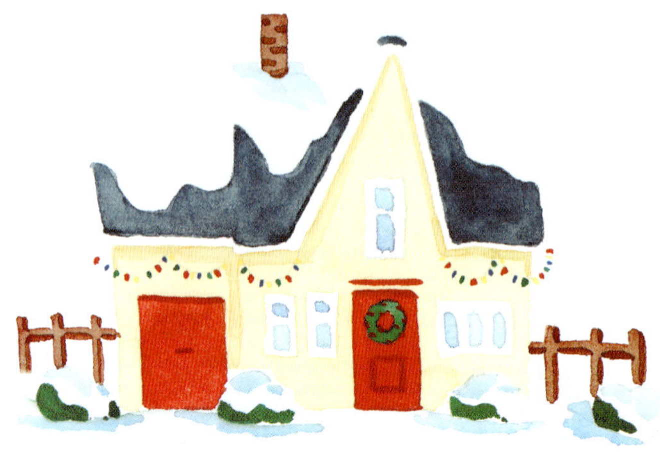

MATERIALS

Pencil

Watercolor paper

Size 8 round brush

Paper towel or cloth

COLORS

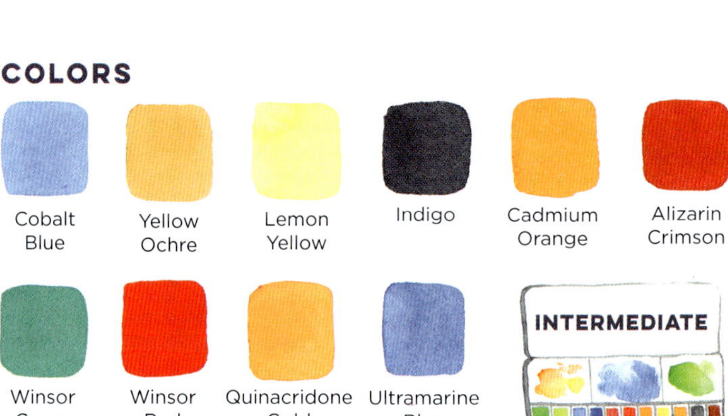

STEP 1: Use your pencil to lightly trace (page 265) or sketch the Home for the Holidays composition on your watercolor paper.

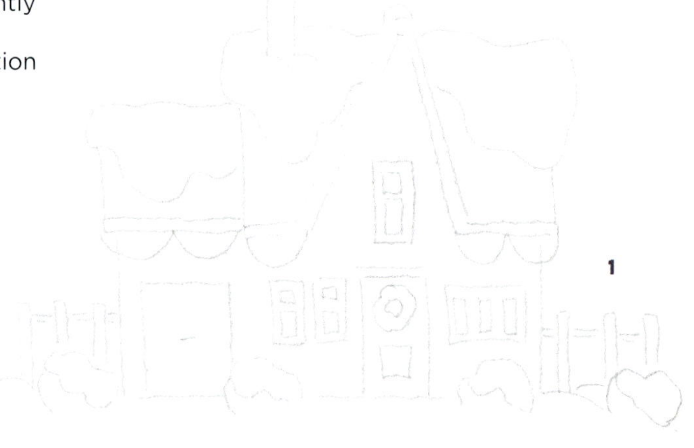

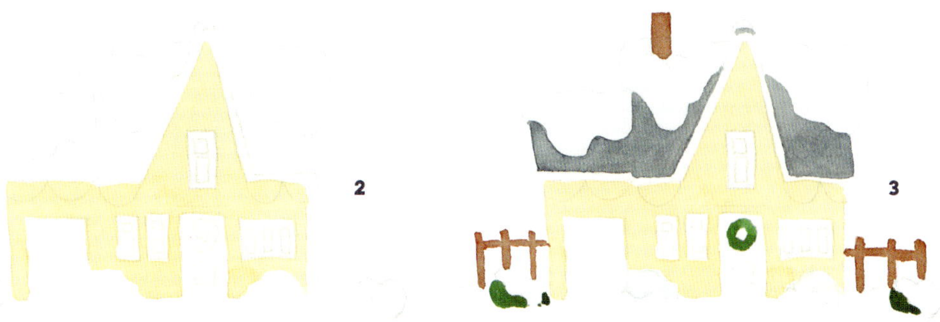

STEP 2: Mix Cobalt Blue into a lot of water for a light **value**. This needs to be light because it's used for the snow on the roof and shrubs. Use your size 8 round brush to paint that snow. **Lift** out some of the paint with a paper towel to get a little variation, leaving some areas a little lighter and some a little darker.

Paint the house using this mixture from your palette: Yellow Ochre (50%) and Lemon Yellow (50%).

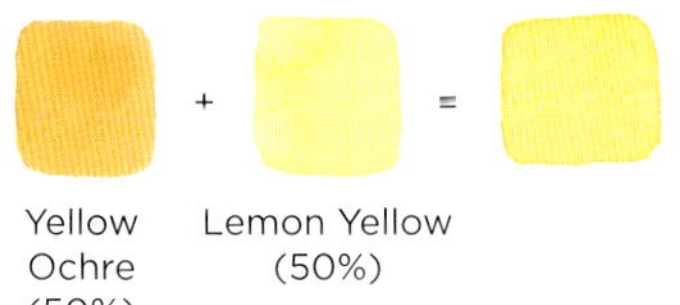

STEP 3: Paint the roof with Indigo. On your palette, mix Cadmium Orange (50%) and Alizarin Crimson (50%). Apply this mixture to the chimney and the fence. For the shrubs in the front of the house and the wreath on the door, mix Winsor Green (50%) with Cadmium Orange (50%) on your palette.

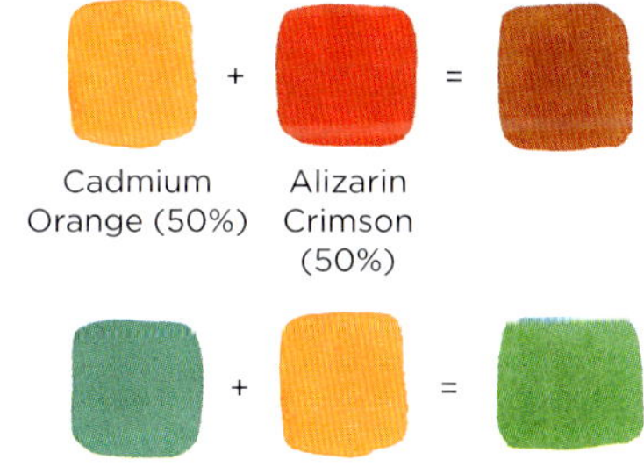

STEP 4: Paint the garage door and the front door with Winsor Red. Paint the glass in the windows using a light **value** of Cobalt Blue because the windows will be reflecting the snow. Add a **shadow** under the roof with Quinacridone Gold.

Mix Cobalt Blue into a lot of water for a light **value**. Paint in the snow on the ground. Try not to get too close to the shrubs because the green color can **bleed** into the snow, and you don't want that to happen.

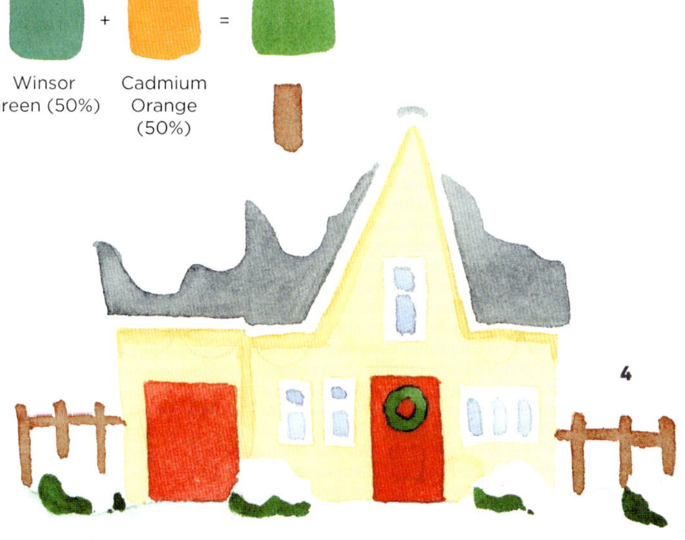

STEP 5: Add details to the garage door and front door with another layer of Winsor Red. Dot in Winsor Red on the door wreath.

For the Christmas lights, use Cobalt Blue, Winsor Red, Winsor Green and Lemon Yellow. You may need to let those dry in between colors so they won't **bleed** together.

Load your brush with a really watered-down Ultramarine Blue and add **shadows** on the snow underneath the shrubs, under the chimney and a little on top of the shrubs. Once again, be careful not to bring the color too close to the green shrubs because you don't want the green to accidentally **bleed** into the snow.

STEP 6: To darken the roof, use Indigo to add another layer. This additional layer is optional; I added the layer to provide contrast so my house would pop.

Lastly, add the final detailing on the chimney and fence using this mixture on your palette: Cadmium Orange (50%) and Alizarin Crimson (50%). Paint on the right side of the fence posts and underneath the horizontal fence. On the chimney, paint in five rectangular bricks.

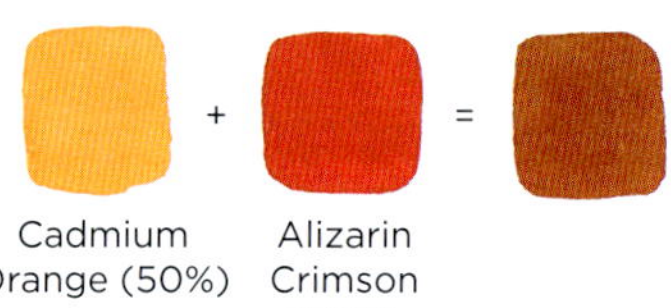

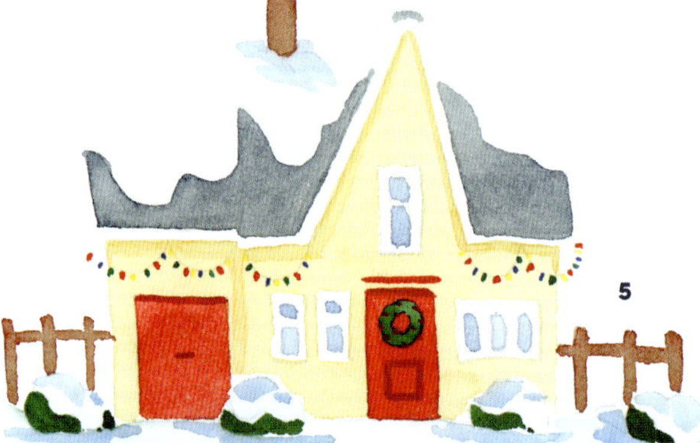

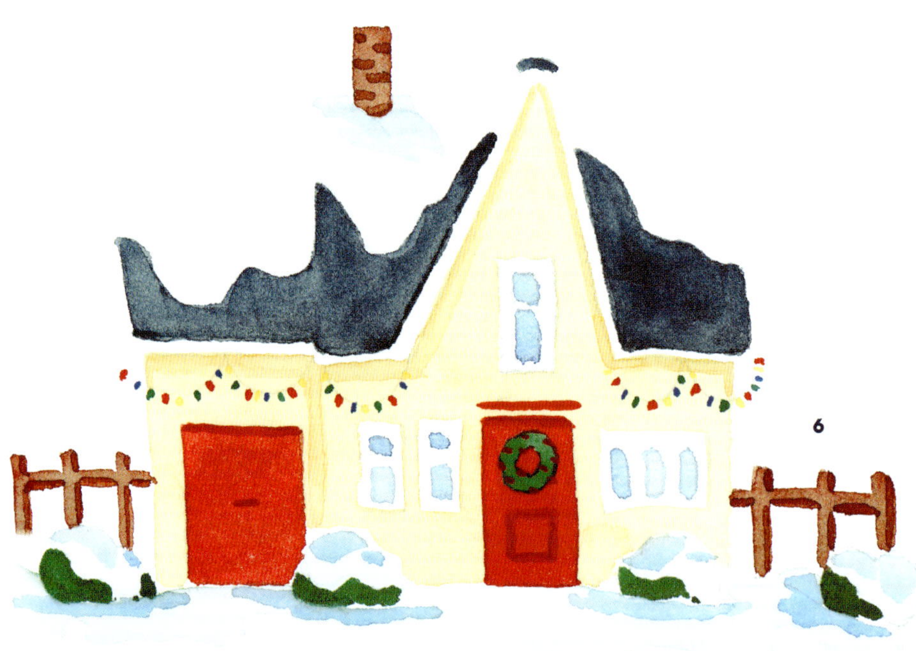

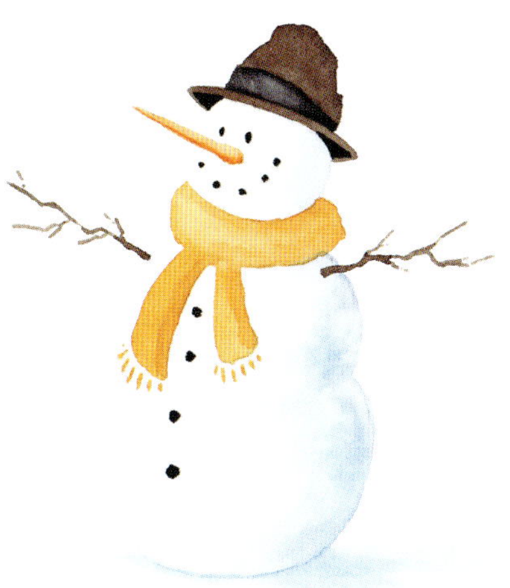

HAPPY SNOWMAN

We are going to "pop" this snowman out from the paper by adding a **shadow** to his right side while keeping his left side solely the white of the paper. Think of the paper as the white "paint" and the brightest **highlight** of this piece.

MATERIALS

Pencil
Watercolor paper
Size 14 round brush
Paper towel
Size 8 round brush

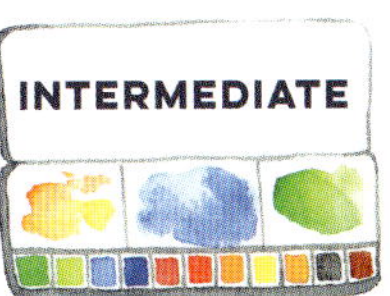

COLORS

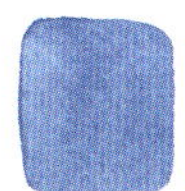 Ultramarine Blue

 Cerulean Blue

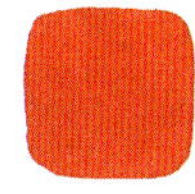 Alizarin Crimson

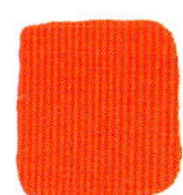 Winsor Red

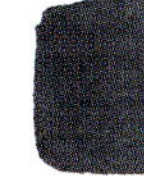 Cadmium Orange

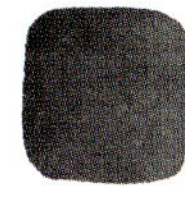 Indigo

 Neutral Tint

Quinacridone Gold

STEP 1: Take your pencil and lightly trace (page 267) or sketch the snowman on your watercolor paper.

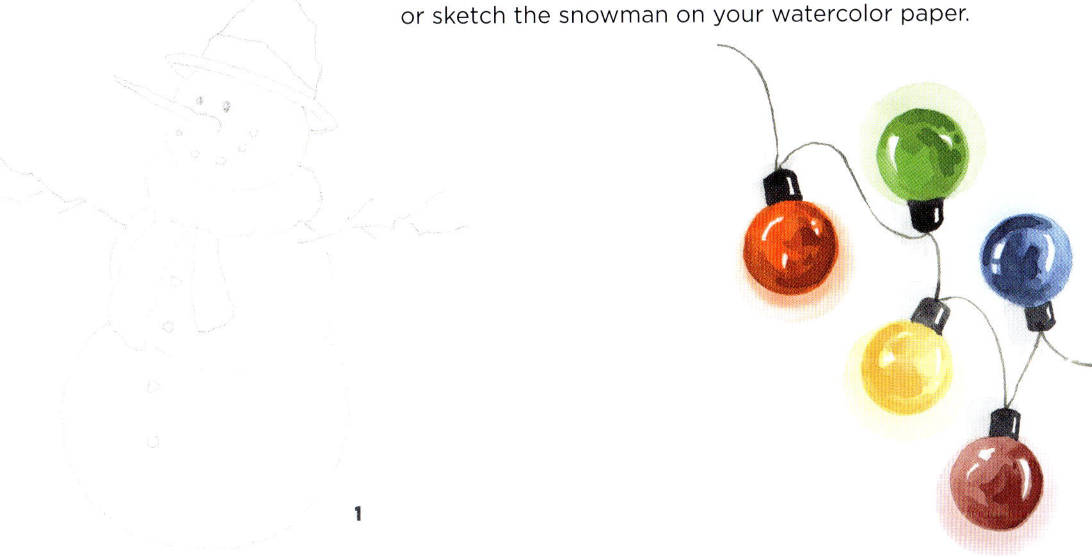

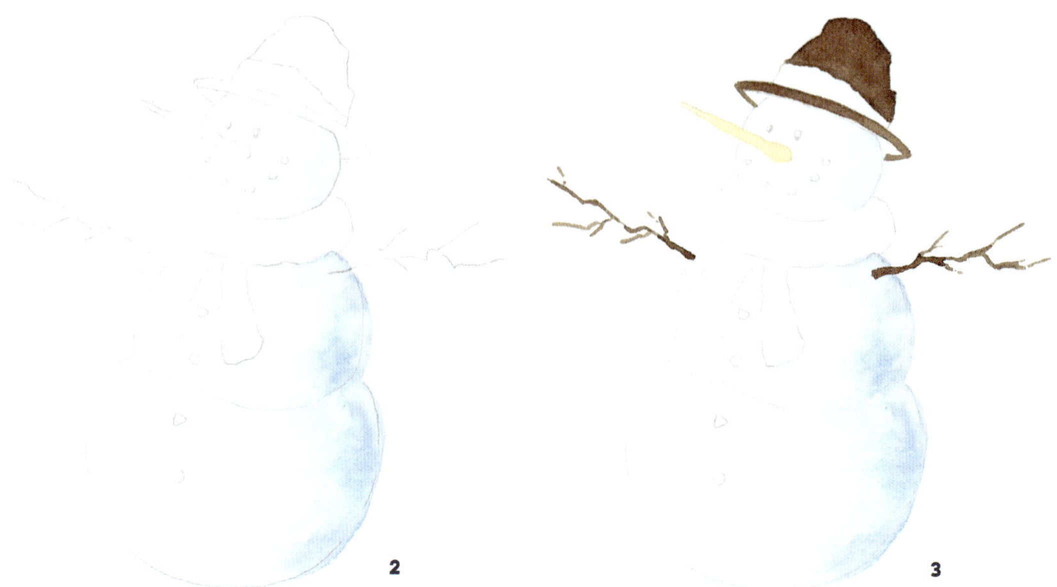

STEP 2: Lightly erase your pencil marks. Using a size 14 round brush, mix Ultramarine Blue (50%) and Cerulean Blue (50%) on your palette. You don't want to make it too dark, so make sure to mix a lot of water into the mixture for a lighter **value**. Clean off your brush and add water to the right side of the snowman (**shadow** side), then lightly lay the color mixture from your palette onto the wet area (**wet-in-wet**). If you get too much paint on the paper, take a paper towel and **blot** it off. While it is still wet, mix Ultramarine Blue (90%) with Alizarin Crimson (10%) on your palette and paint this on the very far right edge of the snowman to get a deeper **shadow**.

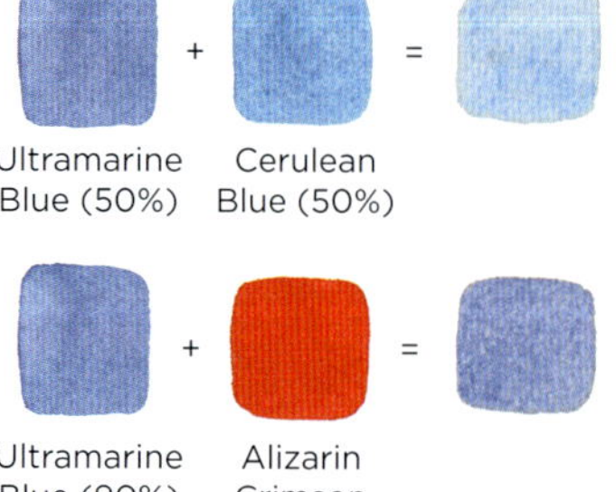

Ultramarine Blue (50%) + Cerulean Blue (50%) =

Ultramarine Blue (90%) + Alizarin Crimson (10%) =

STEP 3: Switch brushes to the size 8 round brush. Paint the carrot a light **value** of Cadmium Orange. On your palette, mix Winsor Red (40%), Cadmium Orange (30%) and Indigo (30%) to create a brown color. (If you have a pre-mixed brown, you can use that; I don't have one because I like to play with the warmth and coolness of the brown as I mix my own.) Use this brown to paint in the hat and stick arms. For the stick arms, paint thin strokes with a variety of little lines.

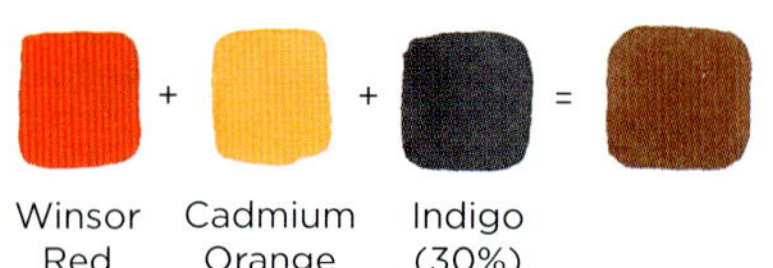

Winsor Red (40%) + Cadmium Orange (30%) + Indigo (30%) =

STEP 4: Paint the coal accents and the strip of ribbon on the hat using Neutral Tint. If you would like these darker, use less water to create a darker **value**.

STEP 5: Paint the scarf with Quinacridone Gold. Use little marks at the end of the scarf to create tassels. Then use Cadmium Orange to add a **shadow** on the bottom of the carrot.

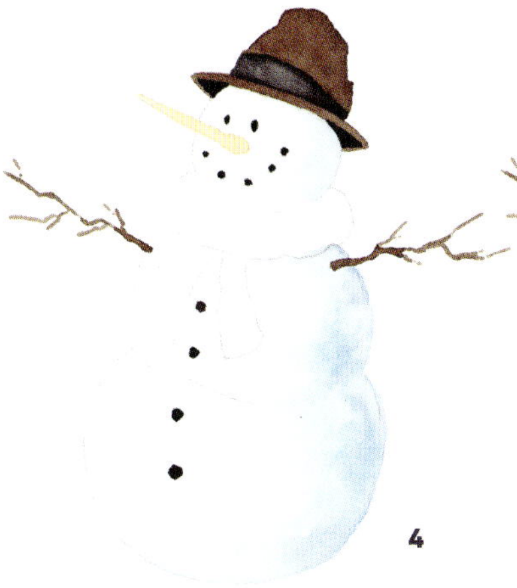

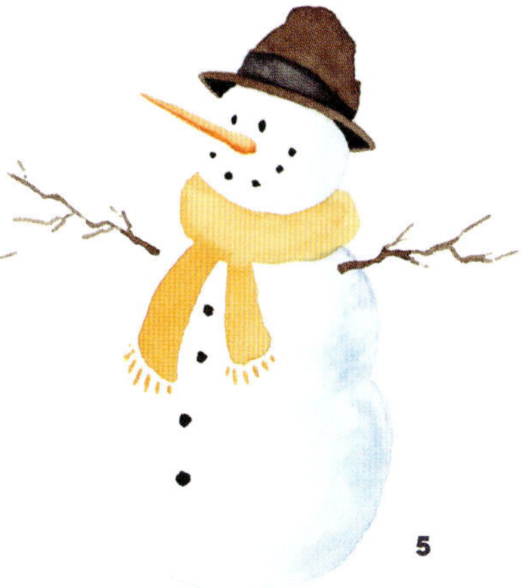

STEP 6: To add a **shadow** on the scarf, use Quinacrid-one Gold, but don't mix in as much water to make the color a darker **value**. On your palette, mix Cerulean Blue (50%), Ultramarine Blue (40%) and Alizarin Crimson (10%). Apply that mixture to the **cast shadow** on the ground; a little bit can be to the left, but the majority of the paint should be on the right side of the snowman. Now you have one happy snowman ready to waltz right off the page!

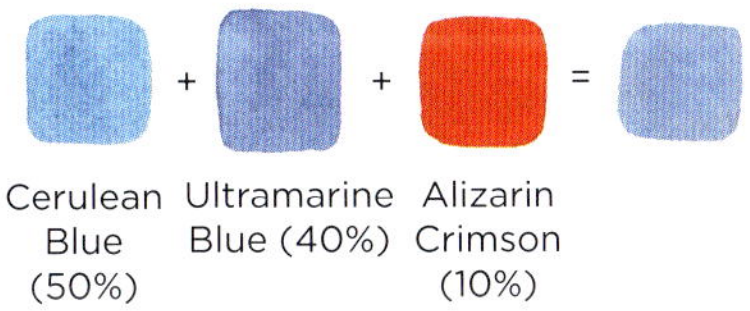

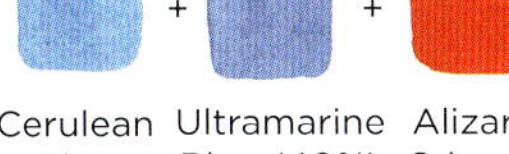

Cerulean Blue (50%) Ultramarine Blue (40%) Alizarin Crimson (10%)

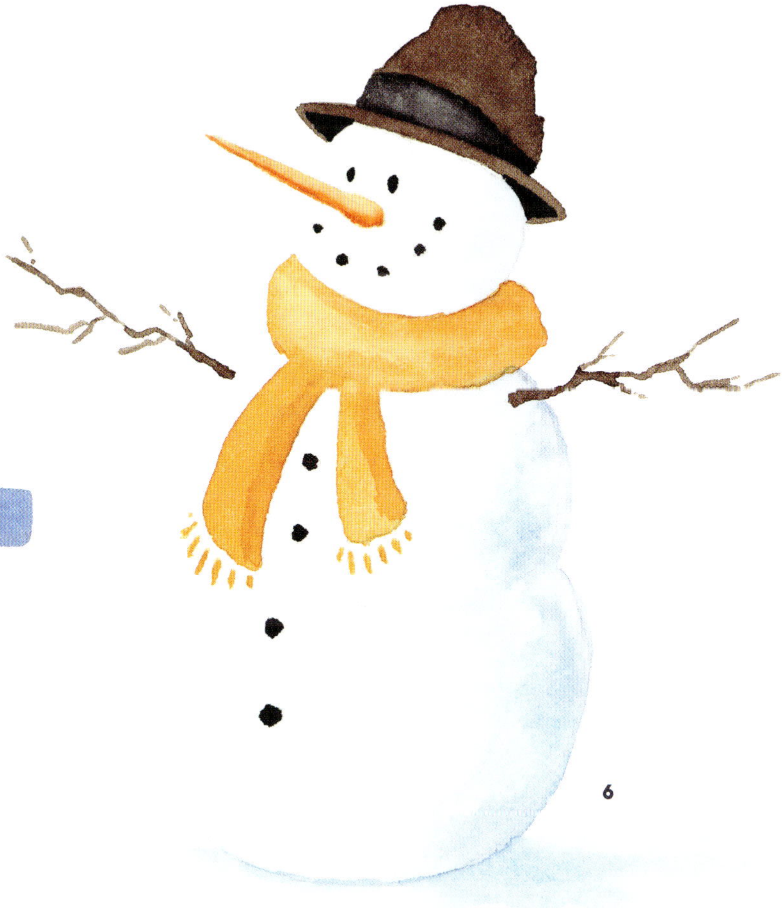

HOLLY

When you are painting an object like holly leaves, you want to give dimension to the leaves by adding more colors besides just a solid green. When you add additional colors, the leaves won't appear flat because you can see light, medium and dark **values**. This will help create depth within each leaf.

MATERIALS

Watercolor paper

Pencil

Size 8 round brush

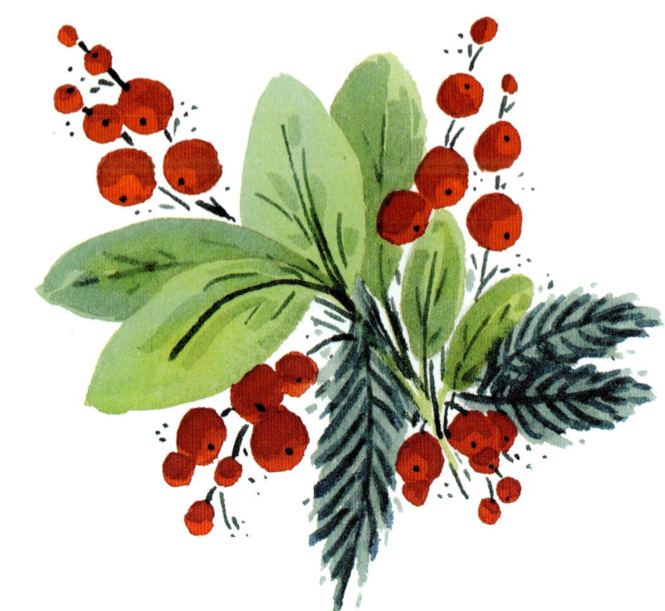

COLORS

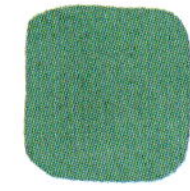

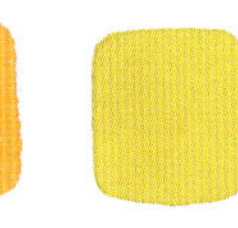
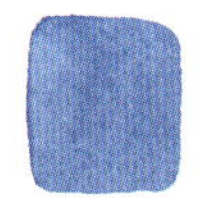
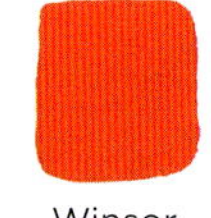
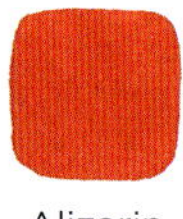

| Winsor Green | Cadmium Orange | Green Gold | Ultramarine Blue | Winsor Red | Alizarin Crimson |

STEP 1: On your water-color paper, trace (page 267) or lightly sketch the holly in pencil.

STEP 2: As you'll be working **wet-in-wet** with a size 8 round brush, it may be helpful to work one leaf at a time. For some leaves, paint Winsor Green and, while that is wet, drop in Cadmium Orange. For other leaves, paint Winsor Green and dab in Green Gold. Mix on your palette Ultramarine Blue (50%) and Winsor Green (50%), then paint the evergreen with a straight line and have "V" strokes coming out. There's no need to wait for the leaves to dry; it's okay if the colors **bleed** together.

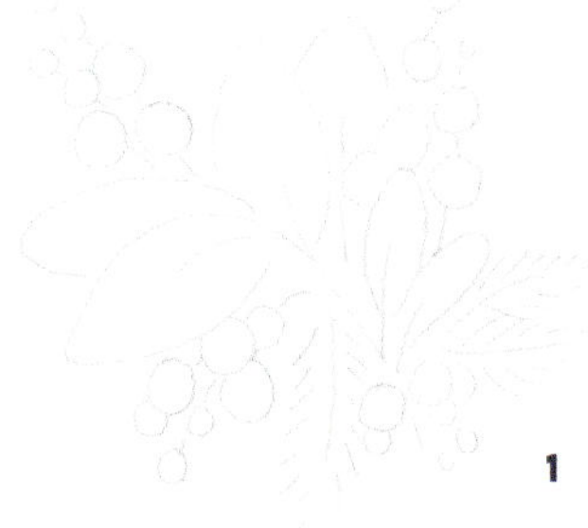

1

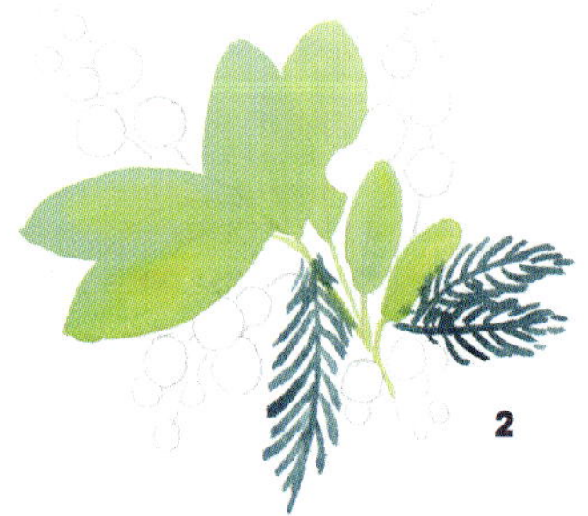

2

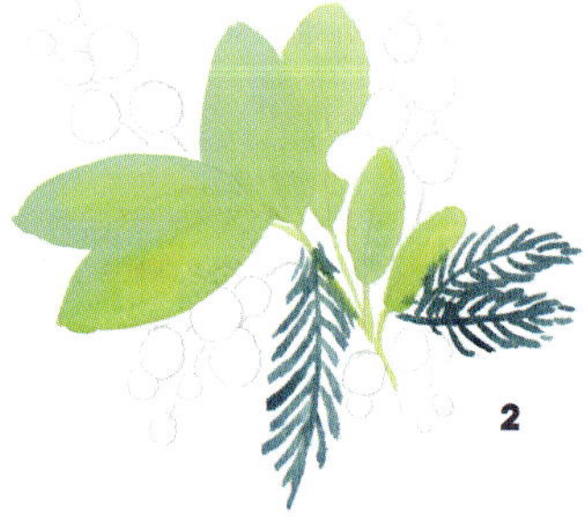

| Ultramarine Blue (50%) | + | Winsor Green (50%) | = | |

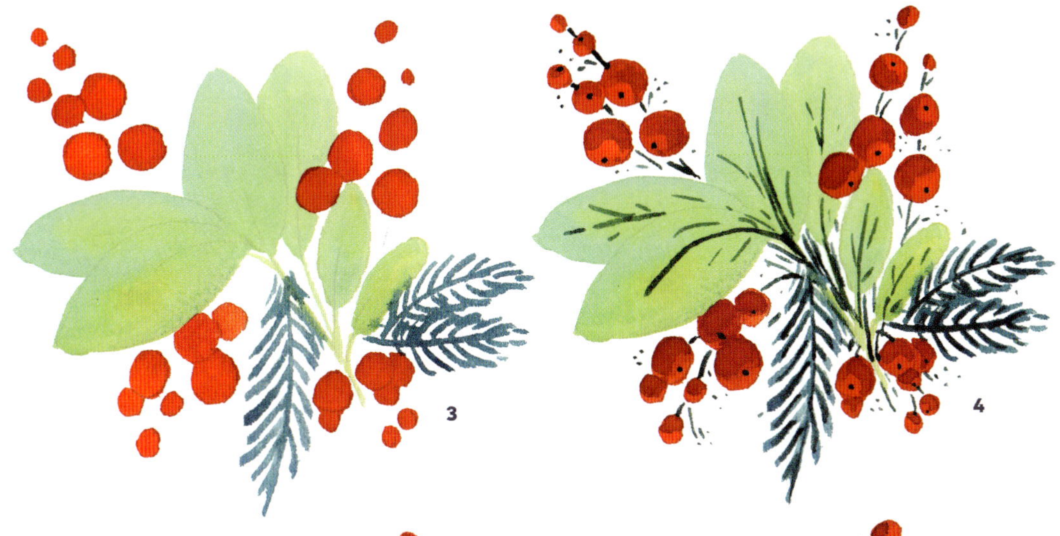

STEP 3: Continue with the **wet-in-wet** technique for the holly berries. Paint the holly berries Winsor Red, then drop in Cadmium Orange while the paint is wet.

STEP 4: Use Alizarin Crimson to paint a **shadow** on the side of the berries. Make a mixture of Winsor Green (60%) and Alizarin Crimson (40%) on your palette and use it for the branches of the holly. Then use this color to put a dot on some of the berries, but make sure the berries are dry before you add that dot. Also add some little dotting around the branches and use the same color to put little veins on the leaves. Lastly, use the color to go over the top of the evergreen to add some dark **shadowing** everywhere.

STEP 5: Darken the holly leaves with a Winsor Green (70%) and Alizarin Crimson (30%) mixture. This should be a lighter mixture than the one used in Step 4. To lighten the **value**, make sure to add more water on your palette.

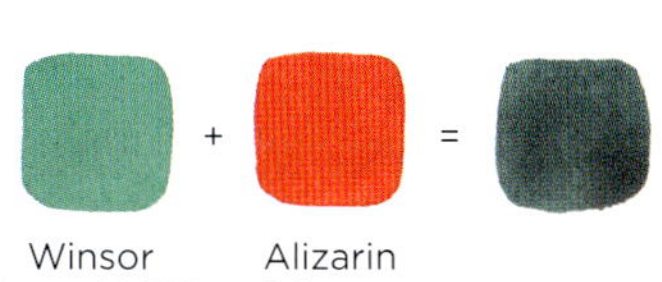

Winsor Green (60%) + Alizarin Crimson (40%) =

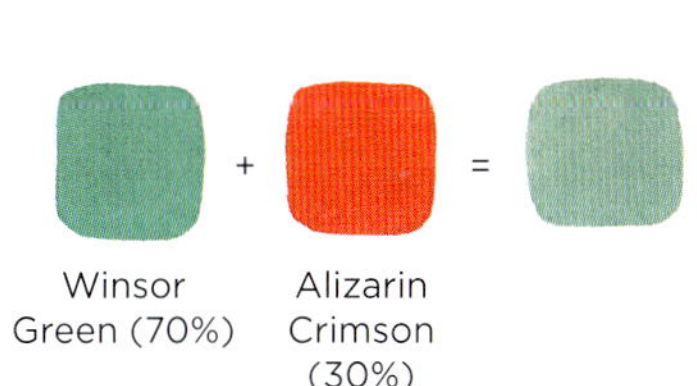

Winsor Green (70%) + Alizarin Crimson (30%) =

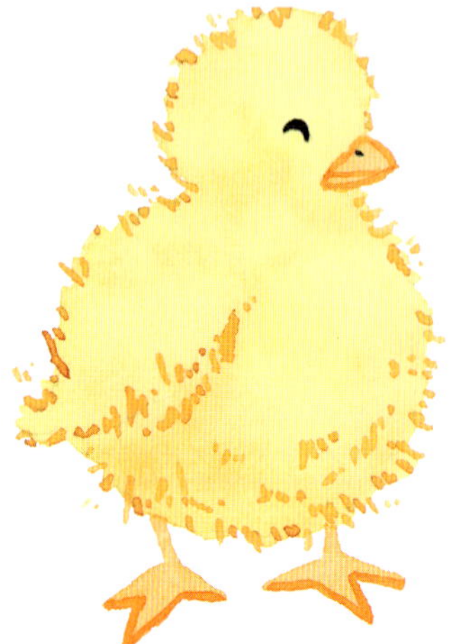

SWEET CHICK

For an artist, sometimes the hardest part is just starting to paint. For the times when you get stuck, a little trick is to paint something simple and quick to feel accomplished. This momentum will help you dive back in. This Sweet Chick painting features simple shapes with colors straight out of the palette to help jump-start your creativity!

MATERIALS

Watercolor paper
Pencil
Size 8 round brush
Sharpie felt-tip pen

COLORS

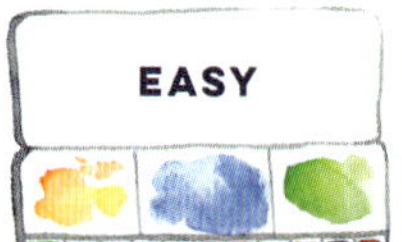

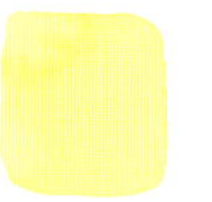
Lemon Yellow

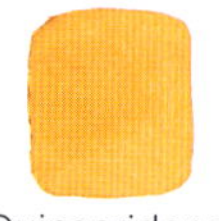
Quinacridone Gold

Cadmium Orange

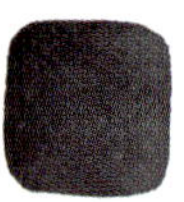
Neutral Tint (optional)

STEP 1: On your watercolor paper, trace (page 267) or sketch the chick in pencil.

1

STEP 2: With a size 8 round brush, use Lemon Yellow to paint across the entire chick, avoiding the beak and feet. While the paint is wet, paint Quinacridone Gold around in a dotting motion so you get nice **texture** (**wet-in-wet**). When you paint the outside of the chick, you don't want it to be a round edge; you want it to look like feathers, so make tiny marks sticking out.

STEP 3: Use Cadmium Orange to paint the feet and beak.

STEP 4: Use your Sharpie to add in the eye and little dot on the beak. If you feel comfortable doing so, you can instead paint the dot and eye using Neutral Tint; however, because these items are so thin, it can be difficult to paint them in with a brush.

Outline the beak and bottom of the feet with Cadmium Orange.

Take Quinacridone Gold and paint some fun swoopy lines around the chick. It is a nice effect if you want some of the marks to go out onto the white paper.

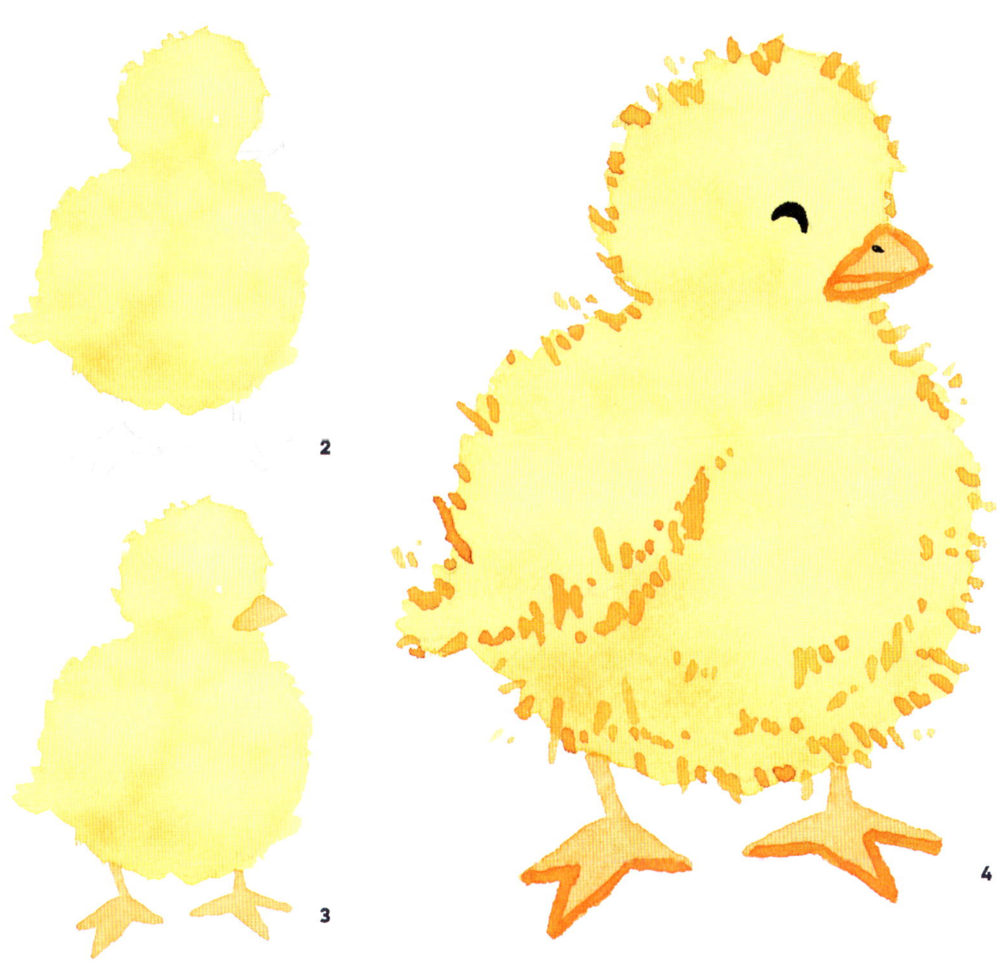

WATERING CAN

A great way to add **texture** is to use a paper towel to **lift** off paint. In this Watering Can painting, we create a fun metal-like **texture** using this **lifting** technique. Paper towels can also be used to **lift** paint off the paper to create clouds in the sky. Anytime you need to create the effect of **texture**, paper towels can be your best friend.

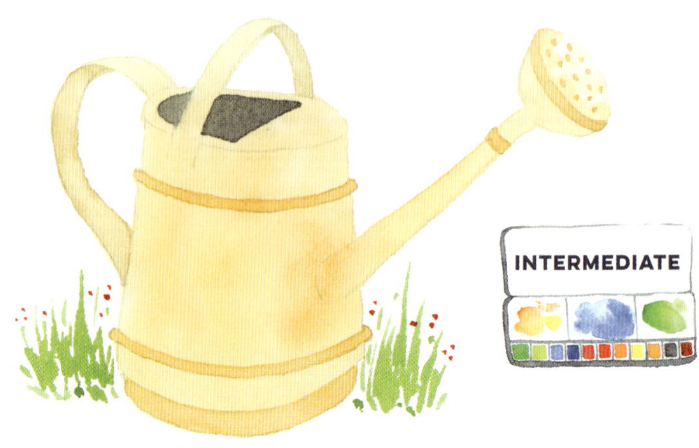

MATERIALS

Watercolor paper

Pencil

Size 8 round brush

Paper towel

COLORS

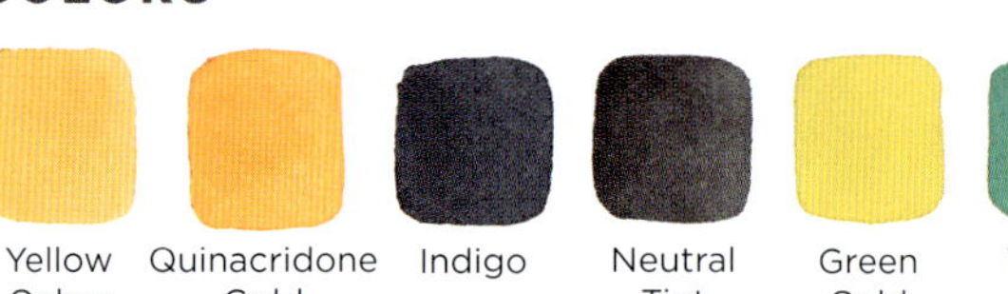

| Yellow Ochre | Quinacridone Gold | Indigo | Neutral Tint | Green Gold | Winsor Green | Winsor Red |

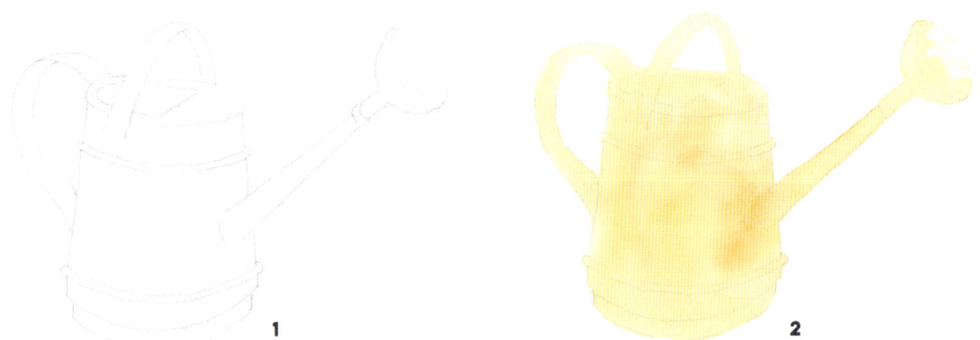

STEP 1: On your watercolor paper, trace (page 269) or sketch the watering can in pencil.

STEP 2: Lightly erase your pencil markings. With a size 8 round brush, paint a **clear water wash** over the entire watering can. Use the **wet-in-wet** technique to lay Yellow Ochre into that **clear water wash**. Also lay in Quinacridone Gold so it will mix with the Yellow Ochre. Try not to move the paint around too much because you want the can to have a metallic **texture**. Take a paper towel and **blot** out the paint.

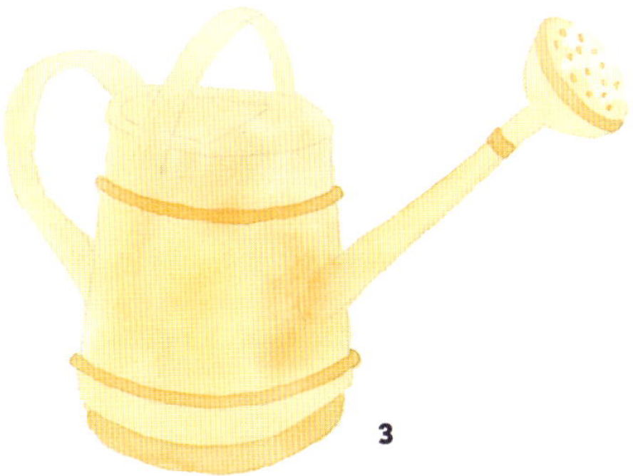

STEP 3: Use a Yellow Ochre **wash** to paint the horizontal lines going across the can and the two lines going around the spout and sprinkler.

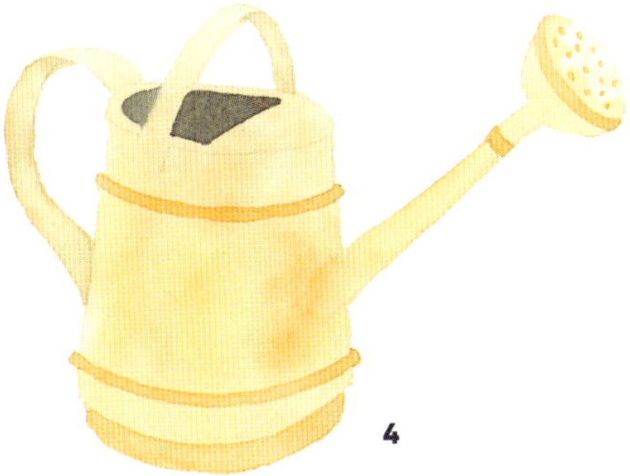

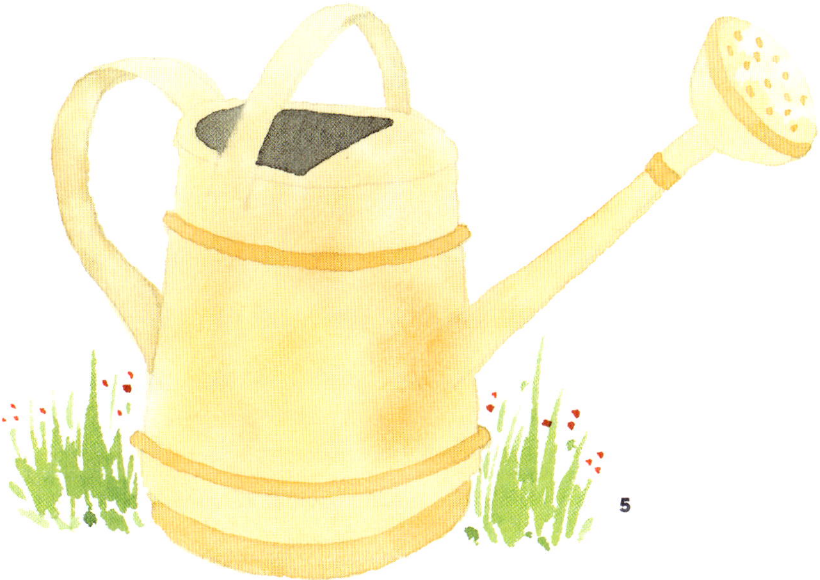

STEP 4: Mix Yellow Ochre (80%) with Indigo (20%) on your palette. Use this color to paint the **shadow** under each of the handles. While that is still wet, **blot** some off to get that metal **texture**. Paint the watering can's opening hole using a Neutral Tint **wash**.

STEP 5: On your palette, combine Green Gold (60%) and Winsor Green (40%). Paint in the blades of grass with this mixture using upstrokes. Take Winsor Red to apply flower dots above the blades of grass.

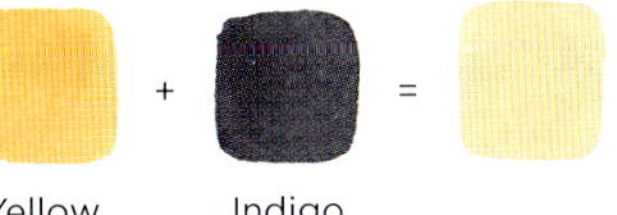

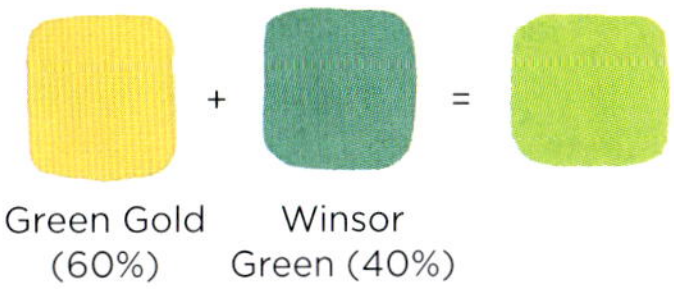

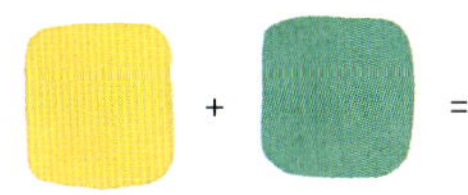

FARM-FRESH EGGS

MATERIALS
Pencil
Watercolor paper
Size 8 round brush

To make a color pastel, you usually add white paint. However, with watercolor, we only have to add more water to dilute the color. Adding more water will allow the white paper to show through more, acting like we added "white" to the paint.

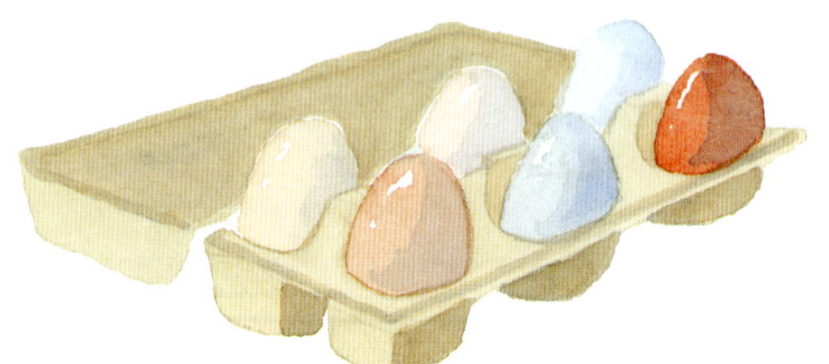

COLORS

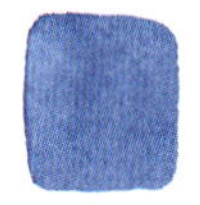 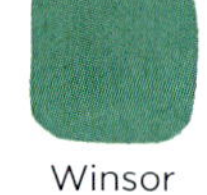 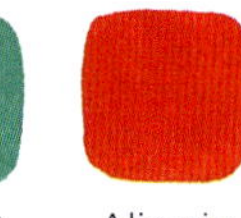 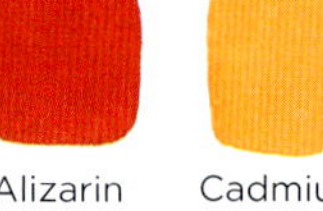 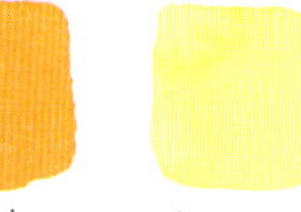 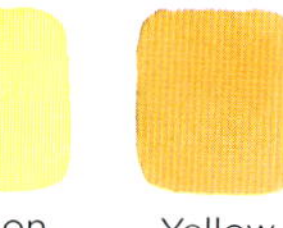 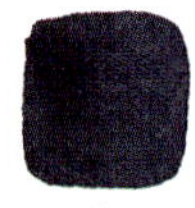 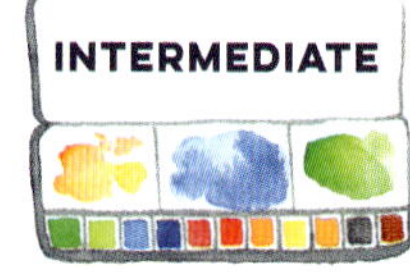

| Ultramarine Blue | Winsor Green | Alizarin Crimson | Cadmium Orange | Lemon Yellow | Yellow Ochre | Indigo |

STEP 1: Use your pencil to lightly trace (page 267) or sketch the eggs and carton on your watercolor paper.

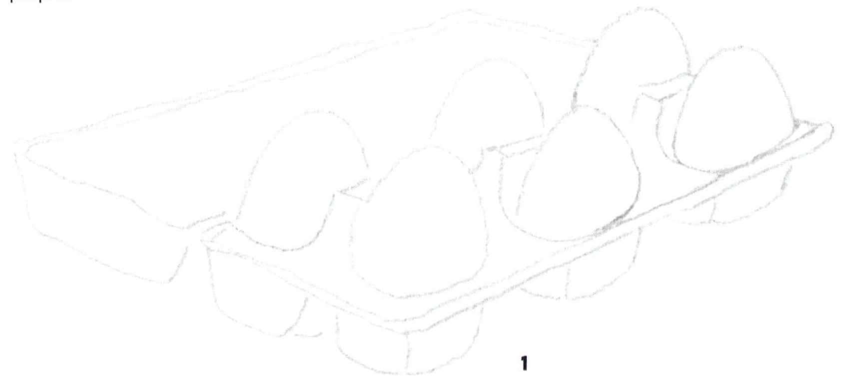

1

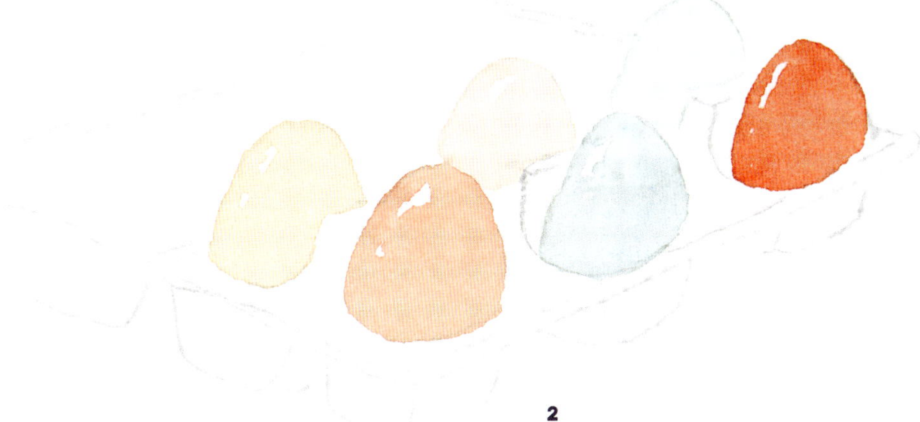

2

STEP 2: Lightly erase the pencil marks. For some of the eggs, the color will be the same, but the **value** will be different. Remember to leave a little **highlight** on the left side of the eggs.

Take Ultramarine Blue (70%) and mix it with Winsor Green (30%) on your palette with a lot of water. With a size 8 round brush, use that color to paint in the darkest blue egg. Then take that same color mixture and add even more water for the lighter blue egg.

For the next three eggs, use the same color mixture but with three different **values**. Create the different **values** by adding more water to the mixture each time. On your palette, mix Cadmium Orange (60%) and Alizarin Crimson (40%). Add water to this mixture and paint the darkest orange egg. Add more water to that mixture and paint the medium **value** for the next orange egg. For the last orange egg, add even more water to the mixture and paint in the lightest color.

For the last egg, mix Lemon Yellow (90%) with Alizarin Crimson (10%) and add a lot of water.

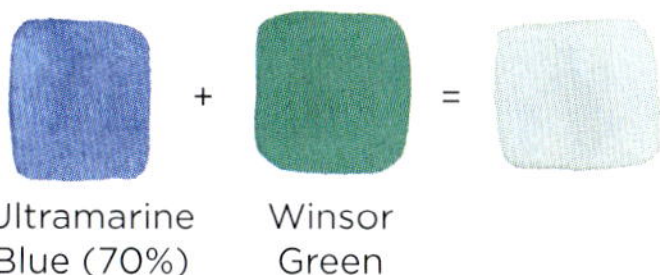

Ultramarine Blue (70%) + Winsor Green (30%) =

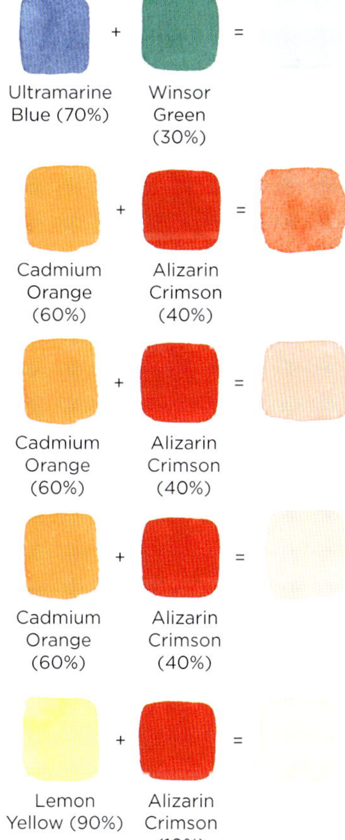

Ultramarine Blue (70%) + Winsor Green (30%) =

Cadmium Orange (60%) + Alizarin Crimson (40%) =

Cadmium Orange (60%) + Alizarin Crimson (40%) =

Cadmium Orange (60%) + Alizarin Crimson (40%) =

Lemon Yellow (90%) + Alizarin Crimson (10%) =

STEP 3: Mix Yellow Ochre (80%) with Indigo (20%) to paint the egg carton.

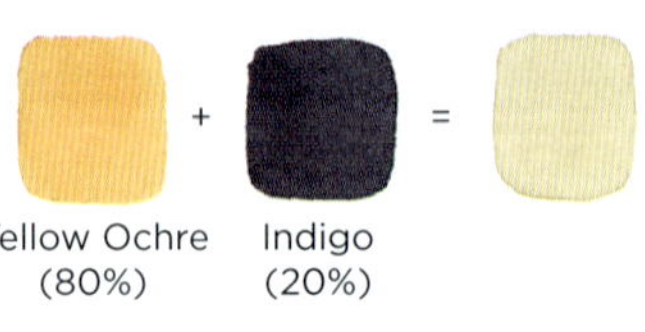

Yellow Ochre (80%)   +   Indigo (20%)   =

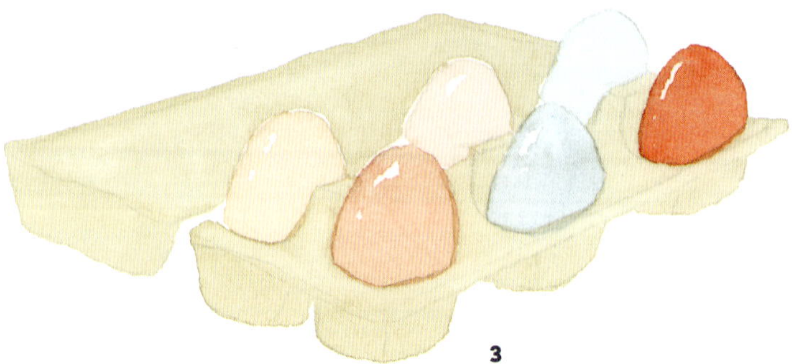

3

STEP 4: Use a light **value** of Ultramarine Blue to add **shadow** on the eggs and on the carton of eggs. Let that dry before moving forward.

Warm up that **shadow** on the egg carton by adding a Yellow Ochre **glaze**.

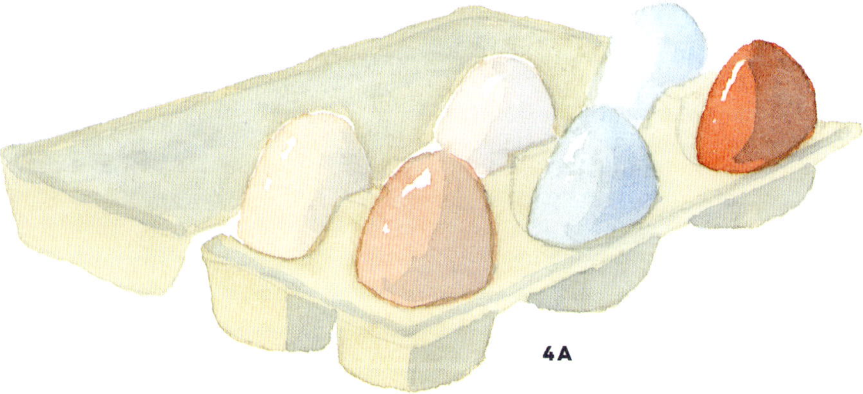

4A

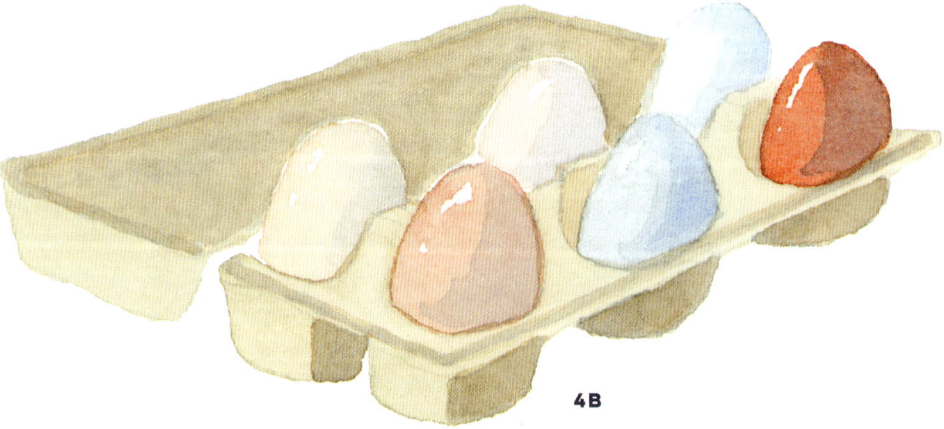

4B

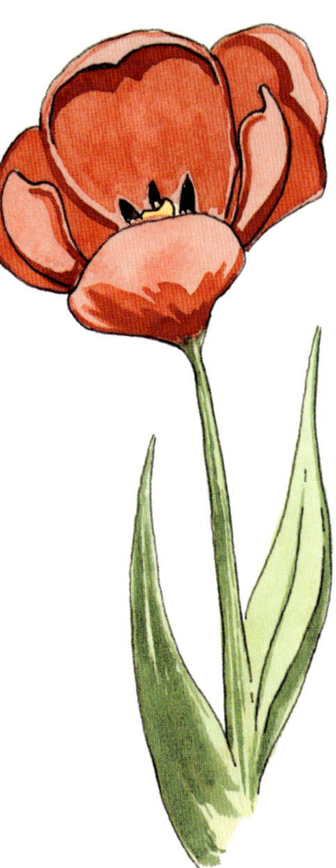

TULIP

When we use water to keep changing the **value** of the color mixture, it makes it appear like we are using many different colors. In this Tulip painting, we use the same mixture with less water each time. Just as we used different **values** to create different shades for eggs in a carton (page 193), for the tulip, we'll gradually change the **water-to-paint ratio** of the color mixture to let our color get darker and darker. Changing the **value** is a great way to add dimension and separate our petals from each other.

MATERIALS

Watercolor paper

Pencil

Size 8 round brush

Sharpie felt-tip pen (optional)

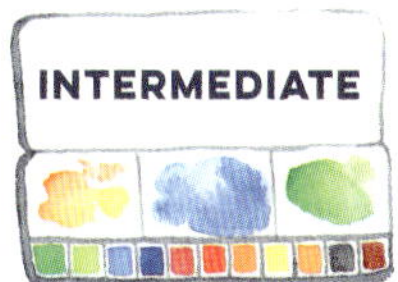

COLORS

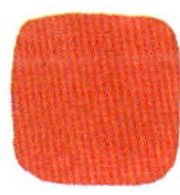

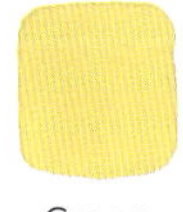
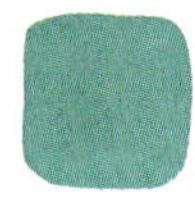
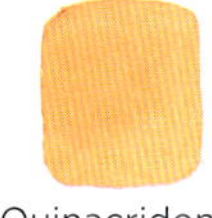
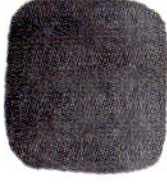

| Alizarin Crimson | Cadmium Orange | Green Gold | Winsor Green | Quinacridone Gold | Neutral Tint |

STEP 1: On your watercolor paper, trace (page 269) or lightly sketch the tulip and stem in pencil.

1

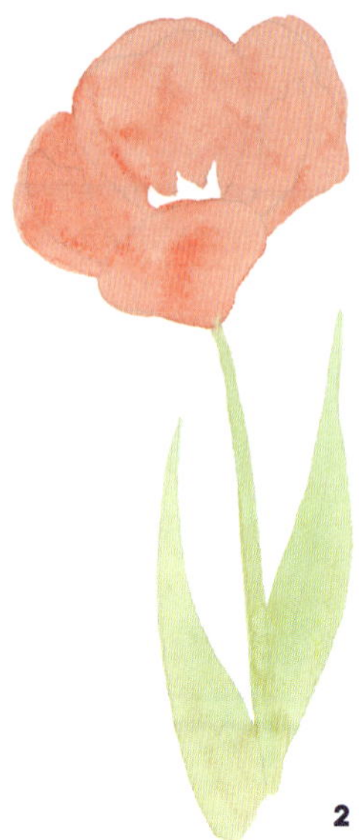

2

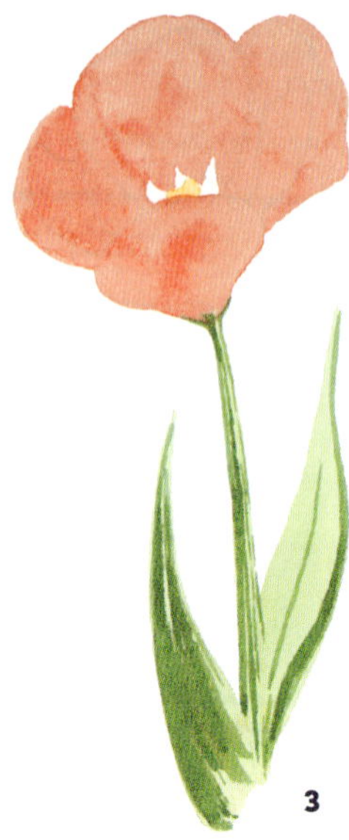

3

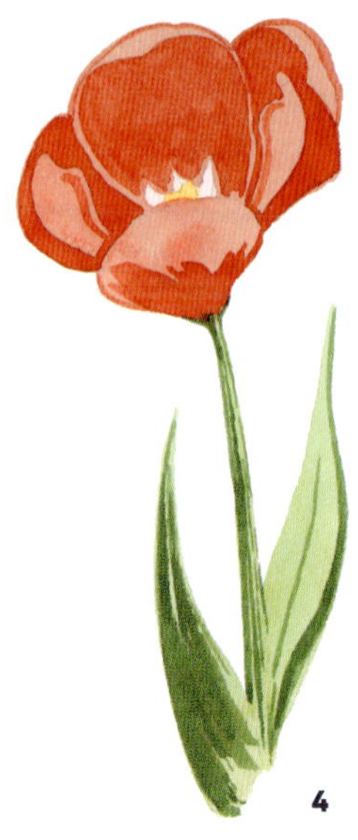

4

STEP 2: Lightly erase your pencil markings. On your palette, combine Alizarin Crimson (50%) and Cadmium Orange (50%). Create a light **value** of this mixture by adding water. With your size 8 round brush, paint in the flower petals, avoiding the center pollen area of the flower.

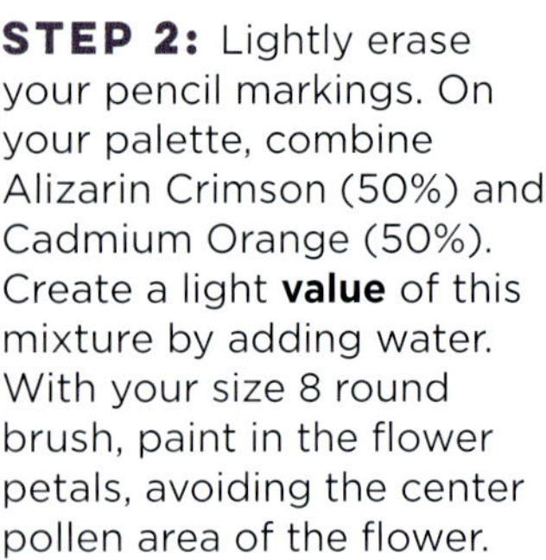

Alizarin Crimson (50%)   Cadmium Orange (50%)

Mix a light **value** of Green Gold (70%) with Winsor Green (30%) on your palette. Use this mixture to paint in the stem and leaves of the tulip.

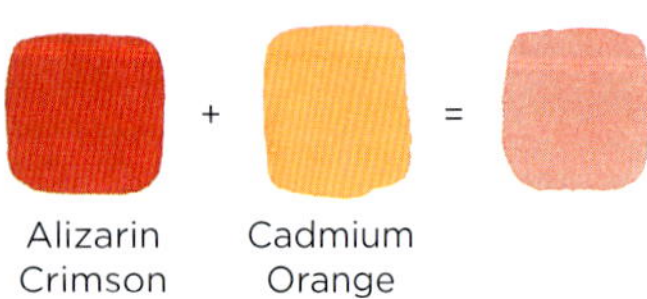

Green Gold (70%)   Winsor Green (30%)

STEP 3: Paint in the pollen patch located in the very center of the flower by using a light **value** of Quinacridone Gold.

Once the pollen is painted, add some darker detailing to the stem and leaves with a mix of Green Gold (60%), Winsor Green (30%) and a touch of Alizarin Crimson (10%). Do not completely paint over the first layer of green.

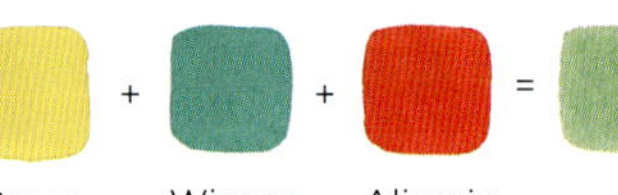

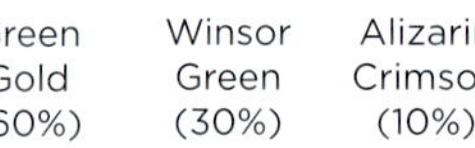

Green Gold (60%)   Winsor Green (30%)   Alizarin Crimson (10%)

STEP 4: Darken part of the flower petals by using Alizarin Crimson (50%) mixed with Cadmium Orange (50%) from your palette. Use less water than you did in Step 2 to make it a more **saturated** mixture that looks darker. Use this mixture to apply a **glaze** to each petal in a decorative design.

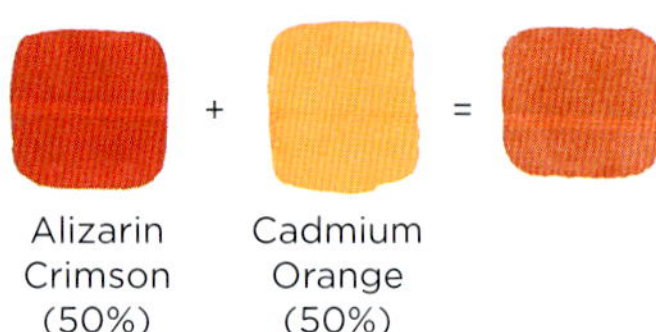

Alizarin Crimson (50%)   Cadmium Orange (50%)

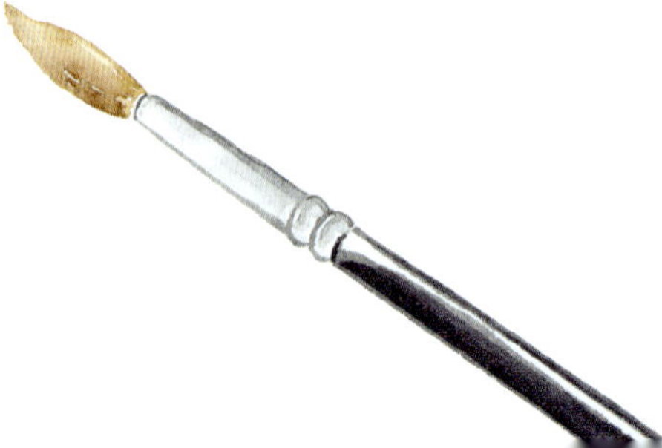

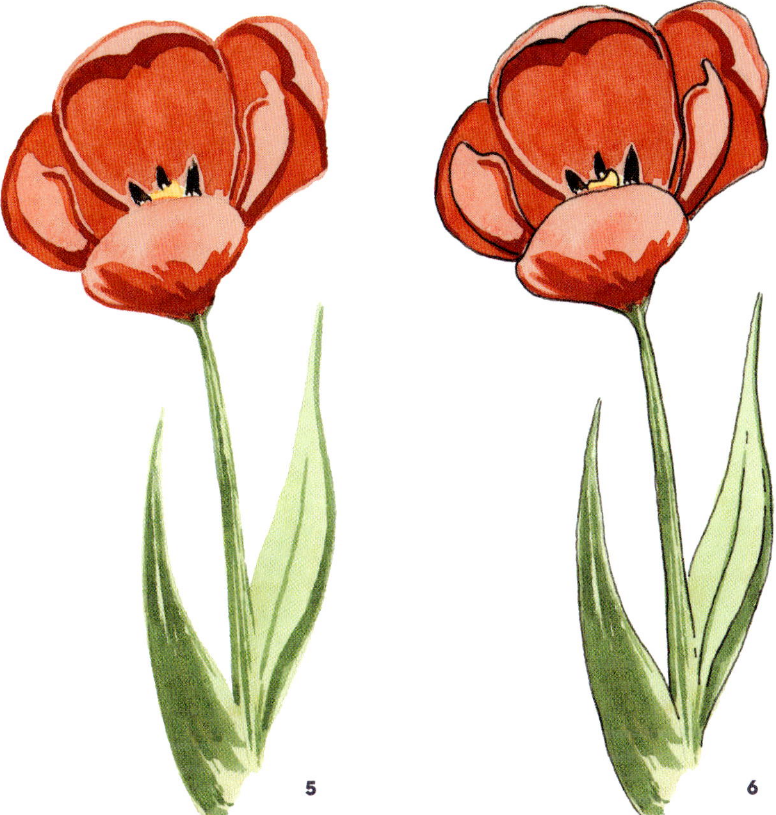

STEP 5: Take Neutral Tint to paint in three seeds next to the yellow pollen. Add more details to the petals where the **shadow** should be with this mixture from your palette: Alizarin Crimson (50%) and Cadmium Orange (50%) with minimal water for a really **saturated** color mixture.

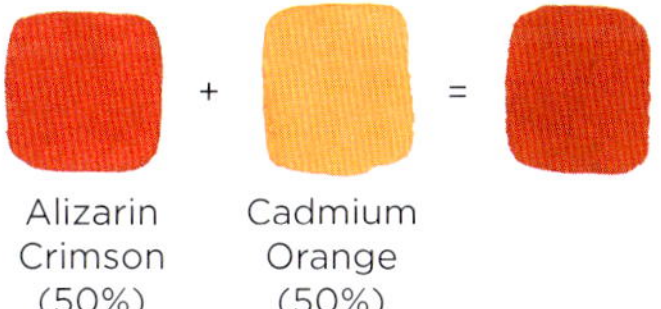

Alizarin
Crimson
(50%)

Cadmium
Orange
(50%)

STEP 6: This is an optional step if you want to add ink on top of your painting. Adding ink to watercolor gives it a different style that can make the art feel bolder because you are adding dark lines. For example, when you change text to bold, it stands out more. If you choose to do so, add the ink by outlining the flower, stem and leaves.

FLUFFY BUNNY

The more variety you can add to a painting, the more engaged the viewer will be. When placing the grass around the bunny in this project, you can apply it in a straight line, but then it won't have any movement. By allowing some of the blades of grass to bend, some to be forward and some in the back, you create variety for a more exciting painting.

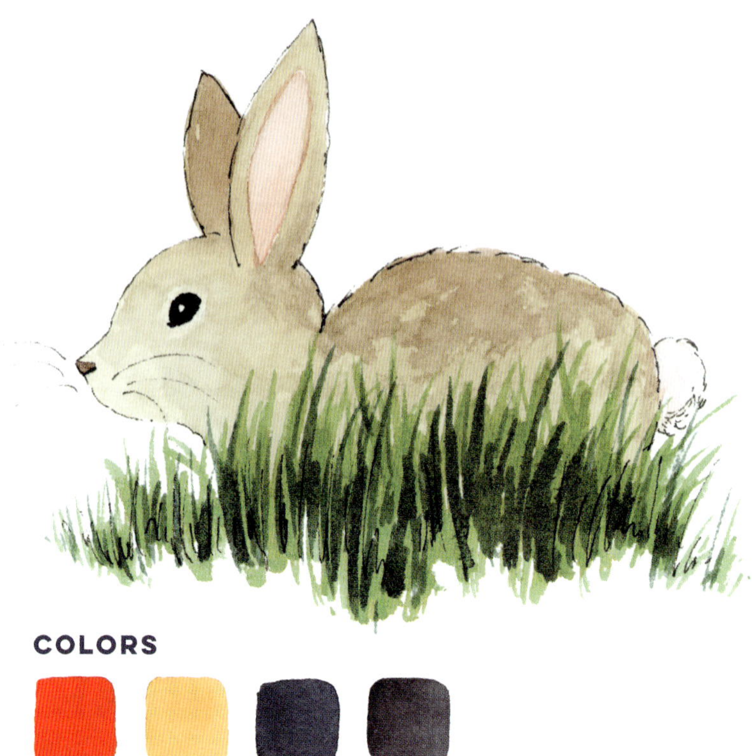

MATERIALS

Pencil

Watercolor paper

Size 8 round brush

Sharpie felt-tip pen

COLORS

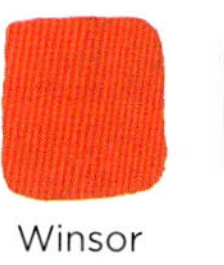
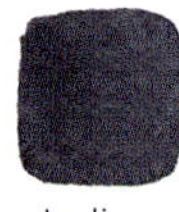
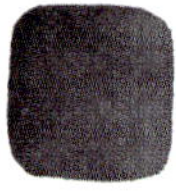

Winsor Red

Yellow Ochre

Indigo

Neutral Tint

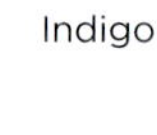
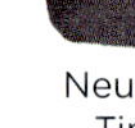
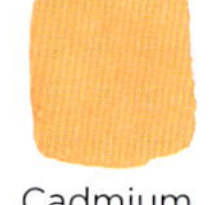
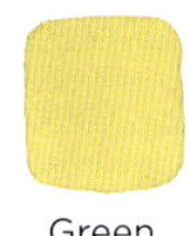
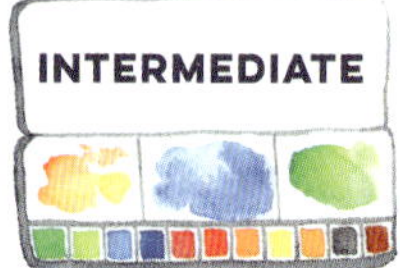

Winsor Green

Cadmium Orange

Green Gold

STEP 1: Use your pencil to trace (page 271) or sketch the bunny on your watercolor paper.

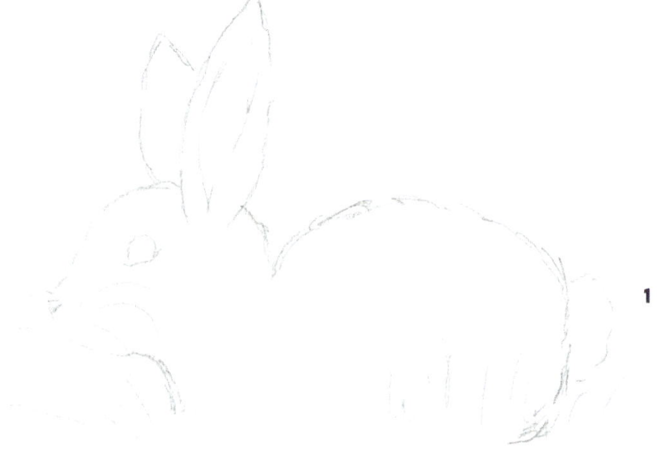

1

STEP 2: With a size 8 round brush, use a light **value** of Winsor Red to paint the inside of the bunny's ears and tail. Don't paint the tail completely; let some of the white paper show through in areas farther away from the body of the bunny. Let that dry.

Yellow Ochre (90%) + Indigo (10%) =

Take Yellow Ochre (90%) with a smidge of Indigo (10%) and combine them on your palette. Use this mixture to paint in the bunny's body. Around the face should be much lighter, so avoid adding too much paint there or add more water to your mixture to make it a lighter **value**.

STEP 3: Paint in the bunny's eye with Neutral Tint. Leave a white dot in the center. If it helps, you can use a pencil to lightly draw a circle so you know where you shouldn't paint.

To create a brown color, mix Yellow Ochre (50%) with Winsor Red (30%) and Indigo (20%) on your palette. Paint the brown nose in a triangular shape with this mixture.

Yellow Ochre (50%) + Winsor Red (30%) + Indigo (20%) =

Then, on your palette, mix Yellow Ochre (90%) with a little Indigo (10%). Use this mixture to paint in the top of the bunny's body. Start at the top of the ears, then bring the paint over the neck and down the back using a **dry brush** technique for fur-like **texture**.

Yellow Ochre (90%) + Indigo (10%) =

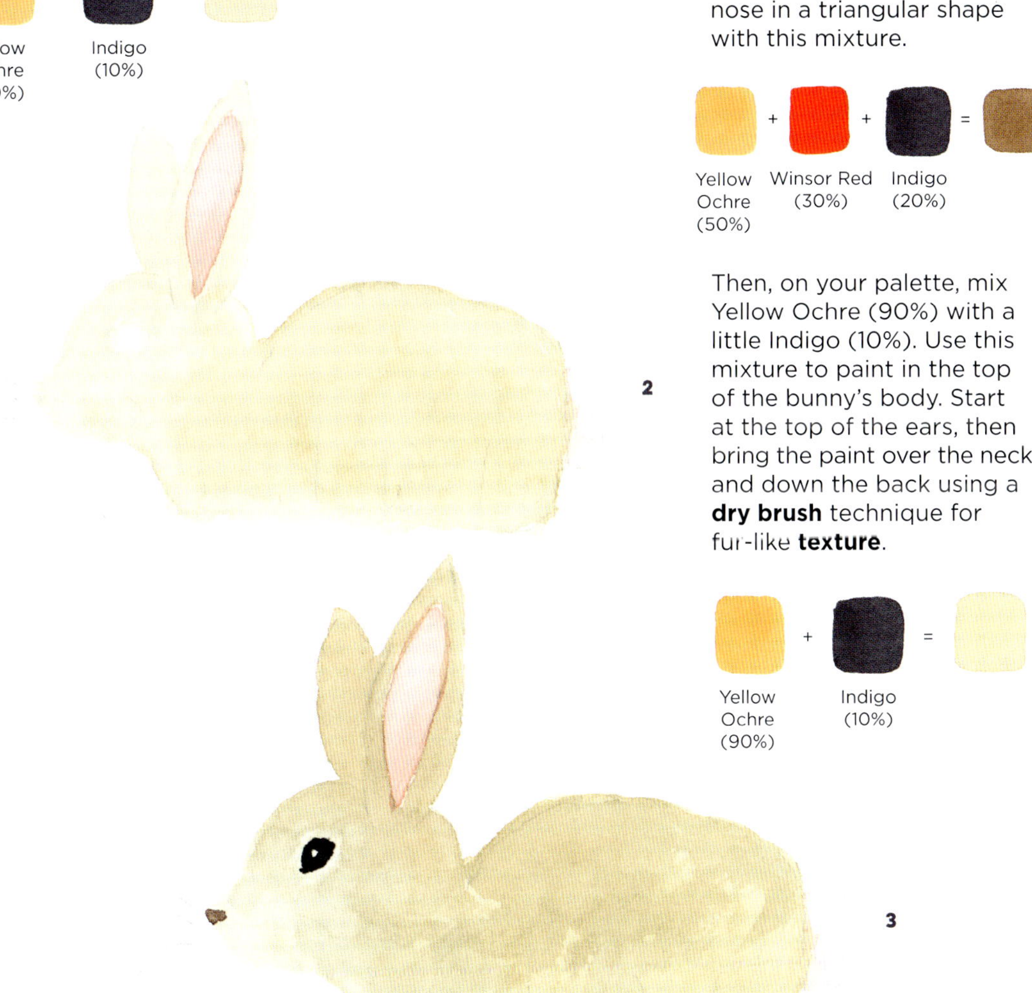

2

3

STEP 4: Mix Cadmium Orange (60%) and Winsor Green (40%) on your palette. Use this mixture to paint in the grass. Start your brush at the base and pull the blade of grass up in quick motions. You can do this both in a straight motion and in a slightly arched motion to the left or right. Add a bit of variety to make the blades of grass look different. Most of the blades of grass will go over the bunny's body.

Mix Yellow Ochre (50%), Winsor Red (30%) and Indigo (20%) on your palette. Use this mixture to paint another layer over the bunny's one ear in the **background**.

With a **dry brush** apply this same color mixture on the bunny's back to continue the fur **texture**.

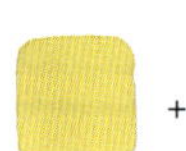
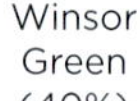

Cadmium Orange (60%) + Winsor Green (40%) =

Yellow Ochre (50%) + Winsor Red (30%) + Indigo (20%) =

STEP 5: Apply darker blades of grass over the top of your first layer. Use this mixture from your palette: Winsor Green (40%), Green Gold (30%) and Winsor Red (30%). Let that dry.

Use your Sharpie to add the whiskers of the bunny. As an optional step, you can outline the body and tail with ink too, and add in ink lines with the blades of grass.

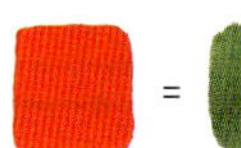

Winsor Green (40%) + Green Gold (30%) + Winsor Red (30%) =

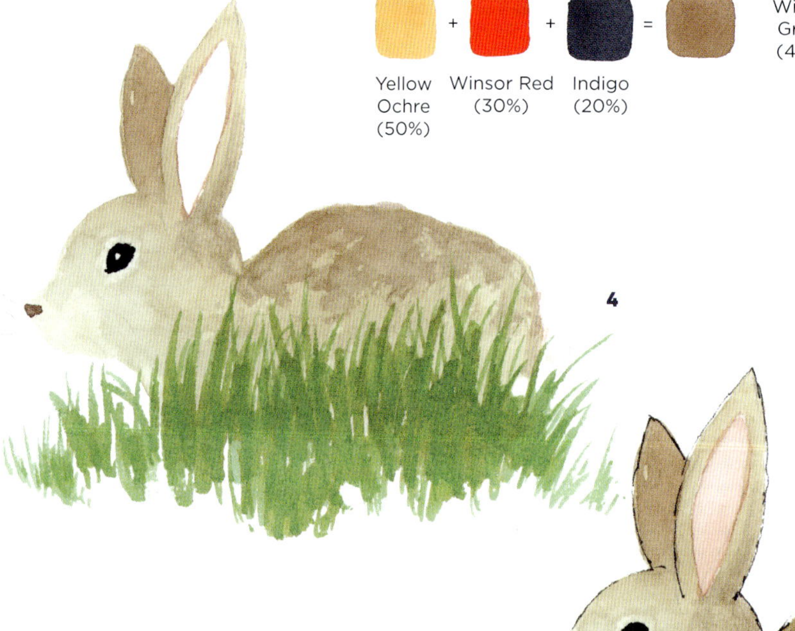

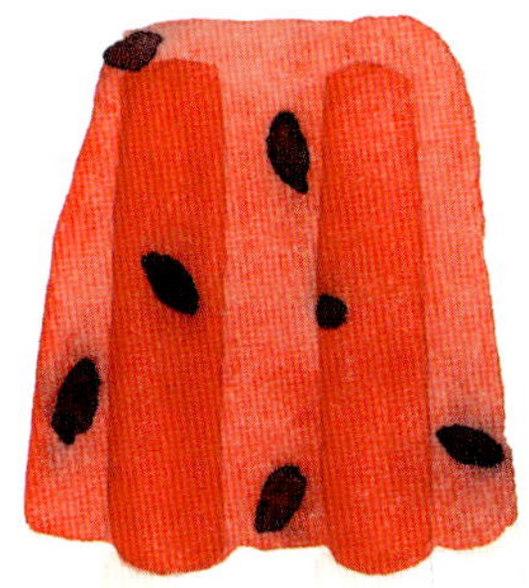
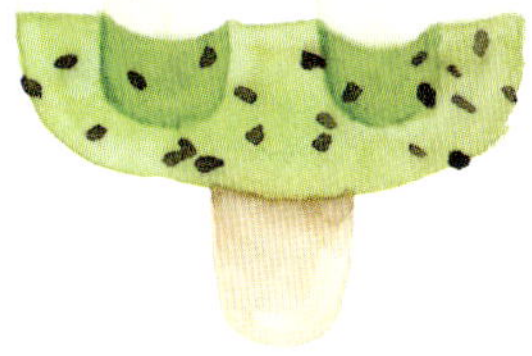

WATERMELON-KIWI POPSICLE

In watercolor, the order in which you paint the layers in your **subject** can significantly impact the final result. For example, in this Watermelon-Kiwi Popsicle painting, we do not paint the seeds at the end because if we did those on the last layer, it would look like the seeds were on top of the popsicle. They would look sharp and defined instead of being slightly blurred by painting them first and allowing the layers on top to make them fuzzy. Building layers on top of the seeds creates the illusion that they are frozen inside the popsicle.

MATERIALS

Pencil

Watercolor paper

Size 8 round brush

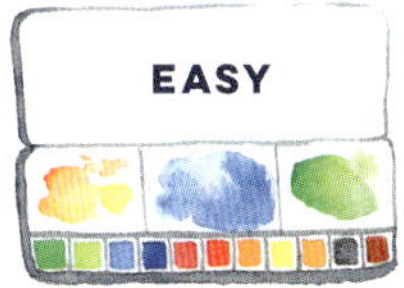

COLORS

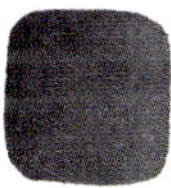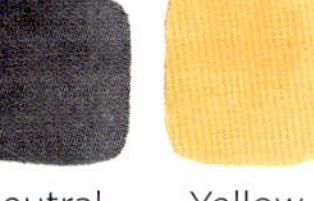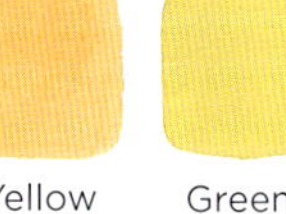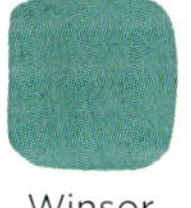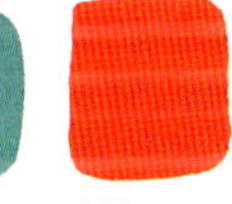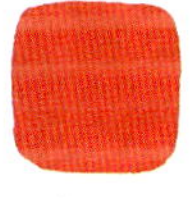

Neutral Tint	Yellow Ochre	Green Gold	Winsor Green	Winsor Red	Alizarin Crimson	Lemon Yellow

STEP 1: Use your pencil to lightly trace (page 269) or sketch the watermelon-kiwi popsicle onto your watercolor paper.

STEP 2: Lightly erase your pencil markings. With your size 8 round brush, use Neutral Tint for the seeds. Paint in tiny seeds at the base for the kiwi flavor. On the top watermelon flavor, add seven seeds. Be careful not to overdo the number of seeds you add for the watermelon layer. No one likes a super seedy watermelon!

Paint the stick of the popsicle using a light **value** of Yellow Ochre.

STEP 3: In this step, it is okay if the next color layer **bleeds** a little with the seeds. The fuzziness will allow them to look like they are under a layer of flavored ice.

Paint in the kiwi color on the bottom with this mixture from your palette: Green Gold (80%) with Winsor Green (20%). Add a decent amount of water to this color mixture so that the seeds will show through from Step 2.

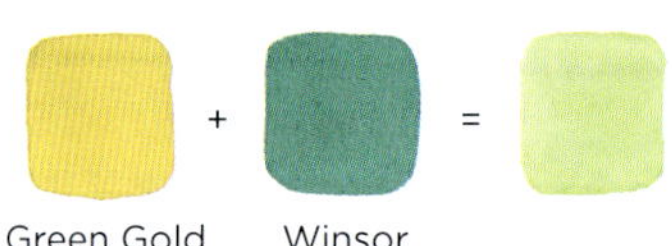

Green Gold (80%) + Winsor Green (20%) =

Take Winsor Red and add water for a light **value**. Apply this color to the watermelon flavor on your popsicle.

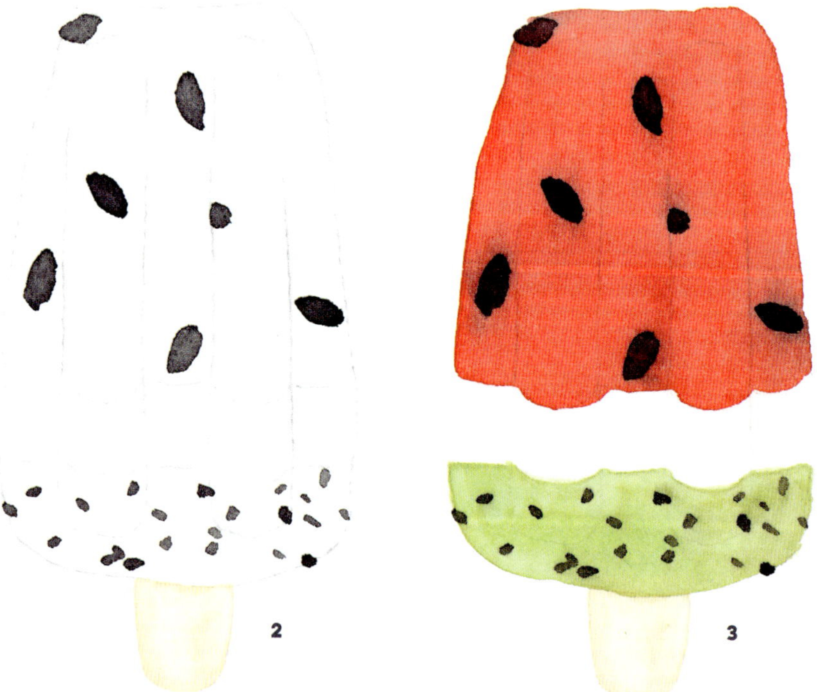

2

3

STEP 4: Starting with the watermelon layer, on your palette combine Winsor Red (80%) with Alizarin Crimson (20%). Use this color to paint the concave grooves of the watermelon portion of the popsicle. Then paint the kiwi concave grooves of the popsicle using Green Gold (70%) mixed with Winsor Green (30%) on your palette.

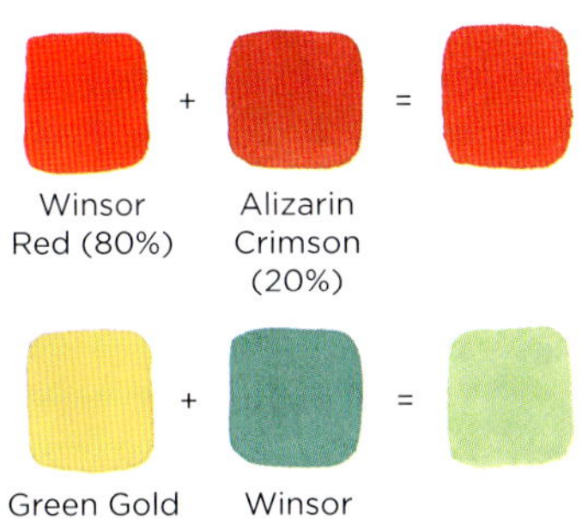

Winsor Red (80%) + Alizarin Crimson (20%) =

Green Gold (70%) + Winsor Green (30%) =

STEP 5: Darken the popsicle stick with a light **value** of Yellow Ochre. Apply this additional layer by focusing directly under the kiwi flavor to appear as a **shadow**.

On your palette, mix Lemon Yellow (80%) with a touch of Winsor Red (20%). Make sure it is a light **value** by adding lots of water. Use this mixture to paint in the white area of the popsicle.

When you paint, add the color to the left and right outside edging of the white area; don't add any to the center ridge. Don't pull this mixture all the way to the concave grooves so there will be a bit of the white paper showing through. Now it's time to paint the concave grooves; start on the left side of both grooves and carry the color into the middle. Don't paint in the white area on the right side of both grooved areas.

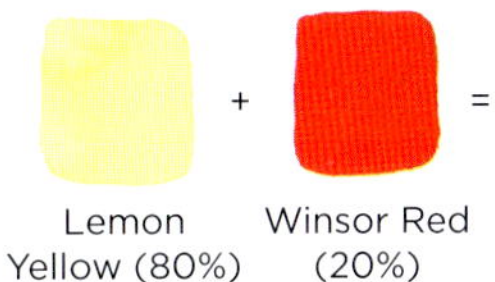

Lemon Yellow (80%) + Winsor Red (20%) =

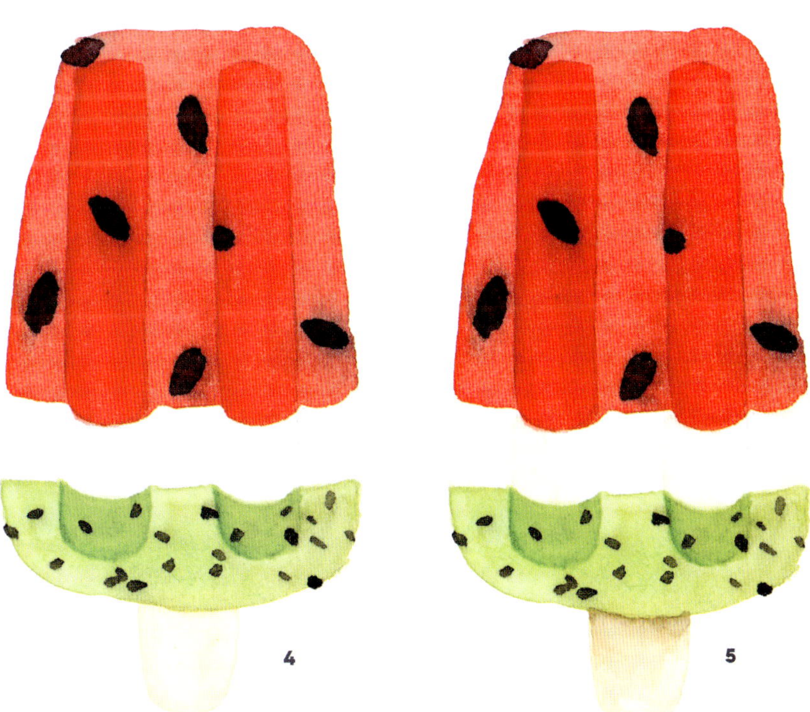

4

5

BIKE

When painting, we sometimes need to remember that we can move our paper around and paint from different angles. Turning the paper upside down can be especially helpful when painting a more detailed object like this bike. Suddenly, an area that seemed complicated to maneuver the paintbrush around is ten times easier when your paper's upside down.

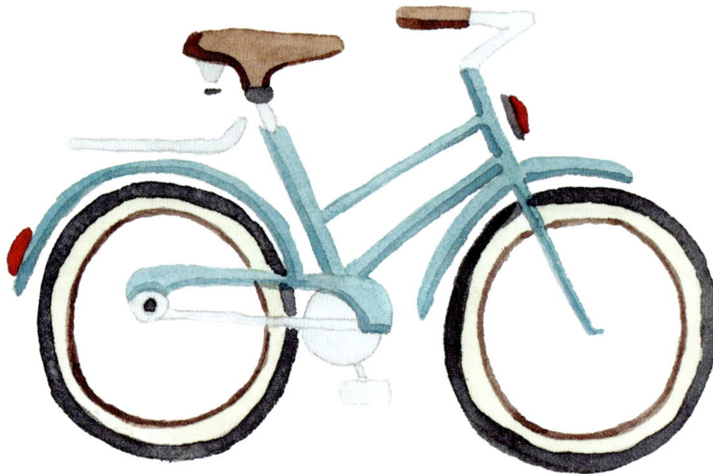

MATERIALS

Pencil

Watercolor paper

Size 8 round brush

COLORS

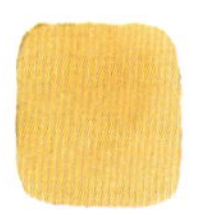

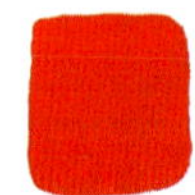

Yellow Ochre · Indigo · Winsor Red

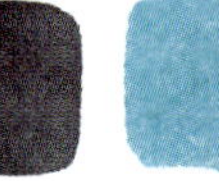
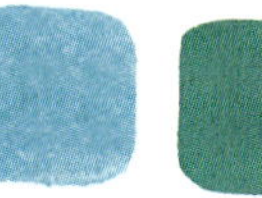

Neutral Tint · Cobalt Teal Blue · Winsor Green

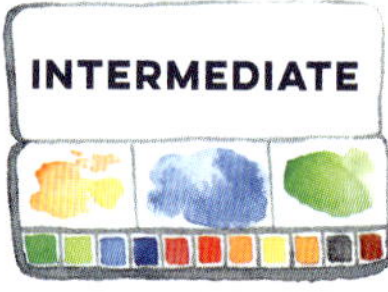

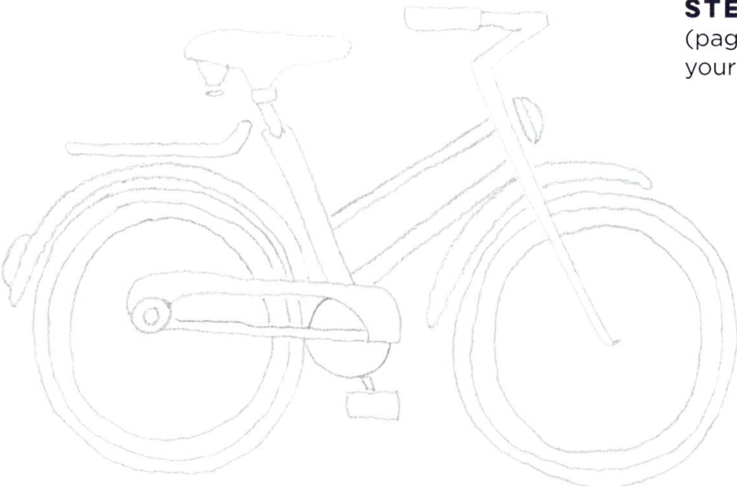

STEP 1: Use a pencil to trace (page 269) or sketch the bike on your watercolor paper.

1

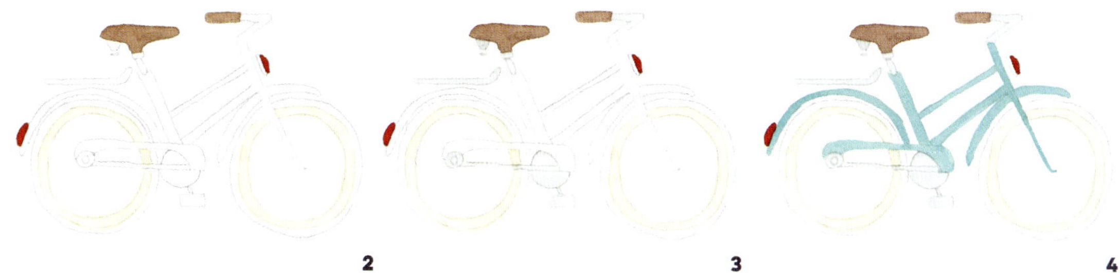

2　　　　　　　**3**　　　　　　　**4**

STEP 2: With your size 8 round brush, paint in the whitewall tire by using a light **value** of this mixture on your palette: Yellow Ochre (80%) and Indigo (20%).

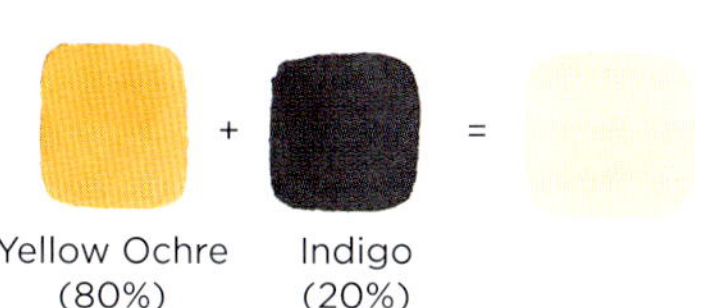

Yellow Ochre (80%)　　Indigo (20%)

Combine Yellow Ochre (60%), Winsor Red (35%) and Indigo (5%) on your palette. Use this mixture to paint the bike seat and handle.

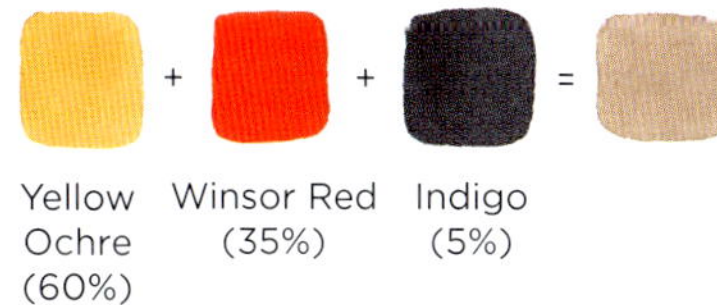

Yellow Ochre (60%)　　Winsor Red (35%)　　Indigo (5%)

Lastly, **load** your brush with Winsor Red and paint the lights on the bike.

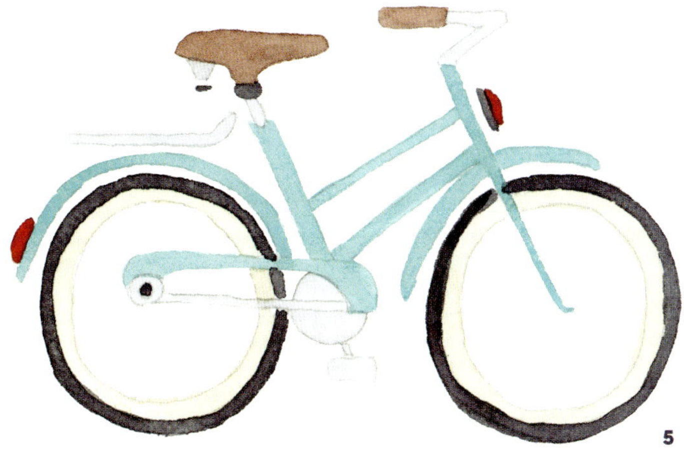

5

STEP 3: Load your brush with a light **value** of Neutral Tint and paint all the silver spots on the bike: bike chain, pedal, handlebars and underneath the seat.

STEP 4: Use a mixture of Cobalt Teal Blue (70%) and Winsor Green (30%) from your palette to paint the main frame of the bike.

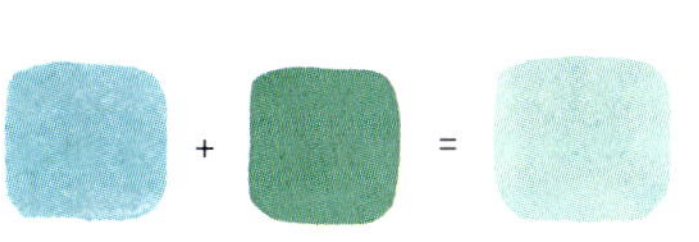

Cobalt Teal Blue (70%)　　Winsor Green (30%)

STEP 5: Use Neutral Tint on the tires, the two little items under the bike seal, the dot in the center of the back tire and the casing around the front light. You will want this to be a dark **value**, so use less water when grabbing the Neutral Tint.

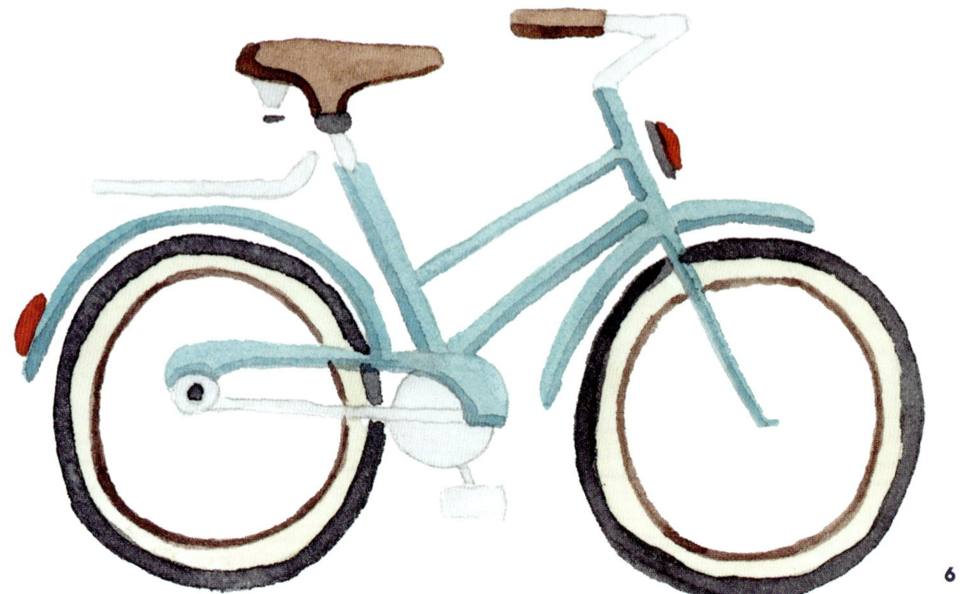

STEP 6: To make the main frame of the bike vibrant, add a thin line of detailing over the main frame of the bike with the same mixture from your palette from Step 4: Cobalt Teal Blue (70%) combined with Winsor Green (30%). If you want a dark **value**, add less water to the mixture.

Load your brush with a mixture of Yellow Ochre (60%), Winsor Red (35%) and Indigo (5%) from your palette. Add dark brown accents under the seat and handle. Also take this mixture and paint the inside lining of the tire. If you need a darker **value**, use less water.

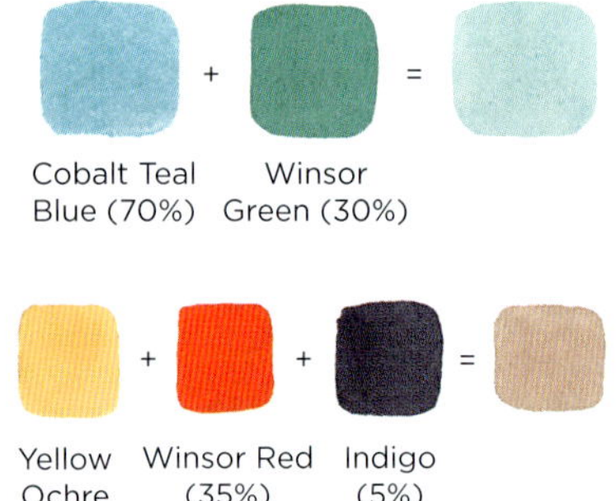

Cobalt Teal Blue (70%)   Winsor Green (30%)

Yellow Ochre (60%)   Winsor Red (35%)   Indigo (5%)

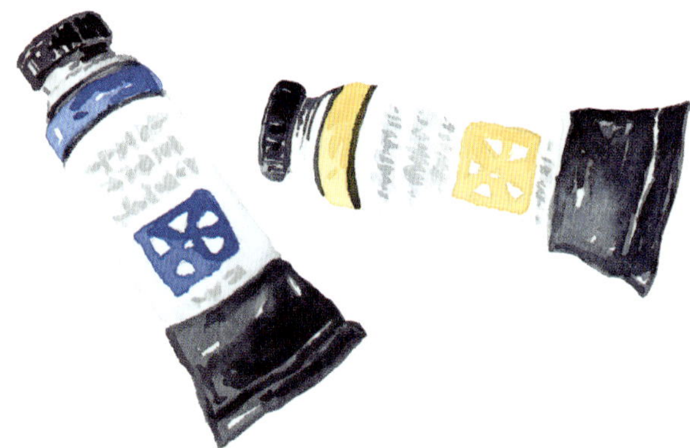

FISHING BOAT

Watercolor can dry extremely fast, especially if it is summertime or you live in a dry climate. One tip for painting free of pressure is to work in sections one at a time so you're not in a rush. In this Fishing Boat painting, instead of painting all the orange buoys at the same time, I painted each one individually; even though the same colors are used, I didn't want one of them to dry before being able to add the red to the orange.

MATERIALS

Pencil

Watercolor paper

Size 8 round brush

Sharpie felt-tip pen (optional)

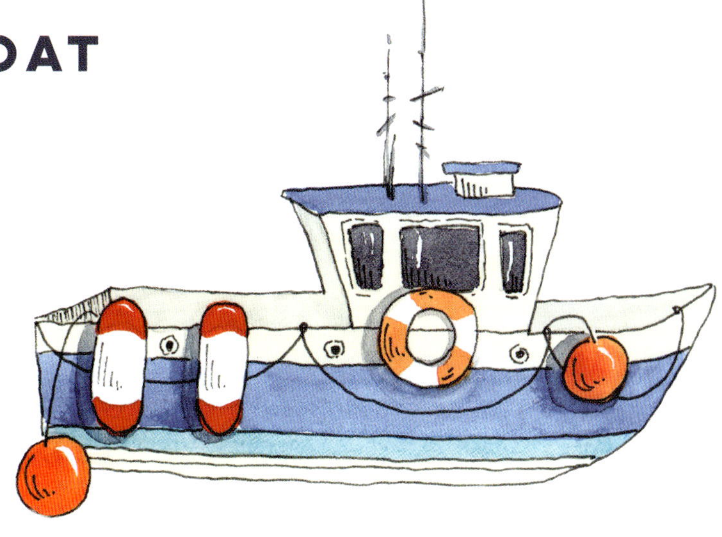

COLORS

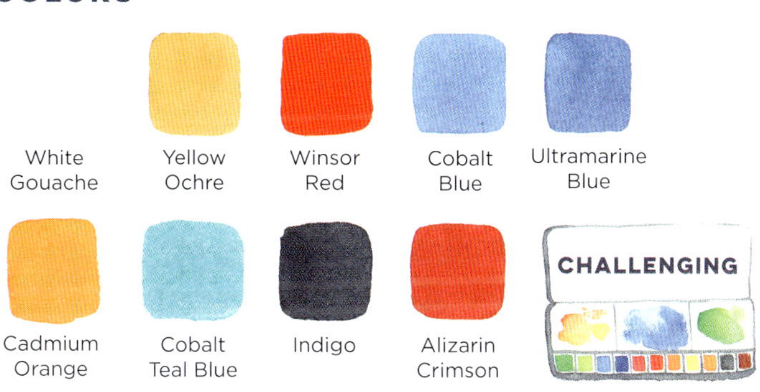

White Gouache

Yellow Ochre

Winsor Red

Cobalt Blue

Ultramarine Blue

Cadmium Orange

Cobalt Teal Blue

Indigo

Alizarin Crimson

STEP 1: Take a pencil and lightly trace (page 271) or sketch the fishing boat on your watercolor paper.

STEP 2: Mix White Gouache (70%) with Yellow Ochre (30%) on your palette. **Load** your size 8 round brush and start applying this mixture as the main color of the boat. Let that dry.

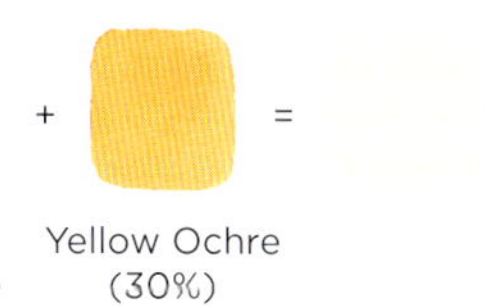

White Gouache (70%)   +   Yellow Ochre (30%)   =

1

Clean your brush well and **load** it with Winsor Red, then apply it to the top and bottom of the oval buoys.

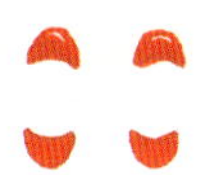

2

STEP 3: Use Cobalt Blue for the thick stripe on the boat and on the roof of the boat. While the paint is still wet on the boat stripe, **load** your brush with Ultramarine Blue and paint **shadows** on the left side of the oval buoys you painted in Step 2.

STEP 4: Paint one buoy at a time so that the first layer doesn't dry before you can lay in the second layer with the **wet-in-wet** technique. Take Cadmium Orange and paint it onto

one circle buoy, leaving a little spot of white as the **highlight**. Now take Winsor Red and drop it onto the wet Cadmium Orange (this helps create more dimension to your buoy instead of having only one color). Do this for the other buoy.

For the circular life preserver buoy, paint three sections using Cadmium Orange and leave three areas on the buoy to show the white of the paper.

STEP 5: **Load** your brush with Cobalt Teal Blue and apply it to the stripe underneath the thicker Cobalt Blue stripe.

Clean off your brush, then **load** it with Indigo (20%) and a lot of water (80%). Add a **shadow** on the inside of the boat.

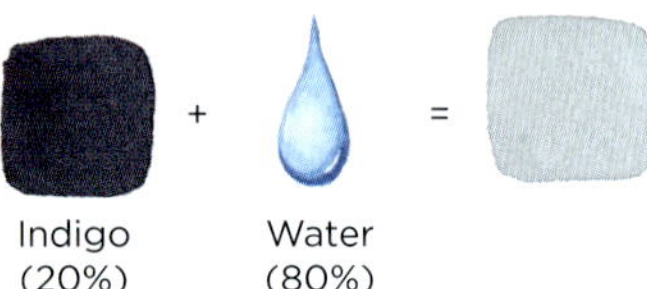

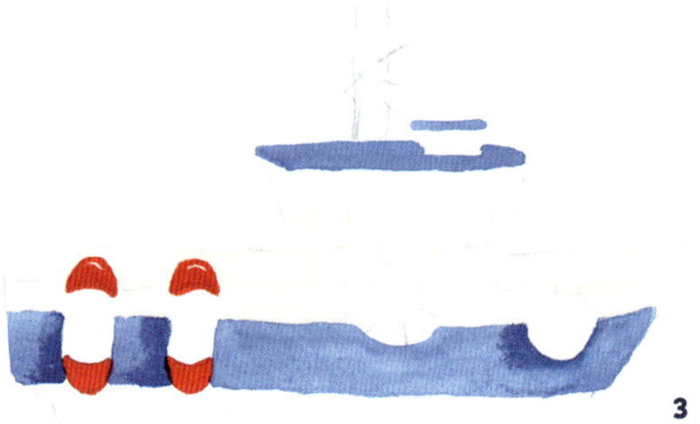

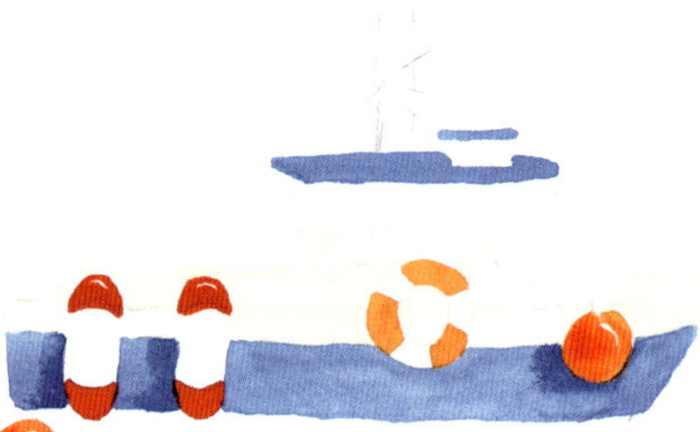

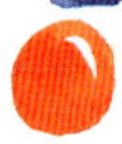

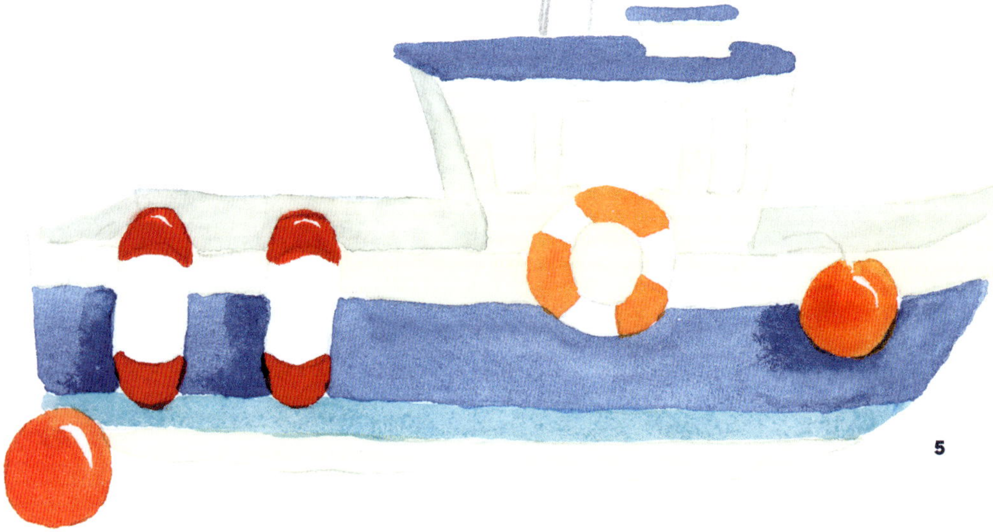

STEP 6: Mix Indigo (70%) with Alizarin Crimson (30%) on your palette and use this mixture for the **shadow** on the left side of the four buoys, following the same shape of each buoy as you paint. Use this same mixture as the color of the windows on the boat. Leave a little thin white stripe for a **highlight** on the windows. There are little antennas on the boat that can be painted with this color mixture as well.

Indigo (70%) + Alizarin Crimson (30%) =

STEP 7: As an optional last step, add ink with your Sharpie. Outline the boat and add in some lines to help indicate curves, **textures** and areas of **shadow**.

6

7

SURFBOARD

One of the beautiful effects from applying water to your paper first and using the **wet-in-wet** technique is achieving a smooth, blended transition. This technique works perfectly on this surfboard because it helps the board's **texture** look slick and shiny without visible brushstrokes.

MATERIALS

Watercolor paper

Pencil

Size 8 round brush

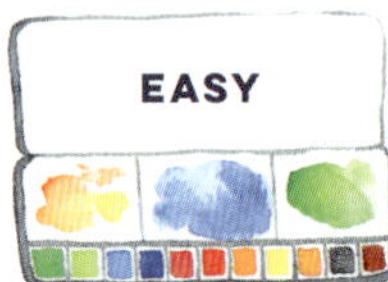

COLORS

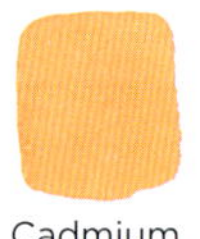
Cadmium Orange

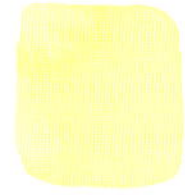
Lemon Yellow

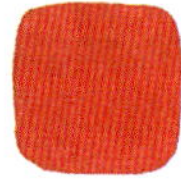
Alizarin Crimson

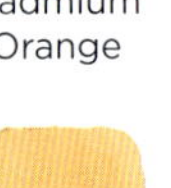
Yellow Ochre

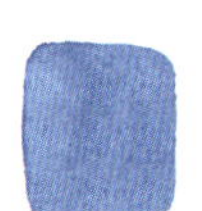
Ultramarine Blue

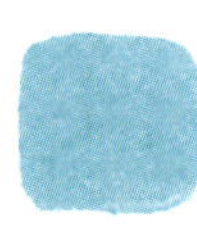
Cobalt Teal Blue

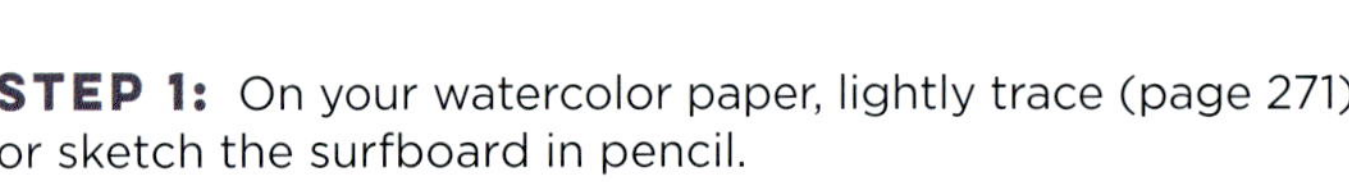

STEP 1: On your watercolor paper, lightly trace (page 271) or sketch the surfboard in pencil.

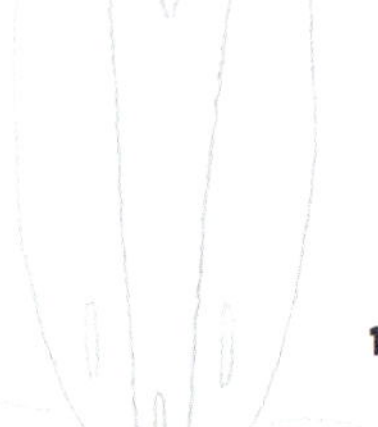

STEP 2: Lightly erase your pencil markings. Move fast with this step or the colors won't blend. **Load** your size 8 round brush with water and paint a **clear water wash** on the top "V" of the surfboard and the left and right sides. Then use the **wet-in-wet** technique by painting Cadmium Orange into the top "V" section. For the left and right sides of the surfboard, continue using a **wet-in-wet** technique by painting a **variegated wash**. At the top of each side, paint Cadmium Orange down 25 percent of the way. Clean your brush and **load** it with Lemon Yellow. Start painting in the Lemon Yellow where the Cadmium Orange ended, allowing those colors to **bleed**. Clean and **load** your brush with Lemon Yellow again, and finish painting the bottom portion with the Lemon Yellow.

STEP 3: Paint the "Y" shape on your surfboard using Alizarin Crimson.

Load your brush with Yellow Ochre and paint the sand. For the edging of the sand, use the **dry brush** technique by not reloading your brush with Yellow Ochre. Use what little remains of the color on your brush to drag out the sand, resulting in a fun, grainy **texture**.

STEP 4: Make a dark purple by mixing Alizarin Crimson (50%) and Ultramarine Blue (50%) on your palette. Use this mixture to paint in the "V" shape on the surfboard.

Alizarin
Crimson
(50%)

Ultramarine
Blue
(50%)

Paint the fins on the surfboard using Cobalt Teal Blue for a contrast (or use your dark purple mixture for a more limited color palette).

STEP 5: Create layers of sand by adding this mixture from your palette: Yellow Ochre (90%) and a touch of Alizarin Crimson (10%). Use the **dry brush** technique at the end of painting in the top layer of sand just like you did in Step 3.

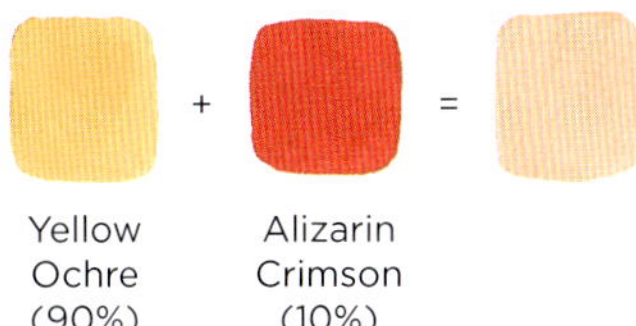

Yellow
Ochre
(90%)

Alizarin
Crimson
(10%)

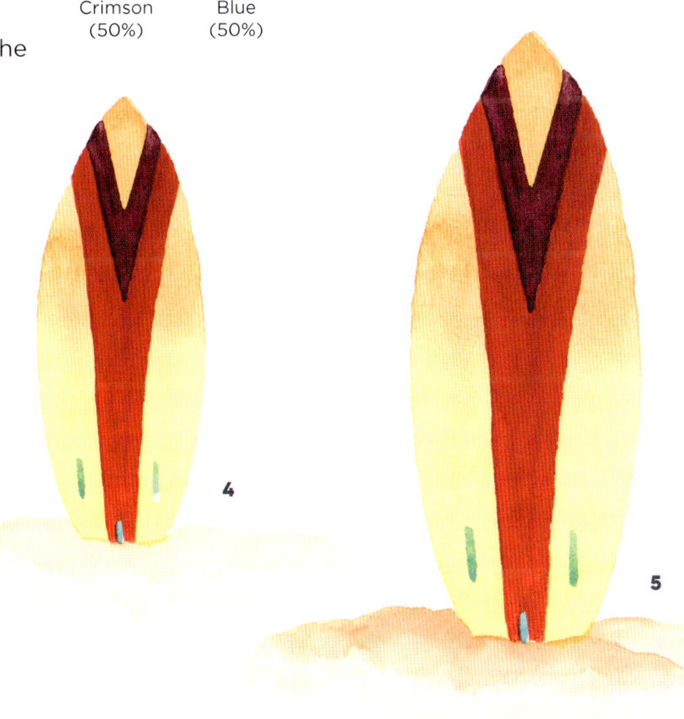

2

3

4

5

MAGNIFIED BUMBLE BEE

Summer reminds me of bright blue skies with colorful flowers and bees dancing around. As a kid, it was a time of adventure and exploration. Because of those memories, I wanted to mash two objects into one for this final summer painting! A tip for drawing or painting circles: You want to lock your wrist and move your arm in a circular motion. You have more control when you use your arm to draw/paint the circle instead of your wrist because your arm is more stabilized.

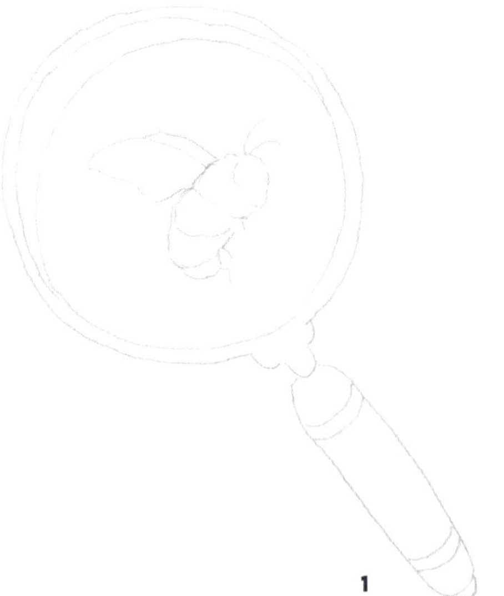

MATERIALS

Watercolor paper

Pencil

Size 8 round brush

COLORS

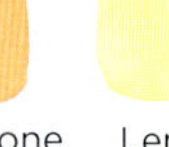

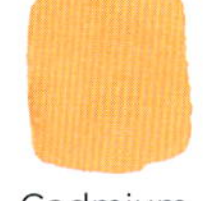
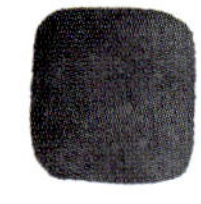
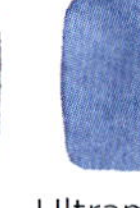
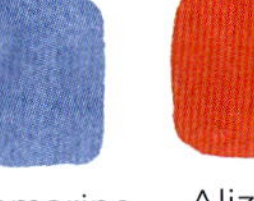
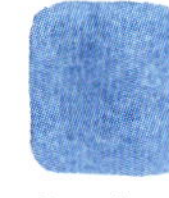

| Quinacridone Gold | Lemon Yellow | Cadmium Orange | Neutral Tint | Ultramarine Blue | Alizarin Crimson | Cerulean Blue |

STEP 1: On your watercolor paper, trace (page 271) or sketch the magnified bumble bee with a pencil.

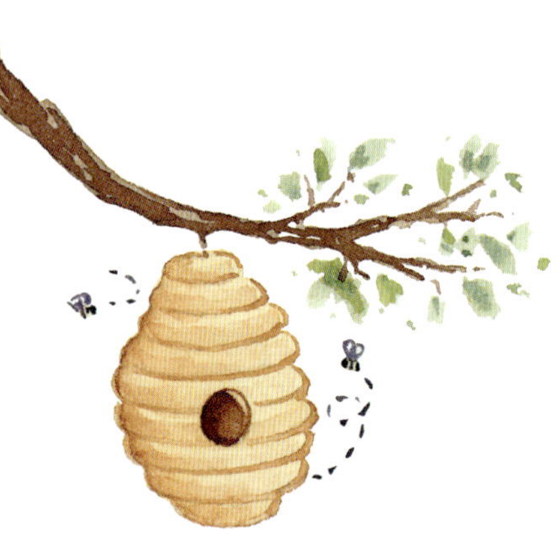

1

STEP 2: Lightly erase your pencil markings. **Load** your size 8 round bush with Quinacridone Gold and paint the three detail areas on the handle of the magnifying glass and the circular case that holds the glass.

STEP 3: On your palette, mix Lemon Yellow (80%) with a little bit of Cadmium Orange (20%). Use this mixture to paint in the yellow areas on the bee's body.

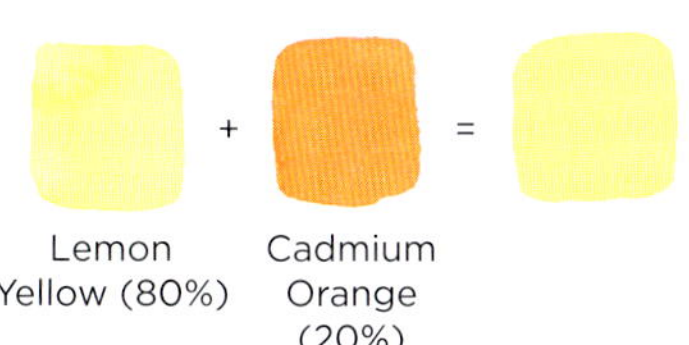

Combine Quinacridone Gold (80%) with a little bit of Neutral Tint (20%) on your palette. With this mixture, add the **shadow** inside the Quinacridone Gold rim that's holding the glass. Also use this mixture to outline the casing holding the glass and then add darker accents on the three detail areas on the handle.

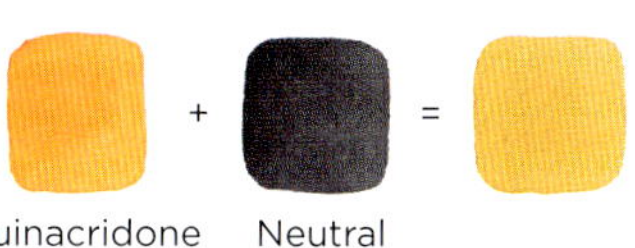

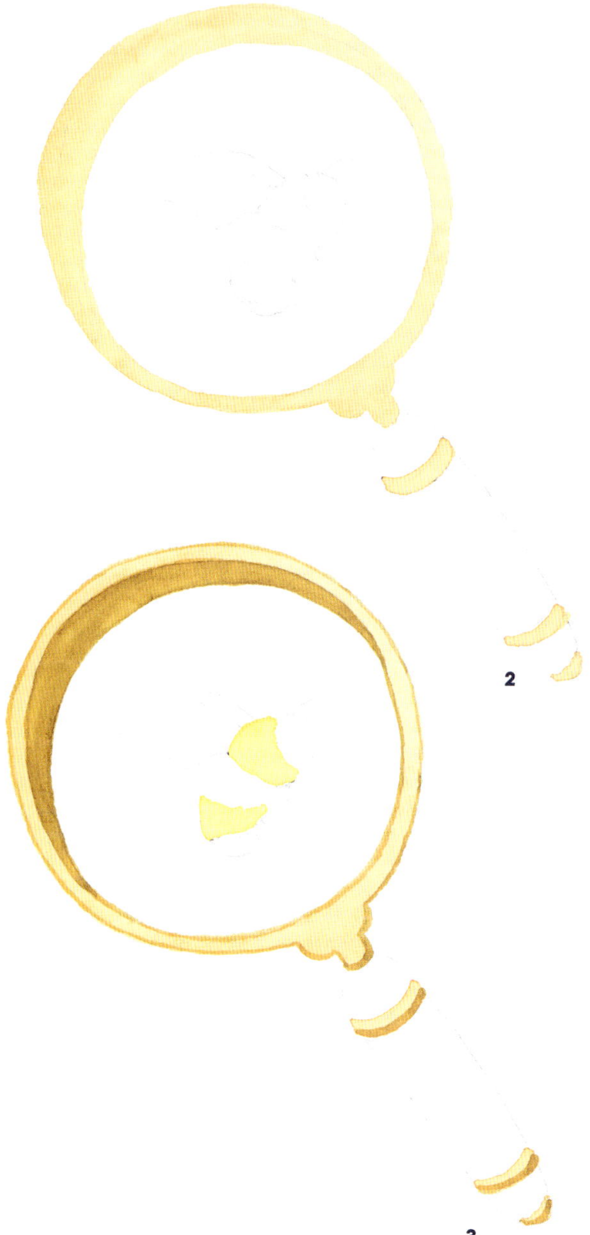

STEP 4: Paint in the black areas on the bee using this mixture from your palette: Neutral Tint (70%) and Ultramarine Blue (30%). You are mixing this color so it isn't just a flat black; it will add dimension to the bee.

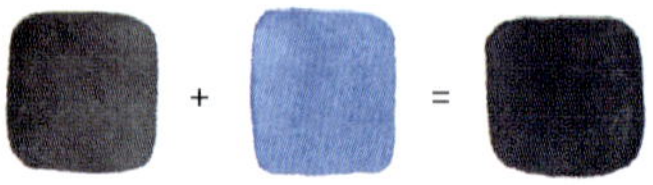

Neutral Tint (70%) + Ultramarine Blue (30%) =

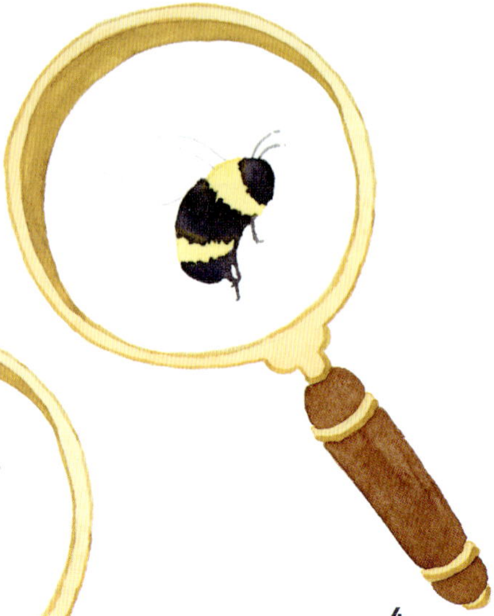

Then mix Cadmium Orange (50%) with Alizarin Crimson (40%) and Neutral Tint (10%) on your palette. Use this color mixture to paint in the wooden handle.

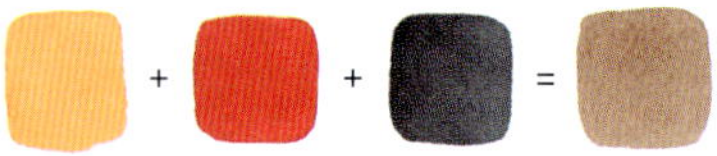

Cadmium Orange (50%) + Alizarin Crimson (40%) + Neutral Tint (10%) =

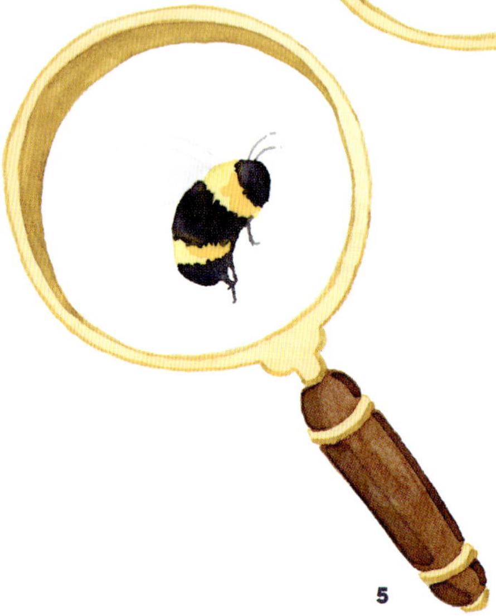

STEP 5: Mix Ultramarine Blue (60%) with Alizarin Crimson (40%). You want this to be a really light **value** by adding lots of water to the color mixture. Apply this color to the wings of the bee.

Mix Lemon Yellow (70%) with Cadmium Orange (30%) on your palette. Take this color and darken the bottom portion of the yellow areas on the bee.

Take the Cadmium Orange (50%) and combine it with Alizarin Crimson (40%) and Neutral Tint (10%) on your palette. You will want this layer to be a dark **value**, so use less water in the mixture. Take this brown color and paint the sides of the wood handle. Make sure to keep these as **hard edges**; there is no need to **soften** the lines on each side of the handle. This will give the wooden handle more texture.

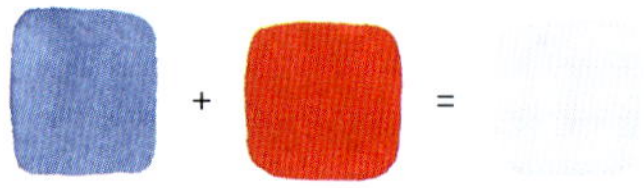

Ultramarine Blue (60%) + Alizarin Crimson (40%) =

Lemon Yellow (70%) + Cadmium Orange (30%) =

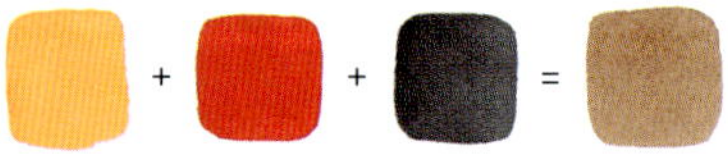

Cadmium Orange (50%) + Alizarin Crimson (40%) + Neutral Tint (10%) =

STEP 6: Use Ultramarine Blue (60%) and mix it with a bit of Alizarin Crimson (40%) on your palette. This is the same mixture you used for the wings in Step 5, but this time you want the color to be a darker **value**, so don't add as much water into the mixture. Use this color to outline and paint the details on the wings.

Darken the black areas on the bee using this mixture from your palette: Neutral Tint (70%) with Ultramarine Blue (30%). This is the same mixture as the one in Step 4, but you want it to be a darker **value**, so don't add as much water into the mixture.

STEP 7: Now it is time to paint the glass. Start by applying a **clear water wash** in the glass area but avoid getting water on the bee. It is okay to leave a space around the bee. Take a light value of Cerulean Blue and start painting it into the **clear water wash**. Add most of the Cerulean Blue on the bottom left side of the glass and pull that color around the rim of the glass. Then slowly pull the color inward toward the bee as it gets lighter in **value**. This is a **gradient wash** but in a circular shape.

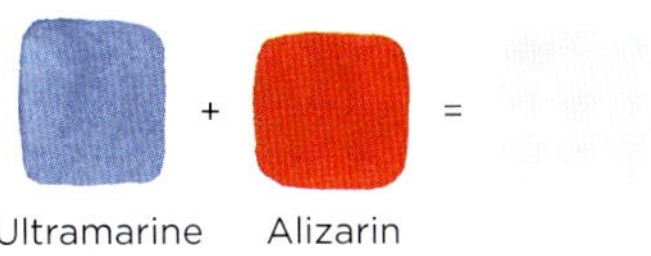

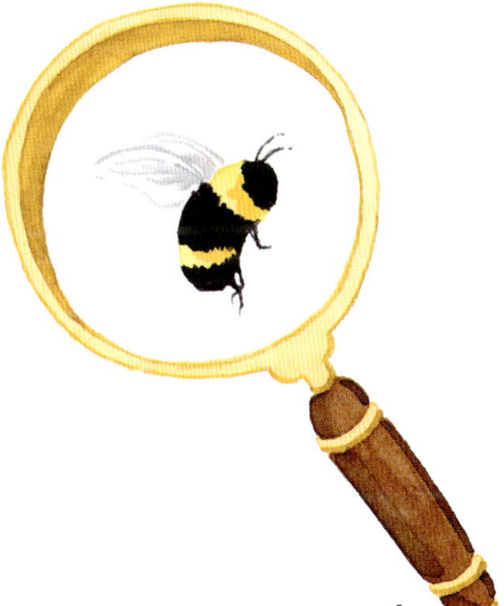

Ultramarine Blue (60%) + Alizarin Crimson (40%) =

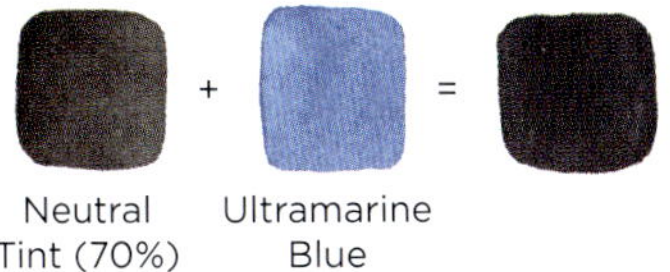

Neutral Tint (70%) + Ultramarine Blue (30%) =

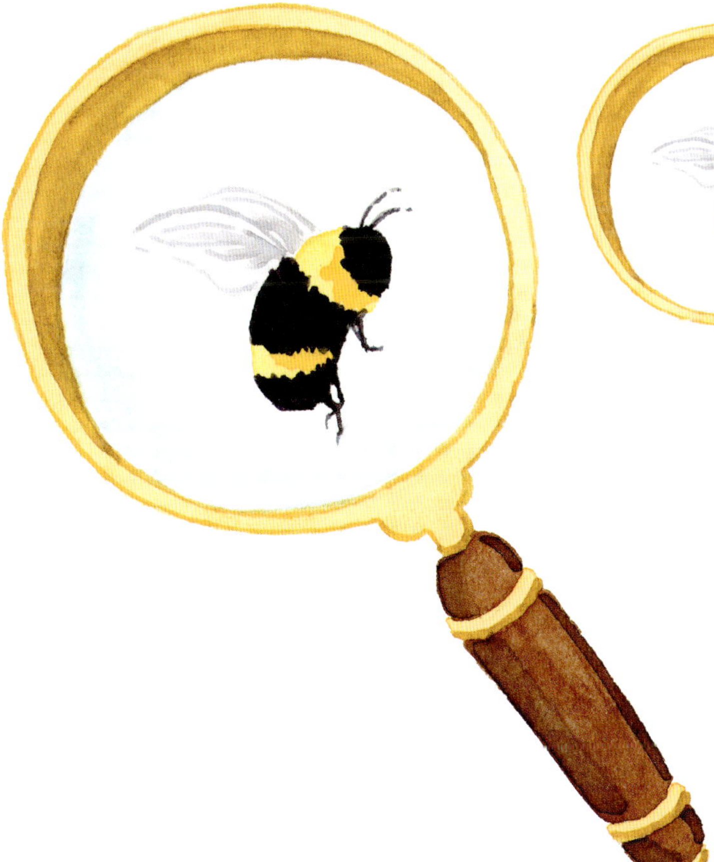

ACKNOWLEDGMENTS

First, I would like to thank my editor, Sadie Hofmeester. Without her, this book would never have happened! Thank you for believing in me and helping me through this crazy process with such kindness. Your passion and enthusiasm for all things books is contagious. I have treasured our chats. To my design team, Meg Baskis and Laura Benton, thank you for working so closely with me to create such a beautiful book. And a huge shout-out to Sarah Monroe, Deb Monti and the rest of the team at Page Street Publishing.

I would also like to thank Sara Erekson, who put just as many hours into this book. I won't forget the late nights and coffee runs while bouncing ideas off each other about making the book the best it can be.

ABOUT THE AUTHOR

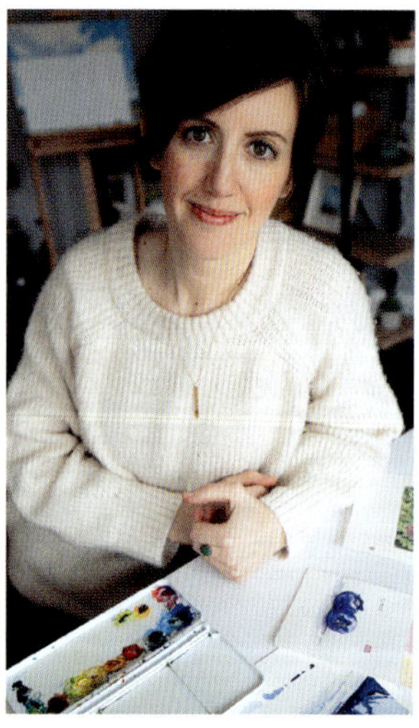

Mallery Jane grew up with a pencil in her hand, loving to draw. She graduated from Arizona State University with a bachelor's degree in art education. For the next seven years, she taught art to thousands of students in the school system.

In 2021, Mallery made one of the most significant decisions of her life—she quit her teaching job to become a full-time artist. Even though she no longer teaches in the school system, she shares her passion for teaching art online at MalleryJane.com. Mallery Jane is most well-known on Instagram, TikTok and YouTube for the unique way she helps others learn how to draw and paint.

When Mallery isn't working on creating tutorials, she is spending quality time with her young golden retriever pup, Jesse, and her love, Sara.

@MalleryJane

@MalleryJaneArt

@MalleryJaneArt

@MalleryJaneArt

INDEX

TEMPLATES

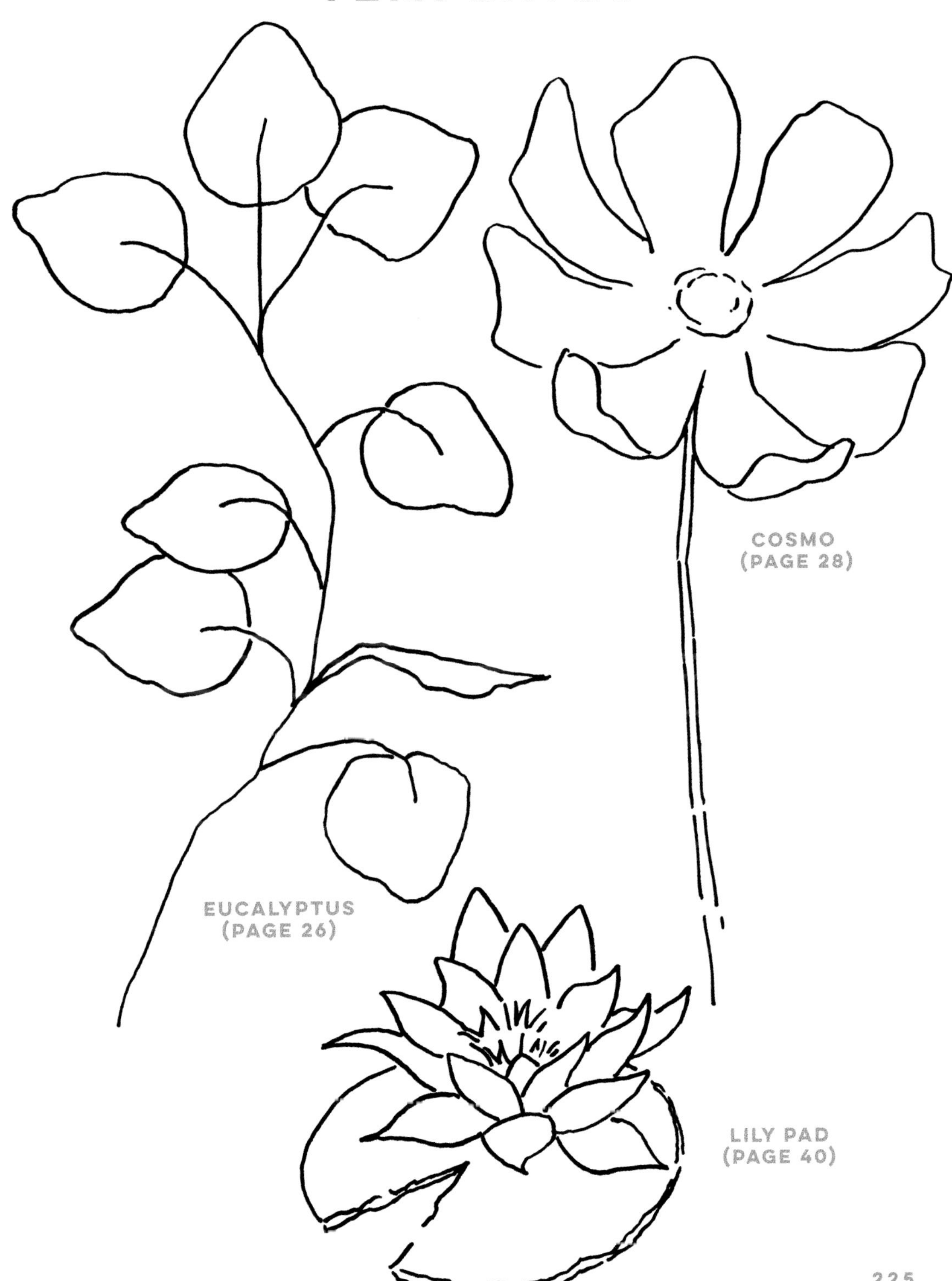

225

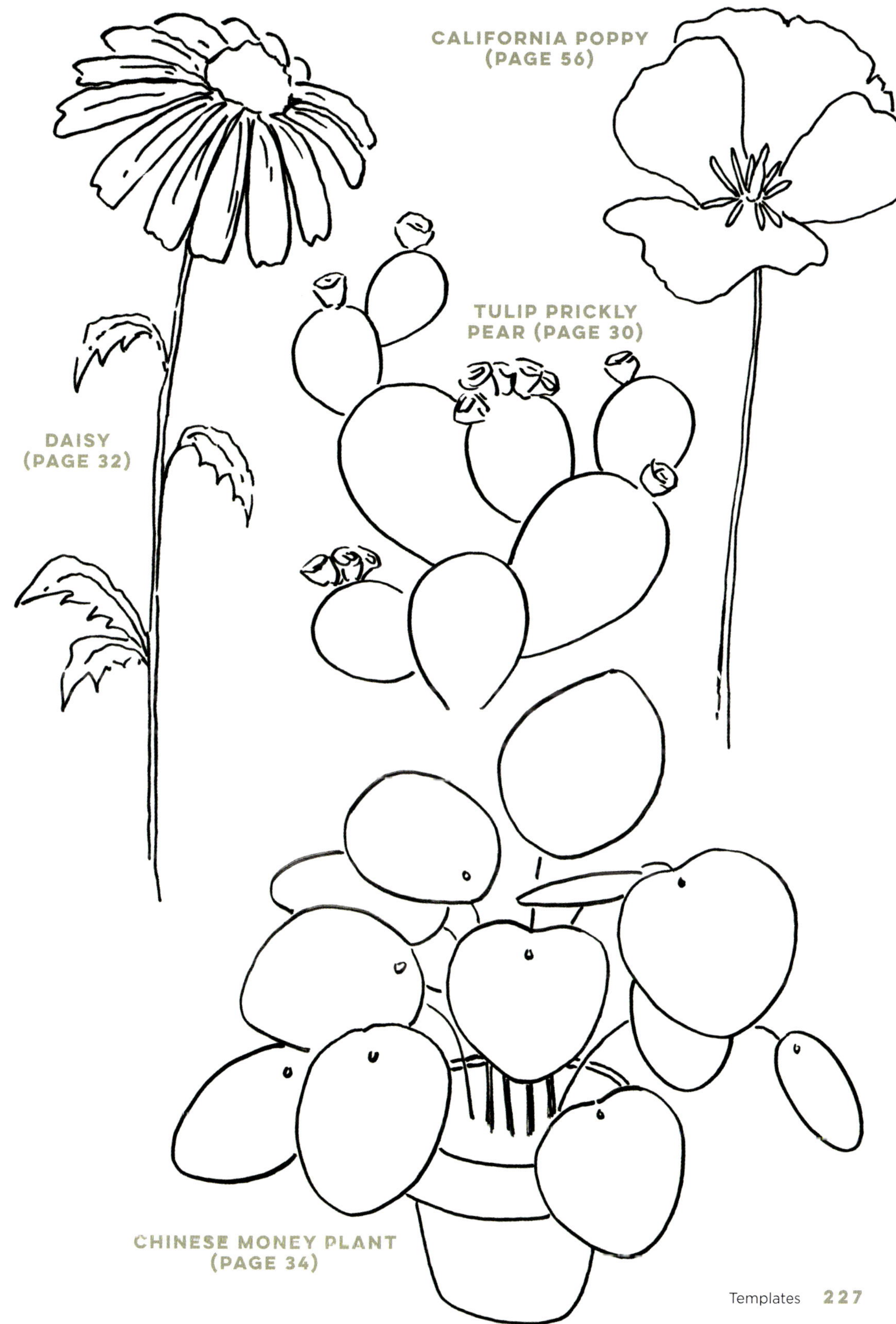

CALIFORNIA POPPY
(PAGE 56)
TULIP PRICKLY
PEAR (PAGE 30)
DAISY
(PAGE 32)
CHINESE MONEY PLANT
(PAGE 34)

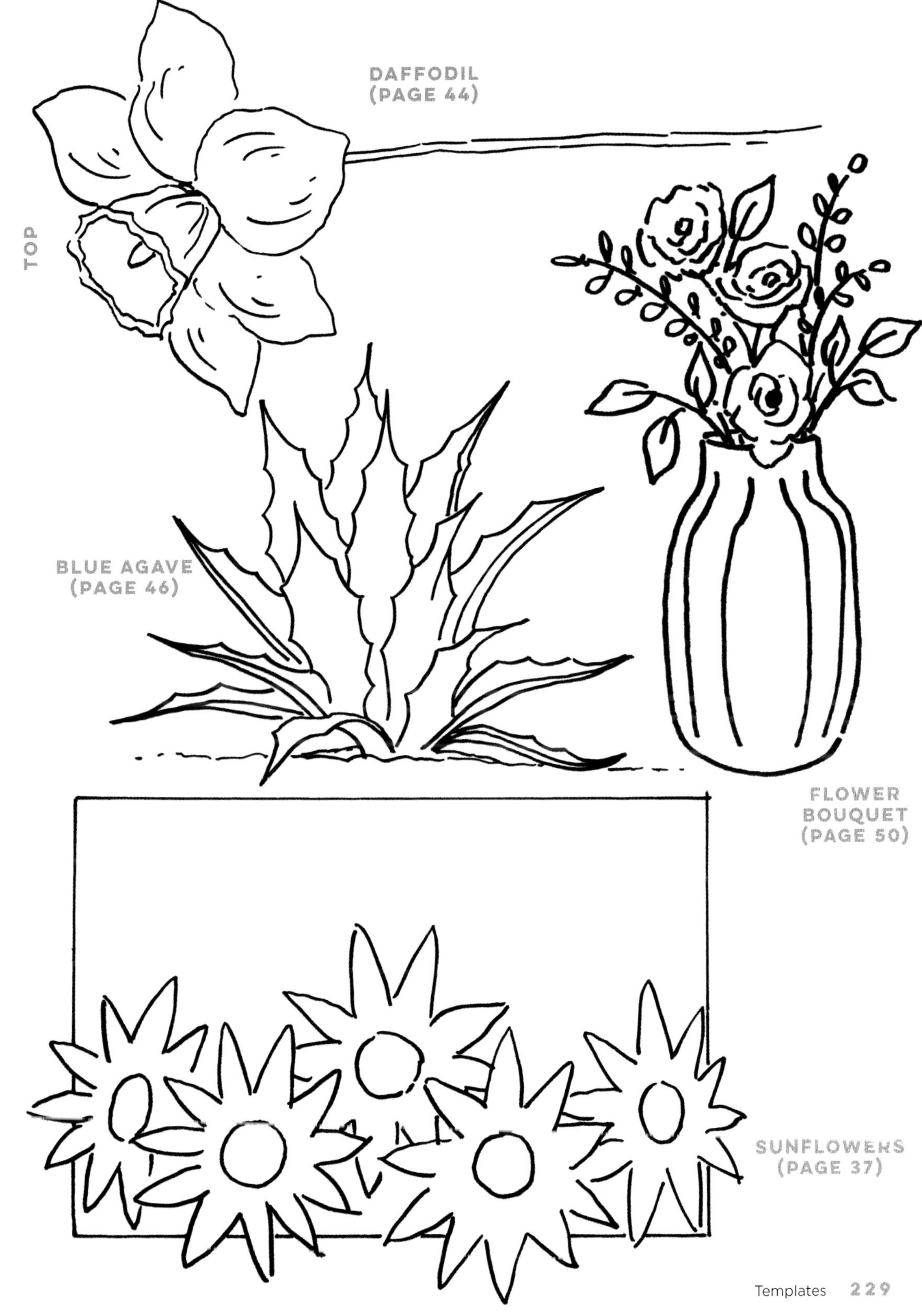

TOP
DAFFODIL
(PAGE 44)
BLUE AGAVE
(PAGE 46)
FLOWER
BOUQUET
(PAGE 50)
SUNFLOWERS
(PAGE 37)

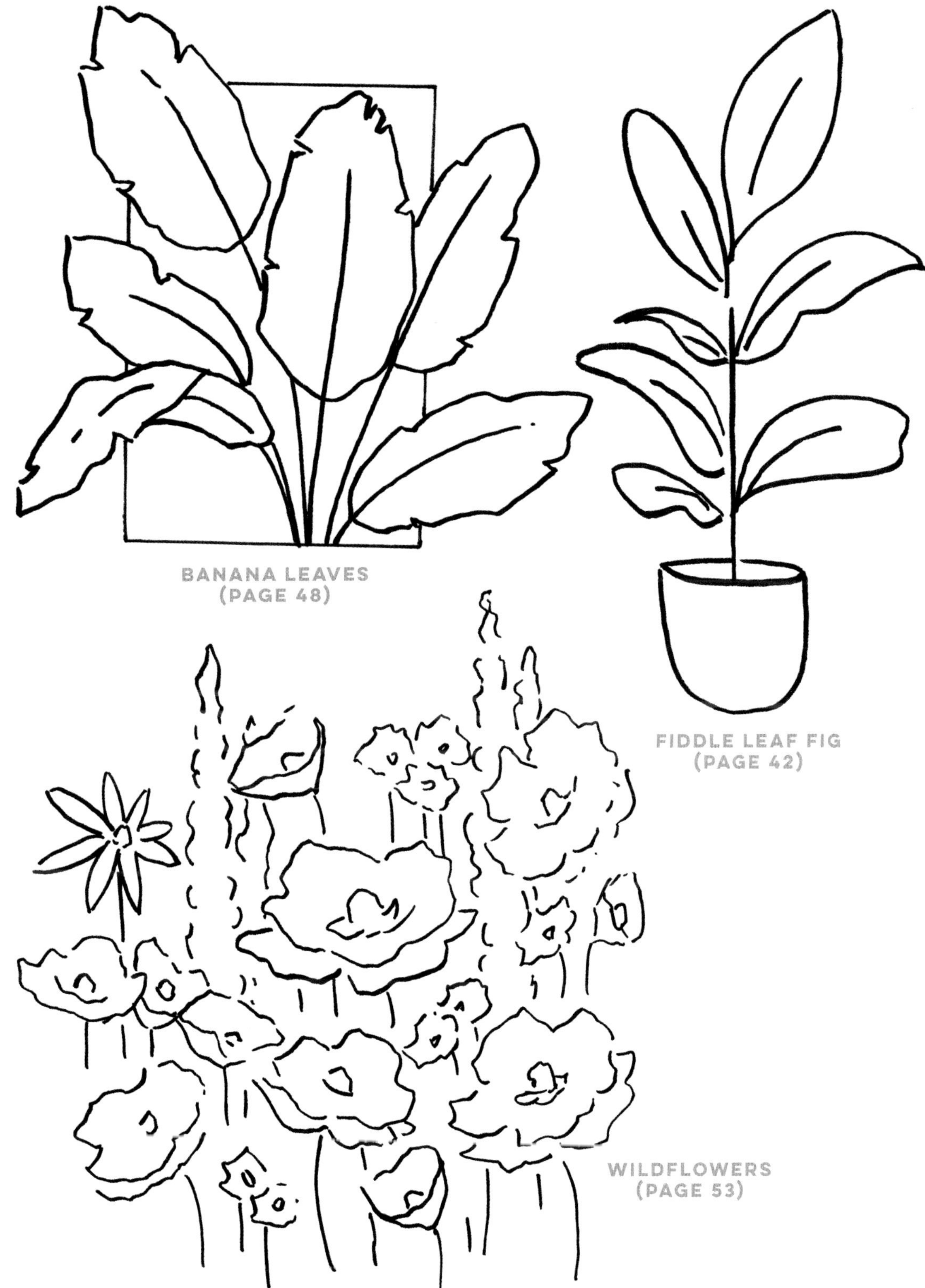

BANANA LEAVES
(PAGE 48)

FIDDLE LEAF FIG
(PAGE 42)

WILDFLOWERS
(PAGE 53)

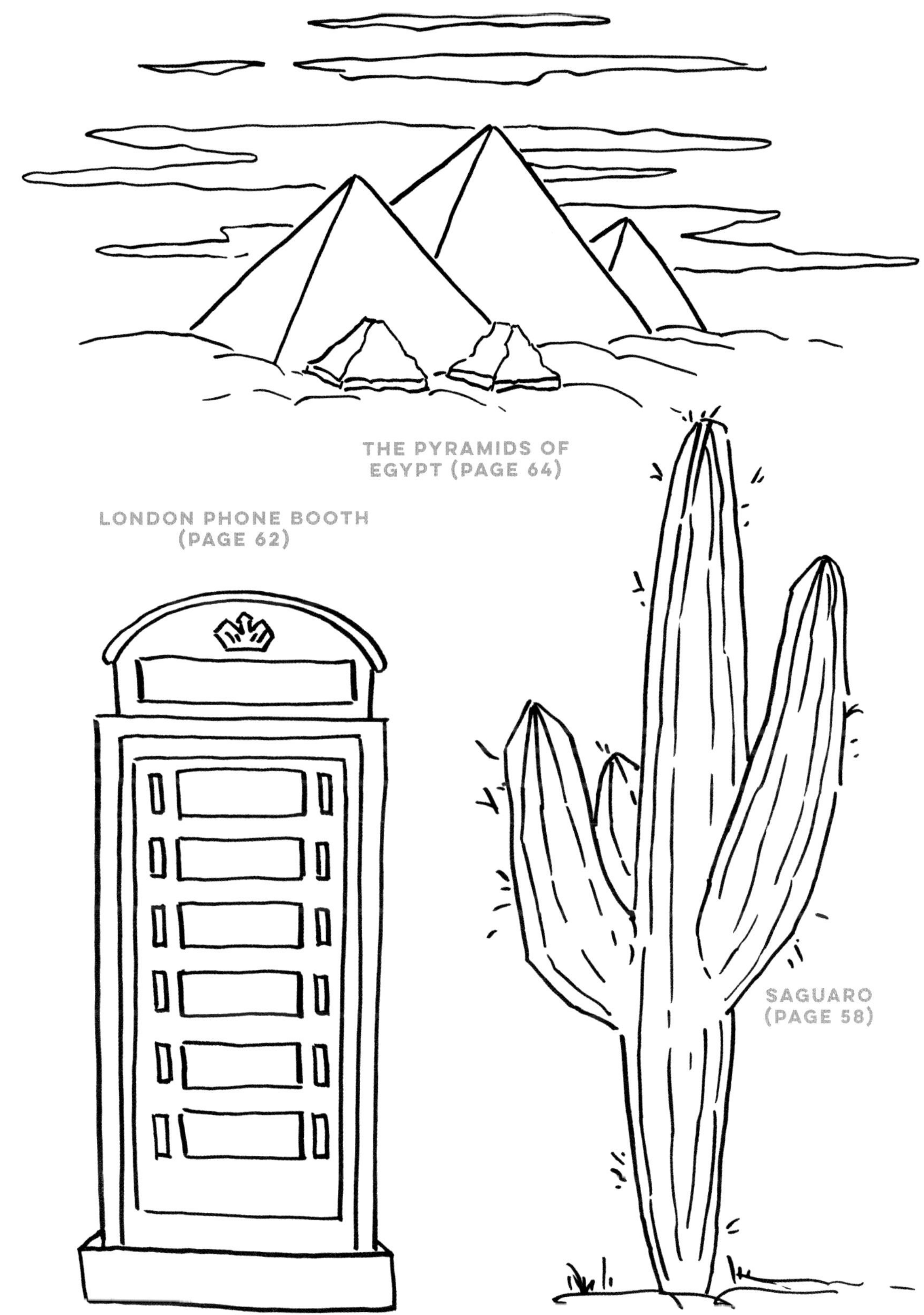

THE PYRAMIDS OF
EGYPT (PAGE 64)

LONDON PHONE BOOTH
(PAGE 62)

SAGUARO
(PAGE 58)

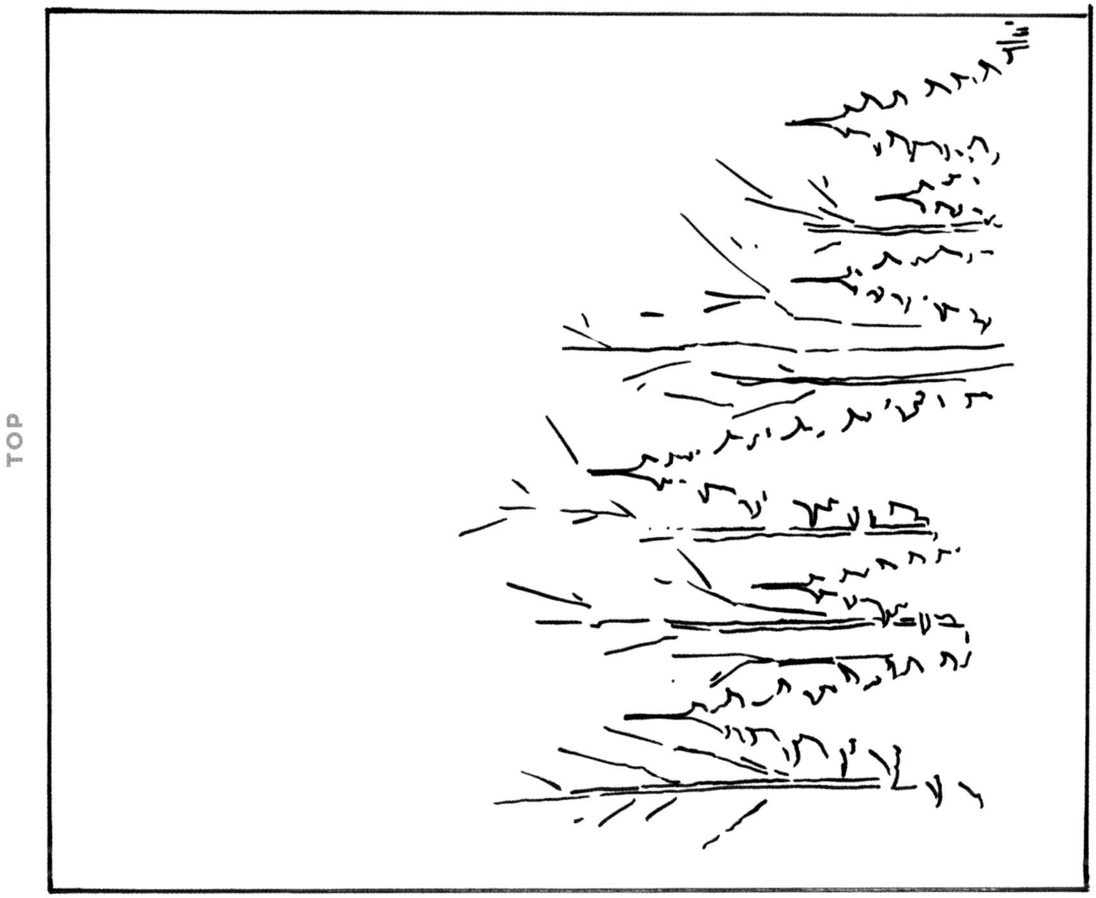

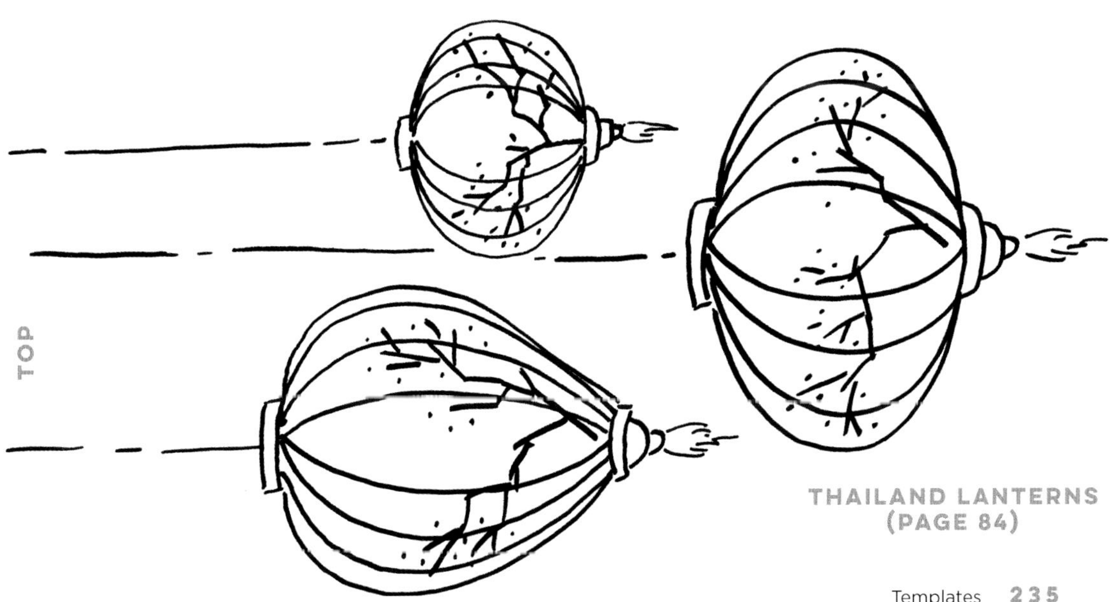

NORTHERN LIGHTS (PAGE 72)

THAILAND LANTERNS
(PAGE 84)

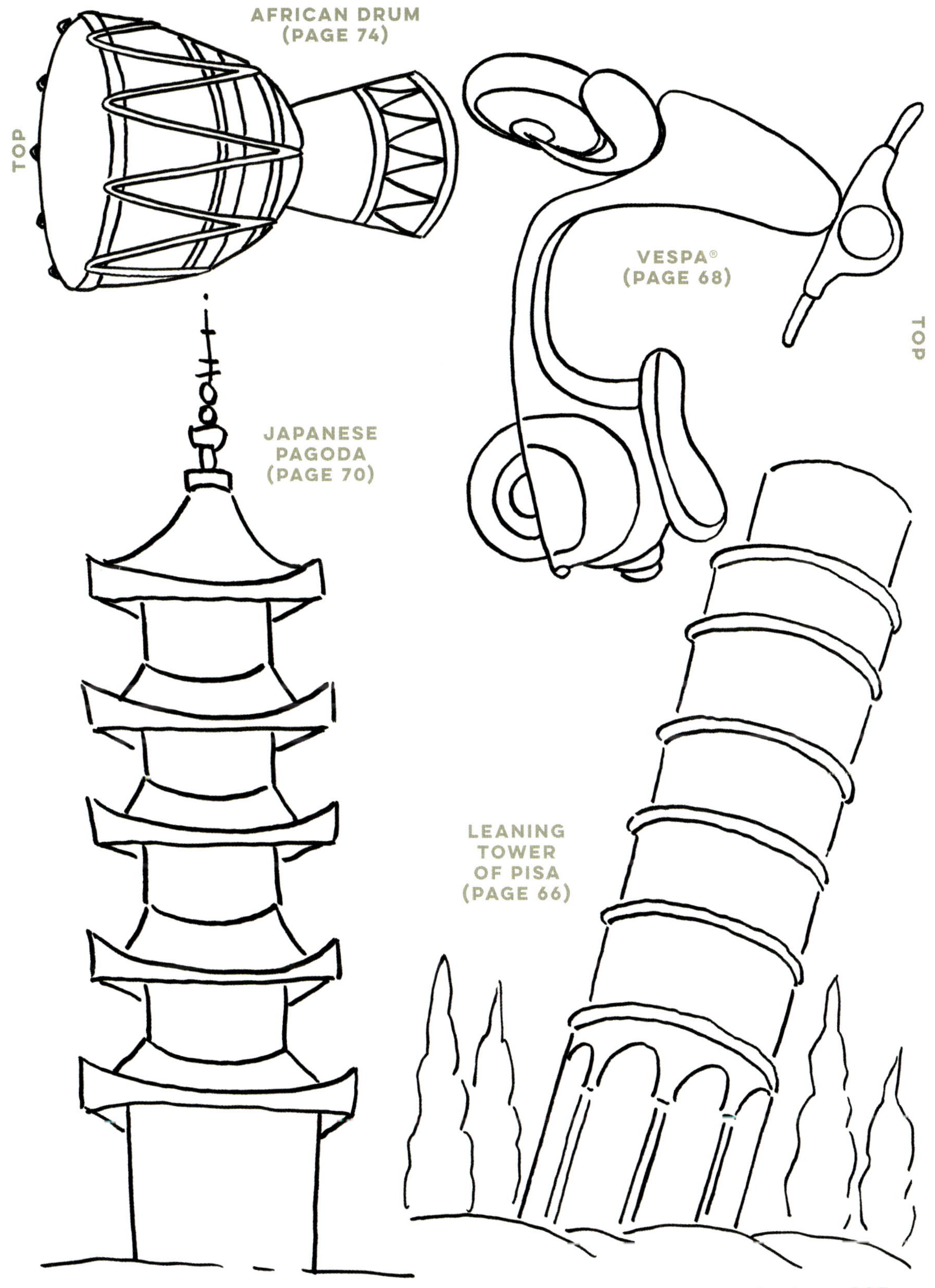

TOP
AFRICAN DRUM
(PAGE 74)
VESPA®
(PAGE 68)
TOP
JAPANESE
PAGODA
(PAGE 70)
LEANING
TOWER
OF PISA
(PAGE 66)

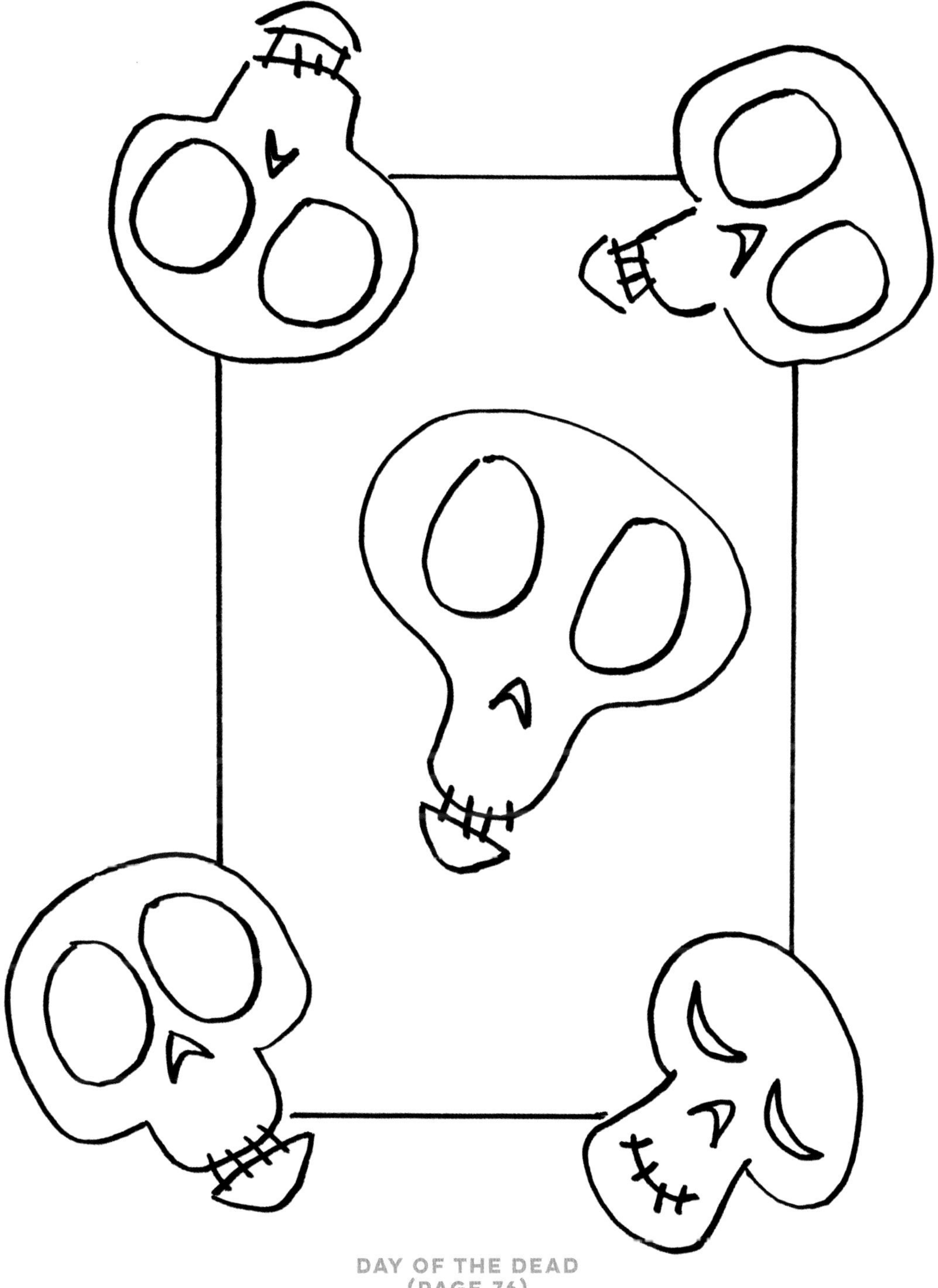

DAY OF THE DEAD
(PAGE 76)

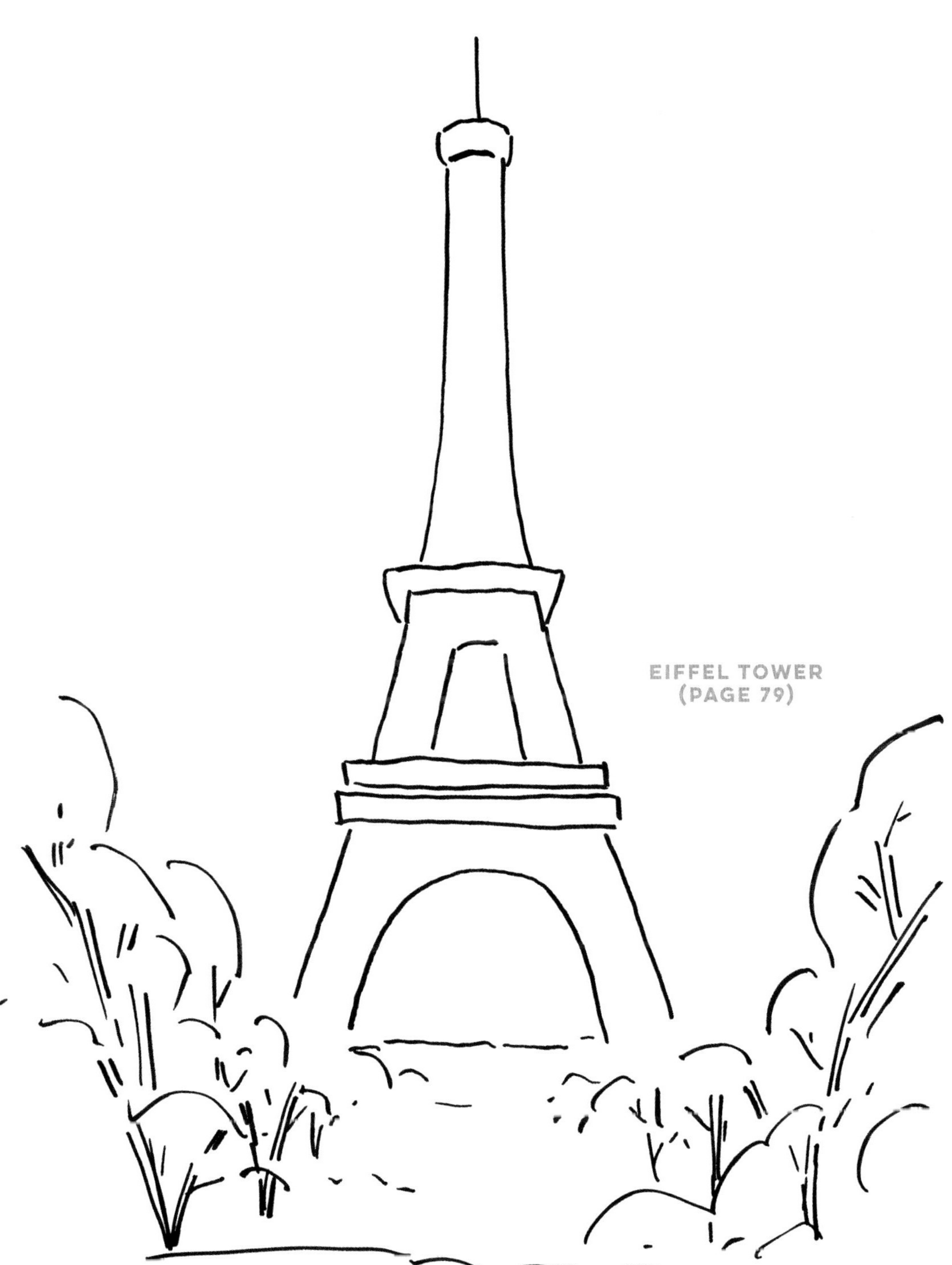
EIFFEL TOWER
(PAGE 79)

TOP

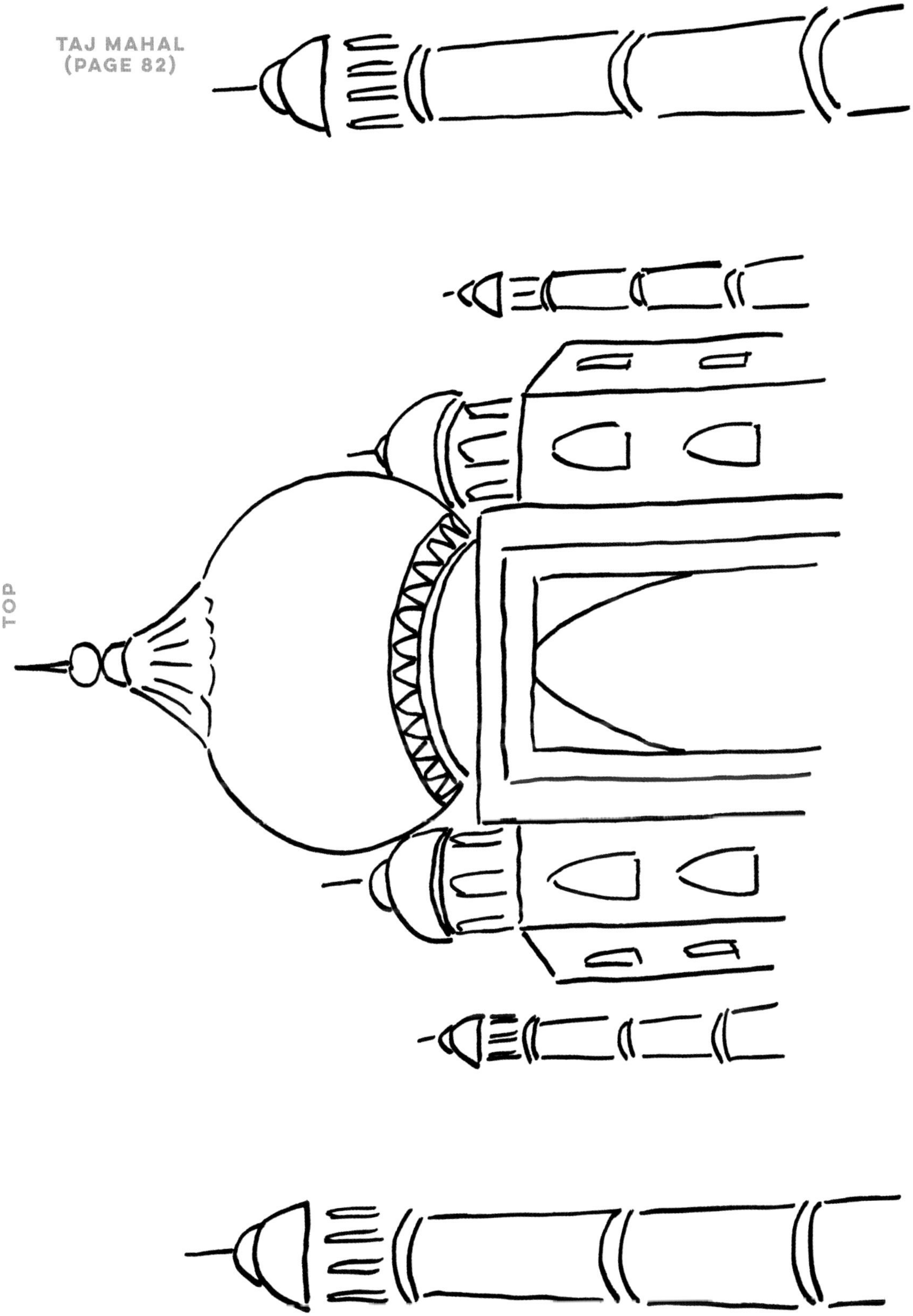

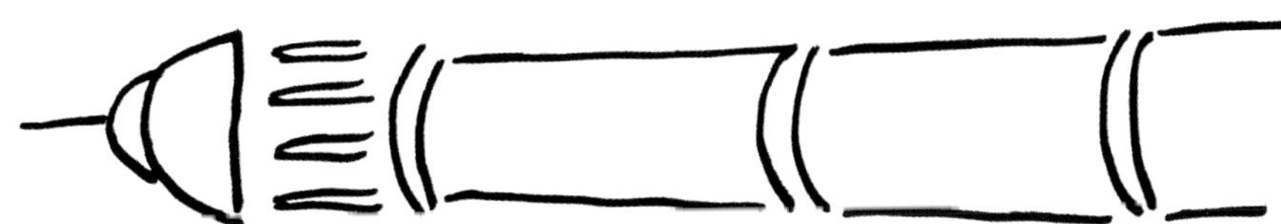

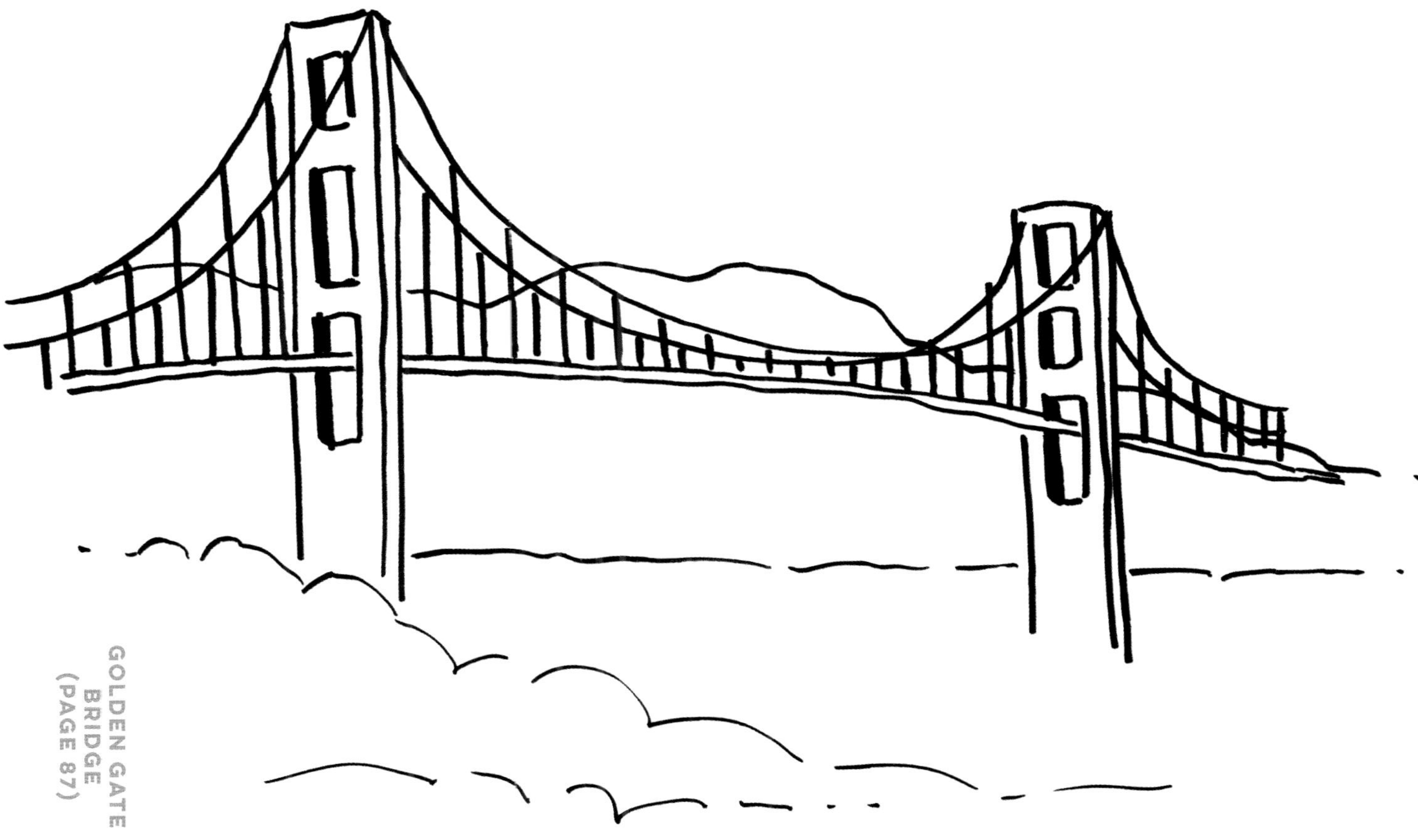
GOLDEN GATE
BRIDGE
(PAGE 87)

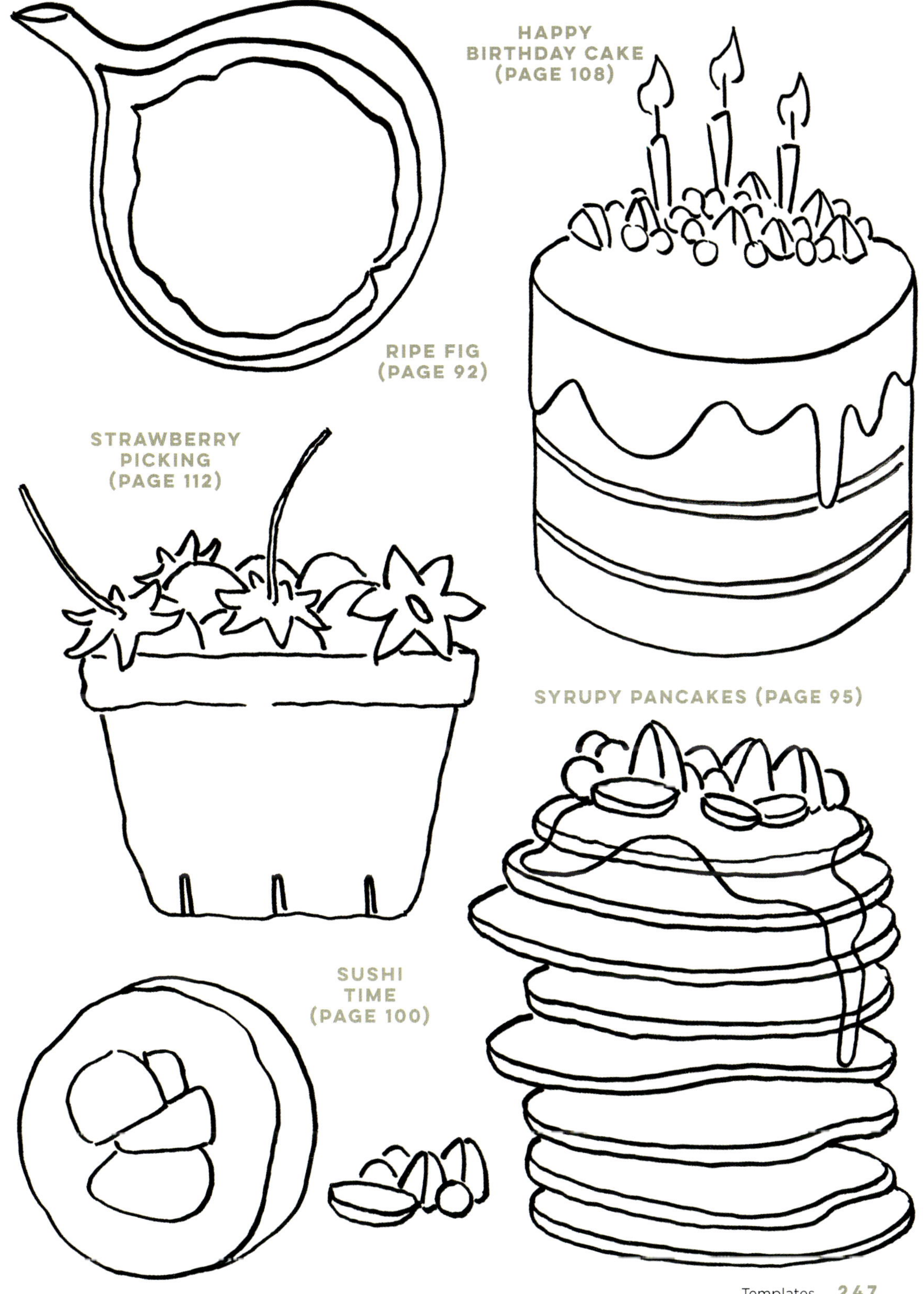

HAPPY
BIRTHDAY CAKE
(PAGE 108)
RIPE FIG
(PAGE 92)
STRAWBERRY
PICKING
(PAGE 112)
SYRUPY PANCAKES (PAGE 95)
SUSHI
TIME
(PAGE 100)

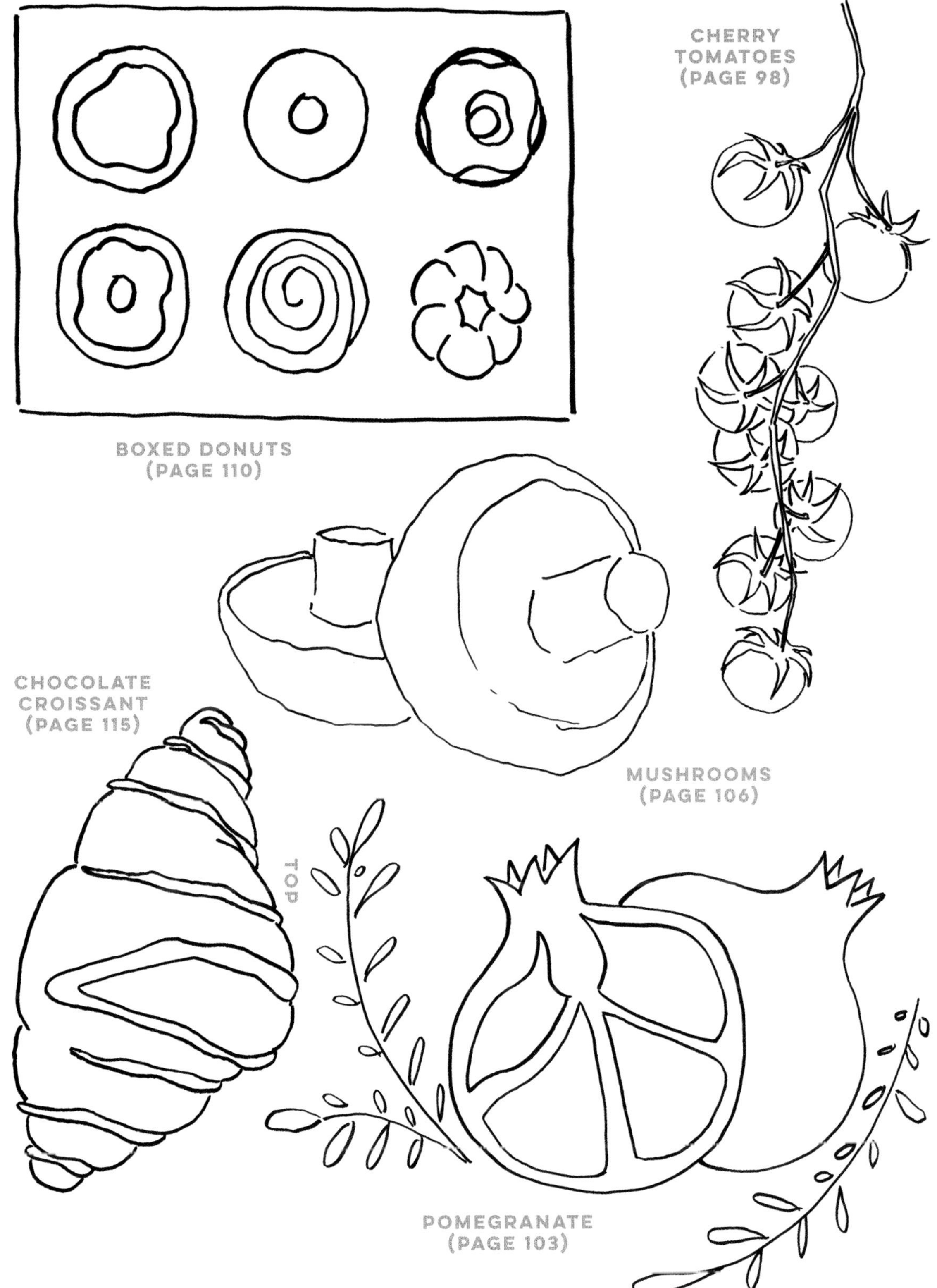

BOXED DONUTS
(PAGE 110)
CHERRY
TOMATOES
(PAGE 98)
CHOCOLATE
CROISSANT
(PAGE 115)
MUSHROOMS
(PAGE 106)
TOP
POMEGRANATE
(PAGE 103)

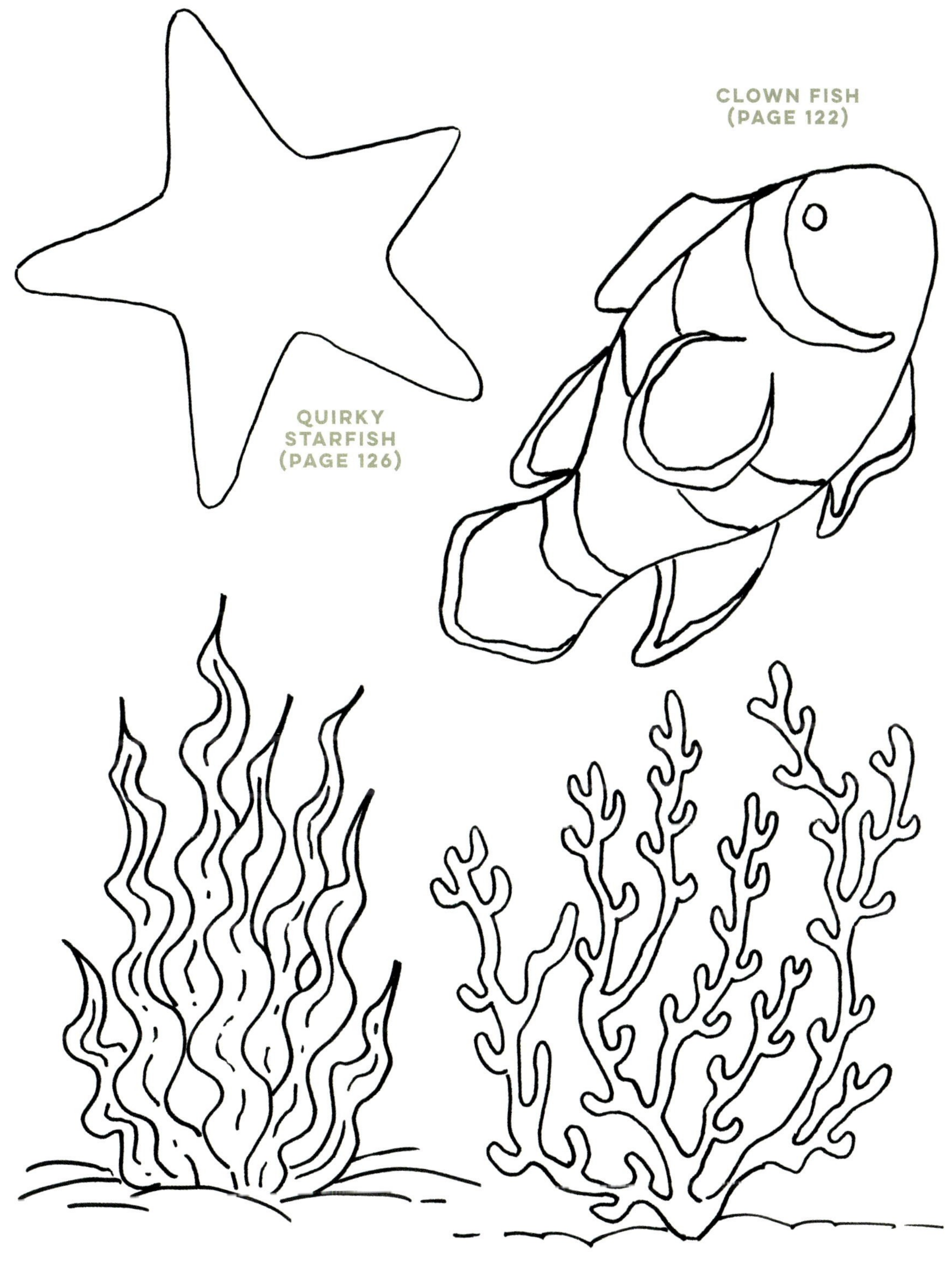

CLOWN FISH
(PAGE 122)
QUIRKY
STARFISH
(PAGE 126)
SEAWEED (PAGE 124)
COLORFUL CORAL
(PAGE 120)

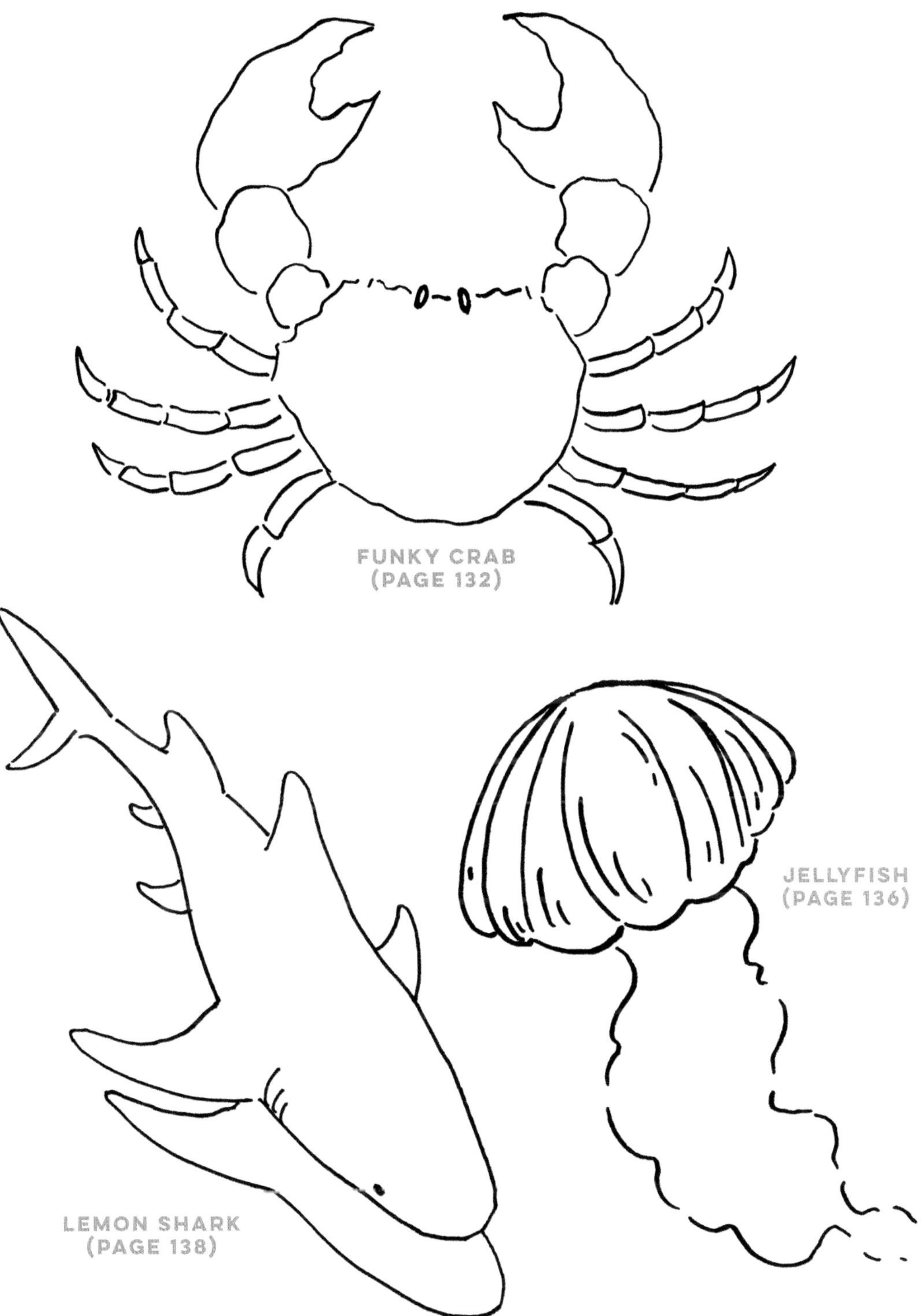

FUNKY CRAB
(PAGE 132)
JELLYFISH
(PAGE 136)
LEMON SHARK
(PAGE 138)

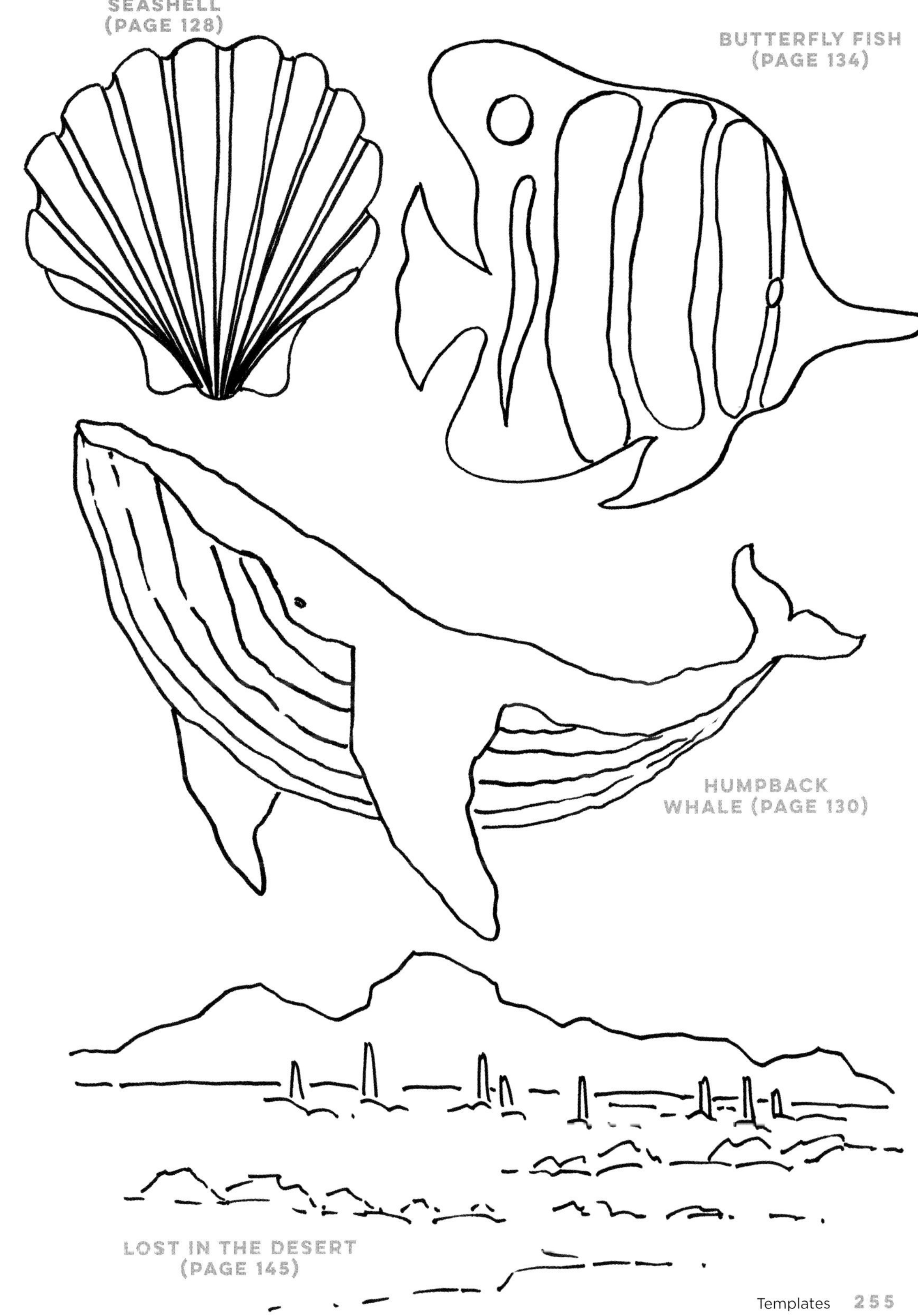

SEASHELL
(PAGE 128)
BUTTERFLY FISH
(PAGE 134)
HUMPBACK
WHALE (PAGE 130)
LOST IN THE DESERT
(PAGE 145)

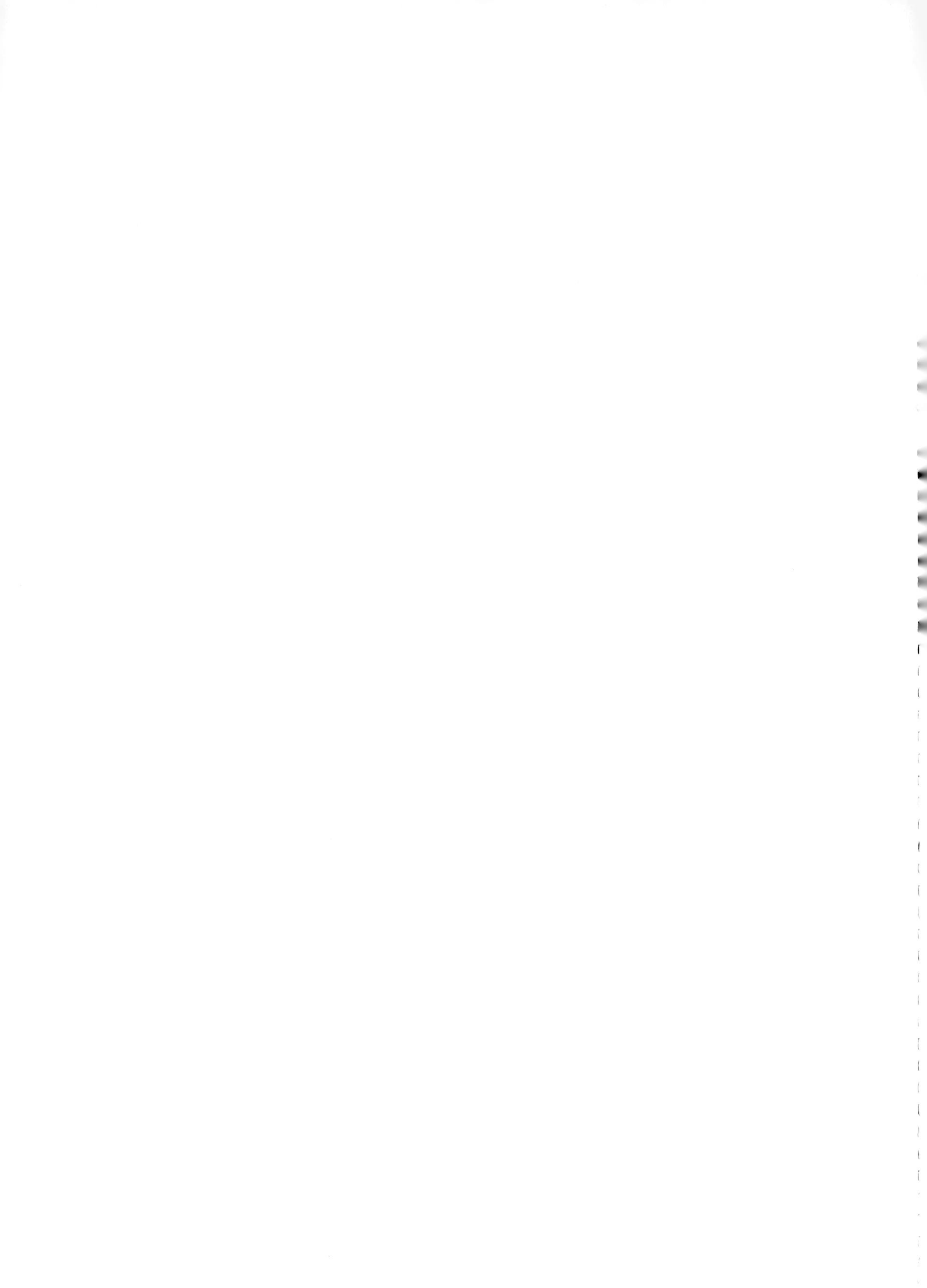

BEACH TIME
(PAGE 142)

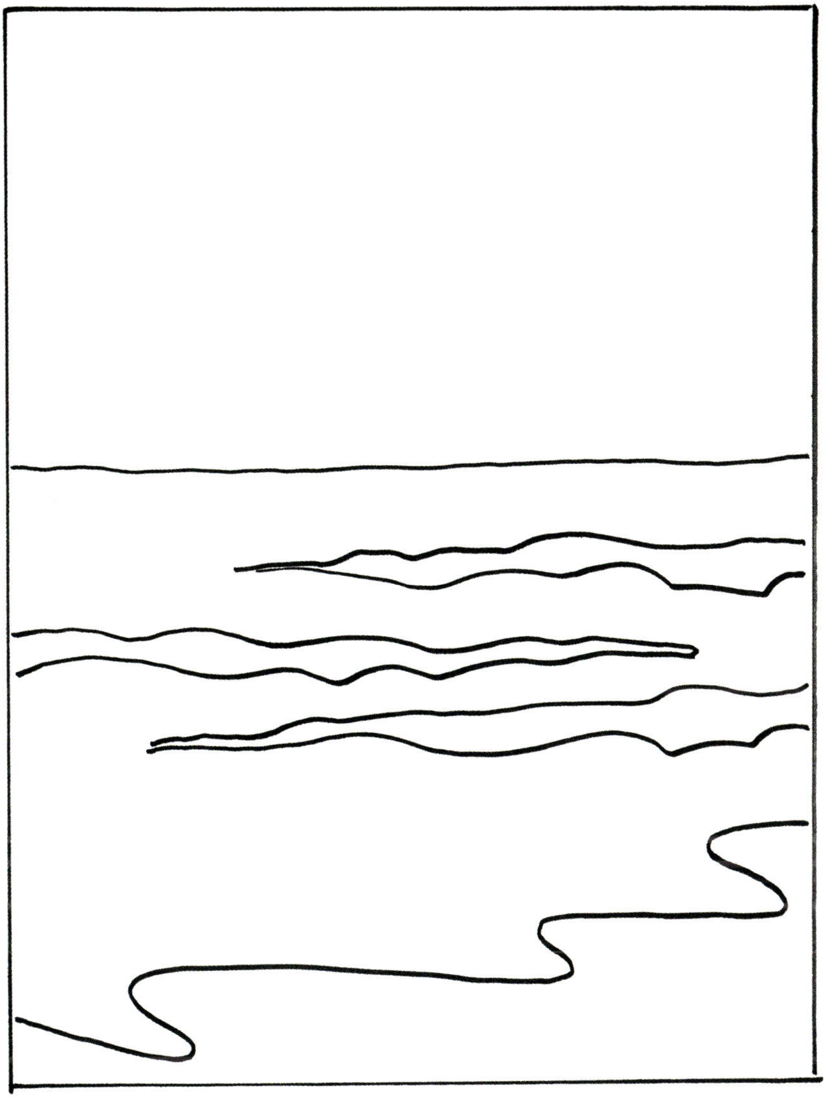

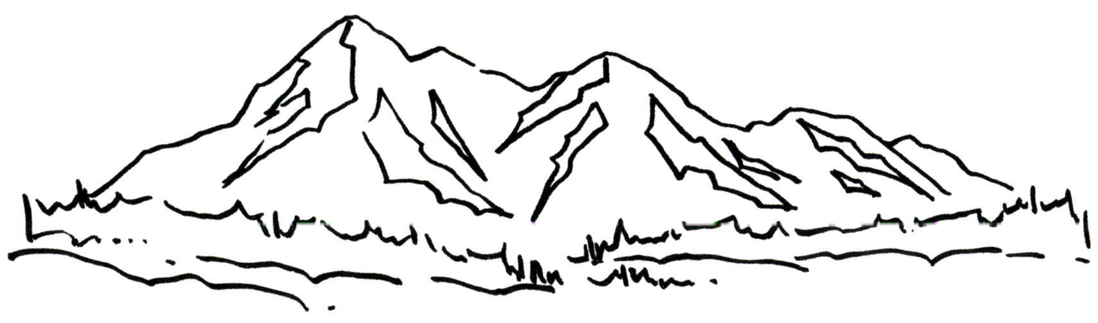

SNOWY MOUNTAIN (PAGE 156)

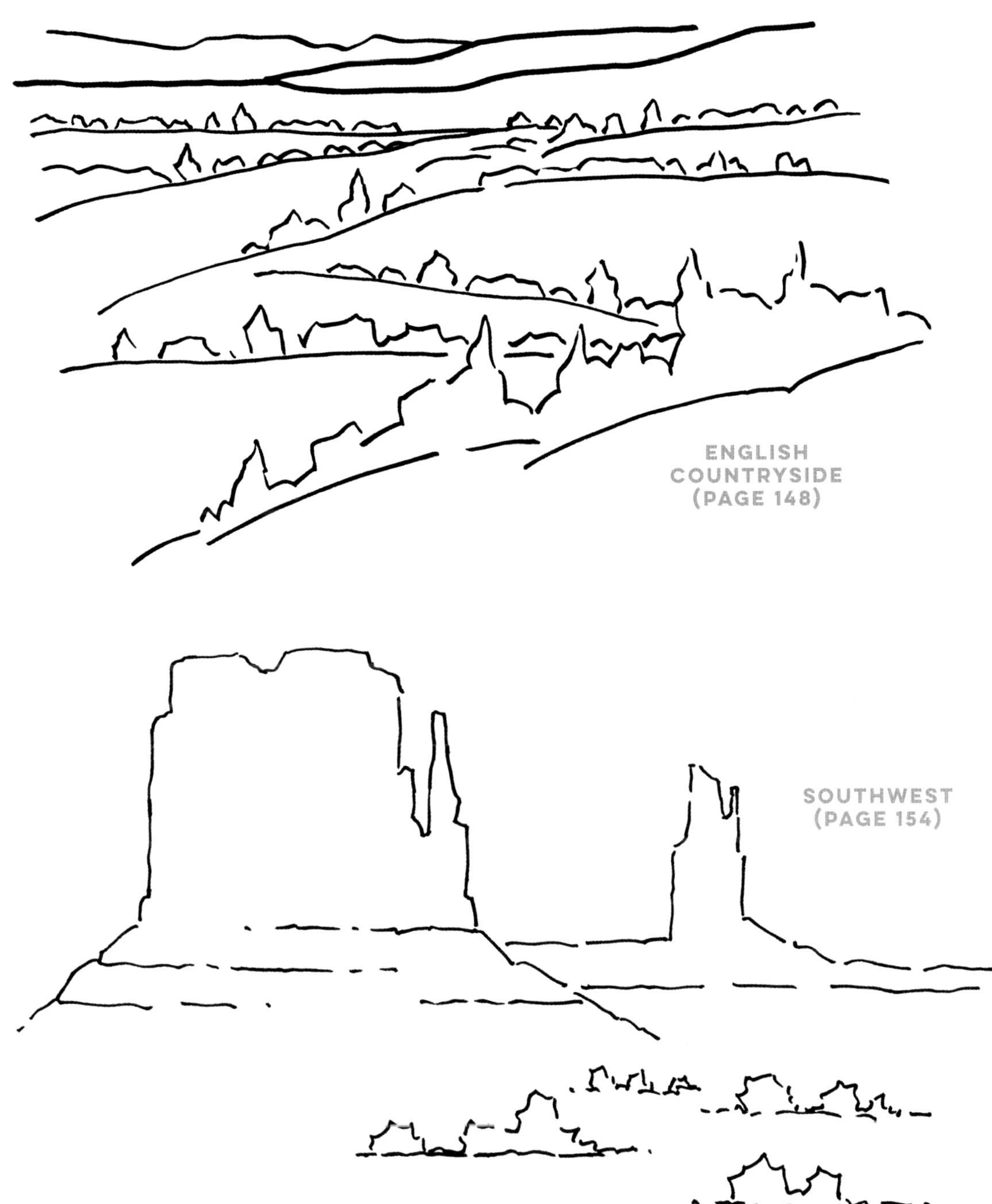

ENGLISH
COUNTRYSIDE
(PAGE 148)

SOUTHWEST
(PAGE 154)

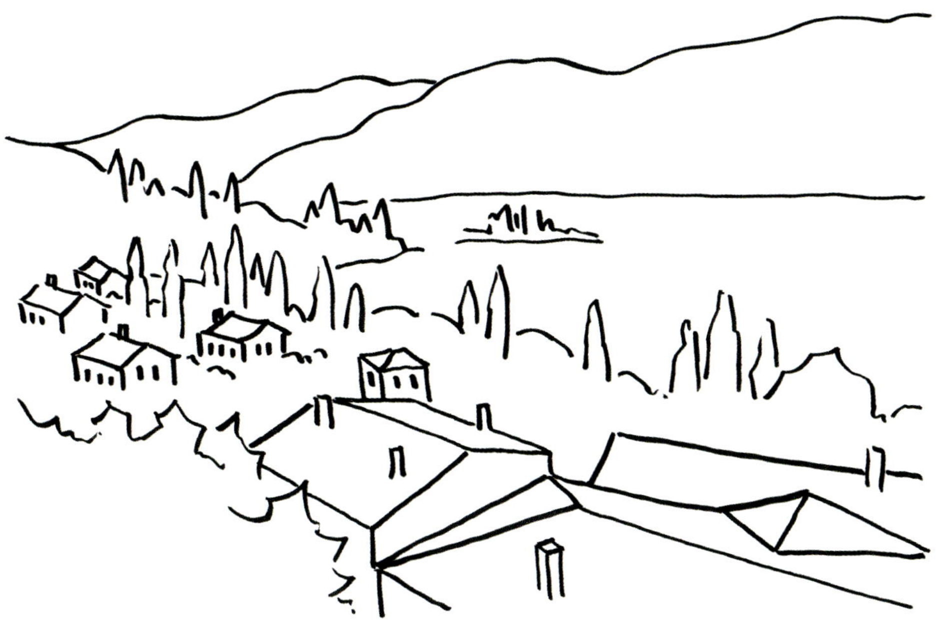

ITALIAN LAKESIDE
(PAGE 158)

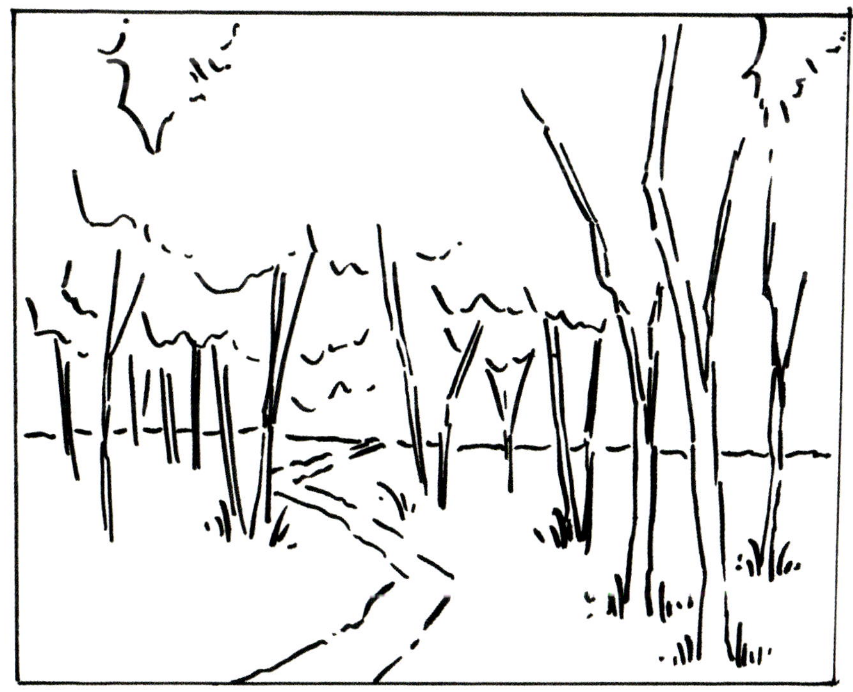

SUNLIT FOREST (PAGE 151)

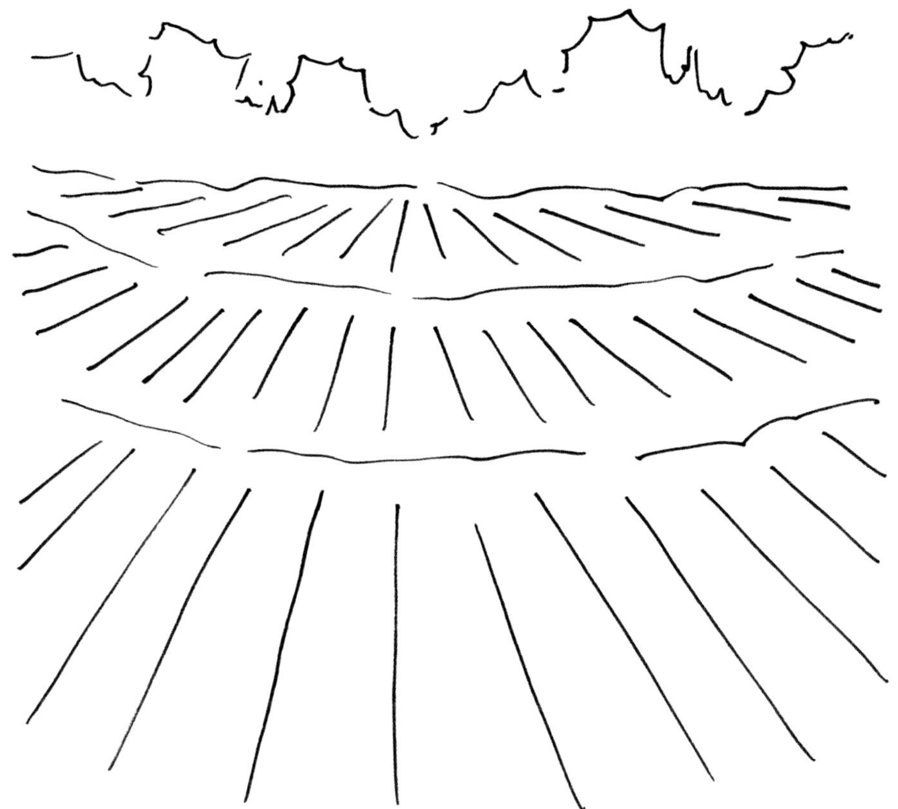

IN THE FIELDS
(PAGE 162)

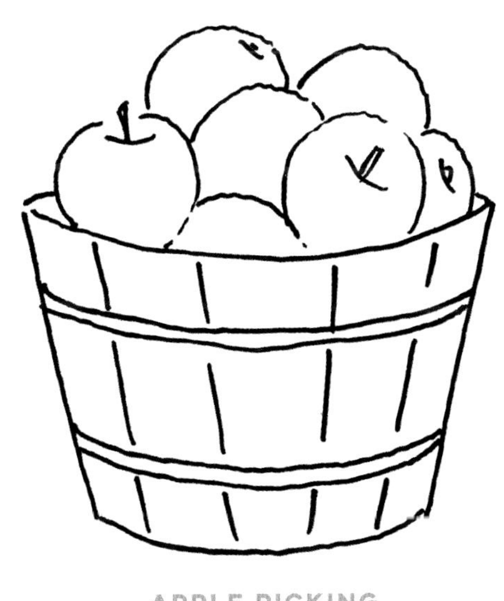

APPLE PICKING
(PAGE 170)

MAPLE LEAF
(PAGE 166)

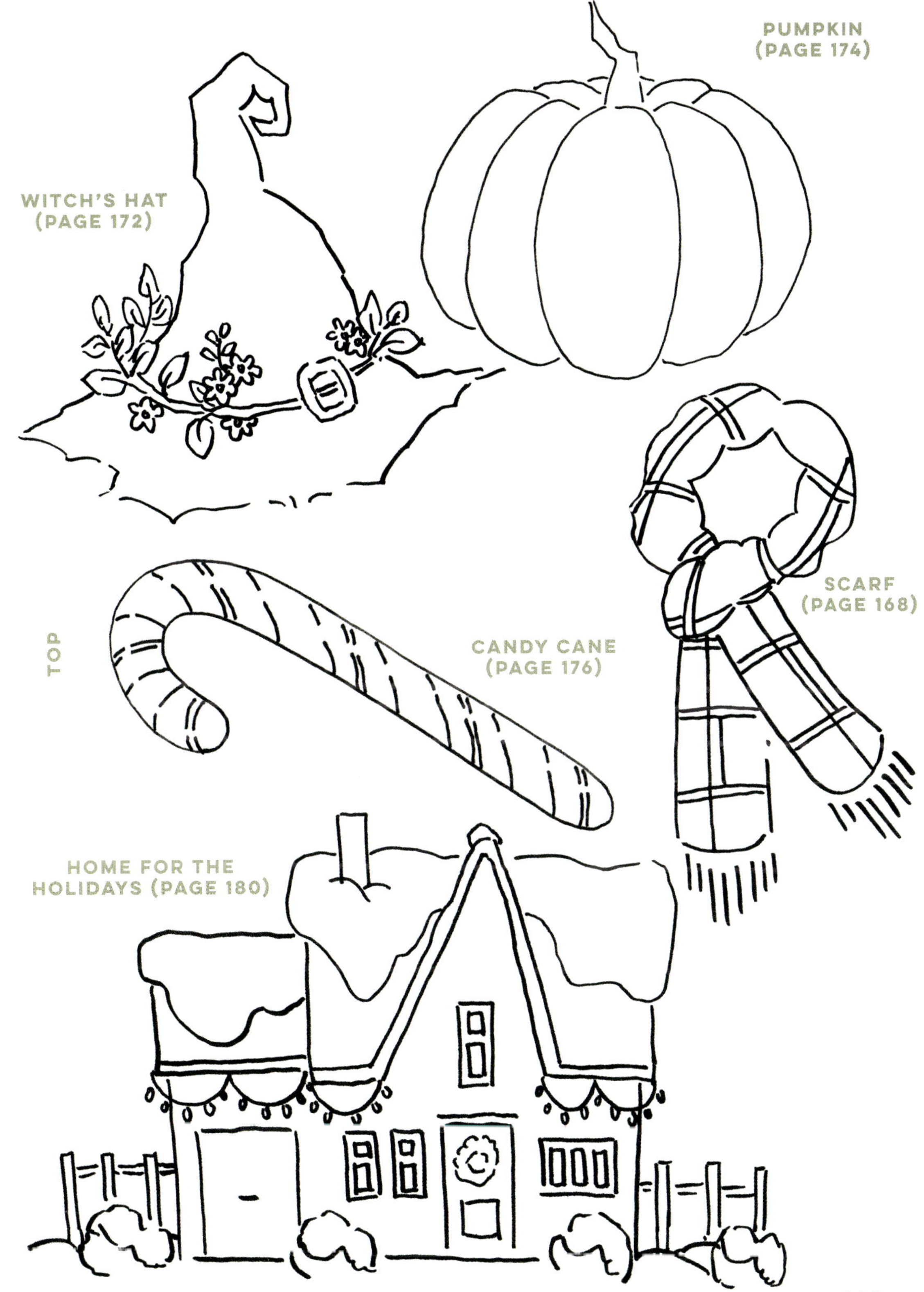

PUMPKIN
(PAGE 174)
WITCH'S HAT
(PAGE 172)
SCARF
(PAGE 168)
TOP
CANDY CANE
(PAGE 176)
HOME FOR THE
HOLIDAYS (PAGE 180)

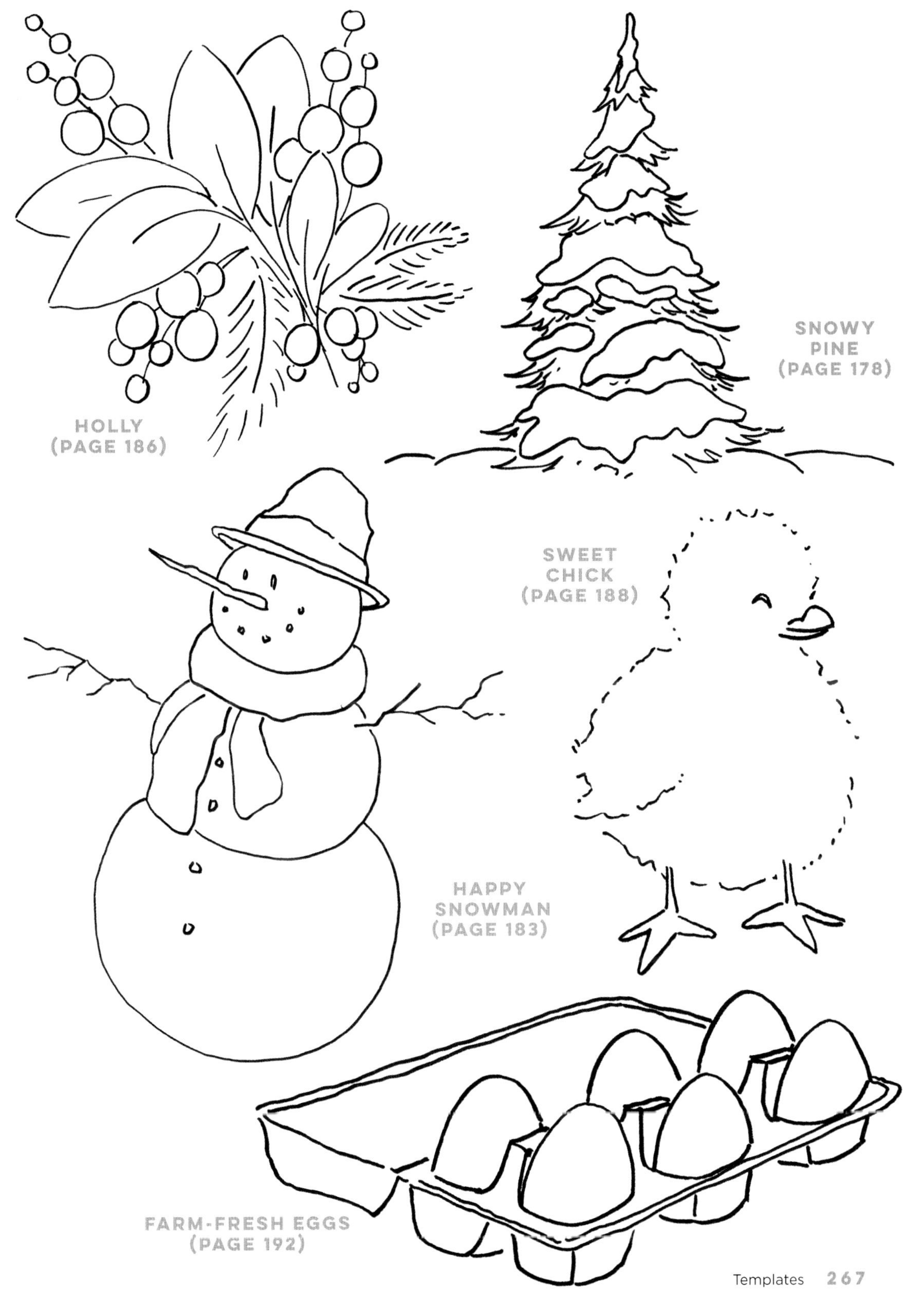

HOLLY
(PAGE 186)
SNOWY
PINE
(PAGE 178)
SWEET
CHICK
(PAGE 188)
HAPPY
SNOWMAN
(PAGE 183)
FARM-FRESH EGGS
(PAGE 192)

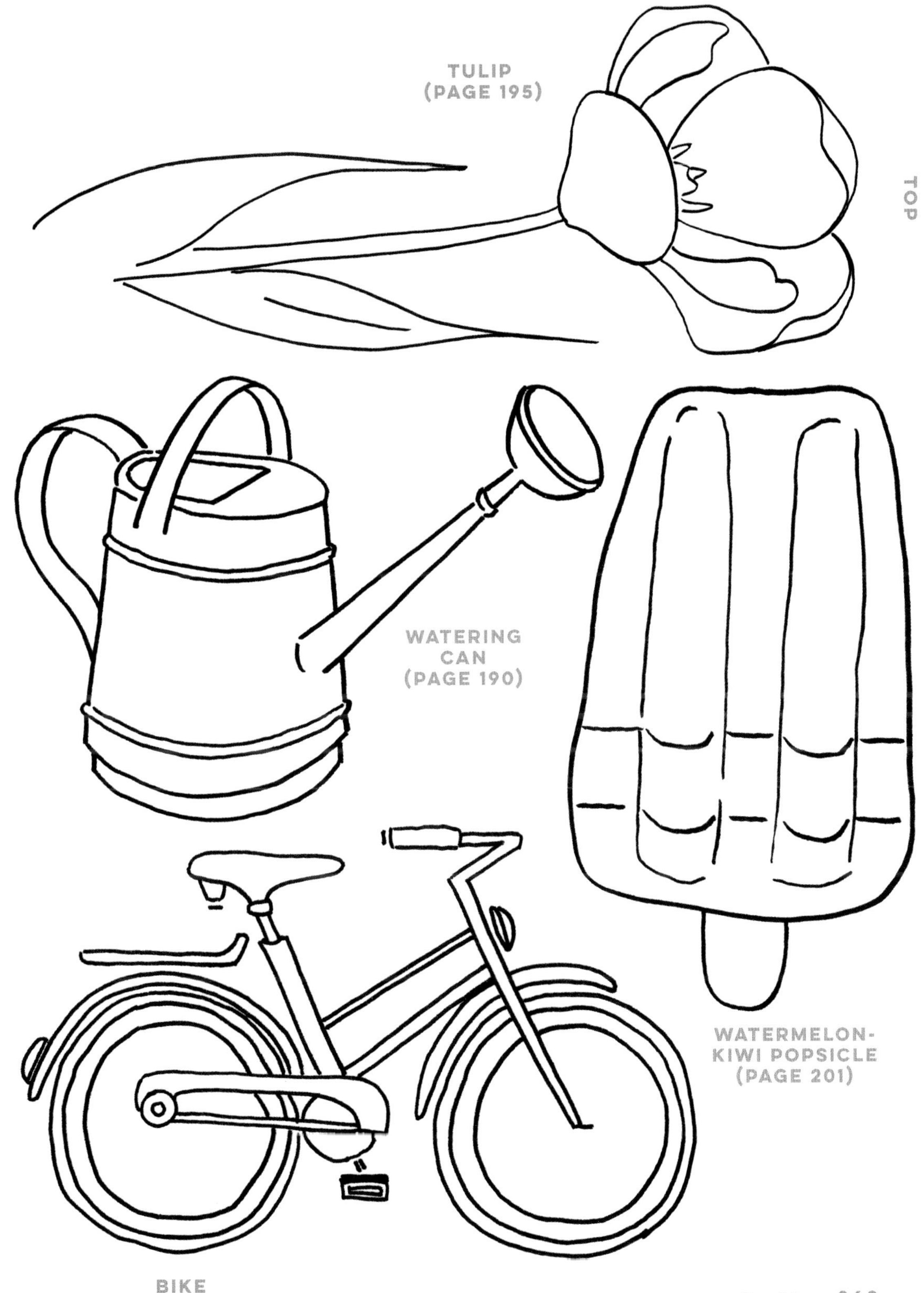

TULIP
(PAGE 195)
TOP
WATERING
CAN
(PAGE 190)
WATERMELON-
KIWI POPSICLE
(PAGE 201)
BIKE
(PAGE 204)

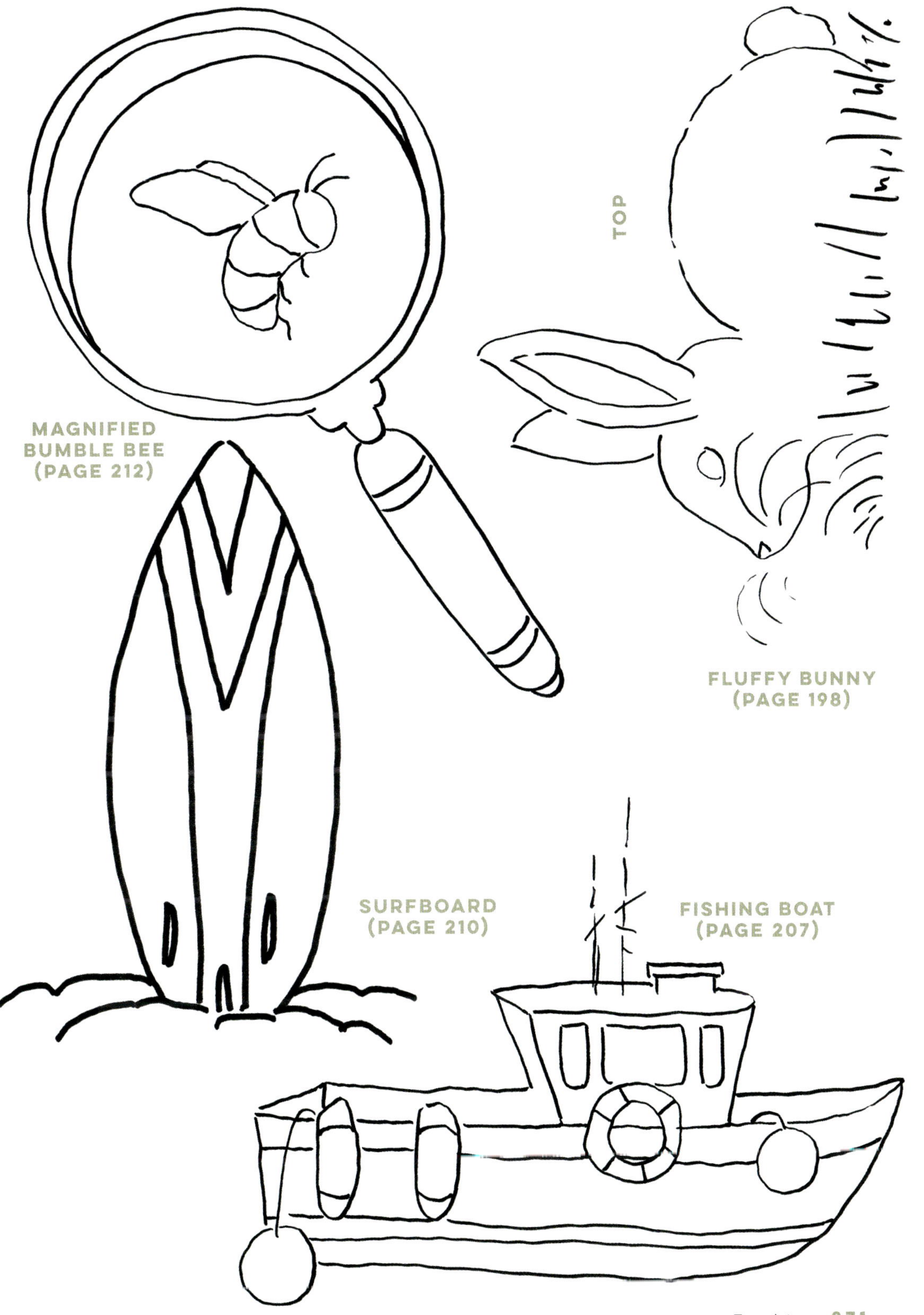

MAGNIFIED
BUMBLE BEE
(PAGE 212)

TOP

FLUFFY BUNNY
(PAGE 198)

SURFBOARD
(PAGE 210)

FISHING BOAT
(PAGE 207)